Verse by Verse Commentary on the Book of

EXODUS

Enduring Word Commentary Series
By David Guzik

The grass withers, the flower fades,
but the word of our God stands forever.
Isaiah 40:8

Commentary on Exodus

Copyright ©2015 by David Guzik

Printed in the United States of America
or in the United Kingdom

ISBN: 978-1-939466- 26-6

Enduring Word Media

5521 San Ardo Way
Santa Barbara, CA 93111

Electronic Mail: enduringwordbooks@gmail.com
Internet Home Page: www.enduringword.com

Table of Contents

Exodus 1 - Israel Multiplies in Egypt

A. Israel's affliction in Egypt.

1. (1-6) The twelve sons of Jacob who came into Egypt.

Now these *are* the names of the children of Israel who came to Egypt; each man and his household came with Jacob: Reuben, Simeon, Levi, and Judah; Issachar, Zebulun, and Benjamin; Dan, Naphtali, Gad, and Asher. All those who were descendants of Jacob were seventy persons (for Joseph was in Egypt *already*). And Joseph died, all his brothers, and all that generation.

a. **Now these are the names of the children of Israel who came to Egypt**: The first verses of Exodus reach back some 430 years. The story of the Exodus begins where the story Genesis ends: a large family with a crucial place in God's plan of the ages and their migration to Egypt.

i. The Hebrew title for the Book of Exodus is taken from its first words: *And These are the Names Of.* In the original language, the first word of Exodus is *and*, marking its continuity from the Genesis account.

b. **And Joseph died**: Joseph was the remarkable great-grandson of Abraham who saved Egypt – and the world – from terrible famine because he listened to God's voice speaking through Pharaoh's dream. Because of his wisdom and administration, he was lifted to high and honored office in Egypt. Yet eventually **Joseph died**, and the status his family enjoyed died with him.

2. (7) The rapid multiplication of the children of Israel in Egypt.

But the children of Israel were fruitful and increased abundantly, multiplied and grew exceedingly mighty; and the land was filled with them.

a. **The land was filled with them**: Genesis 47:27 says, *So Israel dwelt in the land of Egypt, in the country of Goshen; and they had possessions there and grew* *and multiplied exceedingly.* They did indeed multiply exceedingly over the generations - so that the **land was filled with them**.

> i. At Exodus 1:7: "The Hebrew deliberately repeats three verbs used in Genesis 1:21,22 which may be translated 'were fruitful…swarmed… became numerous'." (Cole)

b. **The children of Israel were fruitful and increased abundantly**: This family started with five people back in Haran: Jacob, Rachel, Leah, Zilphah, and Bilhah. Blessed by God, the family of Israel grew rapidly in their years in Egypt.

3. (8-11) Afraid of their growing presence, the Egyptians oppress the Israelites.

Now there arose a new king over Egypt, who did not know Joseph. And he said to his people, "Look, the people of the children of Israel *are* more and mightier than we; come, let us deal shrewdly with them, lest they multiply, and it happen, in the event of war, that they also join our enemies and fight against us, and *so* go up out of the land." Therefore they set taskmasters over them to afflict them with their burdens. And they built for Pharaoh supply cities, Pithom and Raamses.

a. **Look, the people of the children of Israel are more and mightier than we; come, let us deal shrewdly with them**: The ancient Egyptians were famous - or infamous - for their proud sense of racial superiority towards all other people. It isn't surprising to see them afraid and discriminating against this strong minority group in their midst, which looked as if it would not be a minority very long.

b. **In the event of war, that they also join our enemies and fight against us**: At the time, the Egyptians feared invasion from the Hittites of the north. If the Hebrews among them joined with the Hittites, it posed a significant threat to their security.

c. **They set taskmasters over them…they built for Pharaoh supply cities**: When the children of Israel were set to slave labor, they built many of the great cities and monuments in Egypt - though not the pyramids, which were built much earlier. Since we don't know exactly when this forced labor began, we don't know how long it lasted. Some estimate the slavery lasted 284 years, others 134 years.

> i. There is a famous wall painting on an ancient tomb from Thebes, Egypt (modern Luxor) – the tomb of the overseer of brick-making slaves during the reign of Thutmose III. "The painting shows such overseers armed with heavy whips. Their rank is denoted by the long staff held in their hands and the Egyptian hieroglyphic determinative of the head and neck of a giraffe." (Kaiser)

4. (12-14) Israel prospers and grows despite the hard bondage of the Egyptians.

But the more they afflicted them, the more they multiplied and grew. And they were in dread of the children of Israel. So the Egyptians made the children of Israel serve with rigor. And they made their lives bitter with hard bondage; in mortar, in brick, and in all manner of service in the field. All their service in which they made them serve *was* with rigor.

a. **The more they afflicted them, the more they multiplied and grew**: This was God's purpose for Israel's time in Egypt. Egypt served as a mother's womb for Israel, a place where they rapidly grew from a large clan to a mighty nation.

i. The nation could not grow this way in Canaan, because it was practically impossible to avoid intermarriage with the pagan and wicked inhabitants of Canaan. Egypt was so racially biased and had such an entrenched system of racial separation that Israel could grow there over several centuries without being assimilated.

ii. This growth in the face of affliction has consistently been the story of God's people throughout all ages - the more they are afflicted, the more they grow. As the ancient Christian writer Tertullian said, "The blood of the martyrs is the seed of the Church."

iii. Suffering and persecution are like a great wave that comes upon a ship and looks as if it will destroy it but the ship catches the wave and just uses it to speed along.

b. **They made their lives bitter with hard bondage**: Because God's purpose was to bless Israel, and fulfill His role for them in His eternal plan, no amount of affliction could defeat His purpose. The Egyptians tried their best through cruel slavery but it did not work. The principle of Isaiah 54:17 proved true: *No weapon formed against you shall prosper*. The wickedness of the Egyptians could *hurt* the children of Israel, but could never *defeat* God's plan for them.

i. Pharaoh thought it best not to kill them, but he did want them to be slaves.

ii. In the midst of their cruel and harsh service, life must have seemed hopeless to the children of Israel, and the idea that God was working out His plan must have seemed very far away - yet it was true nonetheless.

B. The Hebrew midwives obey God.

1. (15-16) The king of Egypt tries to destroy Israel by ordering the death of all male babies.

Then the king of Egypt spoke to the Hebrew midwives, of whom the name of one *was* Shiphrah and the name of the other Puah; and he said, "When you do the duties of a midwife for the Hebrew women, and see *them* on the birthstools, if it *is* a son, then you shall kill him; but if it *is* a daughter, then she shall live."

a. **Of whom the name of one was Shiphrah and the name of the other Puah**: We shouldn't expect that these two women were the only midwives for all the children of Israel. They were probably the leaders of some association of midwives.

i. "*Shiphrah* and *Puah* are two good Semitic names, of an archaic type....meaning something like 'beauty' and 'splendour' respectively." (Cole)

b. **If it is a son, then you shall kill him**: The king of Egypt commanded them to kill all the male babies to utterly weaken and practically destroy the people of Israel within a generation.

i. We may see the command of Pharaoh as consistent with Satan's plan of Jew-hatred through the centuries, as an attack against God's Messiah and ultimate plan for Israel in His plan of redemption. Satan knew that the Messiah - the Seed of the Woman, the One who would crush his head (Genesis 3:15) - would come from the children of Israel; therefore, he tried to destroy the whole nation in one generation by ordering all the male children killed.

2. (17) The midwives bravely obey God rather than men.

But the midwives feared God, and did not do as the king of Egypt commanded them, but saved the male children alive.

a. **But the midwives feared God**: They probably feared Pharaoh and his power, but they **feared God** more. For them, the choice was clear. The civil government commanded something that was clearly against God's command. The midwives did the only right thing - they obeyed God rather than men.

b. **Saved the male children alive**: They acted on the same principle as did the persecuted apostles in Acts 4:19, when Peter asked the civil authorities: *Whether it is right in the sight of God to listen to you more than to God, you judge.*

i. Though generally we are called to obey the government and honor civic rulers (Romans 13:1-5), we are never called to put government in the place of God. Therefore if the government tells us to do something against God's will, we are to obey God first.

3. (18-22) God blesses the efforts of the midwives.

So the king of Egypt called for the midwives and said to them, "Why have you done this thing, and saved the male children alive?" And the midwives said to Pharaoh, "Because the Hebrew women *are* not like the Egyptian women; for they *are* lively and give birth before the midwives come to them." Therefore God dealt well with the midwives, and the people multiplied and grew very mighty. And so it was, because the midwives feared God, that He provided households for them. So Pharaoh commanded all his people, saying, "Every son who is born you shall cast into the river, and every daughter you shall save alive."

a. **Because the Hebrew women are not like the Egyptian women**: Many people assume that the Hebrew midwives lied to Pharaoh when they said this. However, this may not be the case. The midwives may have told the truth. Perhaps indeed the **Hebrew women** were heartier than the Egyptian women, yet the midwives did not explain *all* the reasons why the babies were spared.

i. "This might be no lie, as many suppose, but a truth concerning many of them, and they do not affirm it to be so with all...So here was nothing but truth, though they did not speak the whole truth, which they were not obliged to do." (Poole)

ii. "We are not told whether the midwives were lying, or whether the quick delivery of 'Hebrew' babies was a biological fact...Even if they lied, it is not for their deceit that they are commended, but for their refusal to take infant lives." (Cole)

b. **Therefore God dealt well with the midwives**: Even if the midwives deceived Pharaoh, that was not what God blessed; He blessed their godly bravery in obeying God before man.

c. **The people multiplied and grew very mightily**: The worse the persecution against God's plan to multiply the children of Israel in Egypt, the more God made sure the plan succeeded. This is a wonderful example of the goodness and the power of God. Pharaoh said, "Less" and God said, "More." Pharaoh said, "Stop" and God said, "Go."

i. If the battle were just between Pharaoh and the people of Israel, Pharaoh would have clearly won. But the real battle included God in the equation, and that changed everything.

ii. God obviously won this battle, but He won His victory through some courageous individuals who were willing to stand up to the power of Pharaoh and do what was right.

d. **He provided households for them**: This was God's blessing on the midwives - He enabled them to have children of their own. Usually, midwives held their occupation because they had no children of their own.

e. **Every son who is born you shall cast into the river**: Seeing that his plan did not work, Pharaoh made a far more radical command, that *all* male children should be killed – apparently even Egyptian boys (**Pharaoh commanded all his people**).

i. The method Pharaoh commanded for the death of the male children of Israel became the divine provision for training the deliverer of Israel.

Exodus 2 - Moses' Birth and Early Career

A. Moses' birth and childhood.

1. (1-2) Moses is born - a beautiful child of the tribe of Levi.

And a man of the house of Levi went and took *as wife* a daughter of Levi. So the woman conceived and bore a son. And when she saw that he *was* a beautiful *child,* she hid him three months.

a. **So the woman conceived and bore a son**: The baby Moses opened his eyes to an unfriendly world. He was born in a powerful nation, but was of a foreign, oppressed race during a time when all babies such as himself were under a royal death sentence. Nevertheless, Moses had something special in his favor - he was the child of believing parents.

i. Moses was not the firstborn in his family. He had at least an older brother (Aaron) and an older sister (Miriam).

b. **A man of the house of Levi went and took as wife a daughter of Levi**: Exodus 6:20 tells us the names of Moses' parents: *Amram* and *Jochebed.* Fanciful Jewish legends say that Moses' birth was painless to his mother; that at his birth his face was so beautiful that the room was filled with light equal to the sun and moon combined; that he walked and spoke when he was a day old; and that he refused to nurse, eating solid food from birth.

c. **She hid him three months**: The parents of Moses did not do this only because of the natural parental instinct; they did it also out of faith in God. Hebrews 11:23 describes the faith of Moses' parents: *By faith Moses, when he was born, was hidden three months by his parents, because they saw he was a beautiful child; and they were not afraid of the king's command.*

2. (3-6) Pharaoh's daughter finds Moses.

But when she could no longer hide him, she took an ark of bulrushes for him, daubed it with asphalt and pitch, put the child in it, and laid *it* in the reeds by the river's bank. And his sister stood afar off, to know

what would be done to him. Then the daughter of Pharaoh came down
to bathe at the river. And her maidens walked along the riverside; and
when she saw the ark among the reeds, she sent her maid to get it. And
when she had opened *it,* she saw the child, and behold, the baby wept.
So she had compassion on him, and said, "This is one of the Hebrews'
children."

a. **Laid it in the reeds by the river's bank**: In a literal sense, Moses'
mother did *exactly* what Pharaoh said to do - put her son into the river
(Exodus 1:22). However, she took care to put him in a waterproofed
basket and strategically floated him in the river.

i. "The word for 'papyrus basket' is used only here and for Noah's
ark." (Kaiser) "The Hebrew would be better translated by 'papyrus
basket'; the word is used elsewhere only of Noah's ark." (Cole)

ii. But more so, this was a great example of trusting the child's welfare
and future to God alone. When Moses' mother let go of the boat
made of bulrushes, she gave up something precious, trusting that
God would take care of it, and perhaps find a way to give it back to
her.

b. **The baby wept. So she had compassion on him**: In God's guidance,
Pharaoh's daughter found baby Moses. She was conditioned by her culture
and upbringing to reject the Hebrews, but the cry of baby Moses melted
her heart.

i. God had this beautifully planned for the deliverance of both
Moses, and eventually for the people of Israel. He skillfully guided
the parents of Moses, the currents of the Nile, and the heart of
Pharaoh's daughter to further His plan and purpose.

3. (7-10) Pharaoh's daughter cares for and raises Moses.

Then his sister said to Pharaoh's daughter, "Shall I go and call a nurse
for you from the Hebrew women, that she may nurse the child for
you?" And Pharaoh's daughter said to her, "Go." So the maiden went
and called the child's mother. Then Pharaoh's daughter said to her,
"Take this child away and nurse him for me, and I will give *you* your
wages." So the woman took the child and nursed him. And the child
grew, and she brought him to Pharaoh's daughter, and he became her
son. So she called his name Moses, saying, "Because I drew him out of
the water."

a. **Take this child away and nurse him for me, and I will give you
your wages**: Using both the clever initiative of Moses' family and the
need of Pharaoh's daughter, God arranged a way for Moses' mother to
train him in his early years and be paid for it.

i. God rewarded the faith of Moses' mother, both as she trusted Him in hiding Moses for three months, and also as she trusted God by setting Moses out on the river.

ii. "No doubt it was in these early years that Moses learnt of the 'God of the fathers' (Exodus 3:15) and realized that the Hebrews were his fellow countrymen (Exodus 2:11)." (Cole)

b. **And he became her son**: Being the adopted son of Pharaoh's daughter, Moses was in the royal family. The ancient Jewish historian Josephus wrote that Moses was heir to the throne of Egypt and that while a young man he led the armies of Egypt in victorious battle against the Ethiopians.

i. Certainly, he was raised with both the science and learning of Egypt. Acts 7:22 says, *Moses was learned in all the wisdom of the Egyptians, and was mighty in words and deeds*. Egypt was one of the most academic and scientific societies among ancient cultures. It is reasonable to think that Moses was instructed in geography, history, grammar, writing, literature, philosophy, and music.

ii. Since he was of the royal family, we expect that as Moses went anywhere, he went in a princely chariot and his guards cried out, "Bow the knee!" If he floated on the Nile, it was in a magnificent ship with musical accompaniment; he lived the royal life. We also know that Moses' Hebrew mother had an influence on his life, so he was certainly raised in the Hebrew heritage of his mother.

iii. An ancient Christian writer named Origen had a fanciful allegorical way of interpreting the Scriptures, and what he does with this account of Moses and Pharaoh's daughter is a good example of the peril of over-allegorizing the Scriptures. In Origen's take on this passage:

- Pharaoh represents the devil
- The male and female Hebrew children represent the animal and rational aspects of the soul
- The devil wants to kill the rational character of man, but keep alive his animal character
- The two midwives are the Old and New Testaments
- Pharaoh wants to corrupt the midwives so that the rational character of man will be destroyed
- Because the midwives were faithful, God builds houses of prayer all over the earth
- Pharaoh's daughter represents the church, and gives refuge to Moses - who represents the law
- The waters of the Nile represent the waters of baptism

- When we come to the waters of baptism and take the law into our heart - the royal palaces - then the law grows up into spiritual maturity

iv. Clarke rightly says of this kind of interpretation: "Every passage and fact might then be obliged to say *something, any thing, every thing,* or *nothing,* according to the *fancy,* peculiar *creed,* or *caprice* of the interpreter."

B. Moses' escape from Egypt.

1. (11) Moses grows and gains sympathy for his fellow Israelites.

Now it came to pass in those days, when Moses was grown, that he went out to his brethren and looked at their burdens. And he saw an Egyptian beating a Hebrew, one of his brethren.

a. **When Moses was grown**: Acts 7:23 says this happened when Moses was forty years old. Up until then, he was trained and groomed to become the next Pharaoh of Egypt (according to Josephus), all the while aware of his true origins because of his mother.

i. **Looked at their burdens**: "The phrase means more than 'to see'. It means, 'to see with emotion', either satisfaction (Genesis 9:16) or, as here, with distress (Genesis 21:16). Moses is one who shares God's heart." (Cole)

ii. Hebrews 11:24-26 tells us some of what happened in the heart and mind of Moses as he **looked at their burdens**. It says that by faith, Moses deliberately decided to identify with the people of Israel rather than his Egyptian prestige and opportunity:

By faith Moses, when he became of age, refused to be called the son of Pharaoh's daughter, choosing rather to suffer affliction with the people of God than to enjoy the passing pleasures of sin, esteeming the reproach of Christ greater riches than the treasures in Egypt; for he looked to the reward. (Hebrews 11:24-26)

iii. *Moses knew who he was.* As much allure and ease as there was in life as an Egyptian, he knew "That's not me." His faith in the God he served helped him to know who *he* was.

b. **He saw an Egyptian beating a Hebrew, one of his brethren**: Because Moses had a heart filled with sympathy and brotherhood (**his brethren**) toward his people, he could not stand by while one of his fellow Israelites endured a **beating**.

2. (12) Moses murders an Egyptian.

So he looked this way and that way, and when he saw no one, he killed the Egyptian and hid him in the sand.

a. **He looked this way and that way**: Moss knew what he was about to do was wrong. Moses had several reasons for doing what he did, but his concern to hide what he did showed a troubled conscience.

b. **He killed the Egyptian**: The Bible itself explains some of Moses' thinking behind this action. Acts 7:23-25 explains that Moses did this to defend and avenge the beaten Israelite, but also with the expectation that his fellow Israelites would recognize him as their deliverer.

> i. *Now when he was forty years old, it came into his heart to visit his brethren, the children of Israel. And seeing one of them suffer wrong, he defended and avenged him who was oppressed, and struck down the Egyptian. For he supposed that his brethren would have understood that God would deliver them by his hand, but they did not understand.* (Acts 7:23-25)

3. (13-14) Moses is rejected by his own people.

And when he went out the second day, behold, two Hebrew men were fighting, and he said to the one who did the wrong, "Why are you striking your companion?" Then he said, "Who made you a prince and a judge over us? Do you intend to kill me as you killed the Egyptian?" So Moses feared and said, "Surely this thing is known!"

a. **Why are you striking your companion**: Moses had reason to believe that his education, royal background, success, and great sympathy for the people of Israel would give him credibility among them. Here, he tried to intervene in a violent dispute between **two Hebrew men**.

i. We could say that Moses was first a *murderer*, and then a *meddler*.

b. **Who made you a prince and a judge over us**: Moses seemed to act like **a prince**, given his royal background. He acted like **a judge** in that he determined that one of these men **did the wrong**. He seemed to be the perfect **prince** and **judge** for Israel, but they did not want him.

i. A **prince** has the right to rule and expects your loyalty. A **judge** has the right to tell you what to do, and to punish you if you don't do it. In rejecting Moses they said to him, "We don't want you to rule over us or tell us what to do." People reject Jesus on the same thinking, and just like Moses, Jesus was rejected at His first coming.

ii. Both Moses and Jesus were:

- Favored by God from birth
- Miraculously preserved in childhood
- Mighty in words and deed
- Offered deliverance to Israel
- Rejected with spite
- Rejected in their right to be *prince and a judge* over Israel

iii. Just like Jesus after him, Moses could not deliver when he lived in the palaces of glory. He had to come down off the throne, away from the palace and into a humble place before he could deliver his people.

iv. Moses planned the deliverance of Israel the way any man would, and logically saw himself as the key man - because of his royal background, education, success, and sympathy for his people.

v. Moses had his plans, and they made sense from his perspective. Yet God's plan was radically different. 40 years later, God led Moses and his brother Aaron to Pharaoh with a special stick that turned into a snake. Moses asked Pharaoh to let Israel go back to Canaan; Pharaoh said no, so God brought plagues of blood, frogs, mosquitoes, flies, cattle disease, boils, hail, locusts, and darkness. Finally, God judged stubborn Pharaoh and Egypt with a plague on the firstborn of Egypt. Israel escaped across the Red Sea. The waters of the Red Sea came back and killed the Egyptian army, and the Israelites crossed the wilderness and came to Canaan. *Such an unlikely plan would never come from man.*

4. (15-19) Moses escapes to Midian.

When Pharaoh heard of this matter, he sought to kill Moses. But Moses fled from the face of Pharaoh and dwelt in the land of Midian; and he sat down by a well. Now the priest of Midian had seven daughters. And they came and drew water, and they filled the troughs to water their father's flock. Then the shepherds came and drove them away; but Moses stood up and helped them, and watered their flock. When they came to Reuel their father, he said, "How *is it that* you have come so soon today?" And they said, "An Egyptian delivered us from the hand of the shepherds, and he also drew enough water for us and watered the flock."

a. **Moses fled from the face of Pharaoh**: Moses, fleeing for his life, probably felt that God's plan for his life was completely defeated. He probably believed that every chance he ever had to deliver his people was now over and there was nothing *he* could do. At this point, Moses was right where God wanted him.

i. Moses probably had little idea of it at the time, but he was too big for God to use. Moses tried to do the Lord's work in man's wisdom and power and it didn't work. After 40 years of seemingly perfect preparation, God had another period of preparation for both Moses, and the people of Israel, to make them ready to receive Moses.

b. **Dwelt in the land of Midian**: If Moses went into the area of Canaan and Syria, he would have found no refuge - there was a treaty between

Rameses II and the Hittite king to the effect that fugitives along the northern route to Syria would be arrested and extradited. So Moses went southeast instead to **Midian**.

> i. In that day, **Midian** described the area on both the west and east sides of the Reed Sea, land that today is both Saudi Arabia (on the east of the Reed Sea) and Egypt (on the Sinai Peninsula, on the west of the Reed Sea).

c. **The priest of Midian had seven daughters**: Finally coming to Midian, Moses met the daughters of a **priest of Midian** - likely a descendant of one of Abraham's other children through Keturah named Midian (Genesis 25:1-2).

> i. Because of this connection with Abraham, we have good reason to believe he was a true priest, and worshipped the true God. God led Moses to this specific family at this specific time.

> ii. Trapp on **they came and drew water, and they filled the troughs to water their father's flock**: "They were not so delicately bred as our dainty dames are now-a-days, but did *earn* before they *eat*."

d. **Moses stood up and helped them, and watered their flock**: In Egypt, Moses enjoyed life as one of the royal family and was waited on hand and foot. In the distant desert of Midian, Moses finally had an opportunity to be a servant and he did a good job, working hard to help water the flocks of Reuel's daughters.

> i. "Since Moses still had his Egyptian clothing on, they judged him to be Egyptian in nationality." (Kaiser)

5. (20-22) Moses is accepted into the family of the priest of Midian.

So he said to his daughters, "And where *is* he? Why *is* it *that* you have left the man? Call him, that he may eat bread." Then Moses was content to live with the man, and he gave Zipporah his daughter to Moses. And she bore *him* a son, and he called his name Gershom; for he said, "I have been a stranger in a foreign land."

a. **Moses was content to live with the man**: By taking a wife and having a son, Moses seems to give up on Egypt and his hope of being a deliverer for Israel. Moses was content with where God put him, even though Midian was very different from Egypt.

> ii. **Zipporah**: "We might translate as 'warbler' or, less kindly, 'twitterer'; it is the name of a small bird." (Cole)

b. **He called his name Gershom**: This name – meaning "stranger" – was evidence of some loneliness, living apart from either the Egyptians or the Hebrews.

i. We make a mistake when we think that the years in Midian were a "waiting" time for Moses. They were instead, *working* years; he had never worked this hard in his life! God trained him, shaping him for his future calling, but Moses was certainly not "on the shelf."

ii. In Egypt, Moses learned how to be somebody. In Midian he learned how to be nobody. "Much he had learned in Egypt, but more in Midian." (Trapp)

6. (23-25) God remembers Israel and turns His attention to them.

Now it happened in the process of time that the king of Egypt died. Then the children of Israel groaned because of the bondage, and they cried out; and their cry came up to God because of the bondage. So God heard their groaning, and God remembered His covenant with Abraham, with Isaac, and with Jacob. And God looked upon the children of Israel, and God acknowledged *them.*

a. **So God heard their groaning, and God remembered**: If Moses "forgot" about Israel in Egypt (in the sense of turning his active attention away from them), God did not. God **remembered** (again, in the sense of turning His active attention towards them) Israel and their affliction.

i. When **Israel groaned because of the bondage**, it could be said, "Misery finally found a voice." (Kaiser)

b. **God remembered His covenant with Abraham, with Isaac, and with Jacob**: God did not turn His attention to Israel because they were such good people, but because of the covenant He made with them. He gives His love and attention to us on the same basis - the covenant relationship we have with God through Jesus.

Exodus 3 - Moses and the Burning Bush

A. God's call to Moses from the burning bush.

1. (1-3) Moses and the burning bush on Mount Horeb.

Now Moses was tending the flock of Jethro his father-in-law, the priest of Midian. And he led the flock to the back of the desert, and came to Horeb, the mountain of God. And the Angel of the LORD appeared to him in a flame of fire from the midst of a bush. So he looked, and behold, the bush was burning with fire, but the bush *was* not consumed. Then Moses said, "I will now turn aside and see this great sight, why the bush does not burn."

a. **Moses was tending the flock of Jethro his father-in-law**: For 40 years Moses lived as an obscure shepherd in the desert of Midian. At this point, his life was so humble that he didn't even have a flock of sheep to call his own - the sheep belonged to his **father-in-law**.

i. **Tending the flock**: "The Hebrew suggests that this was his habitual occupation." (Cole)

b. **The back of the desert, and came to Horeb, the mountain of God**: Moses brought the sheep to this mountain, also later called Mount Sinai. **Horeb** probably means "desert" or "desolation," and the name gives an idea of the terrain.

c. **The bush was burning with fire, but the bush was not consumed**: It wasn't just that Moses saw a bush burning; apparently, it is not uncommon for a plant like this to spontaneously ignite out in that desert. Nevertheless, two things were distinctive about that bush:

- **The Angel of the LORD appeared...from the midst** of the bush
- Though the bush burned, **the bush was not consumed**.

i. "Though the bush burned with fire, it did not crackle or diminish, no leaf curled and no branch charred. It burned, but was not consumed." (Meyer)

ii. The bush burning but not being consumed was a magnetic sight to Moses - it drew him in for a closer examination. Some think the burning bush to be a symbol of Israel, or the people of God more generally – afflicted but not destroyed, because God is in the midst of them.

iii. Yet we can also say that the burning bush was a picture of the cross. The Hebrew word used to describe this bush comes from the words "to stick or to prick," this meaning a thorn-bush or bramble. We can think of the cross – where Jesus, crowned with thorns, endured the fires of judgment and yet was not consumed by them – and be reminded of the cross when we consider the burning bush.

iv. **I will now turn aside to see this great sight**: Whatever exactly Moses saw, it was nothing *normal*. "To explain what happened here as a temporary mirage of reflected sunlight on some red leaves or a campfire of some Bedouin or even the phenomenon of Saint Elmo's fire is to substitute *our* experience for Moses' forty years in that area and his estimate that it was indeed unusual." (Kaiser)

v. Clarke on the **Angel of the LORD**: "Not a created angel certainly, for he is called *Jehovah*, Exodus 3:4 and has the most expressive attributes of the Godhead applied to him…Yet he is an *angel, malach,* a *messenger*, in whom was the name of God….And who is this but JESUS, the Leader, Redeemer, and Saviour of all mankind?"

2. (4-6) From the burning bush, God calls to Moses.

So when the LORD saw that he turned aside to look, God called to him from the midst of the bush and said, "Moses, Moses!" And he said, "Here I am." Then He said, "Do not draw near this place. Take your sandals off your feet, for the place where you stand *is* holy ground." Moreover He said, "I *am* the God of your father; the God of Abraham, the God of Isaac, and the God of Jacob." And Moses hid his face, for he was afraid to look upon God.

a. **When the LORD saw that he turned aside to look**: God didn't speak to Moses until He had Moses' attention. Often God's Word doesn't touch our heart the way that it might, because we don't give it our attention.

i. The burning bush was a spectacular phenomenon that captured Moses' attention, but it changed nothing until Moses received the *Word of God* that came to him there.

b. **God called to him from the midst of the bush**: Moses didn't see anyone in the burning bush; yet God, in the presence of the *Angel of the LORD* (Exodus 3:2), was there calling out to Moses from the midst of the burning bush.

i. Undoubtedly, this was another occasion where Jesus appeared before His incarnation in the Old Testament as *the Angel of the* Lord, as He did many times (Genesis 16:7-13, Judges 2:1-5, Judges 6:11-24, Judges 13:3-22).

ii. We say this is God, in the Person of Jesus Christ, because of God the Father it is said *No one has seen God at any time. The only begotten Son, who is in the bosom of the Father, He has declared Him* (John 1:18); and that no man has ever seen God in the Person of the Father (1 Timothy 6:16).

c. **Moses, Moses**: God's first words to Moses called him by name. This shows that even though Moses was now an obscure, forgotten shepherd on the backside of the desert, God knew who he was, and Moses was important to God.

i. The *double* call (**Moses, Moses!**) implied importance and urgency, as when God called *Abraham, Abraham!* (Genesis 22:11), *Samuel, Samuel!* (1 Samuel 3:10), *Simon, Simon* (Luke 22:31), *Martha, Martha* (Luke 10:41), and *Saul, Saul* (Acts 9:4).

d. **Then He said**: God told Moses to do two things to show special honor to this place because of the immediate presence of God.

- He told Moses to keep a distance (**Do not draw near this place**).

- He commanded Moses to show reverence for God's presence (**Take your sandals off your feet**).

i. **Do not draw near** literally has the sense of "stop coming closer." Moses was on his way for an up-close examination of the burning bush when God stopped him short.

ii. This was a holy place, and because God is holy, there will always be a distance between God and man. Even in perfection man will never be equal to God, though we will be able to have closer fellowship with Him than ever.

iii. **Take your sandals off your feet**: Removing the sandals showed an appropriate *humility*, because the poorest and most needy have no shoes, and servants usually went barefoot. It also recognized the *immediate presence* of God. In many cultures, you take off your shoes when you come into someone's house, and now Moses was in God's "house," a place of His immediate presence.

iv. "As this sole must like in dust, gravel, and sand about the foot when travelling, and render it very uneasy, hence the custom of frequently *washing* the feet in those countries where these sandals were worn. *Pulling off the shoes was*, therefore, an emblem of laying aside the *pollutions* contracted by *walking* in the *way of sin*." (Clarke)

e. **The God of Abraham, the God of Isaac, and the God of Jacob**: God revealed Himself to Moses by declaring His relationship to the patriarchs. This reminded Moses that God is the God of the covenant, and His covenant with Israel was still valid and important. This wasn't a "new God" meeting Moses, but the same God that dealt with **Abraham**, **Isaac**, and **Jacob**.

i. God would reveal Himself to Moses more intimately than He had to any of the patriarchs; yet it all began with God reminding Moses of the bridge of covenant they met on.

ii. Some in the days of Moses might have thought that God neglected or forgot His covenant in the 400 years of Israel's slavery in Egypt, since the time of the patriarchs. Nevertheless, God was at work during that time, preserving and multiplying the nation.

f. **Moses hid his face, for he was afraid to look upon God**: God told Moses to do what was appropriate for a creature before their Creator - to revere and recognize His holiness. Moses responded as a man who knew he was not only a creature, but also a sinful creature - he **hid his face**.

i. In his years in the wilderness of Midan, Moses must have often remembered how he murdered an Egyptian and how proud he was to think he could deliver Israel himself. Moses might have remembered a thousands sins, both real and imagined - now, when God appeared, he responded in a way completely different than he might have 40 years before.

B. God's commission to Moses.

1. (7-10) God explains His general plan to Moses, and Moses' place in the plan.

And the Lord said: "I have surely seen the oppression of My people who *are* in Egypt, and have heard their cry because of their taskmasters, for I know their sorrows. So I have come down to deliver them out of the hand of the Egyptians, and to bring them up from that land to a good and large land, to a land flowing with milk and honey, to the place of the Canaanites and the Hittites and the Amorites and the Perizzites and the Hivites and the Jebusites. Now therefore, behold, the cry of the children of Israel has come to Me, and I have also seen the oppression with which the Egyptians oppress them. Come now, therefore, and I will send you to Pharaoh that you may bring My people, the children of Israel, out of Egypt."

a. **I have come down to deliver them out of the hand of the Egyptians, and to bring them up from that land to a good and large land**: God did not just *then* decide to give Israel the land of Canaan. It was the same land that He promised to the patriarchs some 400 years previous to this.

b. **I have surely seen the oppression of My people who *are* in Egypt, and have heard their cry**: God wanted Moses and Israel to know His compassionate care for them.

i. To this point, Moses' experience emphasized the *separation* between himself and God. Moses could never burn without being consumed. Moses could not speak from the midst of a fire. Moses couldn't keep his sandals on in the divine presence. Moses was not the eternal God of the patriarchs. The separation between God and Moses was real; yet God would soon show His care and compassion to Moses and the people of Israel. God is *separate*, but not necessarily *distant*. God is separate; yet God cares and connects Himself to our needs.

c. **I will send you to Pharaoh that you may bring My people**: In Exodus 3:8 God said, *I have come down to deliver them.* Then at Exodus 3:10 God said, **Come now, therefore, and I will send you**. If God said He would deliver them, why did He use or need Moses at all? This shows that God often uses and chooses to rely on human instruments.

i. God could do it all by Himself, but it is most often God's plan to work with and through people, as we are *workers together with Him* (2 Corinthians 6:1).

2. (11-12) Moses' answer, and God's reply to that answer.

But Moses said to God, "Who *am* I that I should go to Pharaoh, and that I should bring the children of Israel out of Egypt?" So He said, "I will certainly be with you. And this *shall be* a sign to you that I have sent you: When you have brought the people out of Egypt, you shall serve God on this mountain."

a. **Who am I**: 40 years before, Moses thought he knew who he was; he was a prince of Egypt and a Hebrew, God's chosen instrument to deliver Israel. After forty years of chasing sheep around the desert, Moses didn't have the same self-sure confidence that he once had.

b. **I will certainly be with you**: God's reply is intended to take Moses' focus off of himself and on where it *should be* - God. Therefore, God never answered the question "**Who am I?**" Instead, He reminded Moses "**I will certainly be with you.**"

i. This was a great opportunity to deal with Moses' "self-esteem" problem, but God ignored the solutions we usually use regarding this "problem." Moses only had a self-esteem problem when he was too confident in his own ability to deliver Israel.

ii. **Who am I**: This really wasn't the right question; *"Who is God?"* was the proper question. God's identity was more important than who Moses was. When we know the God who is with us, we can step forth confidently to do His will.

iii. **I will certainly be with you**: After this, Moses had no right to protest further. From here, his objections move from a godly lack of self-reliance to an ungodly lack of faith.

c. **When you have brought the people out of Egypt, you shall serve God on this mountain**: As Moses tended his flock in the wilderness, it probably seemed totally unlikely that he would lead all three million of his people to this same **mountain**, but God promised that this would be so.

i. The **sign** that God had truly sent Moses may not have been the coming to Mount Sinai (which did not happen for many, many months). The sign probably refers backwards, to the sign of the burning bush and the encounter with God there.

3. (13-14) The revelation of God's name to Moses.

Then Moses said to God, "Indeed, *when* I come to the children of Israel and say to them, 'The God of your fathers has sent me to you,' and they say to me, 'What *is* His name?' what shall I say to them?" And God said to Moses, "I AM WHO I AM." And He said, "Thus you shall say to the children of Israel, 'I AM has sent me to you.'"

a. **And they say to me, "What *is* His name?" what shall I say to them**: Rightfully, Moses sensed he needed credentials before the people of Israel. Before, he thought he had the credentials because he was a prince of Egypt. 40 years of tending sheep took away his sense of self-reliance.

i. When God revealed Himself to man in the days of the patriarchs, it was often associated with a newly revealed name or title for God.

- Abraham, in the encounter with Melchizedek, called on *God Most High* (Genesis 14:22)
- Abraham later encountered *Almighty God* (Genesis 17:1)
- Abraham came to know the LORD as *Everlasting God* (Genesis 21:33), and *The-LORD-Will-Provide* (Genesis 22:14)
- Hagar encountered *You-Are-the-God-Who-Sees* (Genesis 16:13)
- Jacob met *El Elohe Israel* (Genesis 33:20) and *El Bethel* (Genesis 35:7).

ii. So if Moses were to come to the elders of Israel as a representative of God, it would be logical for them to wonder, "By what name did He reveal Himself to you?"

b. **And God said to Moses, "I AM WHO I AM"**: It might seem nonsensical to refer to one's self with the phrase, **"I AM WHO I AM"**; yet it revealed something important about God – that He has no equal.

i. "There is no equivalent for God but God. If you place God on the one side of your symbol of equation (=), there is nothing to put on the other but Himself." (Meyer)

ii. The *closest* we come to an equivalent is to say, "God is love" (1 John 4:8, 4:16). Yet that is not exactly an equivalent, because you can't turn it around and say, "Love is God." God is love, but He is also greater than love.

iii. This name **I AM WHO I AM** is connected with the name *Yahweh*. "This pithy clause is clearly a reference to the name YHWH. Probably 'Yahweh' is regarded as a shortening of the whole phrase, and a running together of the clause into one word." (Cole)

iv. *Yahweh* was not a new name, nor an unknown name - it appears more than 160 times in the book of Genesis. Moses' mother's name was *Jochabed* meaning *Yahweh is my glory*. Moses and Israel knew the name *Yahweh*. God did not give Moses a previously unknown name of God, but the name they had known before. God called them back to the faith of the patriarchs, not to something "new."

v. In the English-speaking world, for a time people pronounced *Yahweh* as *Jehovah*. The pious Jews of later years did not want to pronounce the name of God out of reverence, so they left the vowels out of His name and simply said the word *Lord* (*Adonai*) instead. If the vowels of the word *Adonai* are put over the consonants for *YHWH*, you can get the name "Jehovah." All this came about much later; in the days of the Bible, the name was pronounced *Yah-weh* or *Yah-veh*.

c. **I AM has sent me to you**: God told Moses His name was **I AM** because God simply *is*; there was never a time when He did not exist, or a time when He will cease to exist.

i. The name **I AM** has within it the idea that God is completely independent; that He relies on nothing for life or existence (Isaiah 40:28-29; John 5:26). Theologians sometimes call this quality *aseity*. It means that God doesn't need anybody or anything - life is in Himself.

ii. It is also connected with the idea that God is eternal and unchanging. "Strictly speaking, there is no past or future tense in the

Divine Vocabulary. When God appears to employ them, it is by way of accommodation to our limited horizons." (Meyer)

iii. Also inherent in the idea behind the name **I Am** is the sense that God is "the becoming one"; God becomes whatever is lacking in our time of need. The name **I Am** invites us to fill in the blank to meet our need - when we are in darkness, Jesus says *I am the light*; when we are hungry, He says *I am the bread of life*; when we are defenseless, He says *I am the Good Shepherd*. God is the becoming one, becoming what we need.

iv. In this, God's name is both an announcement and an introduction. It announces God's presence and invites any interested to know Him by experience, to taste and see that the LORD is good.

d. **I Am**: This is a divine title that Jesus took upon Himself often, clearly identifying Himself with the voice from the burning bush.

i. *Therefore I said to you that you will die in your sins; for if you do not believe that **I Am** [He], you will die in your sins.* (John 8:24)

ii. *Then Jesus said to them, "When you lift up the Son of Man, then you will know that **I Am** [He], and that I do nothing of Myself; but as My Father taught Me, I speak these things."* (John 8:28)

iii. *Jesus said to them, "Most assuredly, I say to you, before Abraham was, **I Am**."* (John 8:58)

iv. *Now I tell you before it comes, that when it does come to pass, you may believe that **I Am*** (John 13:19)

v. *Jesus therefore, knowing all things that would come upon Him, went forward and said to them, "Whom are you seeking?" They answered Him, "Jesus of Nazareth." Jesus said to them, "**I Am** [He]." And Judas, who betrayed Him, also stood with them. Now when He said to them, "I am [He]," they drew back and fell to the ground.* (John 18:4-6)

4. (15-18) God tells Moses what to say to the elders of Israel.

Moreover God said to Moses, "Thus you shall say to the children of Israel: 'The LORD God of your fathers, the God of Abraham, the God of Isaac, and the God of Jacob, has sent me to you. This *is* My name forever, and this *is* My memorial to all generations.' Go and gather the elders of Israel together, and say to them, 'The LORD God of your fathers, the God of Abraham, of Isaac, and of Jacob, appeared to me, saying, "I have surely visited you and *seen* what is done to you in Egypt; and I have said I will bring you up out of the affliction of Egypt to the land of the Canaanites and the Hittites and the Amorites and the Perizzites and the Hivites and the Jebusites, to a land flowing with milk

and honey.'" Then they will heed your voice; and you shall come, you
and the elders of Israel, to the king of Egypt; and you shall say to him,
'The LORD God of the Hebrews has met with us; and now, please, let us
go three days' journey into the wilderness, that we may sacrifice to the
LORD our God.'"

a. **Thus you shall say to the children of Israel**: After 400 years in Egypt,
Moses had the job of announcing that *now* was the time for the children
of Israel to go back to Canaan, and to take the land God promised to
their fathers.

i. This was probably totally contrary to what the elders and people of
Israel desired. In 400 years, you set down roots. They probably had
no desire to return to the Promised Land; all they wanted was to be
made more comfortable in Egypt.

ii. The first word had to come to the people of God (Exodus 3:16)
and then to the world (Exodus 3:18). Often God will not speak to the
wider world until He speaks to His people and He has their attention.

b. **This is My name forever**: God here referred to the name just
previously mentioned in the same verse, the **LORD God** (*Yahweh Elohim*).
"**Forever**" emphasizes the eternal faithfulness of God to His covenant.

c. **Then they will heed your voice**: This was a precious promise to
Moses. Forty years before, when it seemed that he had everything going
for him, the people of Israel rejected him as a deliverer for the nation.
Surely, he must be wondering why they would listen to him now, when it
seemed he had nothing going for him.

i. But Moses had *God* going for him now; they would indeed listen to
Moses' message.

d. **To the king of Egypt; and you shall say to him....let us go three
days' journey into the wilderness**: God presented the smaller request
to Pharaoh first so that the request would be as appealing and as easy to
accept as possible. He did this so Pharaoh would have no excuse at all for
refusing God and hardening his heart.

5. (19-22) God tells Moses how it will go with the Egyptians.

"**But I am sure that the king of Egypt will not let you go, no, not even
by a mighty hand. So I will stretch out My hand and strike Egypt with
all My wonders which I will do in its midst; and after that he will let
you go. And I will give this people favor in the sight of the Egyptians;
and it shall be, when you go, that you shall not go empty-handed. But
every woman shall ask of her neighbor, namely, of her who dwells near
her house, articles of silver, articles of gold, and clothing; and you shall**

put *them* on your sons and on your daughters. So you shall plunder the Egyptians."

a. **I am sure that the king of Egypt will not let you go**: God knew this from the beginning. He knew what it would take to move the heart of Pharaoh, and the plagues and calamities to come were engineered for a specific purpose, and they were not haphazardly planned.

i. Moses asked God about how his fellow Israelites would receive the news of the deliverance from Egypt, but getting the people of Israel behind Moses was only a small part of the struggle ahead - what about the Egyptians? How would they ever agree to let this free labor force leave the country? Without Moses asking, God answered this question.

ii. Clarke insists that the sense of **I am sure that the king of Egypt will not let you go, no, not even by a mighty hand** is better understood as *I am sure that the king of Egypt will not let you go, except with a mighty hand.* The idea is plain enough – Pharaoh would not let go of them easily, so God would bring great judgment against Egypt to persuade him.

b. **I will give this people favor…you shall not go empty-handed**: God promised to arrange things not only to move Pharaoh's heart, but also to move the heart of the Egyptian people so that when Israel did depart, they would be showered with **silver** and **gold** and **clothing**. This was not stealing or extortion; it was the appropriate wages for the years of forced labor.

i. In Deuteronomy 15:12-14, God says that if you have a slave, and his time of service is up, *you shall not let him go away empty-handed.* God was not going to let Israel leave their slavery in Egypt empty-handed; instead, they would **plunder the Egyptians**.

Exodus 4 - Moses' Commission from God

A. God gives Moses signs to confirm his ministry.

1. (1) Moses asks, "How will they believe me?"

Then Moses answered and said, "But suppose they will not believe me or listen to my voice; suppose they say, 'The LORD has not appeared to you.'"

a. **But suppose they will not believe me**: It was not wrong for Moses to initially ask, "*Who am I that I should go to Pharaoh?*" (Exodus 3:11); this was a logical question, considering how great the task was. Yet God answered this question more than adequately in Exodus 3:12: *I will certainly be with you*. After that point, and in this passage, Moses' questions show unbelief more than sincere seeking.

b. **But suppose they will not believe me or listen to my voice**: In Exodus 3:18, God promised that the leaders of Israel *would* listen to Moses. He said, "*They will heed your voice*." When Moses made this protest, he may as well have said, "But what if you are wrong, God?"

i. It was good when Moses had no confidence in the flesh, but it was bad that he then lacked confidence in God. In view of the burning bush, the voice of God, and the divine encounter, there was no place for Moses to say "**but**."

ii. "We are ever prone, when God is calling us to some high service, to say 'But,' and this to introduce our statement of the difficulties as we see them." (Morgan)

2. (2-5) The first sign: Moses' rod turns to a snake and back again.

So the LORD said to him, "What *is* that in your hand?" He said, "A rod." And He said, "Cast it on the ground." So he cast it on the ground, and it became a serpent; and Moses fled from it. Then the LORD said to Moses, "Reach out your hand and take *it* by the tail" (and he reached out his hand and caught it, and it became a rod in his hand), that they

may believe that the LORD God of their fathers, the God of Abraham, the God of Isaac, and the God of Jacob, has appeared to you."

a. **What is that in your hand**: This reflects a precious principle regarding how God uses people - God used what Moses had in his **hand**. Moses' years of tending sheep were not useless. Those years had put into Moses' **hand** things he could use for God's glory. God didn't use the scepter that was in Moses' royal hand when he lived in Egypt, but He did use the simple shepherd's staff.

  i. God likes to use what is in our hand.

  - God used what was in Shamgar's hand (Judges 3:31)
  - God used what was in David's hand (1 Samuel 17:49)
  - God used the jawbone of a donkey in Samson's hand (Judges 15:15)
  - God used five loaves and two fish in the hand of a little boy (John 6:9)

b. **He said, "A rod"**: That rod of Moses would part the Red Sea. It would strike a rock and see water pour forth. It would be raised over battle until Israel won. It would be called *the rod of God* (Exodus 4:20 and 17:9).

c. **It became a serpent**: Not only did Moses' rod become like a snake; it became a real snake that was frightening enough to Moses that he ran from it.

d. **Reach out your hand and take it by the tail**: We see the faith of Moses when he reached out to grab the snake when God commanded him to. The tail is the most dangerous place to grab a snake, yet Moses was unharmed.

  i. In this little incident, Moses learned how to do what God told him to do even when it was uncomfortable.

e. **That they may believe that the LORD God of their fathers...has appeared to you**: This miracle would make the children of Israel realize that **the God of Abraham, the God of Isaac, and the God of Jacob** was with them, and that the God of the covenant had not forsaken them.

3. (6-9) The second and third signs: Moses is made leprous and whole again; water turns to blood and back again.

Furthermore the LORD said to him, "Now put your hand in your bosom." And he put his hand in his bosom, and when he took it out, behold, his hand *was* leprous, like snow. And He said, "Put your hand in your bosom again." So he put his hand in his bosom again, and drew it out of his bosom, and behold, it was restored like his *other* flesh. "Then it will be, if they do not believe you, nor heed the message of

the first sign, that they may believe the message of the latter sign. And it shall be, if they do not believe even these two signs, or listen to your voice, that you shall take water from the river and pour *it* on the dry *land.* And the water which you take from the river will become blood on the dry *land.*"

a. **It was restored like his other flesh**: Each of the first two signs had to do with *transformation*. Something good and useful (a rod or a hand) was made into something evil (a serpent or a leprous hand), and significantly, they were then transformed back again.

i. There was a real message in the first two signs. The first said, "Moses, if you obey Me, your enemies will be made powerless." The second said, "Moses, if you obey Me, your pollution can be made pure." Doubts in each of these areas probably hindered Moses, and before those signs spoke to anyone else, they spoke to Moses. This is the pattern with all God's leaders.

ii. "The Hebrew word for leprosy covered a number of assorted diseases much as our word 'cancer' currently does." (Kaiser)

b. **The water which you take from the river will become blood on the dry land**: The third sign was simply a sign of judgment. Good, pure waters were made foul and bloody by the work of God, and they did not turn back again. This showed that if the miracles of transformation did not turn the hearts of the people, then perhaps the sign of judgment would. **If they do not believe even these two signs, or listen to your voice** shows that the sign of judgment was only given when unbelief persisted despite the miracles of transformation right before them.

4. (10) Moses makes an excuse: "I can't speak well."

Then Moses said to the LORD, "O my Lord, I *am* not eloquent, neither before nor since You have spoken to Your servant; but I *am* slow of speech and slow of tongue."

a. **O my Lord, I am not eloquent**: After these remarkably persuasive signs, Moses still objected to God's call. Moses revealed that he was not confident with his ability to speak - **slow of speech** is literally "heavy of mouth."

b. **I am slow of speech and slow of tongue**: It seems that Moses' excuse was not justified. Clearly 40 years before this, Moses was not **slow of speech and slow of tongue**. Acts 7:22 says *Moses was learned in all the wisdom of the Egyptians, and was mighty in words and deeds.*

i. Those years of eloquence in Egypt ended 40 years before this. For 40 years, Moses only seemed to speak to sheep. His *self* confidence was gone, but he needed *God* confidence instead.

ii. "Thus Moses' complaint was not in defective articulation, but in his inability to take command of Hebrew and Egyptian (cf. Ezekiel 3:5, where 'heavy of tongue' = difficulty with a foreign language...)." (Kaiser)

5. (11-12) God's response to Moses' excuse.

So the LORD said to him, "Who has made man's mouth? Or who makes the mute, the deaf, the seeing, or the blind? *Have* **not I, the LORD? Now therefore, go, and I will be with your mouth and teach you what you shall say."**

a. **Who made man's mouth**: The fact that Moses believed that he was not eloquent is completely beside the point. The God who created the most eloquent mouths who ever lived was on his side.

b. **Who has made man's mouth? Or who makes the mute, the deaf, the seeing, or the blind? Have not I, the LORD**: This is a dramatic statement revealing the sovereignty of God, and God revealed it in the context of an invitation to trust God and to work with Him.

i. There is not the slightest sense of fatalism in this declaration of God's sovereignty. It is *never* "God is so mighty we can't do anything," but it is *always* "God is so mighty, He can work through us if we make ourselves available."

c. **Makes the mute, the deaf...the blind**: Some think this is cruel of God. Nevertheless, the point here was not to analyze the origin of evil, but to show that God is so mighty that He can even call the mute, deaf, and blind to do His work. Moses' perceived inadequacies didn't matter at all.

i. If Moses was a poor speaker, was this news to God? Does God have trouble keeping track of who is deaf, who is blind, and who is mute? Does Moses really think God made a mistake here?

ii. If Moses was a poor speaker, it didn't matter - the mighty God said, **"I will be with your mouth and teach you what you shall say."** By extension, God is sufficient for us, no matter what real or imagined inadequacies we have.

6. (13-17) Moses' unwillingness, and God's reply.

But he said, "O my Lord, please send by the hand of whomever *else* **You may send." So the anger of the LORD was kindled against Moses, and He said: "Is not Aaron the Levite your brother? I know that he can speak well. And look, he is also coming out to meet you. When he sees you, he will be glad in his heart. Now you shall speak to him and put the words in his mouth. And I will be with your mouth and with**

his mouth, and I will teach you what you shall do. So he shall be your spokesman to the people. And he himself shall be as a mouth for you, and you shall be to him as God. And you shall take this rod in your hand, with which you shall do the signs."

a. **Please send by the hand of whomever else You may send**: Finally, Moses was done with excuses and showed the real state of his heart. Simply, he would much rather that God send someone else. His problem wasn't really a lack of ability; it was a lack of willingness.

> i. "It's common for men to give pretended reasons instead of one real one." (Benjamin Franklin)

b. **So the anger of the LORD was kindled against Moses**: God was not angry when Moses asked, *"Who am I?"* (Exodus 3:11). He was not angry when Moses asked, "Who should I say sent me?" (Exodus 3:13). He was not angry when Moses disbelieved God's Word and said, *"Suppose they will not believe me or listen to my voice"* (Exodus 4:1). He was not even angry when Moses falsely claimed that he was not and had never been eloquent (Exodus 4:10). But God *was* angry when Moses was just plain unwilling.

> i. There may be a hundred understandable reasons why Moses was unwilling, some of them making a lot of sense. Perhaps Moses really *wanted* to serve, but was unwilling because of past rejection. Nevertheless, the basic truth was that Moses was *unwilling*, not *unable*.

c. **Is not Aaron the Levite your brother? I know that he can speak well**: When God brought Aaron to help lead with Moses, it was an expression of His chastening to Moses, not of His approval or giving in to Moses. Aaron was more of a *problem* to Moses than help.

> i. Aaron did turn out to be a source of problems for Moses. Aaron instigated the worship of the golden calf, fashioning the calf himself and building the altar himself (Exodus 32:1-6). Aaron's sons blasphemed God with impure offerings (Leviticus 10:1-7). At one time, Aaron openly led a mutiny against Moses (Numbers 12:1-8).

> ii. As these episodes unfolded, Moses surely looked back at why the LORD gave Aaron to Moses as a partner - because God was angry at Moses' unwillingness.

d. **I know that he can speak well**: Aaron was a smooth talker, but a man weak on *content*. Moses had to put the words of God into the mouth of Aaron (**you shall speak to him and put the words in his mouth**). In this sense, Aaron was like a modern-day news reader, who does nothing but read what others have written for him.

> i. Aaron wasn't God's spokesman; he was the spokesman of Moses. God doesn't need leaders like this. It isn't God's way to have a man

minister as a smooth talker but not be qualified for leadership. God wants to combine the offices of "talker" and "leader."

B. Moses leaves Midian, goes to Egypt.

1. (18) Moses asks leave of his father-in-law Jethro to go to Egypt.

So Moses went and returned to Jethro his father-in-law, and said to him, "Please let me go and return to my brethren who *are* in Egypt, and see whether they are still alive." And Jethro said to Moses, "Go in peace."

a. **So Moses went**: When the fire faded from the burning bush and when the voice of God was silent across the desert, then it was upon Moses to *obey*, and to do what God told him to do. More than one person has had a spectacular burning bush type experience and then gone on to live as if nothing really happened.

i. Did Moses have any idea what he was getting into when he agreed to take the LORD's call? Could he see the Egyptian army closing in, and God parting the Red Sea through Moses' hand? Could he see the song of victory, the water from the rock, the manna from heaven, the battles won through prayer? Could he see vision of God on Mount Sinai, the voice of God from heaven, the tablets of stone, the golden calf? Could he see the tabernacle built, the priests consecrated? Could he see the spies sent forth into Canaan, the response of unbelief, and a thirty-eight year sentence to wander the wilderness? Could he see a lonely climb to the top of Mount Pisgah, where he would die looking out over the land of promise? Could he see the honor of sitting beside the LORD on the Mount of Transfiguration? Did Moses have any idea what he was getting into?

b. **Please let me go**: Moses was a good example of the truth that serving God doesn't mean neglecting your employer. Moses made sure that it was clear for him to go.

i. "Even the call of God did not erase the need for human courtesy and respect for one's father-in-law." (Kaiser)

c. **Please let me go and return to my brethren who are in Egypt, and see whether they are still alive**: As well, Moses didn't really tell his father-in-law the story behind his desire to return to Egypt. Perhaps he just felt it was too fantastic, and would rather let God demonstrate His Word through fulfilling it.

i. It is far more important - and more beneficial - for others to see the fruit of God's guidance in your life than to hear you explain all you believe God said to you.

2. (19-23) God tells Moses how events will unfold in Egypt.

And the LORD said to Moses in Midian, "Go, return to Egypt; for all the men who sought your life are dead." Then Moses took his wife and his sons and set them on a donkey, and he returned to the land of Egypt. And Moses took the rod of God in his hand. And the LORD said to Moses, "When you go back to Egypt, see that you do all those wonders before Pharaoh which I have put in your hand. But I will harden his heart, so that he will not let the people go. Then you shall say to Pharaoh, 'Thus says the LORD: "Israel *is* My son, My firstborn. So I say to you, let My son go that he may serve Me. But if you refuse to let him go, indeed I will kill your son, your firstborn."' "

> a. **The men who sought your life are dead...I will harden his heart**: God knew Moses was safe in Egypt, and so eased his mind from this anxiety; but God also knew that He would **harden** Pharaoh's heart, and that it would take the death of the firstborn before Pharaoh would agree to release the children of Israel.

> > i. Sometimes it says that God hardened the heart of Pharaoh (Exodus 4:21). Sometimes it says that Pharaoh hardened his own heart (Exodus 8:15). Sometimes it says simply that Pharaoh's heart was hardened, without saying who did it (Exodus 7:13).

> > ii. Who really hardened Pharaoh's heart? We might say that it was both God and Pharaoh; but whenever God hardened Pharaoh's heart, He never did it *against* Pharaoh's will. Pharaoh never said, "Oh, I want to do what is good and right and I want to bless these people of Israel"; and God answered, "No, for I will harden your heart against them!" When God hardened, He allowed Pharaoh's heart to do what Pharaoh wanted to do - God gave Pharaoh over to his sin (Romans 1:18-32).

> > iii. "God does not harden men by putting evil into them, but by not giving them mercy." (Augustine)

> b. **Israel is My son, My firstborn**: As a picture, God regarded Israel as His **firstborn**, and God knew that there would be an exchange of His **firstborn** (Israel) and Egypt's firstborn.

3. (24-26) Moses' life is spared on the way.

And it came to pass on the way, at the encampment, that the LORD met him and sought to kill him. Then Zipporah took a sharp stone and cut off the foreskin of her son and cast *it* at *Moses'* feet, and said, "Surely you *are* a husband of blood to me!" So He let him go. Then she said, *"You are* a husband of blood!"; because of the circumcision.

a. **The LORD met him and sought to kill him**: This is a mysterious event, but it seems that God is confronting Moses - in the strongest possible way - because Moses had not circumcised his son. God demands that this be set right before Moses enter Egypt and begin to fulfill the call of God.

i. There is often a point of confrontation in the life of the leader where God demands that they lay aside some area of compromise, and will not allow them to progress further until they do.

ii. "There can be no doubt that for some reason unrecorded Moses had failed to carry out the divine instructions concerning circumcision... Obedience completely established, everything moved forward." (Morgan)

b. **Surely you are a husband of blood to me**: Perhaps Zipporah objected to the rite of circumcision. She was not an Israelite and may have thought it a barbaric custom. Perhaps this was why God held Moses accountable (for not doing what was right, even though his wife didn't like it), but disabled Moses so that Zipporah had to perform the circumcision itself.

i. Some wonder why Moses' wife seems so bitter here. Perhaps for the first time, she recognized the serious nature of her husband's call and how important it was for their whole family to walk in the ways of the LORD.

ii. "Stone instruments like [flint knife] were retained for ritual purposes long after the introduction of metal implements." (Kaiser)

4. (27-31) Moses and Aaron present themselves to the people of Israel.

And the LORD said to Aaron, "Go into the wilderness to meet Moses." So he went and met him on the mountain of God, and kissed him. So Moses told Aaron all the words of the LORD who had sent him, and all the signs which He had commanded him. Then Moses and Aaron went and gathered together all the elders of the children of Israel. And Aaron spoke all the words which the LORD had spoken to Moses. Then he did the signs in the sight of the people. So the people believed; and when they heard that the LORD had visited the children of Israel and that He had looked on their affliction, then they bowed their heads and worshiped.

a. **So he went and met him on the mountain of God**: God told Moses that He would send Aaron to him (Exodus 4:14), and now it happens. God is showing Moses that He keeps His promises.

i. "Aaron, who came to meet Moses, could speak well; but he was a weak man, whose alliance with Moses caused his nobler younger brother much anxiety and pain." (Meyer)

b. **So the people believed**: It happened just as God said. God had promised *then they will heed your voice* (Exodus 3:18), and the people of Israel did - and their excitement was real as they anticipated the deliverance of the nation.

c. **When they heard that the LORD had visited the children of Israel**: Years before when Moses offered himself as a deliverer to Israel, they rejected him. Now the time and the circumstances were right, and God's destiny for Moses' life would begin to be fulfilled.

Exodus 5 - Moses Meets Pharaoh; Israel's Burdens Are Increased

A. Pharaoh receives Moses and Aaron and responds with a command.

1. (1-3) Moses asks Pharaoh to let the children of Israel go to the wilderness to worship.

Afterward Moses and Aaron went in and told Pharaoh, "Thus says the LORD God of Israel: 'Let My people go, that they may hold a feast to Me in the wilderness.'" And Pharaoh said, "Who *is* the LORD, that I should obey His voice to let Israel go? I do not know the LORD, nor will I let Israel go." So they said, "The God of the Hebrews has met with us. Please, let us go three days' journey into the desert and sacrifice to the LORD our God, lest He fall upon us with pestilence or with the sword."

a. **Moses and Aaron went in and told Pharaoh**: This confrontation took tremendous courage, and **Moses and Aaron** should be commended for their obedience to God in doing it.

i. Pharaoh was nothing like a public servant; the entire public lived to serve the Pharaoh. His power and authority were supreme, and there was no constitution or law or legislature higher or even remotely equal to him.

ii. The Pharaohs were said to be the children of the sun; they were friends to the greatest gods of Egypt and sat with them in their own temples to receive worship alongside them.

iii. An inscription by a Pharaoh on an ancient Egyptian temple gives the idea: "I am that which was, and is, and shall be, and no man has lifted my veil." (Meyer) The Pharaoh was more than a man; he considered himself a god, and the Egyptians agreed.

iv. Having grown up in the royal courts of Egypt, Moses knew this well, but he also knew that *Pharaoh was only a man*. With the authority of the living God, Moses confronted Pharaoh.

b. **Let My people go**: The fundamental demand of God to Pharaoh (through His messengers Moses and Aaron) was *freedom* for *His people*. God asserted that Israel belonged to *Him*, not Pharaoh; and therefore, that they should be free. Those who belong to God should be free, not bound.

c. **Who *is* the LORD, that I should obey His voice to let Israel go? I do not know the LORD, nor will I let Israel go**: Pharaoh knew of many gods, but did not recognize the LORD or His ownership of Israel; therefore he refused the request.

i. **Who is the LORD**: Pharaoh did not have the right heart, but he did ask the right question. Moses asked *Who am I?* (Exodus 3:11) The relevant questions were not about the identity of Moses or Pharaoh, but **who is the LORD?** *If* Pharaoh really knew who the LORD was, he would have gladly released Israel.

d. **Please, let us go three days' journey into the desert and sacrifice to the LORD our God**: Moses relayed the demand God first gave him back at Exodus 3:18. God presented the smaller request to Pharaoh first so that the request would be as appealing and as easy to accept as possible. He did this so Pharaoh would have no excuse at all for refusing God and hardening his heart.

2. (4-9) Pharaoh increases the burden of the Israelites.

Then the king of Egypt said to them, "Moses and Aaron, why do you take the people from their work? Get *back* to your labor." And Pharaoh said, "Look, the people of the land *are* many now, and you make them rest from their labor!" So the same day Pharaoh commanded the taskmasters of the people and their officers, saying, "You shall no longer give the people straw to make brick as before. Let them go and gather straw for themselves. And you shall lay on them the quota of bricks which they made before. You shall not reduce it. For they are idle; therefore they cry out, saying, 'Let us go *and* sacrifice to our God.' Let more work be laid on the men, that they may labor in it, and let them not regard false words."

a. **Why do you take the people from their work**: Pharaoh not only rejected the idea of giving the Israelites three days off, he saw the request itself as a waste of good working time.

b. **The people of the land are many now**: Pharaoh knew that the previous attempts to cut the population of Israel had failed. They continued to multiply. This was good for Israel, but bad for Pharaoh.

c. **For they are idle; therefore they cry out**: To punish Israel for the request and to give them more work ("You seem to have enough time to make these crazy requests - then you must have enough time to work more!"), Pharaoh commanded that the Israelites must gather their own materials (specifically, straw) for making bricks.

> i. Straw has an acidic content that makes the bricks stronger. The use of straw in making bricks in Egypt during this period is confirmed by archaeology. "Bricks of all sorts have been found in Egypt, some with regularly chopped straw, some with rough roots and oddments, some without straw at all." (Cole)

> ii. "Chopped straw was mixed in with the clay to make the bricks more pliable and stronger by first binding the clay together and then by decaying and releasing a humic acid." (Kaiser)

> iii. "The eastern bricks are often made of *clay* and *straw* kneaded together, and then not burned, but thoroughly dried in the sun. This is expressly mentioned by Philo...'because straw is the bond by which the brick is held together.'" (Clarke)

3. (10-14) The Egyptian taskmasters carry out Pharaoh's orders.

And the taskmasters of the people and their officers went out and spoke to the people, saying, "Thus says Pharaoh: 'I will not give you straw. Go, get yourselves straw where you can find it; yet none of your work will be reduced.'" So the people were scattered abroad throughout all the land of Egypt to gather stubble instead of straw. And the taskmasters forced *them* to hurry, saying, "Fulfill your work, *your* daily quota, as when there was straw." Also the officers of the children of Israel, whom Pharaoh's taskmasters had set over them, were beaten *and* were asked, "Why have you not fulfilled your task in making brick both yesterday and today, as before?"

> a. **I will not give you straw...yet none of your work will be reduced**: The immediate effect of the work of Moses was to make it *worse* for Israel, not better. Confronting the evil of Egyptian bondage would not be quick or easy. This was a significant test of Moses and Israel.

> b. **And the taskmasters forced them to hurry... Also the officers of the children of Israel...were beaten**: The freedom of all Israel was the goal; all Israel endured the difficult struggle before liberty was gained. The workers and their leaders didn't confront Pharaoh, but were still connected to this work of freeing Israel from Egypt.

> > i. "Things commonly go backward with the saints before they come forward, so the corn growth downward ere it grow upward." (Trapp)

B. Pharaoh troubles the children of Israel.

1. (15-19) Pharaoh rebukes the officers of Israel, increasing their burdens.

Then the officers of the children of Israel came and cried out to Pharaoh, saying, "Why are you dealing thus with your servants? There is no straw given to your servants, and they say to us, 'Make brick!' And indeed your servants *are* beaten, but the fault *is* in your *own* people." But he said, "You *are* idle! Idle! Therefore you say, 'Let us go *and* sacrifice to the LORD.' Therefore go now *and* work; for no straw shall be given you, yet you shall deliver the quota of bricks." And the officers of the children of Israel saw *that* they *were* in trouble after it was said, "You shall not reduce *any* bricks from your daily quota."

a. **The officers of the children of Israel came and cried out to Pharaoh**: In their trouble, the children of Israel did not turn to God; they did not turn to Moses. Instead, they looked to **Pharaoh** for help. They felt that their previous bondage was better than their current increased misery.

i. It is wrong to simply say that Israel loved their slavery. Exodus 2:23 says, *the children of Israel groaned because of the bondage, and they cried out; and their cry came up to God because of their bondage.* Yet what God allows and even performs in the work of bringing freedom made it feel worse, at least for a time.

b. **You are idle! Idle**: Pharaoh was absolutely unsympathetic and cruel. He believed the problem was that Israel was lazy; more work and harder work would cure them of laziness. *Pharaoh hated Israel and wanted them in perpetual bondage to him.*

i. "Thus, they would be kept quiet and agitation would cease." (Thomas)

ii. **Your daily quota**: "Brick quotas are abundantly documented in Egypt." (Kaiser)

2. (20-21) The officers cry out against Moses.

Then, as they came out from Pharaoh, they met Moses and Aaron who stood there to meet them. And they said to them, "Let the LORD look on you and judge, because you have made us abhorrent in the sight of Pharaoh and in the sight of his servants, to put a sword in their hand to kill us."

a. **They met Moses and Aaron**: The leaders of the children of Israel were not happy when they came from the presence of Pharaoh, and they thought it was all the fault of Moses and Aaron.

b. **Let the LORD look on you and judge**: The officers of Israel were *certain* that God was on their side, and anything that made the immediate condition of Israel worse was *not* of the LORD.

c. **You have made us abhorrent in the sight of Pharaoh**: They believed this was the wrong Moses did. When Israel was an obedient slave to Pharaoh, they thought he was their friend. Now that the idea of freedom had entered, Pharaoh showed how he felt about them all along.

i. Satan sometimes seems friendly to us when we accept his lordship; but when we start to be free in Jesus, he often will try to make life difficult for us.

ii. Exodus 4:31 said *So the people believed; and when they heard that the LORD had visited the children of Israel and that He had looked on their affliction, then they bowed their heads and worshiped.* After the counter-attack of Pharaoh; the faith, excitement, and worship of Exodus 4:31 was gone pretty quickly.

iii. *God allowed all this*; in fact you could say that He designed it. In theory, God could have freed Israel from Egypt without a struggle on their part. Yet He knew that was not good or best for them; that for them to make the transition from *slaves* to *free people of the promised land*, some testing and stretching was absolutely necessary.

3. (22-23) Moses complains about the problem to God.

So Moses returned to the LORD and said, "Lord, why have You brought trouble on this people? Why *is* it You have sent me? For since I came to Pharaoh to speak in Your name, he has done evil to this people; neither have You delivered Your people at all."

a. **Lord, why have You brought trouble on this people**: It was a good question, and Moses did well to so boldly speak his heart to God. Yet Moses had already forgotten what God told him at the burning bush, that Pharaoh *would not* easily let go of Israel.

i. *Moses did right in speaking his heart to God.* "Happy is the man who when he cannot understand the divine movement and, indeed, doubts it has yet faith enough in God Himself to tell Him all his doubt. Those who face men, having the right to say to them, 'Thus saith Jehovah' have also the right to return to Jehovah and state the difficulties, and expose openly their own doubts and fears." (Morgan)

ii. *Moses did wrong in forgetting what God had said.* The LORD told him, *I am sure that the king of Egypt will not let you go, no, not even by a mighty hand. So I will stretch out My hand and strike Egypt with all My wonders which I will do in its midst; and after that he will let you go.* (Exodus 3:19-20)

iii. If God were to give Moses an extended explanation to answer the question, it might go like this: "Moses, I **brought trouble** because I am interested in more than simply freeing Israel from slavery; I want to transform them from a slave people into a people fit for My promised land. This doesn't happen quickly or easily, and it involves countless expressions of both trust and surrender. Trust Me in this **trouble**, and I will use it for Israel's good and My glory."

b. **Why is it You have sent me**: In this season of testing, the same old fears came crashing in on Moses: "I'm not the man God should send." "God won't come through." "Pharaoh and the Egyptians are too strong." There was still unbelief and lack of focus on God that had to be worked out of Moses.

> i. "The agony of soul through which Moses passed must have been as death to him. He died to his self-esteem, to his castle-building, to pride in his miracles, to the enthusiasm of his people, to everything that a popular leader loves. As he lay there on the ground alone before God, wishing himself back in Midian, and thinking himself hardly used, he was falling as a grain of wheat into the ground to die, no longer to abide alone, but to bear much fruit." (Meyer)

> ii. Moses probably thought that the dying to himself was finished after 40 years of tending sheep in Midian, but it wasn't. It never is. God still will use adversity to train us to trust in Him until the day we go to be with Him in heaven.

c. **Neither have You delivered Your people at all**: It seems that despite God's previous warning, something in Moses hoped that it would all come rather easy. Yet God's deliverance was real, and would soon be seen for Israel. Israel felt that it was sometimes difficult to be in God's will, but they would see how much worse it was to be against God's will.

Exodus 6 - God's Assurance to Moses

A. God comforts Moses.

1. (1) God's promise to Moses: Pharaoh *will* let you go.

Then the LORD said to Moses, "Now you shall see what I will do to Pharaoh. For with a strong hand he will let them go, and with a strong hand he will drive them out of his land."

    a. **Now you shall see what I will do to Pharaoh**: Carrying the story from the previous chapter, Moses was discouraged by what he thought was God's lack of action and help. God's reply to Moses showed that He wanted him to know that the Lord was in control of it all.

        i. Moses was discouraged because he was too impressed by Pharaoh and not impressed enough by God.

    b. **For with a strong hand he will let you go**: God promised that not only would Pharaoh *let* the children of Israel leave; he would **drive them out** with a **strong hand**. This seemed impossible after Pharaoh's initial reaction to Moses and the message from the LORD.

        i. This was a wonderful, grace-filled message to Moses. God said in effect, "Moses, not only will Pharaoh let them go; **with a strong hand he will drive them out** of Egypt."

        ii. "This was the divine declaration made in answer to the statement of human difficulty.... Everything began with a solemn charge to Moses. It is first an answer to the complaint which God's servant uttered in His presence. It was a message of divine self-assertion and, therefore, necessarily a message of grace." (Morgan)

2. (2-5) The God of the covenant confirms His promise.

And God spoke to Moses and said to him: "I *am* the LORD. I appeared to Abraham, to Isaac, and to Jacob, as God Almighty, but *by* My name LORD I was not known to them. I have also established My covenant with them, to give them the land of Canaan, the land of their pilgrimage,

in which they were strangers. And I have also heard the groaning of the children of Israel whom the Egyptians keep in bondage, and I have remembered My covenant."

a. **I am the LORD**: In reminding Moses of the great name of God (Yahweh), He confirmed that He remained the covenant-making and covenant-keeping God, who would absolutely fulfill His promise to Moses.

i. "When all human help has failed, and the soul, exhausted and despairing, has given up hope from man, God draws near, and says, I AM." (Meyer)

b. **I appeared to Abraham, to Isaac, and to Jacob, as God Almighty, but by My name LORD I was not known to them**: The patriarchs were privileged to know the God who made the covenant, but for them the covenant was barely fulfilled. The patriarchs knew God as the *Maker* of the covenant. Moses and the generation of the Exodus would know God as the One who *fulfilled* the covenant.

i. The patriarchs knew the *name* Yahweh (it is used some 160 times in Genesis); but the great application of the name referred to God who kept *and* fulfilled the covenant: **I have also established My covenant with them**. "The patriarchs had only the promises, not *the things* promised." (Kaiser)

c. **As God Almighty**: In addition, though the patriarchs knew **God Almighty** (*El Shaddai*), they did not know Him as extensively and intimately as He would reveal Himself to Moses and his generation. They knew the power of God, but didn't have the same personal relationship and revelation Moses would come to know.

i. For us, God wants to be more than **God Almighty** - He wants us also to know Him as a personal, promise-making and promise-keeping God, whom we can trust in everything. Believers should ask themselves if they really know God by such names.

ii. "The supreme need in every hour of difficulty and depression is a vision of God. To see Him is to see all else in proper proportion and perspective." (Morgan)

d. **I have remembered My covenant**: God had remembered His covenant; now Moses was called to remember his God.

3. (6-8) God's promise of the seven "I wills" to Israel.

"Therefore say to the children of Israel: 'I *am* the LORD; I will bring you out from under the burdens of the Egyptians, I will rescue you from their bondage, and I will redeem you with an outstretched arm

and with great judgments. I will take you as My people, and I will be your God. Then you shall know that I *am* the LORD your God who brings you out from under the burdens of the Egyptians. And I will bring you into the land which I swore to give to Abraham, Isaac, and Jacob; and I will give it to you *as* a heritage: I *am* the LORD.'"

a. **Therefore say to the children of Israel**: The previous statement seemed to be more for Moses himself (Exodus 6:2-5). This following word was given for the benefit of Israel as a whole.

b. **I am the LORD**: God went to the furthest length possible to confirm this covenant with the children of Israel. In seven separate **I will** promises, God said, "I'm going to do it. You can count on me."

i. The promises were glorious, and equally so in their spiritual application to believers today:

- **I will bring you out**
- **I will rescue you from their bondage**
- **I will redeem you**
- **I will take you as My people**
- **I will be your God**
- **I will bring you into the land**
- **I will give it to you as a heritage**

ii. "Each of these verbs are in the Hebrew past (i.e., perfect) tense instead of the future tense, for so certain was God of their accomplishment that they were viewed as having been completed." (Kaiser)

iii. There is a strong contrast with the later five **I will** statements of Satan in Isaiah 14:13-15. The great difference is that Satan was powerless to make any of his "I wills" come to pass. God is more than able to fulfill each of His promises.

c. **And I will bring you into the land which I swore to give to Abraham, Isaac, and Jacob**: For the first plainly stated time, Moses was to tell Israel what God ultimately promised - not only to deliver them from the bondage of Egypt, but also to give them the land promised to the patriarchs.

i. **I will bring you out**: "A great deliverance; but nothing to that which Christ hath wrought for us from the tyranny of sin and terror of hell." (Trapp)

d. **I am the LORD**: With this God, concluded the promise by reminding all of His covenant-making and covenant-keeping name.

4. (9) The response of the children of Israel.

So Moses spoke thus to the children of Israel; but they did not heed Moses, because of anguish of spirit and cruel bondage.

a. **But they did not heed Moses**: After Moses spoke what God told him, the children of Israel were still stuck in miserable unbelief. They probably would have said that they did not doubt God, but they doubted the messenger - Moses.

b. **Because of anguish of spirit and cruel bondage**: This is why Israel doubted both God and His messenger. Their centuries of slavery made them think like slaves instead of people of the covenant. Pharaoh was bigger in their eyes than God was.

i. **Anguish of spirit**: "The NIV weakly translates 'their discouragement'; but it was the inward pressure caused by deep anguish that prevented proper breathing – like children sobbing and gasping for their breath." (Kaiser)

ii. Many Christians find themselves in the same place. They find it hard to trust God and believe that He is *for* them. This is why Paul says we must *not be conformed to this world, but be transformed by the renewing of your mind* (Romans 12:1-2). The children of Israel needed their minds renewed, and we do also.

iii. Ezekiel 20:5-9 shows why God was so small and Pharaoh was so big in Israel's heart during this time. Ezekiel explained that they trusted the gods of their oppressors, worshipping the gods of the Egyptians. This is why they didn't trust God, and His messenger Moses. The reason why God did not judge Israel at the time was because He didn't want His name profaned among the Gentiles.

5. (10-13) God tells Moses to stick with His plan.

And the LORD spoke to Moses, saying, "Go in, tell Pharaoh king of Egypt to let the children of Israel go out of his land." And Moses spoke before the LORD, saying, "The children of Israel have not heeded me. How then shall Pharaoh heed me, for I *am* of uncircumcised lips?" Then the LORD spoke to Moses and Aaron, and gave them a command for the children of Israel and for Pharaoh king of Egypt, to bring the children of Israel out of the land of Egypt.

a. **How then shall Pharaoh heed me**: God told Moses to repeat what he had unsuccessfully done before (Exodus 5:1-2). Moses felt this approach had failed once, so there was no sense in repeating it. This approach failed to persuade even the people of Israel; it seemed that it would never work with Pharaoh.

i. Note the *ground* for Moses' discouragement: **For I am of uncircumcised lips**. Previously, he objected because he believed he was not eloquent (Exodus 4:10). Now he objected because he believed he was not worthy for the task. "That inability was now born of a sense, not as before of his lack of eloquence, but of his uncleanness." (Morgan)

b. **Then the LORD spoke to Moses and Aaron, and gave them a command**: God wanted Moses and Aaron to be persistent in their obedience; not to look at Pharaoh, not to look at the children of Israel, not even to look at self - but to look at God and God alone.

i. Moses wanted to quit after the first setback. God had much to do in his heart before Moses would be ready to deal with all the discouragement ahead as he led Israel to the Promised Land.

ii. God was building endurance in Moses, the ability to stick with God's plan and will even when it didn't seem to work. This is faith; this is patient endurance in the LORD.

c. **A command for the children of Israel and for Pharaoh**: Moses had to understand that this was God's *will*, not merely a few suggestions for Israel and Pharaoh. This was His divine command that *would* be accomplished, one way or another.

B. The genealogies of Jacob's first three children: Reuben, Simeon, and Levi.

"Tread gently here! This is a private burying-ground, the last resting place of the founders of a family to which the world is deeply indebted for priceless service." (F.B. Meyer)

1. (14-15) The immediate descendants of Reuben and Simeon.

These *are* the heads of their fathers' houses: The sons of Reuben, the firstborn of Israel, *were* Hanoch, Pallu, Hezron, and Carmi. These are the families of Reuben. And the sons of Simeon *were* Jemuel, Jamin, Ohad, Jachin, Zohar, and Shaul the son of a Canaanite woman. These *are* the families of Simeon.

2. (16-19) The main families descended from Levi.

These *are* the names of the sons of Levi according to their generations: Gershon, Kohath, and Merari. And the years of the life of Levi *were* one hundred and thirty-seven. The sons of Gershon *were* Libni and Shimi according to their families. And the sons of Kohath *were* Amram, Izhar, Hebron, and Uzziel. And the years of the life of Kohath *were* one hundred and thirty-three. The sons of Merari *were* Mahali and Mushi. These *are* the families of Levi according to their generations.

a. **The sons of Levi according to their generations**: In the tribe of Levi, there were three main families - **Gershon, Kohath, and Merari**. Each of these families would be given specific duties in the service of the LORD and His tabernacle.

3. (20-27) How Moses and Aaron descended from Amram, a son of Kohath.

Now Amram took for himself Jochebed, his father's sister, as wife; and she bore him Aaron and Moses. And the years of the life of Amram *were* one hundred and thirty-seven. The sons of Izhar *were* Korah, Nepheg, and Zichri. And the sons of Uzziel *were* Mishael, Elzaphan, and Zithri. Aaron took to himself Elisheba, daughter of Amminadab, sister of Nahshon, as wife; and she bore him Nadab, Abihu, Eleazar, and Ithamar. And the sons of Korah *were* Assir, Elkanah, and Abiasaph. These are the families of the Korahites. Eleazar, Aaron's son, took for himself one of the daughters of Putiel as wife; and she bore him Phinehas. These *are* the heads of the fathers' houses of the Levites according to their families. These *are the same* Aaron and Moses to whom the LORD said, "Bring out the children of Israel from the land of Egypt according to their armies." These *are* the ones who spoke to Pharaoh king of Egypt, to bring out the children of Israel from Egypt. These *are the same* Moses and Aaron.

> a. **She bore him Aaron and Moses**: This passage not only tells us the ancestors of Moses and Aaron, but also some of Aaron's descendants. His sons listed here are Nadab, Abihu, Eleazar, and Ithamar; and his grandson through Eleazar, whose name was Phinehas.
>
> > i. This portion is important because the priesthood that will eventually come from the family of Aaron will be passed down to his descendants. Therefore it was important to know exactly who his descendants were.
>
> b. **The sons of Korah** (cousins to Moses and Aaron; their father Korah was Moses' uncle) will also play part in a significant event before Israel reaches the Promised Land (Numbers 16).

4. (28-30) Moses objects again.

And it came to pass, on the day the LORD spoke to Moses in the land of Egypt, that the LORD spoke to Moses, saying, "I *am* the LORD. Speak to Pharaoh king of Egypt all that I say to you." But Moses said before the LORD, "Behold, I *am* of uncircumcised lips, and how shall Pharaoh heed me?"

> a. **Speak to Pharaoh king of Egypt all that I say to you**: God previously commanded Moses to speak to Pharaoh. After the first disappointing experience, Moses now hesitated in his obedience.
>
> b. **I am of uncircumcised lips**: This may refer to Moses' idea that he had a speech problem, or it may be his understanding that he was a sinful man, and therefore unworthy to be used.

i. Moses' feeling may be similar to that of Isaiah, later recorded in Isaiah 6:1-8. Isaiah knew that he was a sinner in God's presence, and sensed that the center of his sin was in his lips - as in speaking and communicating in a way that didn't glorify God. God could deal with Isaiah's unclean lips, and He was more than able to deal with Moses' uncircumcised lips. God is also perfectly able to deal with the things in our life - real or imagined - that hinder us from being used by Him.

Exodus 7 - Miracles and Plagues before Pharaoh

A. God explains the plan to Moses again.

1. (1-2) The re-affirmation of the work of Moses and Aaron.

So the LORD said to Moses: "See, I have made you *as* God to Pharaoh, and Aaron your brother shall be your prophet. You shall speak all that I command you. And Aaron your brother shall speak to Pharaoh to send the children of Israel out of his land."

a. **So the LORD said to Moses**: God showed amazing patience with His servant Moses. After the outburst at the end of the previous chapter, we might expect that God had enough with Moses. Yet God didn't even chastise Moses; He simply told him what to do and set him to do it. This is another example of the richness of God's mercy.

b. **I have made you as God to Pharaoh**: Pharaoh had rejected any direct dealing with Yahweh, as he said in Exodus 5:2: *Who is the LORD, that I should obey His voice to let Israel go?* Therefore, God would then deal with Pharaoh through Moses.

i. "He should stand before Pharaoh in the place of God, not only delivering His messages, but accompanying them with such actions of power as should demonstrate the authority of those messages." (Morgan)

ii. This idea carries over into the New Testament, especially when Paul wrote that believers are like letters written by Jesus that the whole world reads (2 Corinthians 3:2-3). People that won't look to God, look at us; those who won't read the Bible, read our lives.

iii. "A prophet is one who represents God to man and, as such, all the Lord's people are prophets. Are we giving those around a true idea of God?" (Thomas)

c. **Aaron your brother shall be your prophet**: If Moses was to be "**as God**" to Pharaoh, then Aaron was to be Moses' "prophet" - his spokesman before Pharaoh.

i. Just as Moses was not to act on his own initiative, but to wait for God's direction, Aaron was not to act on his own initiative, but to wait for Moses' direction.

d. **You shall speak all that I command you**: God would not allow Moses to let the seeming failure of his first encounter with Pharaoh to discourage him. Moses is simply commanded to go.

2. (3) God promises to harden Pharaoh's heart.

"And I will harden Pharaoh's heart, and multiply My signs and My wonders in the land of Egypt."

a. **I will harden Pharaoh's heart**: As in the previous statement of God hardening Pharaoh's heart (Exodus 4:21), we remember that God did not harden Pharaoh's heart *against* Pharaoh's own desire. God confirmed Pharaoh in his wicked inclination against Israel.

b. **Harden Pharaoh's heart**: Pharaoh revealed his heart when he refused the humble request of Moses back at Exodus 5:1-4. Now, God would strengthen Pharaoh in the evil he already chose.

i. God can do the same today. In our rebellion, we may reach the place where God will strengthen us in the evil we desire: *Therefore God also gave them up to their uncleanness, in the lusts of their hearts...and even as they did not like to retain God in their knowledge, God gave them over to a debased mind, to do those things which are not fitting* (Romans 1:24, 28).

c. **And multiply My signs and My wonders in the land**: Even as God hardened Pharaoh's heart, He also gave him reasons to believe and surrender to God – *if he wanted to*.

3. (4-7) Why God will harden Pharaoh's heart.

"But Pharaoh will not heed you, so that I may lay My hand on Egypt and bring My armies *and* My people, the children of Israel, out of the land of Egypt by great judgments. And the Egyptians shall know that I *am* the LORD, when I stretch out My hand on Egypt and bring out the children of Israel from among them." Then Moses and Aaron did *so;* just as the LORD commanded them, so they did. And Moses *was* eighty years old and Aaron eighty-three years old when they spoke to Pharaoh.

a. **But Pharaoh will not heed you**: God knew from the beginning that Pharaoh would not agree to Moses' request. It was no surprise to God that Pharaoh did not heed Moses.

b. **So that I may lay My hand on Egypt…and the Egyptians shall know that I am the** LORD: This explains why the LORD hardened Pharaoh's heart - essentially, to bring righteous judgment upon Egypt. In doing so, God would reveal Himself even to those who rejected Him.

i. Pharaoh claimed that he didn't know who the LORD was (Exodus 5:2). God promised to show Pharaoh who He was, but to do it in a way that would not please Pharaoh or Egypt.

ii. God planned and did His work so that the Egyptians would see that He was the LORD. He does the same in His work among the church, displaying His wisdom to angelic beings, both faithful and fallen (Ephesians 3:10-11). He also does the same in individual lives, displaying His goodness and power to an on-looking world. "Believers are the world's Bibles, by studying which men may come to know the Lord Himself." (Meyer)

iii. "These miracles would also be an invitation for the Egyptians to personally believe in the Lord. Thus the invitation was pressed repeatedly…and some apparently did believe, for there was a 'mixed multitude' (Exodus 12:38) that left Egypt with Israel." (Kaiser)

c. **Moses was eighty years old**: This is retirement age for many, but Moses knew that God's will was more important than retirement. We also see from this that Aaron was Moses' older brother, so God went against the conventional customs of that day by making the younger brother more prominent.

B. Moses and Aaron before Pharaoh.

1. (8-10) Moses and Aaron appear before Pharaoh again.

Then the LORD **spoke to Moses and Aaron, saying, "When Pharaoh speaks to you, saying, 'Show a miracle for yourselves,' then you shall say to Aaron, 'Take your rod and cast** it **before Pharaoh,** and **let it become a serpent.'" So Moses and Aaron went in to Pharaoh, and they did so, just as the** LORD **commanded. And Aaron cast down his rod before Pharaoh and before his servants, and it became a serpent.**

a. **Take your rod and cast it before Pharaoh**: When God first gave Moses a similar sign in Exodus 4:1-9, it seemed those signs were primarily for the leaders of Israel. Now, Moses and Aaron brought the sign before Pharaoh.

b. **So Moses and Aaron went in to Pharaoh**: The first time Moses and Aaron went before Pharaoh, everything seemed to go wrong (Exodus 5:15-19). It took courage for them to go to Pharaoh *again*, but Moses simply obeyed God.

c. **Aaron cast down his rod before Pharaoh and before his servants, and it became a serpent**: This was not *exactly* the same miracle that Moses experienced on Mount Sinai and performed before the elders of Israel (Exodus 4:2-5 and 4:29-30). That saw the rod of Moses turn into a serpent, but a different Hebrew word is used here – something like a crocodile, which was something of a symbol of Egypt itself.

i. "When cast down it became a *tannin* ('great serpent,' 'dragon,' or 'crocodile')….The connection of the name *tannin* with the symbol of Egypt is clear from Psalm 74:13 and Ezekiel 29:3." (Kaiser)

2. (11-13) Pharaoh's magicians imitate the miracle of Aaron's rod.

But Pharaoh also called the wise men and the sorcerers; so the magicians of Egypt, they also did in like manner with their enchantments. For every man threw down his rod, and they became serpents. But Aaron's rod swallowed up their rods. And Pharaoh's heart grew hard, and he did not heed them, as the LORD had said.

a. **So the magicians of Egypt, they also did in like manner with their enchantments**: In the midst of an unmistakable miracle, Satan provided Pharaoh with a reason to doubt - and Pharaoh seized on the doubt and hardened his heart.

i. "Magic was very prevalent in Egypt, and a number of papyri deal with the subject." (Cole)

b. **For every man threw down his rod, and they became serpents**: Apparently, this wasn't mere magic; the **enchantments** of the Egyptian magicians were examples of dark, demonic power showing itself in what at least appeared to be miracles.

i. Miracles – or at least apparent miracles – are part of Satan's arsenal. Paul later wrote on this theme: *The coming of the lawless one is according to the working of Satan, with all power, signs, and lying wonders, and with all unrighteous deception among those who perish, because they did not receive the love of the truth, that they may be saved* (2 Thessalonians 2:9-10).

ii. This means that miracles can prove that something is *supernatural*, but they cannot prove that something is *true*.

iii. These Egyptian magicians were intelligent, learned men; but they lacked the wisdom of God, as Paul observed concerning them in 2 Timothy 3:7-9: *Always learning and never able to come to the knowledge of the truth. Now as Jannes and Jambres resisted Moses, so do these also resist the truth: men of corrupt minds, disapproved concerning the faith; but they will progress no further, for their folly will be manifest to all, as theirs also was.*

c. **Aaron's rod swallowed up their rods. And Pharaoh's heart grew hard, and he did not heed them**: By showing God's superior power regarding a symbol of Egypt (the crocodile or similar creature) was a clear message to Pharaoh and everyone else. It was a message that Pharaoh ignored, hardening his heart.

i. Charles Spurgeon preached a wonderful message titled *The Power of Aaron's Rod*, in which he used this as an example of the truth that God's power is greater than anything else, and can "swallow up" our idols and sins and such.

3. (14-18) God sends Moses to warn Pharaoh about the coming of the first plague.

So the LORD said to Moses: "Pharaoh's heart *is* hard; he refuses to let the people go. Go to Pharaoh in the morning, when he goes out to the water, and you shall stand by the river's bank to meet him; and the rod which was turned to a serpent you shall take in your hand. And you shall say to him, 'The LORD God of the Hebrews has sent me to you, saying, "Let My people go, that they may serve Me in the wilderness"; but indeed, until now you would not hear! Thus says the LORD: "By this you shall know that I *am* the LORD. Behold, I will strike the waters which *are* in the river with the rod that *is* in my hand, and they shall be turned to blood. And the fish that *are* in the river shall die, the river shall stink, and the Egyptians will loathe to drink the water of the river."' "

a. **Pharaoh's heart is hard; he refuses to let the people go**: The first plague - as all the plagues - came because Pharaoh hardened his heart against God and His people. In mercy, God warned Pharaoh, but Pharaoh disregarded the warning.

b. **By this you shall know that I am the LORD**: If Pharaoh really recognized and honored the God of Israel, he would have freed the children of Israel. Pharaoh sinned against Israel because he sinned against the LORD.

4. (19-21) The first plague comes upon Egypt: The Nile turns to blood.

Then the LORD spoke to Moses, "Say to Aaron, 'Take your rod and stretch out your hand over the waters of Egypt, over their streams, over their rivers, over their ponds, and over all their pools of water, that they may become blood. And there shall be blood throughout all the land of Egypt, both in *buckets of* wood and *pitchers of* stone.'" And Moses and Aaron did so, just as the LORD commanded. So he lifted up the rod and struck the waters that *were* in the river, in the sight of Pharaoh and in the sight of his servants. And all the waters that *were* in

the river were turned to blood. The fish that *were* in the river died, the river stank, and the Egyptians could not drink the water of the river. So there was blood throughout all the land of Egypt.

a. **That they may become blood**: This is the first of the plagues. There are nine in total (the tenth is the slaying of the firstborn, which is in a class by itself), and they are grouped together in threes. In this structure of threes, the first two plagues come only after warning and a call to repentance; the third plague in each set comes without warning.

b. **All the waters that were in the river were turned to blood**: Some say the plagues each have a naturalistic explanation. In the case of this first plague, some point out that when the Nile reaches an extremely high flood stage, it collects finely powdered red earth, and this red earth carries organisms that color the water and kill fish. But if this were the cause, it is hard to explain how Pharaoh could possibly be impressed.

i. God may or may not have used natural mechanisms to accomplish these plagues; even if He did, the timing and character of the plagues come from God's hand alone.

ii. It is important to understand that these plagues were all literal; there was nothing symbolic about them. Each plague pointed to a greater meaning than the event itself, *but they really happened.* This guides our understanding about the plagues in the Book of Revelation; there is no reason to see them as merely symbolic either.

iii. The plagues God brought against Egypt had a definite strategy and purpose. Each of them confronts and attacks a prized Egyptian deity. Not only did they bring punishment against Egypt, the plagues also answered Pharaoh's original question: *Who is the* LORD, *that I should obey His voice to let Israel go?* (Exodus 5:2) The plagues show the LORD God to be greater than any of the deities of Egypt.

c. **So there was blood throughout the land of Egypt**: Specifically, this first plague was directed against the numerous Egyptian river deities. The Nile itself was virtually worshipped as a god by the Egyptians, and the LORD God shows that *He* has complete power over the Nile, not some river god.

i. "The 'plagues' are described by cognate Hebrew words, all meaning 'blow' or 'stroke'." (Cole) Each plague was as if God were to strike or beat a deity worshipped by the Egyptians.

ii. The Egyptian god *Khnum* was said to be the guardian of the Nile, and this showed he was unable to protect his territory. The god *Hapi* was said to be the spirit of the Nile, and was brought low by this plague. The great god *Osiris* was thought to have the Nile as his bloodstream; in this plague, he truly bled. The Nile itself was worshipped as a god, and there are papyri recording hymns sung in praise of the river.

iii. There is a significant mention of something like this in a papyrus from this general period known as the Ipuwer Papyrus. It actually says (Ipuwer 2.10) that the Nile was blood and undrinkable. The same papyrus repeatedly mentions that servants left their masters.

5. (22-25) The magicians of Egypt copy the miracle.

Then the magicians of Egypt did so with their enchantments; and Pharaoh's heart grew hard, and he did not heed them, as the LORD had said. And Pharaoh turned and went into his house. Neither was his heart moved by this. So all the Egyptians dug all around the river for water to drink, because they could not drink the water of the river. And seven days passed after the LORD had struck the river.

a. **The magicians of Egypt did so with their enchantments**: Digging in wells, the magicians of Egypt found fresh water to replicate the LORD's plague upon the Nile. The magicians turned fresh *well water* into blood.

b. **The magicians of Egypt did so with their enchantments**: Bible scholars warmly debate if this was a magician's trick or if these **enchantments** were miracles from Satan's hand. The evidence seems to lean in favor of them being miracles from Satan's hand.

i. If the magicians of Egypt really wanted to do a miracle, they should have turned the bloody river clean again. They didn't because it seems that Satan cannot perform a constructive, cleansing miracle. He can bring supernatural destruction, but not goodness. All they did was make more bloody water!

ii. "Alleviation of human suffering is no part of the programme of the devil or his agents. That can only come from Jehovah, through the believing cry of his servants." (Meyer)

c. **Pharaoh's heart grew hard...Neither was his heart moved by this**: One way or another, the result in the heart of Pharaoh was the same. Pharaoh took another opportunity to reject and dishonor the LORD God.

Exodus 8 - Plagues Upon Egypt

A. The second plague: Frogs.

1. (1-4) The warning of the second plague.

And the LORD spoke to Moses, "Go to Pharaoh and say to him, 'Thus says the LORD: "Let My people go, that they may serve Me. But if you refuse to let *them* go, behold, I will smite all your territory with frogs. So the river shall bring forth frogs abundantly, which shall go up and come into your house, into your bedroom, on your bed, into the houses of your servants, on your people, into your ovens, and into your kneading bowls. And the frogs shall come up on you, on your people, and on all your servants."' "

a. **Go to Pharaoh**: This series of plagues will end with death coming to almost every home in Egypt. God could have brought that terrible last plague early in this series, but did not – and did not for a determined purpose. God used this series of plagues to glorify Himself (especially above the gods of the Egyptians), *and* to give Pharaoh chance to repent.

i. We should see the good mercy of God in doing this. He might have gone directly to the more severe judgment, but instead gave Pharaoh many chances to repent and change.

b. **I will smite all your territory with frogs**: God threatened a plague of **frogs** for a specific reason. The Egyptian goddess *Heqet* (or, *Heket*) was always pictured with the head of a frog. Among the ancient Egyptians, frogs were considered sacred and could not be killed.

i. Egyptians worshipped the frog as a female goddess because frogs were common around the Nile, because they reproduced rapidly, and because being amphibians they are part of two worlds, creatures of both land and water.

2. (5-7) God brings frogs upon the land through Moses and Aaron and the magicians of Egypt do the same.

Then the LORD spoke to Moses, "Say to Aaron, 'Stretch out your hand with your rod over the streams, over the rivers, and over the ponds, and cause frogs to come up on the land of Egypt.'" So Aaron stretched out his hand over the waters of Egypt, and the frogs came up and covered the land of Egypt. And the magicians did so with their enchantments, and brought up frogs on the land of Egypt.

a. **The frogs came up and covered the land of Egypt**: Since the Egyptians worshipped the frog, God gave them a plague of frogs. We see both God's determined plan and His sense of humor.

i. "Though he is the Lord of hosts he has no need of powerful armies, the ministry of angels, or the thunderbolts of justice to punish a sinner or a sinful nation; the *frog* or the *fly* in his hands is a sufficient instrument of vengeance." (Clarke)

ii. "Thus the first and this second plague are about the water; the third and fourth about the earth; the five next about the air; and the last about man." (Trapp)

b. **And the magicians did so with their enchantments, and brought up frogs**: The ability of the magicians to do the same **with their enchantments** points to a supernatural power present. This wasn't the work of a skilled illusionist; this was occult power at work.

i. For all their occult powers, all the magicians could do was make *more* frogs! They could only make the problem worse; yet their work gave Pharaoh an excuse to further harden his heart.

3. (8-15) Pharaoh asks Moses for help.

Then Pharaoh called for Moses and Aaron, and said, "Entreat the LORD that He may take away the frogs from me and from my people; and I will let the people go, that they may sacrifice to the LORD." And Moses said to Pharaoh, "Accept the honor of saying when I shall intercede for you, for your servants, and for your people, to destroy the frogs from you and your houses, *that* they may remain in the river only." So he said, "Tomorrow." And he said, *"Let it be* according to your word, that you may know that *there is* no one like the LORD our God. And the frogs shall depart from you, from your houses, from your servants, and from your people. They shall remain in the river only." Then Moses and Aaron went out from Pharaoh. And Moses cried out to the LORD concerning the frogs which He had brought against Pharaoh. So the LORD did according to the word of Moses. And the frogs died out of the houses, out of the courtyards, and out of the fields. They gathered them together in heaps, and the land stank. But when Pharaoh saw

that there was relief, he hardened his heart and did not heed them, as the LORD had said.

a. **Entreat the LORD that He may take away the frogs**: Here, God's previous promise (Exodus 7:1) was fulfilled. As a prophet of God, Moses stood in the place of God before Pharaoh, and Pharaoh made his request to God through Moses.

i. **Entreat**: "An unusual word, meaning 'intercede', the first occasion on which pharaoh has been really moved, and on which he makes a promise to let Israel go, a promise which he does not keep." (Cole)

ii. "The frogs could not be killed because of their sacredness, and yet such large numbers of them would be revolting in their loathsomeness, especially because cleanliness was a particular mark of the Egyptians." (Thomas)

b. **So the LORD did according to the word of Moses**: When Moses prayed, God answered - and all the frogs died. The understated description **"the land stank"** gives a hint at how nauseating it was.

c. **He hardened his heart**: Even when Pharaoh's plea was granted, his heart did not change - **he hardened his heart** - yet Pharaoh did just as God said he would.

i. "This becomes a familiar pattern: when he did not keep it the first time, no doubt it became easier and easier to do the same again." (Cole)

ii. "Pharaoh *increased his guilt*. His vows heaped up his transgressions. He forgot his promises; but God did not. They were laid by in store against him." (Spurgeon)

iii. "As to Pharaoh, it is the story of a strong will, making itself stupid, while all the way, until the condition was utterly beyond hope of remedy, God gave him opportunity to use that strong will in surrender." (Morgan)

B. The third plague: Lice.

1. (16-17) God tells Moses to initiate the plague of lice.

So the LORD said to Moses, "Say to Aaron, 'Stretch out your rod, and strike the dust of the land, so that it may become lice throughout all the land of Egypt.'" And they did so. For Aaron stretched out his hand with his rod and struck the dust of the earth, and it became lice on man and beast. All the dust of the land became lice throughout all the land of Egypt.

a. **Stretch out your rod**: This plague came unannounced. This time God did not show Pharaoh the mercy of a warning and an invitation to repentance.

  i. We must never think God is unfair when He does not show mercy. If someone were *totally* fair, they would *never* show mercy.

b. **Struck the dust of the earth, and it became lice on man and beast**: This plague struck at the heart of all Egyptian worship, especially at their priests. The Egyptian priesthood was extremely careful about hygiene and ritual cleansing; an infestation of lice made them unable to worship their gods.

  i. The plague of lice was also upon every **beast**. The gods of Egypt would not receive the sacrifice of lice-infested animals, so this stopped their sacrificial system.

2. (18-19) The magicians of Egypt are unable to duplicate this plague.

Now the magicians so worked with their enchantments to bring forth lice, but they could not. So there were lice on man and beast. Then the magicians said to Pharaoh, "This *is* the finger of God." But Pharaoh's heart grew hard, and he did not heed them, just as the LORD had said.

a. **Now the magicians so worked with their enchantments to bring forth lice, but they could not**: These magicians could use occult powers to change a rod into a snake, to turn water into blood, and to summon frogs – yet they could not bring forth lice. This shows that as great as Satan's power is, it is limited - and it comes to its limit rather early.

b. **This is the finger of God**: When the magicians said this to Pharaoh, it showed they knew there was a power greater than their own, yet it was a power that they did not honor and serve.

c. **Pharaoh's heart grew hard, and he did not heed them**: The hardness of Pharaoh's heart is shown when he would not even listen to the analysis of his own advisers. There was no *rational* reason why he insisted on resisting and rejecting the LORD God.

C. The fourth plague: Flies.

1. (20-23) Moses warns Pharaoh of a plague of flies.

And the LORD said to Moses, "Rise early in the morning and stand before Pharaoh as he comes out to the water. Then say to him, 'Thus says the LORD: "Let My people go, that they may serve Me. Or else, if you will not let My people go, behold, I will send swarms *of flies* on you and your servants, on your people and into your houses. The houses of the Egyptians shall be full of swarms *of flies,* and also the ground on which they *stand.* And in that day I will set apart the land of Goshen, in

which My people dwell, that no swarms *of flies* shall be there, in order that you may know that I *am* the LORD in the midst of the land. I will make a difference between My people and your people. Tomorrow this sign shall be."'

a. **Let My people go, that they may serve Me**: There is no record of a specific reply from Pharaoh to this request, but since the plague came, he obviously did not soften his heart towards the LORD God of Israel. Perhaps the reaction was not described because there was no reaction; perhaps he ignored Moses' message.

b. **In that day I will set apart the land of Goshen**: This is the first mention of the idea that **the land of Goshen** (where most the Israelites lived) was spared in the plagues. Possibly, the people of Israel suffered at least somewhat under the previous plagues. To a large extent, they would be spared in this fourth plague.

c. **In order that you may know that I am the LORD in the midst of the land**: To *ignore* someone demonstrates hatred just as much as *attacking* them does. If Pharaoh thought he could ignore God and His messenger, he was wrong, and the plagues would continue.

d. **I will make a difference between My people and your people**: God wanted Pharaoh to know that there was something special about the people of Israel. Pharaoh refused to recognize this, so the plagues continued.

> i. "If only we will let the Spirit of God work unhindered, He will effect an inward division. Our tastes and desires, our hopes and aims, will become different, and we shall be aware of a growing dissimilarity between ourselves and the world." (Meyer)

2. (24) The plague of flies comes.

And the LORD did so. Thick swarms *of flies* came into the house of Pharaoh, *into* his servants' houses, and into all the land of Egypt. The land was corrupted because of the swarms *of flies*.

a. **Thick swarms of flies came**: Literally, it says God sent *a swarm* (Hebrew, *awrob*) upon Egypt; it does not specify what the swarm was. It may have been a variety of insects. Psalm 78:45 says these swarms *devoured them*, and this indicates that there were biting insects in the swarm.

> i. **Thick swarms of flies**: "The word occurs only here and in passages based on this context, and its exact meaning is conjectural. 'Fleas' or 'sandflies' are other suggestions: but 'mosquitoes' may be the best translation." (Cole)

b. **Into the house of Pharaoh, into his servants' houses, and into all the land of Egypt**: No one was spared this terrible plague – except for the people of Israel, who largely lived in the land of Goshen (Exodus 8:22).

c. **The land was corrupted because of the swarms of flies**: This shows that the point of this plague was probably the same as the plague of lice. The Egyptian gods could not be worshipped amidst this uncleanness.

3. (25-27) Pharaoh tries to compromise with Moses.

Then Pharaoh called for Moses and Aaron, and said, "Go, sacrifice to your God in the land." And Moses said, "It is not right to do so, for we would be sacrificing the abomination of the Egyptians to the LORD our God. If we sacrifice the abomination of the Egyptians before their eyes, then will they not stone us? We will go three days' journey into the wilderness and sacrifice to the LORD our God as He will command us."

a. **Go, sacrifice to your God in the land**: In this, Pharaoh suggested a compromise, allowing Israel a holiday for their God, but demanding they stay within the land of Egypt to worship. Pharaoh wanted to negotiate with Moses (and the LORD), and find some compromise, common ground.

i. "That is the true attitude of the man of faith. Evil is always suggesting some compromise. To listen to it, is to remain enslaved. The only way into liberty is to leave the land of evil; to go accompanied by the women and the children; and to take all property also. It is when that attitude is assumed, that men pass out from all bondage, and find the liberty which is in the purpose of God for them." (Morgan)

b. **If we sacrifice the abomination of the Egyptians before their eyes, then will they not stone us?** Moses reminded Pharaoh of the social uproar this would cause, and held to the original request, refusing to compromise. Moses' character has grown strong before Pharaoh.

i. "Moses refuses on the grounds that to sacrifice in Egypt would be like killing a pig in a Muslim mosque, or slaughtering a cow in a Hindu temple...In the sense that the Egyptians would consider the sacrifice of a sacred animal as blasphemous." (Cole)

4. (28-32) Pharaoh's false repentance.

And Pharaoh said, "I will let you go, that you may sacrifice to the LORD your God in the wilderness; only you shall not go very far away. Intercede for me." Then Moses said, "Indeed I am going out from you, and I will entreat the LORD, that the swarms *of flies* may depart tomorrow from Pharaoh, from his servants, and from his people. But let Pharaoh not deal deceitfully anymore in not letting the people go to sacrifice to the LORD." So Moses went out from Pharaoh and

entreated the LORD. And the LORD did according to the word of Moses; He removed the swarms *of flies* from Pharaoh, from his servants, and from his people. Not one remained. But Pharaoh hardened his heart at this time also; neither would he let the people go.

a. **I will let you go, that you may sacrifice to the LORD your God in the wilderness**: This was a clear promise, and one that Pharaoh did not live up to. We cannot tell if Pharaoh deliberately lied to Moses or simply changed his mind once the plague of flies was gone.

> i. Many people turn to God in a time of calamity, and when things get better, they almost immediately turn their hearts back in hardness to God. Pharaoh was not an unusual example of humanity; he was like many or most of us, ancient or modern.

> ii. **I will let you go** carries the tone that Pharaoh believed that he owned or controlled Israel. "They were not Pharaoh's people; Pharaoh never chose them, he had never brought them where they were. He had not fought with them and overcome them. They were not captives in war, nor did they dwell in a territory which was the spoil of fair conflict." (Spurgeon)

b. **Intercede for me**: This shows Pharaoh knew exactly who the plagues came from, and how they could be stopped (by humbly appealing to the LORD God).

c. **Pharaoh hardened his heart at this time also**: Despite God's kindness to him and to Egypt, Pharaoh continued to harden **his heart**. This is a demonstration of how deep and severe the gradual hardening of a heart may become.

> i. As we continue in sin and reject God's opportunities for us to repent and return, the hardening continues. It is commonly seen. A man doesn't start by gambling away his paycheck; it starts with continuing on in friendly betting, and his heart grows hard. A man doesn't start with shameful perversion; it starts with a few magazines, a couple of videos, and his heart grows hard. A woman doesn't start addicted to alcohol; it starts with some social drinking, and her heart grows hard.

> ii. "The drunkard, the murderer himself, is a man who at first did evil as far as he dared, and afterwards dared to do evil which he would once have shuddered at." (Chadwick)

Exodus 9 - More Plagues Upon Egypt

A. The fifth plague: Disease on livestock.

1. (1-4) God tells Moses to warn Pharaoh.

Then the LORD said to Moses, "Go in to Pharaoh and tell him, 'Thus says the LORD God of the Hebrews: "Let My people go, that they may serve Me. For if you refuse to let *them* go, and still hold them, behold, the hand of the LORD will be on your cattle in the field, on the horses, on the donkeys, on the camels, on the oxen, and on the sheep; a very severe pestilence. And the LORD will make a difference between the livestock of Israel and the livestock of Egypt. So nothing shall die of all *that* belongs to the children of Israel."'"

a. **Go in to Pharaoh and tell him**: In mercy, God told Moses to give another warning, so that Pharaoh would have opportunity to repent.

b. **Let My people go, that they may serve Me**: In this appeal, two things were clear. First, the people of Israel belonged to God, not to Pharaoh. Second, it was clear that God wanted Pharaoh to let the children of Israel go for the sake of the LORD Himself, not even so much for the sake of the children of Israel.

i. Pharaoh was responsible to treat Israel well for the sake of the LORD, not so much for the sake of Israel. In the same way, we must treat each other well not only for the sake of our fellow brother or sister, but also for the sake of the LORD. We owe it to Him even more than we owe it to them.

c. **A very severe pestilence...nothing shall die of all that belongs to the children of Israel**: Pharaoh was warned that another plague was on the way, one that would severely damage the livestock of Egypt – but *not* the livestock owned by the people of Israel.

2. (5-7) The disease and death of the livestock.

Then the LORD appointed a set time, saying, "Tomorrow the LORD will do this thing in the land." So the LORD did this thing on the next day, and all the livestock of Egypt died; but of the livestock of the children of Israel, not one died. Then Pharaoh sent, and indeed, not even one of the livestock of the Israelites was dead. But the heart of Pharaoh became hard, and he did not let the people go.

a. **All the livestock of Egypt died**: This plague was directed against the Egyptian god *Hathor* who was thought to be a mother goddess in the form of a cow. In addition, Egyptian religion considered cattle sacred, and the cow was often a symbol of fertility. God shows Pharaoh and all of Egypt that He was mightier than this imagined pagan god.

i. Cole cites an ancient record of a battle the Egyptians lost because their enemies put a herd of cattle in front of their advancing troops. It worked because the Egyptian soldiers would not shoot at the opposing army for fear of accidentally killing what they considered to be the sacred cattle.

b. **The Pharaoh sent, and indeed, not even one of the livestock of the Israelites was dead**: Moses told Pharaoh that the Israelites would be spared, and Pharaoh believed it enough to confirm this. Nevertheless, he did not change his heart when it was proven that Moses and his God were exactly right.

B. The sixth plague: Boils.

1. (8-10) The plague of boils comes without previous announcement.

So the LORD said to Moses and Aaron, "Take for yourselves handfuls of ashes from a furnace, and let Moses scatter it toward the heavens in the sight of Pharaoh. And it will become fine dust in all the land of Egypt, and it will cause boils that break out in sores on man and beast throughout all the land of Egypt." Then they took ashes from the furnace and stood before Pharaoh, and Moses scattered *them* toward heaven. And *they* caused boils that break out in sores on man and beast.

a. **Ashes from a furnace**: "Would be black and fine. Perhaps 'soot' would be the best English rendering, for it is described as very fine 'dust' blowing in the wind." (Cole)

b. **They caused boils that break out in sores on man and beast**: As the third plague in this second set of three, this plague came without warning. This time, God chose *not* to mercifully give Pharaoh a previous opportunity to turn.

i. "For the first time the lives of humans are attacked and endangered, and thus it was a foreshadowing of the tenth and most dreadful of all the plagues." (Kaiser)

c. **Boils that break out in sores**: The idea behind the ancient Hebrew word for *boil* is "to burn." It has the idea of a swelling, painful, skin inflammation. These painful **boils** and **sores** affected people *and* animals.

2. (11-12) The effect of the boils on the magicians of Egypt.

And the magicians could not stand before Moses because of the boils, for the boils were on the magicians and on all the Egyptians. But the LORD hardened the heart of Pharaoh; and he did not heed them, just as the LORD had spoken to Moses.

a. **The magicians could not stand before Moses because of the boils**: This plague was probably directed against the Egyptian god *Imhotep*, who was said to be the god of medicine. Even those who were thought to be closest to the Egyptian gods (the court **magicians**) were stricken with this plague.

b. **The LORD hardened the heart of Pharaoh**: Here, for the first time, it is said that **the LORD hardened the heart of Pharaoh**. Previously, God announced that he *would* harden Pharaoh's heart (Exodus 4:21 and 7:3), and this was the fulfillment of it. Yet it is said at least six times before this that Pharaoh hardened his own heart (Exodus 7:13, 7:22, 8:15, 8:19, 8:32, 9:7). We see that God's hardening of Pharaoh's heart was the strengthening of what he already had set himself towards.

i. "This is the first occasion on which this form of words is used after an actual plague. Previously, the position has always been put from the other side: pharaoh has hardened his own heart. The moral would be that God hardens those who harden themselves." (Cole)

ii. " 'Harden' is the expression, not of the divine purpose but of the result of disobedience to the divine appeals. As a matter of fact, all the plagues were intended and calculated to soften, if Pharaoh had been willing to yield." (Thomas)

c. **Just as the LORD had spoken to Moses**: All went according to God's plan, even the hardness of Pharaoh's heart.

C. The seventh plague: Hail.

1. (13-21) Moses warns Pharaoh and the Egyptians of the plague of hail.

Then the LORD said to Moses, "Rise early in the morning and stand before Pharaoh, and say to him, 'Thus says the LORD God of the Hebrews: "Let My people go, that they may serve Me, for at this time I will send all My plagues to your very heart, and on your servants and on your people, that you may know that *there is* none like Me in all the earth. Now if I had stretched out My hand and struck you and your people with pestilence, then you would have been cut off from

the earth. **But indeed for this** *purpose* **I have raised you up, that I may show My power** *in* **you, and that My name may be declared in all the earth. As yet you exalt yourself against My people in that you will not let them go. Behold, tomorrow about this time I will cause very heavy hail to rain down, such as has not been in Egypt since its founding until now. Therefore send now** *and* **gather your livestock and all that you have in the field, for the hail shall come down on every man and every animal which is found in the field and is not brought home; and they shall die."' " He who feared the word of the** LORD **among the servants of Pharaoh made his servants and his livestock flee to the houses. But he who did not regard the word of the** LORD **left his servants and his livestock in the field.**

a. **I will send all My plagues to your very heart**: In this extended warning, God wanted Pharaoh to know who was in control. As bad as it had been to this point, it was only by God's mercy that Pharaoh and Egypt had not already been **cut off from the earth**.

b. **That I may show My power in you, and that My name may be declared in all the earth**: In this bold declaration, God told Pharaoh through Moses that his resistance was being used for God's glory.

i. If Pharaoh thought he was accomplishing anything with his resistance against God, he was completely wrong. All his stubborn rebellion merely glorified the LORD more in the end.

c. **Gather your livestock and all that you have in the field**: God invited Pharaoh and the Egyptians to trust Him by recommending precautions before the plague. Some took God's invitation and spared their livestock, but others did not.

i. "Rainfall comes so occasionally in Upper Egypt that the prediction of a severe hailstorm accompanied by a violent electrical storm must have been greeted with much skepticism." (Kaiser)

2. (22-26) A plague of hail and lightning bringing fire from the heavens.

Then the LORD **said to Moses, "Stretch out your hand toward heaven, that there may be hail in all the land of Egypt; on man, on beast, and on every herb of the field, throughout the land of Egypt." And Moses stretched out his rod toward heaven; and the** LORD **sent thunder and hail, and fire darted to the ground. And the** LORD **rained hail on the land of Egypt. So there was hail, and fire mingled with the hail, so very heavy that there was none like it in all the land of Egypt since it became a nation. And the hail struck throughout the whole land of Egypt, all that** *was* **in the field, both man and beast; and the hail struck every**

herb of the field and broke every tree of the field. Only in the land of Goshen, where the children of Israel *were,* there was no hail.

a. **There was hail, and fire mingled with the hail, so very heavy that there was none like it**: This was perhaps the most frightening plague thus far. The Egyptians must have believed that the wrath of God was poured down from heaven in all severity.

i. **So there was hail, and fire mingled with the fire hail**: "A strange mixture; a miracle within a miracle, saith Rabbi Solomon. Fire and water made a peace betwixt themselves, that they might obey the will of their Creator." (Trapp)

b. **The hail struck throughout the whole land of Egypt**: This plague was directed against several Egyptian gods. Notable among them was *Nut,* the sky goddess.

3. (27-35) Pharaoh falsely repents and his heart grows harder.

And Pharaoh sent and called for Moses and Aaron, and said to them, "I have sinned this time. The LORD *is* righteous, and my people and I *are* wicked. Entreat the LORD, that there may be no *more* mighty thundering and hail, for *it is* enough. I will let you go, and you shall stay no longer." So Moses said to him, "As soon as I have gone out of the city, I will spread out my hands to the LORD; the thunder will cease, and there will be no more hail, that you may know that the earth *is* the Lord's. But as for you and your servants, I know that you will not yet fear the LORD God." Now the flax and the barley were struck, for the barley *was* in the head and the flax *was* in bud. But the wheat and the spelt were not struck, for they *are* late crops. So Moses went out of the city from Pharaoh and spread out his hands to the LORD; then the thunder and the hail ceased, and the rain was not poured on the earth. And when Pharaoh saw that the rain, the hail, and the thunder had ceased, he sinned yet more; and he hardened his heart, he and his servants. So the heart of Pharaoh was hard; neither would he let the children of Israel go, as the LORD had spoken by Moses.

a. **I have sinned this time. The LORD is righteous, and my people and I are wicked**: This sounds like perfect words of repentance from Pharaoh, but true repentance had not worked its way into his heart. Pharaoh was grieved at the *consequences* of sin, but not at the sin itself.

i. "Pharaoh's 'I have sinned' (Exodus 9:27) is one of eight such confessions in Scripture, four sincere and four insincere." (Thomas) Perhaps it is better to see it as 5 insincere and 3 sincere.

• Pharaoh – a hardened sinner (Exodus 9:27)
• Balaam – a double-minded man (Numbers 22:34)

- Achan – a doubtful penitent (Joshua 7:20)
- Saul – an insincere man (1 Samuel 15:24)
- Judas – the repentance of despair (Matthew 27:4)
- Job – a godly repentance (Job 6:20)
- David – a repentance after a delay (2 Samuel 12:13)
- The Prodigal – the blessed confession of sin (Luke 15:18)

b. **I know that you will not yet fear the LORD God**: Moses' response to Pharaoh showed that he was starting to learn and to discern. Moses knew the promise to touch Pharaoh's firstborn had not yet been fulfilled (first described by God back in Exodus 4:22-23).

i. "Moses does not believe that pharaoh will keep his word, yet he grants the request so that pharaoh may be without excuse." (Cole)

c. **He sinned yet more; and he hardened his heart**: Hardening the heart against God is sin; failing to repent when God graciously answers our plea is to ignore His rich mercy and is to sin **yet more**.

Exodus 10 - The Plagues Continue

A. The eighth plague: Locusts.

1. (1-6) God tells Moses to bring another warning to Pharaoh.

Now the LORD said to Moses, "Go in to Pharaoh; for I have hardened his heart and the hearts of his servants, that I may show these signs of Mine before him, and that you may tell in the hearing of your son and your son's son the mighty things I have done in Egypt, and My signs which I have done among them, that you may know that I *am* the LORD." So Moses and Aaron came in to Pharaoh and said to him, "Thus says the LORD God of the Hebrews: 'How long will you refuse to humble yourself before Me? Let My people go, that they may serve Me. Or else, if you refuse to let My people go, behold, tomorrow I will bring locusts into your territory. And they shall cover the face of the earth, so that no one will be able to see the earth; and they shall eat the residue of what is left, which remains to you from the hail, and they shall eat every tree which grows up for you out of the field. They shall fill your houses, the houses of all your servants, and the houses of all the Egyptians; which neither your fathers nor your fathers' fathers have seen, since the day that they were on the earth to this day.' " And he turned and went out from Pharaoh.

a. **I have hardened his heart**: Here the LORD says that He **hardened** Pharaoh's heart, yet in Exodus 9:34 it says that *he* [Pharaoh] *hardened his heart*. Both were true, and one does not deny the other. In hardening Pharaoh's heart, God allowed him to have what he sinfully desired - a hard heart against the LORD and His people.

b. **That you may tell in the hearing of your son and your son's son the mighty things I have done in Egypt**: God's work was not only for the sake of the generation of Moses and Pharaoh; it was also for **your son and your son's son**. God does mighty works among us so that we can encourage generations to come.

c. **How long will you refuse to humble yourself before Me**: Getting to the heart of the matter, God warned Pharaoh to **humble** himself or the worst plague of locusts ever seen would come upon Egypt. *Pride* was at the heart of Pharaoh's problem; he simply didn't want to give in to God.

i. It's an important question that God would ask to anyone: **How long will you refuse to humble yourself before Me?**

2. (7-11) Pharaoh seems to relent - with qualifications.

Then Pharaoh's servants said to him, "How long shall this man be a snare to us? Let the men go, that they may serve the LORD their God. Do you not yet know that Egypt is destroyed?" So Moses and Aaron were brought again to Pharaoh, and he said to them, "Go, serve the LORD your God. Who *are* the ones that are going?" And Moses said, "We will go with our young and our old; with our sons and our daughters, with our flocks and our herds we will go, for we must hold a feast to the LORD." Then he said to them, "The LORD had better be with you when I let you and your little ones go! Beware, for evil is ahead of you. Not so! Go now, you *who are* men, and serve the LORD, for that is what you desired." And they were driven out from Pharaoh's presence.

a. **How long shall this man be a snare to us**: These men, known as **Pharaoh's servants**, hardened their hearts before (Exodus 9:34). Yet even *they* relented in light of the destruction that came upon Egypt, but Pharaoh's heart was harder still!

b. **Who are the ones that are going**: Pharaoh again wanted to bargain with God and Moses. He wanted to allow some to go into the wilderness to worship, but to keep the women and children home as hostages.

i. Pharaoh offered a compromise in Exodus 8:25-26, suggesting that they could have a day to sacrifice to the LORD while still in Egypt. Moses rejected that compromise, and would reject this one also. God would not make this bargain, because He didn't need to. This time, and every time, God holds all the negotiating leverage.

ii. What Pharaoh wanted is what many of us want in the flesh: a way to "give in" to God, without fully submitting to Him. Sometimes we look for a way to bargain with God as an equal, instead of submitting to Him as Creator and LORD.

iii. When Moses first came to Pharaoh, Pharaoh said: *Who is the LORD, that I should obey His voice to let Israel go?* (Exodus 5:2). The fact that Pharaoh still would not submit to the LORD showed that he didn't know who the LORD was yet. This was despite the fact that the LORD God had made it clear that He was:

• Greater than the god *Khnum* (the guardian of the Nile)

- Greater than the god *Hapi* (the spirit of the Nile)
- Greater than the god *Osiris* (who had the Nile as his bloodstream)
- Greater than the goddess *Heqt* (the frog-goddess of fertility)
- Greater than the goddess *Hathor* (a cow-like mother goddess)
- Greater than the god *Imhotep* (the god of medicine)
- Greater than *Nut* (the sky goddess)
- Able to stop the whole worship system of the Egyptian gods with loathsome lice and swarms of insects

iv. Despite all this, Pharaoh showed he still did not know the LORD God; therefore, God would show him more.

3. (12-15) The plague of locusts comes.

Then the LORD said to Moses, "Stretch out your hand over the land of Egypt for the locusts, that they may come upon the land of Egypt, and eat every herb of the land; all that the hail has left." So Moses stretched out his rod over the land of Egypt, and the LORD brought an east wind on the land all that day and all *that* night. When it was morning, the east wind brought the locusts. And the locusts went up over all the land of Egypt and rested on all the territory of Egypt. *They were* very severe; previously there had been no such locusts as they, nor shall there be such after them. For they covered the face of the whole earth, so that the land was darkened; and they ate every herb of the land and all the fruit of the trees which the hail had left. So there remained nothing green on the trees or on the plants of the field throughout all the land of Egypt.

a. **They ate every herb of the land and all the fruit of the trees which the hail had left**: Yahweh showed Himself greater than the Egyptian god *Set*, thought to be the protector of crops.

b. **There remained nothing green on the trees or on the plants of the field**: God did for Pharaoh what He will do in our lives – expose and topple every false god. When we trust in these gods, it hurts to see them fall, but it is always best to have them exposed.

4. (16-20) Another false repentance by Pharaoh.

Then Pharaoh called for Moses and Aaron in haste, and said, "I have sinned against the LORD your God and against you. Now therefore, please forgive my sin only this once, and entreat the LORD your God, that He may take away from me this death only." So he went out from Pharaoh and entreated the LORD. And the LORD turned a very strong west wind, which took the locusts away and blew them into the Red Sea. There remained not one locust in all the territory of Egypt. But

the LORD hardened Pharaoh's heart, and he did not let the children of Israel go.

a. **I have sinned against the LORD your God and against you**: Pharaoh did the same thing in Exodus 9:27-28. He said the *words* of repentance but did not follow through with the actions. His heart was only hardened more after God relented and showed mercy.

i. "Once again comes the easy confession of sin, and the shallow repentance that springs only from a desire to avert the consequences." (Cole)

B. The ninth plague: Darkness.

1. (21-23) A plague of darkness comes without warning.

Then the LORD said to Moses, "Stretch out your hand toward heaven, that there may be darkness over the land of Egypt, darkness *which* may even be felt." So Moses stretched out his hand toward heaven, and there was thick darkness in all the land of Egypt three days. They did not see one another; nor did anyone rise from his place for three days. But all the children of Israel had light in their dwellings.

a. **Stretch out your hand toward heaven, that there may be darkness over the land of Egypt**: As was the pattern with the previous plagues, the third in this set of three came without warning.

b. **Darkness which may even be felt**: This was no normal darkness; it had a supernatural element to it that could **be felt**. Light is not only a physical property; it is an aspect of God's character (*God is light and in Him is no darkness at all*, 1 John 1:5). In judgment, God can withdraw His presence so significantly that the void remaining is **darkness which may even be felt**.

i. Seemingly, God did not even allow artificial light sources to work. The Egyptians attempted to use candles and lamps but were unable to produce light. This was a dramatic show of greatness over the prominent Egyptian god *Ra*, thought to be the sun god.

c. **All the children of Israel had light in their dwellings**: We don't know if this was because God spared them the plague or because God granted them His unique presence, bringing a supernatural light.

2. (24-29) Pharaoh's last attempt at a compromise with Moses.

Then Pharaoh called to Moses and said, "Go, serve the LORD; only let your flocks and your herds be kept back. Let your little ones also go with you." But Moses said, "You must also give us sacrifices and burnt offerings, that we may sacrifice to the LORD our God. Our livestock also shall go with us; not a hoof shall be left behind. For we must take some

of them to serve the LORD our God, and even we do not know with what we must serve the LORD until we arrive there." But the LORD hardened Pharaoh's heart, and he would not let them go. Then Pharaoh said to him, "Get away from me! Take heed to yourself and see my face no more! For in the day you see my face you shall die!" And Moses said, "You have spoken well. I will never see your face again."

a. **Go, serve the LORD; only let your flocks and your herds be kept back**: With this, Pharaoh made his last offer to Moses. All the children of Israel could go into the wilderness for three days of sacrifice unto the LORD God, but they must leave their livestock behind.

> i. Undoubtedly, Pharaoh felt God was a hard bargainer and made the best deal for Himself that He could. Pharaoh still saw things as someone who thought he could bargain with the Creator. This shows that he still didn't really know who the LORD God was, because He still had not submitted to Him.

b. **Not a hoof shall be left behind**: The LORD God, and the prophet Moses representing Him, was absolutely unwilling to compromise on these points. God wanted deliverance for *all of Israel* and for *all that belonged to Israel*, and was not willing to deal on the point.

> i. This reflects the response of God to every attempt we make to surrender less than everything to Him, or to willingly leave some things in bondage. He says, "**Not a hoof shall be left behind**."

c. **Get away from me! Take heed to yourself and see my face no more**: In exasperation, Pharaoh ordered Moses out and told him to never come back. Moses assured Pharaoh, "**You have spoken well. I will never see your face again**" - but this was not good news for Pharaoh.

> i. "Pharaoh was now beyond reason, and God did not reason with him." (Morgan)

> ii. This ends the account of the nine plagues, and though there is one yet to come - the plague upon the firstborn - it is so unique that it must be considered by itself.

> iii. The Bible tells us there were several reasons why God sent these plagues upon Pharaoh and Egypt.
>
> - To answer Pharaoh's question, *Who is the LORD?* (Exodus 5:2). In the plagues, God showed Himself greater than any of the false gods of Egypt
> - To show the power of God through Moses (Exodus 9:16)
> - To give a testimony to the children of Israel for future generations (Exodus 10:2)

- To judge the false gods - demons, really - of Egypt (Exodus 12:12, Numbers 33:4)
- To warn the nations; more than 400 years later, the Philistines remembered the LORD God of Israel as the One who plagued the Egyptians (1 Samuel 4:8)
- As a testimony of the greatness of God to Israel (Exodus 15:11, Deuteronomy 4:34)

Exodus 11 - God Announces the Death of the Firstborn

A. God's instructions to Moses concerning the final calamity.

1. (1-3) Israel plunders the Egyptians.

And the LORD said to Moses, "I will bring yet one *more* plague on Pharaoh and on Egypt. Afterward he will let you go from here. When he lets *you* go, he will surely drive you out of here altogether. Speak now in the hearing of the people, and let every man ask from his neighbor and every woman from her neighbor, articles of silver and articles of gold." And the LORD gave the people favor in the sight of the Egyptians. Moreover the man Moses *was* very great in the land of Egypt, in the sight of Pharaoh's servants and in the sight of the people.

a. **He will surely drive you out of here altogether**: Long before this, God told Moses that He would plague Egypt with the death of the firstborn (Exodus 4:21-23). After this final plague, Pharaoh wouldn't merely allow Israel to leave, he would *compel* them to go.

b. **The LORD gave the people favor in the sight of the Egyptians**: Pharaoh was still not quite convinced, but the people of Egypt were willing to see the people of Israel immediately leave. They were more than willing to give them gifts of silver and gold to persuade them to leave. This was how the slaves of Israel received their past wages from their time of slavery, and how they did not leave Egypt empty-handed.

i. "These jewels were employed afterwards in the adornment and enrichment of the Sanctuary. They flashed in the breastplate of the High Priest, and shone in the sacred vessels." (Meyer)

c. **The man Moses *was* very great in the land of Egypt, in the sight of Pharaoh's servants and in the sight of the people**: Though Pharaoh's heart was not yet persuaded, all of Egypt (including **Pharaoh's servants**) knew the LORD God was greater than the gods of Egypt and that Moses was a servant of this great God.

2. (4-8) The death of the firstborn is announced to Pharaoh.

Then Moses said, "Thus says the LORD: 'About midnight I will go out into the midst of Egypt; and all the firstborn in the land of Egypt shall die, from the firstborn of Pharaoh who sits on his throne, even to the firstborn of the female servant who *is* behind the handmill, and all the firstborn of the animals. Then there shall be a great cry throughout all the land of Egypt, such as was not like it *before,* nor shall be like it again. But against none of the children of Israel shall a dog move its tongue, against man or beast, that you may know that the LORD does make a difference between the Egyptians and Israel.' And all these your servants shall come down to me and bow down to me, saying, 'Get out, and all the people who follow you!' After that I will go out." Then he went out from Pharaoh in great anger.

a. **Then Moses said**: As Moses still stood before Pharaoh, for the first time God led him to specifically say what would happen to the firstborn of Egypt. They **shall die**, all of them, because the Egyptians would not let God's firstborn (Israel) go. Therefore, **there shall be a great cry throughout all the land of Egypt**.

i. **Even to the firstborn of the female servant who is behind the handmill**: "To sit 'behind the two mill stones' (so the Hebrew reads literally) is to do the work of the lowest woman slave in the household, grinding corn (Isaiah 47:2)." (Cole)

ii. "In view of the law of primogeniture [right of the firstborn], the blow would be the most terrible that could be inflicted." (Thomas)

b. **Against none of the children of Israel shall a dog move its tongue**: Despite the great calamity to come, God would grant the Egyptians the ability to see the situation as it really was - the fault of their own Pharaoh, not the fault of Moses or the children of Israel.

i. This was even worse news to Pharaoh. Perhaps a politician doesn't mind calamity if he can blame it on someone else. Here, God promised that Pharaoh himself would bear the blame.

ii. "An unprecedented outpouring of grief would follow, but among the Israelites there would be such tranquility on that evening that not a dog would have occasion to bark." (Kaiser)

iii. "They had made Israel cry: and God usually retaliates spoil to spoil (Ezekiel 39:10), number to number (Isaiah 65:11, 12), choice to choice (Isaiah 66:3, 4), cry to cry (James 5:1, 4)." (Trapp)

c. **That you may know that the LORD does make a difference between the Egyptians and Israel**: Perhaps some in that day (including Pharaoh) found it easy to say, "The Egyptians have gods, and the Israelites have a God. What is the difference?" In His overwhelming demonstration of power over the deities of Egypt, Yahweh showed that there *was* a difference.

> i. "The Lord hath put a difference between those who are his people and those who are not. There are many distinctions among men which will one day be blotted out; but permit me to remind you at the outset that this is an eternal distinction." (Spurgeon)

d. **All these your servants shall come down to me and bow down to me, saying, 'Get out, and all the people who follow you!'** Moses' final words to Pharaoh told him that he and the rest of the Egyptians would *command* the people of Israel to go.

3. (9-10) God tells Moses that Pharaoh will still not heed.

But the LORD said to Moses, "Pharaoh will not heed you, so that My wonders may be multiplied in the land of Egypt." So Moses and Aaron did all these wonders before Pharaoh; and the LORD hardened Pharaoh's heart, and he did not let the children of Israel go out of his land.

a. **Pharaoh will not heed you**: If nine plagues had come from the hand of God, one might expect that the warning about a tenth plague would be believed; but Pharaoh's heart remained hard, and God strengthened Pharaoh in his hardness of heart.

> i. **So that My wonders may be multiplied in the land of Egypt**: "The nine plagues can now be seen as a whole. They touched every phase of nature: mineral, animal, vegetable, human. They affected persons and property, and included all, from the highest to the lowest." (Thomas)

b. **And the LORD hardened Pharaoh's heart**: Here, for the *fourth* time, we are told that God hardened Pharaoh's heart (Exodus 9:12, 10:20, 10:27, and 11:10). Yet God never hardened Pharaoh's heart until Pharaoh himself first hardened it against the LORD and His people (Exodus 7:13, 7:22, 8:15, 8:19, 8:32, and 9:7).

Exodus 12 - God Institutes Passover

A. Passover instructions.

1. (1-6) Each household should take a lamb.

Now the LORD spoke to Moses and Aaron in the land of Egypt, saying, "This month *shall be* your beginning of months; it *shall be* the first month of the year to you. Speak to all the congregation of Israel, saying: 'On the tenth *day* of this month every man shall take for himself a lamb, according to the house of *his* father, a lamb for a household. And if the household is too small for the lamb, let him and his neighbor next to his house take *it* according to the number of the persons; according to each man's need you shall make your count for the lamb. Your lamb shall be without blemish, a male of the first year. You may take *it* from the sheep or from the goats. Now you shall keep it until the fourteenth day of the same month. Then the whole assembly of the congregation of Israel shall kill it at twilight.'"

a. **This month shall be your beginning of months**: The coming deliverance from Egypt was such a significant act that God told the children of Israel to remake their calendar. The new year would now start with the month of their redemption from Egypt. It was a dramatic way of saying that *everything* was to change.

i. "God is ever the God of new beginnings in the history of failure. The ultimate statement is found in the Apocalypse in the words: 'Behold, I make all things new.'" (Morgan)

ii. "Commence a nation's annals from its evangelization. Begin the chronicle of a people from the day when they bow at the feet of Jesus." (Spurgeon)

iii. **Speak to all the congregation of Israel**: "This is the first occurrence in the Pentateuch of what was to become a technical term, describing Israel in its religious sense...and which underlies the New Testament use of *ekklesia*, 'church'." (Cole)

b. **Every man shall take for himself a lamb**: On the tenth of this first month, each family - or household - was to take a lamb, and the lamb was to live with the family for the four days until Passover (**on the tenth day of this month...until the fourteenth day of the same month**).

i. In this way, the lamb became part of the family. By the time it was sacrificed on the fourteenth, it was both cherished and mourned. God wanted the sacrifice of something precious.

ii. **If the household is too small for the lamb**: The rabbis later determined that there should be at least ten people for each Passover lamb, and not more than twenty.

iii. "Passover was a domestic and family festival, and thus shows its early origin. It has here no temple, no meeting-tent, no altar and no priest: but representation, if not substitution, is clearly implied." (Cole)

c. **Your lamb shall be without blemish**: The lamb was also to be **without blemish**. This sacrifice unto the LORD had to be as perfect as a lamb could be.

d. **You may take it from the sheep or from the goats**: The Hebrew word for **lamb** can refer to either a young sheep or a young goat.

i. "The Hebrew *seh* is quite a neutral word and should be translated 'head of (small) stock', applying equally to sheep and goats of any age. The Hebrews, like the Chinese, seem to have regarded any distinction between sheep and goats as a minor subdivision. Probably because of this, to 'separate the sheep from the goats' is proverbial of God's discernment in New Testament times (Matthew 25:32)." (Cole)

ii. **Israel shall kill it at twilight**: "Christ came in the evening of the world; in the 'last hour' (1 John 2:11); when all lay buried in darkness; in the eventide of our sin and death." (Trapp)

2. (7-11) Instructions for eating the Passover.

'And they shall take *some* of the blood and put *it* on the two doorposts and on the lintel of the houses where they eat it. Then they shall eat the flesh on that night; roasted in fire, with unleavened bread *and* with bitter *herbs* they shall eat it. Do not eat it raw, nor boiled at all with water, but roasted in fire; its head with its legs and its entrails. You shall let none of it remain until morning, and what remains of it until morning you shall burn with fire. And thus you shall eat it: *with* a belt on your waist, your sandals on your feet, and your staff in your hand. So you shall eat it in haste. It *is* the LORD's Passover.'

a. **Take some of the blood and put it on the two doorposts and on the lintel of the houses**: Before the Passover lamb could be eaten, its blood had to be applied to the doorway of the home, to the top and upon each side the blood was applied. The only part of this sacrifice given to God was the blood; the rest was eaten by each family or discarded (**what remains of it until morning you shall burn with fire**).

    i. As the blood was applied to the top and each side of the doorway, this blood dripped down, forming a figure of a cross in the doorway.

    ii. The blood on the doorposts showed that the sacrifice of the Passover lamb was to be remembered in daily life. You would see it every time you went in or out of the house.

b. **And thus you shall eat it**: Then the lamb could be eaten, but only if it had been **roasted in fire**, with the lamb itself coming into contact with the fire, and with **bitter herbs** accompanying the meal.

    i. "The paschal lamb was not killed in order to be looked at only, but to be eaten; and our Lord Jesus Christ has not been slain merely that we may hear about him and talk about him, and think about him, but that we may feed upon him." (Spurgeon)

c. **Let none of it remain until morning**: The Passover lamb had to be eaten completely; a family had to totally consume the sacrifice.

    i. The idea behind eating it all was that you had to take it all then, and not store up some of the leftover lamb for later. It was for right then, right now, and you had to receive all of it without thinking you could take a bit then and come back to it later if you pleased. We take *all of Jesus*, not just the parts that please us.

d. **With a belt on your waist, your sandals on your feet, and your staff in your hand**: The Passover lamb had to be eaten in faith, trusting that the deliverance promised to Israel was present, and that they would walk in that deliverance immediately.

    i. Faith was essential to the keeping of Passover: *By faith he* [Moses] *kept the Passover and the sprinkling of blood, lest he who destroyed the firstborn should touch them.* (Hebrews 11:28)

e. **It is the LORD's Passover**: The Passover was the Lord's in the sense that He provided it:

- As a rescue, to deliver Israel from the plague of the firstborn.
- As an institution, to remember God's rescue and deliverance for Israel through every generation.
- As a powerful drama, acting out the perfect sacrifice and rescue Jesus would later provide.

i. By the inspiration of the Holy Spirit, Paul made it perfectly clear: *For indeed Christ, our Passover, was sacrificed for us* (1 Corinthians 5:7). John the Baptist drew on a similar image when he said of Jesus, *Behold! The Lamb of God who takes away the sin of the world!* (John 1:29) It seems that Jesus was actually crucified on Passover (John 19:14). *We see Jesus in the Passover.*

- Jesus lived with and became bonded to the human family before He was sacrificed for them.
- The sacrifice of Jesus has to be appropriate to each home, not simply on a national or community basis.
- Jesus the Passover Lamb was spotless – perfectly so, not stained by any sin, any moral or spiritual imperfection.
- It was only the blood of Jesus, His actual poured-out life that atoned for sin.
- In His death, Jesus was touched with fire, the fire of God's judgment and wrath.
- In His death, Jesus received the bitter cup of God's judgment.
- The work of Jesus has to be received fully, with none left in reserve.
- The Passover work of Jesus for His people is the dawn and prelude to their freedom.

3. (12-13) The protection of the blood.

'For I will pass through the land of Egypt on that night, and will strike all the firstborn in the land of Egypt, both man and beast; and against all the gods of Egypt I will execute judgment: I *am* the LORD. Now the blood shall be a sign for you on the houses where you *are*. And when I see the blood, I will pass over you; and the plague shall not be on you to destroy *you* when I strike the land of Egypt.'

a. **When I see the blood, I will pass over you**: For Israel to be spared the judgment on the firstborn, they had to apply the blood just as God said they should. The blood of the lamb was essential to what God required.

i. If an Israelite home *didn't* believe in the power of **the blood** of the lamb, they could sacrifice the lamb and eat it, but they would still be visited by judgment.

ii. If an Egyptian home *did* believe in the power of **the blood** of the lamb, and made a proper Passover sacrifice, they would be spared the judgment.

iii. Additionally, an intellectual agreement with what God said about **the blood** was not enough; they actually had to *do* what God said must be done with the blood.

b. **I will strike all the firstborn in the land of Egypt**: God regarded Israel as His firstborn, His favored people. If Egypt refused to release God's firstborn, then God required the firstborn of Egypt as a penalty and judgment.

4. (14-20) The institution of Passover and Unleavened Bread as feasts.

'**So this day shall be to you a memorial; and you shall keep it as a feast to the L**ORD **throughout your generations. You shall keep it as a feast by an everlasting ordinance. Seven days you shall eat unleavened bread. On the first day you shall remove leaven from your houses. For whoever eats leavened bread from the first day until the seventh day, that person shall be cut off from Israel. On the first day** *there shall be* **a holy convocation, and on the seventh day there shall be a holy convocation for you. No manner of work shall be done on them; but** *that* **which everyone must eat; that only may be prepared by you. So you shall observe** *the Feast of* **Unleavened Bread, for on this same day I will have brought your armies out of the land of Egypt. Therefore you shall observe this day throughout your generations as an everlasting ordinance. In the first** *month,* **on the fourteenth day of the month at evening, you shall eat unleavened bread, until the twenty-first day of the month at evening. For seven days no leaven shall be found in your houses, since whoever eats what is leavened, that same person shall be cut off from the congregation of Israel, whether** *he is* **a stranger or a native of the land. You shall eat nothing leavened; in all your dwellings you shall eat unleavened bread.'**

a. **Seven days you shall eat unleavened bread**: Passover began on the 10th; on the 14th they ate the Passover, and this was the first day of unleavened bread. Then for the next seven days, they ate only unleavened bread.

b. **So you shall observe the Feast of Unleavened Bread, for on this same day I will have brought your armies out of the land of Egypt**: For the first Passover, the unleavened bread was a practical necessity - they left Egypt in such a hurry there was no time to allow for the dough to rise. After the first Passover, the **Feast of Unleavened Bread** was a testimony **throughout your generations**.

c. **For seven days no leaven shall be found in your houses**: Leaven was also a picture of sin and corruption, because of the way a little leaven influences a whole lump of dough, and also because of the way leaven "puffs up" the lump - even as pride and sin makes us "puffed up."

i. Significantly, God called them to walk "unleavened" after their initial deliverance from Egypt. Symbolically, they were being called to a life in moral purity before the L ORD.

ii. Some suggest there was also a hygienic aspect in getting rid of all the leaven. Since they used a piece of dough from the previous batch to make the bread for that day, and did so repeatedly, that harmful bacteria could take hold in the dough; so it was good to remove all leaven and start all over at least once a year.

B. Moses leads the people in the observance of Passover.

1. (21-23) Moses tells the elders to do as God said.

Then Moses called for all the elders of Israel and said to them, "Pick out and take lambs for yourselves according to your families, and kill the Passover *lamb.* **And you shall take a bunch of hyssop, dip** *it* **in the blood that** *is* **in the basin, and strike the lintel and the two doorposts with the blood that** *is* **in the basin. And none of you shall go out of the door of his house until morning. For the LORD will pass through to strike the Egyptians; and when He sees the blood on the lintel and on the two doorposts, the LORD will pass over the door and not allow the destroyer to come into your houses to strike** *you.*"

a. **Moses called for all the elders of Israel and said to them**: The elders were expected to lead the way. Moses instructed them to observe the Passover, knowing the rest of the nation would follow.

b. **Take a bunch of hyssop**: They used **hyssop** to apply the blood to the doorposts and the lintel. Through the Scriptures, hyssop was often used to apply blood for the cleansing of sin.

i. In Leviticus 14:6, the ceremony for the cleansing of a leper used **hyssop** to apply blood. In Numbers 19:6, **hyssop** was used to make the ashes of a red heifer for the water of purification. In Numbers 19:18, **hyssop** was used to apply the purification water.

ii. David, in his great Psalm of repentance, said *purge me with hyssop, and I shall be clean* (Psalm 51:7). **Hyssop** was always connected with purification through sacrifice.

iii. **Hyssop** was even connected with Jesus' great sacrifice for sin. John 19:29 points out when Jesus was offered sour wine to drink on the cross, the sponge soaked with it was put on a bunch of **hyssop**.

c. **When He sees the blood...the LORD will pass over**: The LORD looked for blood. This blood sacrifice was the basis for sparing people from judgment.

i. Rescue from the angel of death didn't happen by a prayer or a fasting or a good work; it was accomplished by a life given on behalf of others.

2. (24-27a) Passover as an enduring ordinance.

"And you shall observe this thing as an ordinance for you and your sons forever. It will come to pass when you come to the land which the LORD will give you, just as He promised, that you shall keep this service. And it shall be, when your children say to you, 'What do you mean by this service?' that you shall say, 'It *is* the Passover sacrifice of the LORD, who passed over the houses of the children of Israel in Egypt when He struck the Egyptians and delivered our households.'"

a. **An ordinance for you and your sons forever:** The deliverance of Passover was not only for them, but also for their children, and all generations to follow. Passover was the greatest work of redemption performed on the Old Testament side of the cross.

i. In the same way, Jesus gave the new Passover saying that His work on the cross was not only for that generation, but should be remembered and applied to all generations (Luke 22:14-20).

b. **When He struck the Egyptians and delivered our households:** In Passover, there was a two-fold work. First, an enemy was defeated (**He struck the Egyptians**). Second, God's people were set free and given a new identity with new promises, a new walk, a new life altogether (**delivered our households**).

3. (27b-28) The obedience of the people.

So the people bowed their heads and worshiped. Then the children of Israel went away and did *so;* just as the LORD had commanded Moses and Aaron, so they did.

a. **So the people bowed their heads and worshipped:** Rightfully, the immediate reaction of Israel to this announcement (before it actually happened) was *worship*. They honored the God who said He would do all this for them.

b. **Then the children of Israel went away and did so:** In many ways, these were the most important words of the whole account. As great as God's deliverance was, the people would have never received it if they had failed to do what God told them to do.

i. We wonder if any Israelites suffered under the judgment of the firstborn because they *did not* believe and obey. We wonder if any Egyptians were spared judgment because they *did* believe and obey.

C. The final plague: the death of Egypt's firstborn.

1. (29-30) God slays the firstborn of Egypt.

And it came to pass at midnight that the LORD struck all the firstborn in the land of Egypt, from the firstborn of Pharaoh who sat on his

throne to the firstborn of the captive who *was* in the dungeon, and all the firstborn of livestock. So Pharaoh rose in the night, he, all his servants, and all the Egyptians; and there was a great cry in Egypt, for *there was* not a house where *there was* not one dead.

a. **The LORD struck all the firstborn in the land of Egypt**: God told Moses that Pharaoh would not let them go until he was forced to by God's mighty works (Exodus 3:19-20), and that this work would somehow touch the firstborn of Egypt (Exodus 4:21-23). Now the situation unfolded just as God said it would.

> i. **To the firstborn of captive who was in the dungeon: Dungeon** is "Literally, the 'pit-house'. Pits were a common prison. Here the opposite to pharaoh is not the 'mill girl' (Exodus 11:15), but the prisoner of war in the dungeon." (Cole)

b. **All the firstborn in the land of Egypt**: This plague was directed against two significant Egyptian gods. First, *Osiris* was the Egyptian god thought to be the giver of life. Second, this was against the supposed deity of Pharaoh himself, because his own household was touched (**the firstborn of Pharaoh who sat on his throne**).

> i. An inscription was found in a shrine connected with the great Sphinx that records a solemn promise from the Egyptian gods vowing that Thutmose IV would succeed his father Amenhotep II - whom many believe to be the pharaoh of the Exodus. This unique, emphatic promise from the gods that something so natural would happen – that the eldest son would take his father's place as Pharaoh – was perhaps because Thutmose IV was not his father's firstborn son, and the firstborn was struck dead at the first Passover. Therefore, they believed that the second-born son needed special protection from the gods and the inscription sought to provide that.

c. **So Pharaoh rose in the night, he, all his servants, and all the Egyptians; and there was a great cry in Egypt**: In dealing with Pharaoh, God first had to inform his *mind*, and then break his *will*. Pharaoh's problem wasn't that there was insufficient intellectual evidence; his heart had to be broken and made soft towards God.

> i. Egypt and Pharaoh would not give God *His* firstborn - Israel (Exodus 4:22-23); so God took the firstborn of Egypt. Finally, Pharaoh knew that the LORD God was greater than all the Egyptian gods, and was greater than Pharaoh himself - who was thought to be a god.

ii. **A great cry in Egypt**: Israel cried to God for deliverance (Exodus 2:23), and they cried to Pharaoh for relief (Exodus 5:15). Now the Egyptians had reason to cry.

2. (31-36) The response of Pharaoh and the Egyptians.

Then he called for Moses and Aaron by night, and said, "Rise, go out from among my people, both you and the children of Israel. And go, serve the LORD as you have said. Also take your flocks and your herds, as you have said, and be gone; and bless me also." And the Egyptians urged the people, that they might send them out of the land in haste. For they said, "We *shall* all *be* dead." So the people took their dough before it was leavened, having their kneading bowls bound up in their clothes on their shoulders. Now the children of Israel had done according to the word of Moses, and they had asked from the Egyptians articles of silver, articles of gold, and clothing. And the LORD had given the people favor in the sight of the Egyptians, so that they granted them *what they requested.* Thus they plundered the Egyptians.

a. **Rise, go out from among my people**: Pharaoh didn't simply allow Israel to leave; now he *commanded* them to go. This was just what the LORD told Moses would happen: *When he lets you go, he will surely drive you out of here altogether* (Exodus 11:1).

b. **Bless me also**: This shows that now Pharaoh knew who the LORD was, the God who was greater than Pharaoh and whom Pharaoh must seek for blessing. Pharaoh only came to this knowledge through being broken.

c. **Egyptians urged the people, that they might send them out of the land in haste...they plundered the Egyptians**: The Egyptian people also agreed that the Israelites must go, to the extent that they essentially *paid* the Israelites to leave. Therefore, the children of Israel left in a hurry, so quickly that there was no time to let the bread rise. This is why they had to eat unleavened bread as the LORD had commanded.

i. We can imagine that some of the Israelites did not follow God's instruction to get all the leaven out (Exodus 12:15). Now because of the haste of their departure, they *had* to do what God had told them because God arranged the circumstances so that they couldn't use leaven.

ii. In the same way, sometimes God arranges circumstances to where obedience is simply made *necessary*, even if we would not normally choose it. For example, God may want a man to give up friends that bring a bad influence, and the man finds that his friends leave him first.

D. Israel leaves Egypt.

1. (37-39) The children of Israel go out of Egypt.

Then the children of Israel journeyed from Rameses to Succoth, about six hundred thousand men on foot, besides children. A mixed multitude went up with them also, and flocks and herds; a great deal of livestock. And they baked unleavened cakes of the dough which they had brought out of Egypt; for it was not leavened, because they were driven out of Egypt and could not wait, nor had they prepared provisions for themselves.

a. **The children of Israel journeyed**: This was the moment all the previous chapters of Exodus anticipated. Israel was now *free*, and Pharaoh and his armies did not hold them back as they traveled from their center of **Rameses to Succoth**.

i. Since **Succoth** means *shelters*, it may not describe a temporary encampment instead of an existing Egyptian city. It's easy to imagine the celebrations (and tension) at Succoth that night.

b. **About six hundred thousand men on foot, besides children**: Assembling together at Succoth, about 600,000 men (besides children or women) left Egypt. The count of **six hundred thousand men** makes for a total population of perhaps two million that left Egypt for the Promised Land.

i. Cole discusses a few ideas that would make the number 600,000 much less, such as saying that *thousand* really means *clan* and that 600 extended family-clans left Egypt. Even so, "By the time they reached Canaan they were certainly a sizable horde (to use the historian's term), to judge from the archaeological impact on Canaanite civilization." (Cole)

ii. "All attempts to explain *elep* ('thousand') as 'clan' or 'tribe' in this context fail to meet the test of inconsistency in other contexts." (Kaiser)

c. **A mixed multitude went up with them**: Not all of the 600,000 were Israelites. Many Egyptians (and perhaps other foreigners) went with them, because the God of Israel demonstrated that He was more powerful than the gods of the Egyptians.

i. **Mixed multitude**: "The Hebrew says 'swarm', from the same root as that used in 8:21 to describe the plague of gadflies." (Cole)

d. **It was not leavened, because they were driven out of Egypt and could not wait**: Again, God made obedience a *necessity* in the case of the unleavened bread.

2. (40-42) Passover as a **solemn observance**.

Now the sojourn of the children of Israel who lived in Egypt *was* four hundred and thirty years. And it came to pass at the end of the four hundred and thirty years; on that very same day; it came to pass that all the armies of the LORD went out from the land of Egypt. It *is* a night of solemn observance to the LORD for bringing them out of the land of Egypt. This *is* that night of the LORD, a solemn observance for all the children of Israel throughout their generations.

a. **At the end of the four hundred and thirty years; on that very same day**: Apparently the Exodus from Egypt began on the same calendar day as the 430th anniversary of Israel's time in Egypt. It's remarkable evidence that God often fulfills promises on anniversaries of prior or prophesied events.

b. **It is a night of solemn observance to the LORD for bringing them out of the land of Egypt**: God intended this event to be as a memorial of His redemptive work for Israel. In this sense, the deliverance from Egypt was the cross-like event of the Old Testament.

c. **Out from the land of Egypt**: The phrase **out of Egypt** is repeated 56 times in the Bible after this point. God wanted His people to remember His deliverance of Israel from Egypt.

3. (43-49) Regulations for Passover.

And the LORD said to Moses and Aaron, "This *is* the ordinance of the Passover: No foreigner shall eat it. But every man's servant who is bought for money, when you have circumcised him, then he may eat it. A sojourner and a hired servant shall not eat it. In one house it shall be eaten; you shall not carry any of the flesh outside the house, nor shall you break one of its bones. All the congregation of Israel shall keep it. And when a stranger dwells with you *and wants* to keep the Passover to the LORD, let all his males be circumcised, and then let him come near and keep it; and he shall be as a native of the land. For no uncircumcised person shall eat it. One law shall be for the native-born and for the stranger who dwells among you."

a. **No foreigner shall eat it**: To share in the Passover, one had to make himself part of the people of Israel. Receiving the covenant of circumcision and taking Passover were all part of the same package.

b. **In one house it shall be eaten**: Passover was commemorated on a family level. Each household celebrated it.

c. **Nor shall you break one of its bones**: None of the bones of the Passover lamb were to be broken. This looked forward to Jesus, the ultimate Passover Lamb, who had not one bone broken even in His crucifixion (Psalm 22:17 and John 19:31-36).

d. **All the congregation of Israel shall keep it**: All who were part of Israel had to commemorate the Passover redemption. You couldn't be part of God's people and *not* share in Passover.

i. In this sense, Passover means all this and more to Christians: *Therefore purge out the old leaven, that you may be a new lump, since you truly are unleavened. For indeed Christ, our Passover, was sacrificed for us. Therefore let us keep the feast, not with old leaven, nor with the leaven of malice and wickedness, but with the unleavened bread of sincerity and truth.* (1 Corinthians 5:7-8)

4. (50-51) Departure from Egypt: the Exodus begins.

Thus all the children of Israel did; as the LORD commanded Moses and Aaron, so they did. And it came to pass, on that very same day, that the LORD brought the children of Israel out of the land of Egypt according to their armies.

a. **Thus all the children of Israel did**: Israel kept the commandments of God that Moses delivered. Their faith and obedience saved their firstborn, plundered the Egyptians, and set them free from Egypt.

b. **The LORD brought the children of Israel out of the land of Egypt**: When Israel left Egypt, it was a nation born in a day. It was as if the 430 years were a time of gestation when the baby grew large. The plagues were like labor pains before birth and now the nation was born.

Exodus 13 - God's Instruction to Israel upon Their Departure

A. Instructions for a new nation.

1. (1-2) The firstborn belongs to God.

Then the LORD spoke to Moses, saying, "Consecrate to Me all the firstborn, whatever opens the womb among the children of Israel, *both* of man and beast; it is Mine."

a. **Consecrate to Me**: The idea was that the firstborn was to be set apart to God, whether **of man** or **beast** - the firstborn belonged to God.

i. "*Consecrate* could either mean 'sacrifice' or merely 'consider as belonging to God'. Instances of both meanings could be found in the Pentateuch." (Cole)

ii. "Not that the rest were exempt, but the first-born were, like the Sabbath day and the first ears of corn, a pledge of the dedication of the whole nation." (Thomas)

b. **It is Mine**: This was for three reasons. First, because Israel was God's firstborn (Exodus 4:22), and this practice honored that fact. Second, because the firstborn was thought to be the best, and the best was always given to God. Finally, as a reminder to all generations of when God redeemed Israel, *His* firstborn, from Egypt.

i. "Israel had been saved through the destruction of Egypt's first-born, and now they were required to dedicate their own first-born as a constant memorial of their deliverance." (Thomas)

2. (3-7) The feast of Unleavened Bread.

And Moses said to the people: "Remember this day in which you went out of Egypt, out of the house of bondage; for by strength of hand the LORD brought you out of this *place*. No leavened bread shall be eaten. On this day you are going out, in the month Abib. And it shall

be, when the LORD brings you into the land of the Canaanites and the Hittites and the Amorites and the Hivites and the Jebusites, which He swore to your fathers to give you, a land flowing with milk and honey, that you shall keep this service in this month. Seven days you shall eat unleavened bread, and on the seventh day *there shall be* a feast to the LORD. Unleavened bread shall be eaten seven days. And no leavened bread shall be seen among you, nor shall leaven be seen among you in all your quarters."

a. **Seven days you shall eat unleavened bread**: The purity of the feast of Unleavened Bread followed upon the blood-deliverance of Passover. This illustrates the principle that we can only walk in purity before the LORD after the blood-deliverance at the cross.

b. **And on the seventh day there shall be a feast to the LORD**: At the same time, the days of Unleavened Bread were not joyless. The time began and ended with **a feast** - a party. A walk of purity in the LORD is a life filled with joy.

3. (8-10) Remember to tell your children why you do these things.

"And you shall tell your son in that day, saying, *'This is done* because of what the LORD did for me when I came up from Egypt.' It shall be as a sign to you on your hand and as a memorial between your eyes, that the Lord's law may be in your mouth; for with a strong hand the LORD has brought you out of Egypt. You shall therefore keep this ordinance in its season from year to year."

a. **It shall be as a sign to you on your hand and as a memorial between your eyes**: God wanted the deliverance from Egypt to be constantly at hand and before their eyes. The Jews used this passage (along with Deuteronomy 6:4-9 and 11:13-21) to institute the practice of the wearing of phylacteries - small boxes holding parchment with scriptures on them, held to the forehead or hand with leather straps.

i. Later, Jesus condemned the abuse of the wearing of phylacteries among the Pharisees. They made their phylactery boxes large and ostentatious as a display of supposedly greater spirituality (Matthew 23:5).

ii. In the end times, there will be a Satanic imitation of this practice when the number of the Antichrist will be applied to either the hand or forehead of all who will take it (Revelation 13:16).

b. **That the LORD's law may be in your mouth**: This shows that God did not command for literal boxes to be tied to the hands and forehead, because to take it in this way means that there should also be a phylactery box to put in the mouth.

i. "The very fact that language like this can be used of the feast of unleavened bread shows it to be pure metaphor."

4. (11-16) How and why to give the firstborn to the LORD.

"And it shall be, when the LORD brings you into the land of the Canaanites, as He swore to you and your fathers, and gives it to you, that you shall set apart to the LORD all that open the womb, that is, every firstborn that comes from an animal which you have; the males *shall be* **the LORD's. But every firstborn of a donkey you shall redeem with a lamb; and if you will not redeem** *it,* **then you shall break its neck. And all the firstborn of man among your sons you shall redeem. So it shall be, when your son asks you in time to come, saying, 'What** *is* **this?' that you shall say to him, 'By strength of hand the LORD brought us out of Egypt, out of the house of bondage. 'And it came to pass, when Pharaoh was stubborn about letting us go, that the LORD killed all the firstborn in the land of Egypt, both the firstborn of man and the firstborn of beast. Therefore I sacrifice to the LORD all males that open the womb, but all the firstborn of my sons I redeem.' It shall be as a sign on your hand and as frontlets between your eyes, for by strength of hand the LORD brought us out of Egypt."**

a. **When the LORD brings you into the land of the Canaanites**: The law of dedicating the firstborn to God (Exodus 13:1-2) was only to take effect when in the Promised Land. By then the need for a reminder of the work of deliverance from Egypt would be all the more necessary.

b. **But every firstborn of a donkey you shall redeem with a lamb... And all the firstborn of man among your sons you shall redeem**: If the firstborn was unacceptable to sacrifice (if it was an unclean animal or a human), a substitute was offered to **redeem** the firstborn from God. If the firstborn was an animal, the substitute was a clean animal. If the firstborn was a human, the substitute was money.

i. "For *set apart* translate 'make them pass over' (*i.e.* by fire) and understand the meaning as 'offer up as a whole burnt offering'. This is the sinister phrase which is used in 2 Kings 16:3 of Ahaz sacrificing his own son 'to Molech'." (Cole)

c. **It shall be as a sign on your hand and as frontlets between your eyes**: This practice of dedicating the firstborn to God would be a reminder through ritual of God's great work and strong power for Israel.

B. Israel's journey out of Egypt.

1. (17-18) God leads them out in the way not expected, the way by the wilderness.

Then it came to pass, when Pharaoh had let the people go, that God did not lead them *by* way of the land of the Philistines, although that *was* near; for God said, "Lest perhaps the people change their minds when they see war, and return to Egypt." So God led the people around *by* way of the wilderness of the Red Sea. And the children of Israel went up in orderly ranks out of the land of Egypt.

a. **God did not lead them by way of the land of the Philistines, although that was near**: The coastal route (the *Via Maris*, known as "the way of the sea") was the shortest and most common way to go from Egypt to Canaan. Yet it was also the road where Egypt's military outposts were. God knew the people of Israel were not ready to face this yet (**lest perhaps the people change their minds when they see war, and return to Egypt**), so He led them a different way.

i. It would have been easy for the Israelites to think that the *Via Maris* was the way to go; it had good, easy roads, the shortest distance; it was a trade route so food and water could be bought. But the dangers of the way were too great, though they could not see them. God anticipated dangers they could not see.

ii. In the same way, God will never allow us to face more than we are able to bear; He knows what we can handle (1 Corinthians 10:13). "He carefully chose their way out of Egypt; not the nearer, but the safer. He tempts not above what we are able: but so orders the matter, that evils are not ready for us until we for them." (Trapp)

iii. "The nation delivered and consecrated is seen at once as under the direct government and guidance of God." (Morgan)

b. **By way of the wilderness of the Red Sea**: The **Red Sea** first mentioned here is not the huge expanse of the Red Sea (some 100 miles wide), but the western "finger" of the Red Sea that extends up unto the border areas of Egypt - the modern day Gulf of Suez.

2. (19) The promise to Joseph fulfilled.

And Moses took the bones of Joseph with him, for he had placed the children of Israel under solemn oath, saying, "God will surely visit you, and you shall carry up my bones from here with you."

a. **Moses took the bones of Joseph with him**: In a great act of faith Joseph asked that his bones be taken from Egypt (Genesis 50:25). He did this because he knew that Egypt was not their final resting place, but that God had a Promised Land for them.

b. **God will surely visit you, and you shall carry up my bones from here with you**: Genesis 50:25-26 says specifically that Joseph was never buried. His coffin laid above ground for the four hundred or so years until it was taken back to Canaan. It was a silent witness all those years that Israel *was* going back to the Promised Land, just as God had promised. Now the promise was being fulfilled.

3. (20-22) Israel led by the cloud by day and the fire by night.

So they took their journey from Succoth and camped in Etham at the edge of the wilderness. And the LORD went before them by day in a pillar of cloud to lead the way, and by night in a pillar of fire to give them light, so as to go by day and night. He did not take away the pillar of cloud by day or the pillar of fire by night *from* before the people.

a. **The LORD went before them**: God showed His presence to Israel in a dramatic way, by giving them constant assurance, with a pillar of cloud by day and a pillar of fire by night.

i. The pillar of cloud by day and of fire by night was also there as a sun and a shield: *He spread a cloud for a covering, and fire to give light in the night* (Psalm 105:39); or as it says in Psalm 84:11: *For the LORD God is a sun and shield; the LORD will give grace and glory; no good thing will He withhold from those who walk uprightly.*

ii. "The exact location of Etham is unknown." (Kaiser)

b. **A pillar of cloud to lead the way, and by night in a pillar of fire to give them light**: According to Cole, the ancient Hebrew for **pillar** literally means "something standing." It was probably more of what we would think of as a *column* than a pillar.

i. "This was the *Shechinah* or Divine dwelling place, and was the continual proof of the presence and protection of GOD." (Clarke)

c. **He did not take away the pillar of cloud by day or the pillar of fire by night from before the people**: Israel could draw great assurance from this visible evidence of God's presence. Nevertheless, there were still many occasions after this when they seemed to doubt, to rebel, and to act as if God was distant.

Exodus 14 - The Crossing of the Red Sea

A. The pursuit of Pharaoh's armies.

1. (1-4) God draws Pharaoh to come out against Israel.

Now the LORD spoke to Moses, saying: "Speak to the children of Israel, that they turn and camp before Pi Hahiroth, between Migdol and the sea, opposite Baal Zephon; you shall camp before it by the sea. For Pharaoh will say of the children of Israel, 'They *are* bewildered by the land; the wilderness has closed them in.' Then I will harden Pharaoh's heart, so that he will pursue them; and I will gain honor over Pharaoh and over all his army, that the Egyptians may know that I *am* the LORD." And they did so.

a. **You shall camp before it by the sea**: We could say that God set an ambush for Pharaoh. Even after the horror of the death of the firstborn, the change in Pharaoh's heart was only temporary (**he will pursue them**). He was quick to strike at Israel when he had the chance.

b. **They are bewildered by the land**: This was exactly what God wanted Pharaoh to believe. God told Moses to lead Israel in a way that looked confused. God told Moses and Israel to do something that look confused because God would **gain honor over Pharaoh** through it.

2. (5-9) Pharaoh decides to force Israel back to Egypt.

Now it was told the king of Egypt that the people had fled, and the heart of Pharaoh and his servants was turned against the people; and they said, "Why have we done this, that we have let Israel go from serving us?" So he made ready his chariot and took his people with him. Also, he took six hundred choice chariots, and all the chariots of Egypt with captains over every one of them. And the LORD hardened the heart of Pharaoh king of Egypt, and he pursued the children of Israel; and the children of Israel went out with boldness. So the Egyptians pursued them, all the horses *and* chariots of Pharaoh, his horsemen and his

army, and overtook them camping by the sea beside Pi Hahiroth, before Baal Zephon.

a. **Why have we done this, that we have let Israel go from serving us**: This was a strange question for Pharaoh to ask. It wasn't difficult to think of at least ten good reasons - namely, ten powerful plagues - why Pharaoh **let Israel go**. This demonstrates how we are often quick to forget what God has done and demonstrated.

i. Perhaps Pharaoh thought that plagues were the limit of God's power; that *now* he could successfully strike against Israel.

ii. There is an analogy in this to the spiritual life. We sometimes think that Satan will let us go easily, or we think that once we leave his kingdom, he forgets about us. Yet just like Pharaoh after Israel, Satan pursues us, attempting to keep us at least on the fringes of his domain and hoping to destroy us if he can.

iii. **Made ready his chariot**: "This is not merely his personal chariot. The meaning is probably 'his chariotry', a collective." (Cole)

b. **Six hundred choice chariots, and all the chariots of Egypt**: Pharaoh had the best military resources. **Chariots** were the most sophisticated military technology available at that time. Israel had nothing except that **the children of Israel went out with boldness**.

i. The idea behind the Hebrew words **with boldness** (*ruwn yad*) includes the idea of rebellion against authority (1 Kings 11:26-27). The rebellious nature of Israel was *good* when it was against Pharaoh and all it stood for; it was *bad* when it was against the LORD, Moses, and all they stood for. The trouble with most rebels is that they rebel against the wrong things.

3. (10-12) The response of the children of Israel.

And when Pharaoh drew near, the children of Israel lifted their eyes, and behold, the Egyptians marched after them. So they were very afraid, and the children of Israel cried out to the LORD. Then they said to Moses, "Because *there were* no graves in Egypt, have you taken us away to die in the wilderness? Why have you so dealt with us, to bring us up out of Egypt? *Is* this not the word that we told you in Egypt, saying, 'Let us alone that we may serve the Egyptians?' For *it would have been* better for us to serve the Egyptians than that we should die in the wilderness."

a. **They were very afraid**: It made sense for Israel to be afraid. They could see Pharaoh's armies on one side and the Red Sea on the other. They seemed to have no chance for escape.

i. God led Israel into what seemed to be a trap. There was no way of escape except the way they had come in, and the Egyptian army had that path blocked.

ii. "Humanly speaking, they might easily overcome the unarmed and encumbered Israelites, who could not be supposed to be able to make any resistance against *cavalry* and *war-chariots*." (Clarke)

iii. "There were no two ways to choose from: they could not miss the way, for they must needs march through the sea. No room for wandering remained: their road was walled up and they could not miss it." (Spurgeon)

b. **The children of Israel cried out to the LORD**: Israel did the right thing. When we find ourselves in dangerous places with no easy escape, we must cry out to God, because *God is our refuge and strength, a very present help in trouble* (Psalm 46:1).

i. "The panic of the people is hardly to be wondered at when we think of their circumstances." (Morgan)

c. **Because there were no graves in Egypt, have you taken us away to die in the wilderness**: Their fear, and their cry to the LORD made sense. Yet their words to Moses showed little faith and a loss of confidence in God. No reasonable mind could really think that Moses planned all this to lead the people of Israel to their deaths in the wilderness.

i. Moses said or did nothing that would support such an accusation, but the children of Israel still thought this way.

ii. "They mocked in the most satirical tone possible (since Egypt specialized in graves and had about three-fourths of its land are available for grave sites)." (Kaiser)

d. **Let us alone that we may serve the Egyptians**: Israel was not yet a week out of Egypt and they already distorted the past, thinking that it was better for them in Egypt than it really was.

4. (13-14) Moses responds with great courage.

And Moses said to the people, "Do not be afraid. Stand still, and see the salvation of the LORD, which He will accomplish for you today. For the Egyptians whom you see today, you shall see again no more forever. The LORD will fight for you, and you shall hold your peace."

a. **Do not be afraid**: At this point, Moses had no idea how God would help them in the situation. All he knew was God certainly *would* help. In a sense, Moses knew he was in such a bad situation that God *had* to come through.

i. When we see that our only help is God, we are more likely to trust Him. Sometimes it is the little things - the things we *think* we can do in our own strength - that get us down, not the big things that we *know* only God can do.

b. **Stand still**: Moses told the people of Israel to *stop*. This is often the LORD's direction to the believer in a time of crisis. *Despair* will cast you down, keeping you from standing. *Fear* will tell you to retreat. *Impatience* will tell you to do something now. *Presumption* will tell you to jump into the Red Sea before it is parted. Yet as God told Israel, He often tells us to simply **stand still** and **hold your peace** as He reveals His plan.

c. **See the salvation of the LORD**: Moses didn't know what God would do; yet, he knew what the result would be. He knew that God would save His people and that the enemies of the LORD would be destroyed. He could say to Israel, "**the LORD will fight for you.**"

i. "*Salvation* is used here in its literal sense of saving life, or of victory instead of defeat in war. As the Old Testament moves on, 'salvation' will gain a more spiritual and less material sense (Psalm 51:12), although the Hebrew was not conscious of any sharp contrast between the two." (Cole)

d. **You shall see them no more forever**: The idea behind this implies much more than at first look. Moses perhaps spoke in terms of eternity as well as their present time.

B. God leads Israel across the Red Sea.

1. (15-18) God's instructions to Moses: stop praying and start doing.

And the LORD said to Moses, "Why do you cry to Me? Tell the children of Israel to go forward. But lift up your rod, and stretch out your hand over the sea and divide it. And the children of Israel shall go on dry *ground* through the midst of the sea. And I indeed will harden the hearts of the Egyptians, and they shall follow them. So I will gain honor over Pharaoh and over all his army, his chariots, and his horsemen. Then the Egyptians shall know that I *am* the LORD, when I have gained honor for Myself over Pharaoh, his chariots, and his horsemen."

a. **Why do you cry to Me**: Before the people, Moses was full of faith; before God, he cried out in desperate prayer. This was good because Moses had to show confidence before the nation to encourage *their* faith.

b. **Why do you cry to Me**: There is a time to pray, and a time to act. It can actually be *against* God's will to stop *doing* and to *only* pray in a particular situation. This was a time for action, and Moses could pray along the way.

i. "There is a time for praying, but there is also a time for holy activity. Prayer is adapted for almost every season, yet not prayer alone, for there comes, every now and then, a time when even prayer must take a secondary place." (Spurgeon)

ii. "There is something more to be done than to pray. We must not only crave God's help, but be forward in the course whereby to make way for God's help." (Trapp)

iii. "There is a favourite sin, of which he has long been guilty; he does not give it up, but he says that he will pray about it. God says to such a man, ' "Where fore criest thou unto me?" Give up thy sin; this is not a matter for thee to pray about, but to repent of.' The man says, "I was asking for repentance." Ask, if thou wilt, for repentance, but exercise it as well." (Spurgeon)

c. **Lift up your rod, and stretch out your hand**: These were simple instructions connected to a mighty miracle. In the same manner, the greatest miracle of salvation happens with simple actions on our part. As the **rod** of Moses did not actually perform the miracle, so we do not save ourselves with what we do, but we connect with God's saving miracle.

i. "Neither Moses nor his rod could be any effective instrument in a work which could be accomplished only by the omnipotence of God; but it was necessary that he should appear in it, in order that he might have credit in the sight of the Israelites, and that they might see that God had chosen him to be the instrument of their deliverance." (Clarke)

d. **Then the Egyptians shall know that I am the LORD**: God was not finished answering Pharaoh's question from Exodus 5:2 when Pharaoh asked, "*Who is the LORD, that I should obey His voice to let Israel go?*" God used the miracle of the parting of the Red Sea to speak to *Egypt* as much as He used it to speak to *Israel*.

i. This is an aspect of the spiritual life rarely reflected upon, yet Ephesians 3:10-11 tells us that God uses His people to teach angelic beings. When God delivers us from a temptation or crisis, it is as much a testimony to our invisible adversaries as it is to us. God uses each victory in our life to tell our unseen enemies of His power and ability to work in and through frail humanity.

2. (19-20) God neutralizes the Egyptian army with the fire.

And the Angel of God, who went before the camp of Israel, moved and went behind them; and the pillar of cloud went from before them and stood behind them. So it came between the camp of the Egyptians and the camp of Israel. Thus it was a cloud and darkness *to the one,* and it

gave light by night *to the other,* so that the one did not come near the other all that night.

a. **And the Angel of God…moved and went behind them**: God sent both a specially commissioned **Angel** and **the pillar of cloud** (Exodus 13:21-22) as a barrier between Israel and the pursuing Egyptian army. God protected Israel from the Egyptian attack until a way was made through the Red Sea.

i. We often have little idea how much God does to protect us from the attacks of our unseen enemies. We sometimes feel that we are overwhelmed in a present spiritual struggle, but we may not know what it would be like if the LORD pulled back His protection.

b. **It came between the camp of the Egyptians and the camp of Israel**: The Egyptians didn't know it, but the same pillar that prevented their pursuit of Israel also protected their lives, at least for a while. If they had submitted to the LORD, who blocked their way with His presence, they would have been spared their coming destruction.

c. **Thus it was a cloud and darkness to the one, and it gave light by night to the other**: The pillar was a source of darkness to the Egyptians but a source of light to Israel. This is a vivid picture of how the glory of God or work of God can be light to one person yet seem dark to another.

i. "Thus the double nature of the glory of God in salvation and judgment, which later appears so frequently in Scripture, could not have been more graphically depicted." (Kaiser)

ii. The word of God has a dark side to sinners, as do also the gospel and even Jesus Himself.

3. (21-22) The waters of the Red Sea are parted, and the children of Israel cross over safely on dry ground.

Then Moses stretched out his hand over the sea; and the LORD caused the sea to go *back* by a strong east wind all that night, and made the sea into dry *land,* and the waters were divided. So the children of Israel went into the midst of the sea on the dry *ground,* and the waters *were* a wall to them on their right hand and on their left.

a. **Moses stretched out his hand over the sea**: Other passages (such as Exodus 13:18 and 15:14) identify this body of water as the *Red Sea.* The Hebrew phrase for *Red Sea* is *yam suph,* which clearly means "Reed Sea." Scholars and archeologists have attempted for years to positively identify this body of water.

i. "The term aptly describes the lake region north of the Gulf of Suez comprising the Bitter Lakes and Lake Timsah. It is possible that the Israelites went along the narrow neck of land on which Baal-zephon stood and that the Biblical Sea of Reeds was modern Lake Sirbonis. We are certain that the crossing was in this area because the Israelites found themselves in the Wilderness of Shur after crossing the sea (Exod. 15:22)." (Pfeiffer)

ii. We don't know exactly where the place was, and what the exact geography was. This is especially true because an area like this will change geography every flood or drought season. We do know there was enough water there to trap the Israelites and to later drown the Egyptians. We can surmise that this was perhaps 10 feet of water or so. We also can surmise that there was enough width in the crossing for the large group of Israelites to cross over in one night.

iii. Much recent research has proposed an alternative route for the Exodus of Israel from Egypt, one that sets Mount Sinai in the Arabian Peninsula instead of the Sinai Peninsula. This alternative route puts the crossing at the Red Sea's Gulf of Aqaba, instead of at the Bitter Lakes, the Port of Suez, or the Gulf of Suez. At the Gulf of Aqaba, crossings have been suggested at the northern tip (at Ezion Geber), in the middle (at Nuweiba Beach), or at the southern end (at the Straits of Tiran).

b. **The LORD caused the sea to go back by a strong east wind all that night, and made the sea into dry land, and the waters were divided**: Some believe this is simply an ancient legend and did not actually happen. However, modern research has demonstrated that it was completely plausible, according to a *Los Angeles Times* article by Thomas H. Maugh titled "Research Supports Bible's Account of Red Sea Parting" (3/14/92):

i. "Sophisticated computer calculations indicate that the biblical parting of the Red Sea, said to have allowed Moses and the Israelites to escape from bondage in Egypt, could have occurred precisely as the Bible describes it. Because of the peculiar geography of the northern end of the Red Sea, researchers report Sunday in the Bulletin of the American Meteorological Society, a moderate wind blowing constantly for about 10 hours could have caused the sea to recede about a mile and the water level to drop 10 feet, leaving dry land in the area where many biblical scholars believe the crossing occurred."

ii. It's important to note that this research does not prove that the crossing of the Red Sea happened at any particular place speculated on in the research; only that natural phenomenon exists, which God *may have* used to part the waters and allow Israel an exit from the

Egyptian army. Even if God used natural phenomenon, it was still a great miracle.

iii. "An infidel may deny the revelation in toto, and from such we expect nothing better; but to hear those who profess to believe this to be a Divine revelation endeavouring to prove that the passage of the Red Sea *had nothing miraculous in it*, is really intolerable. Such a mode of interpretation requires a miracle to make itself credible. Poor infidelity! how miserable and despicable are thy *shifts!*" (Clarke)

c. **The waters were a wall to them on their right hand and on their left**: Psalm 77:16-20 gives more detail in the description of the course of events during the Red Sea crossing. It poetically describes how it rained, thundered, and struck lightning at the crossing of the Red Sea.

4. (23-28) God troubles the Egyptian army, and they are drowned.

And the Egyptians pursued and went after them into the midst of the sea, all Pharaoh's horses, his chariots, and his horsemen. Now it came to pass, in the morning watch, that the LORD looked down upon the army of the Egyptians through the pillar of fire and cloud, and He troubled the army of the Egyptians. And He took off their chariot wheels, so that they drove them with difficulty; and the Egyptians said, "Let us flee from the face of Israel, for the LORD fights for them against the Egyptians." Then the LORD said to Moses, "Stretch out your hand over the sea, that the waters may come back upon the Egyptians, on their chariots, and on their horsemen." And Moses stretched out his hand over the sea; and when the morning appeared, the sea returned to its full depth, while the Egyptians were fleeing into it. So the LORD overthrew the Egyptians in the midst of the sea. Then the waters returned and covered the chariots, the horsemen, *and* all the army of Pharaoh that came into the sea after them. Not so much as one of them remained.

a. **He took off their chariot wheels**: God miraculously worked on the side of Israel against the Egyptians. He **troubled the army of the Egyptians** until Israel had crossed over the Red Sea. Only then did He allow the Egyptian army to continue their pursuit through the parted waters.

b. **So the LORD overthrew the Egyptians in the midst of the sea**: Though some also regard this as simply an ancient legend, modern research again shows it is completely possible.

i. Thomas H. Maugh continued in his *Los Angeles Times* article: "An abrupt change in the wind would have allowed the waters to come crashing back into the area in a few moments, a phenomenon that the Bible says inundated the Israelites' pursuers."

c. **Stretch out your hand over the sea, that the waters may come back upon the Egyptians**: God told Moses to *do* something with his hand connected with the motion of the sea. We know that it was not really the power of Moses' hand that held back the sea or allowed it to come crashing back upon the Egyptian army. It was the power of God at work.

i. God could have performed this miracle just as easily without Moses' cooperation. Yet, God often uses people to take part in His miraculous works. We can say that many miraculous works of God are yet to be done because no person has stepped forth to be the one who will stretch out their hand.

ii. In addition, this was God's vindication of Moses. Israel previously accused him of the lowest of motivations, and the most evil state of heart (Exodus 14:10-12). With this work through Moses, God showed the whole nation that Moses was their chosen leader.

d. **Not so much as one of them remained**: The deliverance at the Red Sea became a turning point in Israel's history. In this era of Israel's history, they had many troubles ahead, but *Pharaoh and the Egyptians* never troubled them again.

5. (29-31) Summary: another act of redemption on Israel's behalf.

But the children of Israel had walked on dry *land* in the midst of the sea, and the waters *were* a wall to them on their right hand and on their left. So the LORD saved Israel that day out of the hand of the Egyptians, and Israel saw the Egyptians dead on the seashore. Thus Israel saw the great work which the LORD had done in Egypt; so the people feared the LORD, and believed the LORD and His servant Moses.

a. **Israel saw the Egyptians dead on the seashore**: This was confirmation to Israel that their deliverance from Egypt was real and complete. An oppressed people are slow to believe they are free while their tyrants still live. God wanted Israel to know that their oppressors were dead.

i. "This is a very graphic touch, an eye-witness account. The drowned Egyptian soldiers stand for an old way of life in slavery, now gone for ever. Somehow the sight of those dead bodies was the concrete sign that salvation and a new life for Israel were now assured." (Cole)

ii. This principle applies to the day-to-day struggles of life. "Though the pressure of your trial is almost unbearable, you will one day see your Egyptian dead." (Meyer)

iii. This principle also applies to our ultimate victory. "But as the morning of eternity breaks, they will awake with songs of joy to see death and the grave and all the evils that they dreaded, like Egyptians, strewn on the shores of the sea of glass." (Meyer)

iv. Clarke speculates that the Israelites plundered these dead Egyptian soldiers and thereby gained weapons they would later use in battles against the Amalekites, Amorites, and others.

b. **So the LORD saved Israel that day out of the hand of the Egyptians**: God delivered Israel in seemingly impossible circumstances. He demonstrated His faithfulness to Israel and to all His people.

i. Spurgeon told the story of an old saint who lay on her deathbed and declared that Jesus would never forsake her, because He had promised so. Someone asked her, "But suppose that He did not keep His promise, and you were to be lost?" She answered, "Then He would be the greater loser than I. It is true I would lose my soul, but God would lose all His honor and glory if He were not true." God's motive for delivering us is not only His love for us, but also a desire to guard His own glory and honor.

ii. "Brethren, if we have trusted in God, and have come out of the Egypt of the world through his grace, and have left all its sins behind us, if we were left to die in the wilderness, the Lord Jesus Christ would lose his glory as a Saviour, the divine Father would lose his name for immutable faithfulness, and the Holy Ghost would lose his honour for perseverance in completing every work which he undertakes." (Spurgeon).

c. **The people feared the LORD, and believed the LORD and His servant Moses**: This was just the result God intended. Sadly for Israel, they did not stay in this place of respect and faith toward the LORD. This was probably more a circumstance of feelings than it was of true faith, because they left this place of respect for the LORD and Moses quickly.

i. We can say that the deliverance of Passover and the miracle of the Red Sea go together. If not for the victory won at the Red Sea, the redemption at Passover would have meant nothing. But they would have never made it to the Red Sea without the miracle of God's redemption at Passover. In the same way, the redemption of the cross would mean nothing without the miracle of the resurrection. The two works of deliverance must go hand in hand.

ii. "The new nation walked through a threatened death toward a new life in a consciousness of the presence and power of Jehovah from which they could not escape." (Morgan)

Exodus 15 - *The Song of Moses*

A. The Song of Moses.

1. (1-5) First stanza: **The Lord is a man of war.**

Then Moses and the children of Israel sang this song to the Lord, and spoke, saying:
"I will sing to the Lord,
For He has triumphed gloriously!
The horse and its rider He has thrown into the sea!
The Lord *is* my strength and song,
And He has become my salvation;
He *is* my God, and I will praise Him;
My father's God, and I will exalt Him.
The Lord *is* a man of war;
The Lord *is* His name.
Pharaoh's chariots and his army He has cast into the sea;
His chosen captains also are drowned in the Red Sea.
The depths have covered them;
They sank to the bottom like a stone."

a. **Then Moses and the children of Israel sang this song to the Lord:** This remarkable song is assumed to have come spontaneously as Moses led the nation into the wilderness on the other side of the Red Sea. They sang this song when their salvation was real to them. They sang it when the power and the presence of God were real to them.

i. God prizes these spontaneous expressions of praise and worship. This was a *new song* sung unto the Lord (as in Psalm 40:3). "There are moods of the soul that can only be expressed in poetry and in music." (Morgan)

ii. "This is the very first of those sacred songs preserved in Scripture, and in some respects it is first in merit as well as in time." (Spurgeon)

b. **I will sing to the LORD:** One of the great principles of worship is that it is unto **the LORD**, not unto man. When we worship God in song, our audience is the LORD Himself and not the people around us.

    i. "The first verse of this song was quoted by David. I think you will find it in almost the same words three times in the Psalms." (Spurgeon)

c. **The horse and its rider He has thrown into the sea:** They praised God because He did what Israel could not do.

d. **The LORD is my strength and song**: When we let God be our **strength**, He will also be our **song**. We will sing because of the victory won by the great strength of the LORD. We will have a singing joy in our life because His strength will not let us down.

    i. "Notice, the song is all of God; there is not a word about Moses. Read this song through, and neither Moses, nor Aaron, nor Miriam are in it: God is all in all." (Spurgeon)

    ii. "Note, the word is not 'The Lord gives me strength,' but 'The Lord *is* my strength'! How strong is a believer? I say it with reverence, he is as strong as God - 'The Lord is my strength.'" (Spurgeon)

e. **He has become my salvation**: This is a glorious phrase. It recognizes that we cannot save ourselves, but God must **become** our salvation.

    i. "He who has God for his *strength*, will have him for his *song*; and he to whom Jehovah is become *salvation*, will *exalt his name*." (Clarke)

2. (6-10) Second stanza: **You have overthrown those who rose against You.**

"Your right hand, O LORD, has become glorious in power;
Your right hand, O LORD, has dashed the enemy in pieces.
And in the greatness of Your excellence You have overthrown those
who rose against You;
You sent forth Your wrath;
It consumed them like stubble.
And with the blast of Your nostrils
The waters were gathered together;
The floods stood upright like a heap;
The depths congealed in the heart of the sea.
The enemy said, 'I will pursue, I will overtake, I will divide the spoil;
My desire shall be satisfied on them. I will draw my sword, My hand
shall destroy them.'
You blew with Your wind,
The sea covered them;
They sank like lead in the mighty waters."

a. **Your right hand, O Lord, has dashed the enemy in pieces**: Moses and the people described what God did to the Egyptians, and they gloried in the defeat of God's enemies. If we really love the Lord, we should glory in the defeat of God's enemies.

b. **Your right hand**: The **right hand** was thought to be the hand of skill and power. When God works with His **right hand**, it is a work of skill and power.

   i. Obviously, this is the use of *anthropomorphism*, understanding something about God by using a human figure of speech, even though it does not literally apply.

   ii. This idea of the **right hand** is used in the Scriptures more than fifty times, including these passages:

   • Psalm 45:4: God's right hand teaches us
   • Psalm 48:10: God's right hand is full of righteousness
   • Psalm 77:10: Remembrance of *the years of the right hand of the Most High*
   • Psalm 110:1: The Father invites the Son to sit at His right hand
   • Habakkuk 2:16: The cup of God's judgment is held in His right hand
   • Ephesians 1:20: Jesus is seated at the right hand of the Father

3. (11-13) Third stanza: **Who is like You, O Lord, among the gods?**

"Who *is* like You, O Lord, among the gods?
Who *is* like You, glorious in holiness,
Fearful in praises, doing wonders?
You stretched out Your right hand;
The earth swallowed them.
You in Your mercy have led forth
The people whom You have redeemed;
You have guided *them* in Your strength
To Your holy habitation."

a. **Who is like You, O Lord, among the gods**: If the people of Egypt still did not know who the Lord was, the people of Israel did. They knew the Lord was not like any of the false gods of Egypt or Canaan.

b. **Who is like You**: Worship should proclaim the superiority of the Lord God over anything else that claims to be god. Israel soon and often forgot this, but we can remember it.

4. (14-18) Fourth and fifth stanza: **The people will hear and be afraid**.

"The people will hear *and* be afraid;
Sorrow will take hold of the inhabitants of Philistia.

Then the chiefs of Edom will be dismayed;
The mighty men of Moab,
Trembling will take hold of them;
All the inhabitants of Canaan will melt away.
Fear and dread will fall on them;
By the greatness of Your arm
They will be *as* still as a stone,
Till Your people pass over, O LORD,
Till the people pass over
Whom You have purchased.
You will bring them in and plant them
In the mountain of Your inheritance,
***In* the place, O LORD, *which* You have made**
For Your own dwelling,
The sanctuary, O LORD, *which* Your hands have established.
The LORD shall reign forever and ever."

a. **All the inhabitants of Canaan will melt away**: Moses and the children of Israel knew that the victory also said something to the enemies of Israel. They would become afraid when they heard of the great things God did for Israel.

b. **Fear and dread will fall on them**: Some 40 years later, Rahab the prostitute from Jericho told the Israeli spies: *For we have heard how the LORD dried up the water of the Red Sea for you when you came out of Egypt* (Joshua 2:10). The people of Canaan *did* hear of what God did for Israel and some responded with godly fear.

c. **The LORD shall reign forever and ever**: After such a great victory, we can sense that Israel really believed this, and they were really ready to let the LORD **reign** over them. This state of victory and surrender did not last very long.

i. Yet, the enduring truth remains - **the LORD shall reign forever and ever**. This *Song of Moses* echoes all the way to the Book of Revelation, where a multitude that has come from great suffering, has experienced great victory, and stands on the shores of a great sea, sing this song:

They sing the song of Moses, the servant of God, and the song of the Lamb, saying: "Great and marvelous are Your works, Lord God Almighty! Just and true are Your ways, O King of the saints! Who shall not fear You, O Lord, and glorify Your name? For You alone are holy. For all nations shall come and worship before You, For Your judgments have been manifested."

ii. The heart, the spirit of this *song of Moses* rings true in the people of God, who want to praise Him and thank Him for all the good He has done for His people. They sing in view of deliverance, of victory, of defense, of confidence.

iii. "It is obvious, then, from the plentiful allusions to this song in holy scripture, that it is full of deep spiritual significance. It teaches us not only to praise God concerning the literal overthrow of Egypt, but to praise him concerning the overthrow of all the powers of evil, and the final deliverance of all the chosen." (Spurgeon)

5. (19-21) Miriam, Moses' sister, leads the women in worship.

For the horses of Pharaoh went with his chariots and his horsemen into the sea, and the LORD brought back the waters of the sea upon them. But the children of Israel went on dry *land* in the midst of the sea. Then Miriam the prophetess, the sister of Aaron, took the timbrel in her hand; and all the women went out after her with timbrels and with dances. And Miriam answered them:

"Sing to the LORD,
For He has triumphed gloriously!
The horse and its rider He has thrown into the sea!"

a. **Miriam the prophetess, the sister of Aaron**: This is the first mention of **Miriam** by name, and she is described as **the sister of Aaron**, so she is therefore also the sister of Moses (Exodus 4:14).

i. Numbers 26:59 seems to indicate that Moses had only one sister. We do know that it was his sister who supervised the launching of the basket onto the Nile River to preserve his life (Exodus 2:4) and arranged the hiring of Moses' mother as his nurse. Based on Numbers 26:59, we can say this was probably - almost certainly - Miriam. She was the older sister of Moses.

b. **Miriam the prophetess**: We also see that Miriam had some kind of prophetic gift. Later she used her leadership position in an unwise and ungodly way - to challenge the authority of Moses (Numbers 12).

c. **All the women went out after her with timbrels and with dances**: On this occasion, Miriam led the women's choir.

B. The bitter water is made drinkable.

1. (22) Three days into the wilderness.

So Moses brought Israel from the Red Sea; then they went out into the Wilderness of Shur. And they went three days in the wilderness and found no water.

a. **Moses brought Israel...they went out into the Wilderness of Shur**: God's man led them, but he led them an unusual way. Into **the Wilderness of Shur** was outside the major trade route along the sea.

b. **They went three days in the wilderness and found no water**: Three days is not a very long time, but it is long enough to forget the great victory and power of God. Now Israel faced a long trip through difficult and dry desert.

i. "Three days is the maximum time the human body can go without water in the desert." (Buckingham)

ii. "The Egyptians found enough water, and even too much of it, for they were drowned in the sea, but the well-beloved Israelites had no water at all. So is it with the wicked man; he often has enough of wealth, and too much of it, till he is drowned in sensual delights and perishes in floods of prosperity." (Spurgeon)

2. (23-25a) Bitter waters made sweet at Marah.

Now when they came to Marah, they could not drink the waters of Marah, for they *were* bitter. Therefore the name of it was called Marah. And the people complained against Moses, saying, "What shall we drink?" So he cried out to the LORD, and the LORD showed him a tree. When he cast *it* into the waters, the waters were made sweet. There He made a statute and an ordinance for them.

a. **They could not drink the waters of Marah, for they were bitter**: It must have seemed like a cruel joke - after three waterless days, they finally came upon water - and found that water undrinkable.

b. **So he cried out to the LORD, and the LORD showed him a tree**: By following God's direction, Moses made the waters drinkable, and Israel found water in the wilderness.

i. "I think, if I had been there, I should have suggested that Moses should use that rod of his. Did he not divide the Red Sea with it? Why not just put his rod into the water, and stir it up, and make it sweet? Oh, yes, you know, we are always for running to old methods! But God is a Sovereign, and he will work as he pleases." (Spurgeon)

ii. In his work on the Exodus journey, Buckingham explains how this may have worked. The chemicals in the sap of the broken limb drew the mineral content down to the bottom of the pools, and left only good water on top.

iii. He further speculates that even though the waters were now drinkable, there was still a significant magnesium and calcium content in the water. The laxative effect of this would clean out the digestive systems of the children of Israel, cleansing them of common Egyptian ailments such as amoebic dysentery and bilharzia, a weakening disease common among Egyptian peasants. In addition, calcium and magnesium together form the basis of a drug called dolomite - used by some athletes as a performance enhancer in hot weather conditions. At Marah, God provided the right medicine to both clean out their systems and prepare them for a long, hot march to Sinai.

iv. We can say that God was not only interested in getting the children of Israel out of Egypt, He also wanted to get Egypt out of the children of Israel - both physically and spiritually.

v. **A tree**: "Medieval commentators delighted to see here a reference to the cross, by which the bitterest of life's waters is sweetened." (Cole)

3. (25b-27) The testing of Israel.

And there He tested them, and said, "If you diligently heed the voice of the LORD your God and do what is right in His sight, give ear to His commandments and keep all His statutes, I will put none of the diseases on you which I have brought on the Egyptians. For I *am* the LORD who heals you." Then they came to Elim, where there *were* twelve wells of water and seventy palm trees; so they camped there by the waters.

a. **And there He tested them**: God **tested** Israel by giving them a command to obey. When God tells us what to do, He really gives us a test. Our obedience determines if we pass the test or not.

i. It had yet to be demonstrated by testing whether the children of Israel were a worshipping people who occasionally murmured, or if they were a murmuring people who occasionally worshipped. Their true nature would be revealed in times of testing.

b. **I will put none of the diseases on you which I have brought on the Egyptians**: This was God's promise to an obedient Israel. In many ways, their physical health was directly connected to their obedience.

i. Dr. S.I. McMillen in his book *None of These Diseases* noted that many of God's laws to Israel had a direct impact of hygiene and health. Practices such as circumcision, quarantine, washing in running water, and eating kosher made a real medical difference in keeping Israel free from disease.

ii. Beyond the direct medical implications, obedience also means we are at peace with God - and free from a tremendous amount of stress and anxiety in life. This has an obvious benefit to the health of any person.

iii. "This miracle was connected with a promise; viz., from now on obedience to commands and statutes would bring healing, both physically and morally." (Kaiser)

iv. Marah was a place of bitterness and testing, but because Israel endured and received provision from God, they genuinely gained from their time at Marah. They learned prayer, they learned self-distrust, they learned daily dependence, they learned obedience, and they even learned a new name for God.

- Israel gained by *examination* at Marah
- Israel gained by *experience* at Marah
- Israel gained by *education* at Marah

c. **Then they came to Elim, where there were twelve wells of water and seventy palm trees**: After the time of testing, God had a time of refreshing for the people of Israel. He knew exactly what they needed, and He knew when to test them and when to rest them.

i. Elim was wonderful – a place of provision, with 12 wells and 70 palm trees. Yet there was no new revelation of God at Elim as there was at Marah, where God revealed Himself as *Jehovah-Rapha*.

ii. "Israel had no miracle at Elim. Wells and palm trees they had; but they had no miracle there, no miraculous change of the bitter into the sweet; and they had no statute, and no ordinance, and no promise, and no new revelation of God, and no new name for Jehovah there." (Spurgeon)

Exodus 16 - Manna for the Children of Israel

A. God's promise to provide.

1. (1) From Elim to the Wilderness of Sin.

And they journeyed from Elim, and all the congregation of the children of Israel came to the Wilderness of Sin, which is between Elim and Sinai, on the fifteenth day of the second month after they departed from the land of Egypt.

a. **On the fifteenth day of the second month**: This marked one month after leaving Egypt, since they left on the fifteenth of the previous month (Exodus 12:18).

b. **The Wilderness of Sin, which is between Elim and Sinai**: They came out from **Elim**, an oasis of rest and comfort (Exodus 15:27). They headed towards **Sinai**, a place to meet with God and receive His law. In between **Elim and Sinai** was **the wilderness of Sin**.

i. In the original text, the name "**Wilderness of Sin**" has nothing to do with *sin* and could just as easily be translated *Wilderness of Zin*. Yet as the story unfolds, we see that this wilderness had a lot to do with sin.

2. (2-3) Israel complains against Moses and Aaron.

Then the whole congregation of the children of Israel complained against Moses and Aaron in the wilderness. And the children of Israel said to them, "Oh, that we had died by the hand of the LORD in the land of Egypt, when we sat by the pots of meat *and* when we ate bread to the full! For you have brought us out into this wilderness to kill this whole assembly with hunger."

a. **Then the whole congregation of the children of Israel complained against Moses and Aaron in the wilderness**: They complained because they did not have enough food. The supplies they carried with them from Egypt began to run out, and they had to be sustained in the wilderness.

i. It would seem that starvation was more *anticipated* than *experienced*. In other words, they did not live through weeks and weeks of famine, nor did they see their family and friends die of malnutrition, or even have to kill all their livestock for food. Instead, they started to feel hungry and anticipated starvation.

ii. They went from *singing* to *complaining* very quickly.

b. **When we sat by the pots of meat and when we ate bread to the full**: Israel selectively remembered the past and thought of their time in Egypt as a good time. They lost sight of God's future for them, and they also twisted the past to support their complaining. This thinking is common among those who complain.

c. **You have brought us out into this wilderness to kill this whole assembly**: This is another common practice among those who complain. They insisted that Moses and Aaron had bad or evil intentions. Of course, Moses and Aaron had no interest in killing the people of Israel, and this was a horrible accusation to make. Yet a complaining heart often finds it easy to accuse the person they complain against of the worst motives.

i. "Human nature can never be reduced to a more abject state in this world than that in which the body is enthralled by *political slavery*, and the soul debased by the influence of *sin*. These poor Hebrews were both *slaves* and *sinners*, and were therefore capable of the meanest and most disgraceful acts." (Clarke)

3. (4-5) God announces to Moses the coming of **bread from heaven**.

Then the LORD said to Moses, "Behold, I will rain bread from heaven for you. And the people shall go out and gather a certain quota every day, that I may test them, whether they will walk in My law or not. And it shall be on the sixth day that they shall prepare what they bring in, and it shall be twice as much as they gather daily."

a. **Behold, I will rain bread from heaven for you**: This was a remarkable promise. **Bread** doesn't normally **rain** from **heaven**. Yet God promised that He would provide for Israel in this unexpected way.

i. This reminds us that God may provide from resources that we never knew existed. Sometimes He provides from familiar resources, sometimes from unexpected resources.

ii. Murmuring Israel called this **bread from heaven** "manna" (Exodus 16:31). God almost always called it *bread from heaven* (Nehemiah 9:15, Psalm 78:24 and Psalm 105:40) or sometimes it was called *angels' food* (Psalm 78:25).

b. **The people shall go out and gather a certain quota every day**: God promised to send **bread from heaven**, but He didn't promise to drop it into their mouths. They still had to **go out and gather** what they needed for every day.

c. **That I may test them**: The blessing of **bread from heaven** came with the responsibility of obedience. This responsibility would test Israel and measure their obedience. The test came on the **sixth day**, when they were to gather twice as much, so the seventh day could be received as a day of rest.

4. (6-8) Moses tells the people about God's coming provision.

Then Moses and Aaron said to all the children of Israel, "At evening you shall know that the LORD has brought you out of the land of Egypt. And in the morning you shall see the glory of the LORD; for He hears your complaints against the LORD. But what *are* we, that you complain against us?" Also Moses said, *"This shall be seen* when the LORD gives you meat to eat in the evening, and in the morning bread to the full; for the LORD hears your complaints which you make against Him. And what *are* we? Your complaints *are* not against us but against the LORD."

a. **At evening you shall know that the LORD has brought you out of the land of Egypt**: One would think that with the experience of the plagues, Passover, and the deliverance at the Red Sea, Israel would *already know* that the LORD had brought them out of Egypt. Yet experiences, even great experiences, don't change the heart as much as we often think.

b. **In the morning you shall see the glory of the LORD**: They would not see the glory of God as in His enthroned radiance but in His great, loving provision for His people. That is a *real* display of God's **glory**.

i. **The glory of the LORD**: "The sheer weight, gravity (*kabed*, 'to be heavy,' then 'to glorify') of his divine presence." (Kaiser)

ii. One way that God showed His glory was through this display of *mercy* and *goodness*. God didn't send them *hell* from heaven; He sent bread instead. Nor did He demand that they stop their complaining before they ate. Just like Jesus would later command us, God loved and fed those who acted like His enemies.

c. **He hears your complaints against the LORD...your complaints against the LORD...Your complaints are not against us, but against the LORD**: The people thought they complained against Moses and Aaron (Exodus 16:2). Really, they complained against the LORD.

d. **When the LORD gives you meat to eat in the evening**: At Exodus 16:4, God promised to give bread from heaven in the morning. Here, He also promised to give **meat to eat in the evening**.

B. God's provision of Manna.

1. (9-12) God shows His glory and promises to provide.

Then Moses spoke to Aaron, "Say to all the congregation of the children of Israel, 'Come near before the LORD, for He has heard your complaints.'" Now it came to pass, as Aaron spoke to the whole congregation of the children of Israel, that they looked toward the wilderness, and behold, the glory of the LORD appeared in the cloud. And the LORD spoke to Moses, saying, "I have heard the complaints of the children of Israel. Speak to them, saying, 'At twilight you shall eat meat, and in the morning you shall be filled with bread. And you shall know that I *am* the LORD your God.'"

a. **The glory of the LORD appeared in the cloud. And the LORD spoke to Moses**: It's difficult to know if *everyone* heard the LORD speak to Moses, or if Moses alone heard this. Certainly, everyone knew God spoke to Moses because of the display of glory, but we don't know if they could hear what the LORD said to him.

b. **I have heard the complaints of the children of Israel**: Since Moses already knew this (based on Exodus 16:4-5), these words give more weight to the idea that God said this publicaly, more for the benefit of Israel than for the benefit of Moses.

2. (13-14) God provides quail for meat and bread from heaven.

So it was that quails came up at evening and covered the camp, and in the morning the dew lay all around the camp. And when the layer of dew lifted, there, on the surface of the wilderness, was a small round substance, *as* fine as frost on the ground.

a. **So it was that quails came up at evening and covered the camp**: In a miraculous way, God provided Israel with plenty of meat in the wilderness. This was a significant display of the mercy of God. When Israel complained, God *could* have answered with judgment or discipline, and He gave them meat instead.

i. The **quails** mentioned here "migrate regularly between south Europe and Arabia across the Sinai Peninsula. They are small, bullet-headed birds, with a strong but low flight, usually roosting on the ground or in the low bushes at nightfall. When exhausted, they would be unable to...take off again. The birds are good eating, and were a favorite delicacy of the Egyptians." (Cole)

b. **A small round substance, as fine as frost on the ground**: The bread from heaven came with the dew each morning, as some kind of residue from the dew. It was **small, round** and **fine as frost on the ground.**

Therefore, it was not easy to gather. It had to be swept up from the ground.

i. Exodus 16:31 further describes the bread from heaven as *like coriander seed* (about the size of a sesame seed), and sweet like *honey*. Numbers 11:7 says it was the color of *bdellium* (a pearl-like color). It was either baked or boiled (Exodus 16:23).

ii. Numbers 11:8 says that they *ground it on millstones or beat it in the mortar, cooked it in pans, and made cakes of it; and its taste was like the taste of pastry prepared with oil.*

iii. Jewish legends supposedly tell us what this bread from heaven tasted like. "One only had to desire a certain dish, and no sooner had he thought of it, than manna had the flavor of the dish desired. The same food had a different taste to everyone who partook of it, according to his age; to the little children, it tasted like milk, to the strong youths like bread, to the old men like honey, to the sick like barley steeped in oil and honey." But they also wrote that manna was bitter in the mouth of Gentiles. (Ginzberg)

iv. Jewish legends also supposedly tell us how they could sweep it up off the desert floor and not have dirt in it. These legends say that when God sent manna, He first sent a north wind to sweep the floor of the desert and then a rain to wash it clean. Then the manna descended on clean ground.

c. **A small round substance**: It is difficult to precisely identify what this **substance** was. Some researchers identify it with what the Arabs today call *mann*, which is formed when "A tiny insect punctures the bark of the tamarisk tree, drinks the sap, and exudes a clear liquid that solidifies as a sugary globule when it hits the ground. When the sun comes up, it melts quickly and disappears." (Buckingham)

i. Though the bread from heaven may have been similar to the modern-day *mann* in the Sinai Peninsula, it wasn't the same thing. The modern-day *mann* never appears in great quantities, it doesn't last year round, and it is confined to a small geographic region.

d. **As fine as frost on the ground**: The purpose for giving the bread from heaven was not only to provide for the material needs of Israel, but also to teach them eternal lessons of dependence on God. This is demonstrated in passages like Deuteronomy 8:3: *So He humbled you, allowed you to hunger, and fed you with manna which you did not know nor did your fathers know, that He might make you know that man shall not live by bread alone; but man lives by every word that proceeds from the mouth of the* LORD. When God puts us in a place of need, He wants to do more than meet the need. He wants to teach eternal lessons.

> i. Feeding Israel through bread from heaven was an example of God's way of cooperating with man. Israel could not bring the manna, and God would not gather it for them. Each had to do their part.

> ii. "Animals are often taught through their food. When they could not be reached in any other way, they have been instructed by their hunger, and by their thirst, and by their feeding." (Spurgeon)

3. (15) The people call the bread from heaven **manna**.

So when the children of Israel saw *it,* they said to one another, "What is it?" For they did not know what it *was.* And Moses said to them, "This *is* the bread which the LORD has given you to eat."

> a. **They said to one another, "What is it"**: The name **manna** (given later in Exodus 16:31) means, "What is that?" and the name comes from the question asked in this verse.

> b. **For they did not know what it was**: God provided for them, but they did not recognize it. When God's provision comes, we often do not recognize it. God met the needs of Israel, but He did it in a way they did not expect.

4. (16-19) Instructions on the gathering of bread from heaven.

"This is the thing which the LORD has commanded: 'Let every man gather it according to each one's need, one omer for each person, *according to the* number of persons; let every man take for *those* who *are* in his tent.'" Then the children of Israel did so and gathered, some more, some less. So when they measured *it* by omers, he who gathered much had nothing left over, and he who gathered little had no lack. Every man had gathered according to each one's need. And Moses said, "Let no one leave any of it till morning."

> a. **Let every man gather it according to each one's need**: The bread from heaven was to be gathered on an individual or a family basis. God did not command the creation of a tribal manna gathering and distribution center. Every household had to provide for itself, and a rich family could not hire a poor family to do their work for them.

> b. **One omer for each person**: An **omer** could be as much as a gallon, especially in the later history of Israel. But at this early point in Israel's history, it may have meant only a *cupful.* It is an imprecise measure.

5. (20-21) Some of the people fail God's test.

Notwithstanding they did not heed Moses. But some of them left part of it until morning, and it bred worms and stank. And Moses was angry

with them. So they gathered it every morning, every man according to his need. And when the sun became hot, it melted.

a. **Notwithstanding they did not heed Moses**: They clearly heard God's command and they clearly knew God's command; yet, for some reason they felt they did not have to obey God's command. There was a harsh penalty for their disobedience - what they gathered in disobedience **bred worms and stank.**

b. **So they gathered it every morning, every man according to his need**: The bad experience of their disobedience led them reluctantly to obedience.

c. **When the sun became hot, it melted**: Apparently the bread from heaven had to be gathered and prepared early in the morning. This was God's gracious way of forcing a work ethic upon the nation of Israel.

6. (22-30) God provides double on the day before the Sabbath.

And so it was, on the sixth day, *that* they gathered twice as much bread, two omers for each one. And all the rulers of the congregation came and told Moses. Then he said to them, "This *is what* the LORD has said: 'Tomorrow *is* a Sabbath rest, a holy Sabbath to the LORD. Bake what you will bake *today,* and boil what you will boil; and lay up for yourselves all that remains, to be kept until morning.'" So they laid it up till morning, as Moses commanded; and it did not stink, nor were there any worms in it. Then Moses said, "Eat that today, for today *is* a Sabbath to the LORD; today you will not find it in the field. Six days you shall gather it, but on the seventh day, *which is* the Sabbath, there will be none."

a. **So it was, on the sixth day, that they gathered twice as much bread**: God promised to provide twice as much on the sixth day, and He did. Perhaps this came as somewhat of a surprise to the people of Israel, because they felt they had to report it to Moses (**came and told Moses**).

b. **Tomorrow is a Sabbath rest, a holy Sabbath to the LORD**: This was the first time God spoke to Israel about the Sabbath. God essentially *forced* them to honor the Sabbath by not providing any bread from heaven on the Sabbath day (**today you will not find it in the field**).

7. (27-30) No manna comes on the Sabbath.

Now it happened *that some* of the people went out on the seventh day to gather, but they found none. And the LORD said to Moses, "How long do you refuse to keep My commandments and My laws? See! For the LORD has given you the Sabbath; therefore He gives you on the sixth day bread for two days. Let every man remain in his place; let no man

go out of his place on the seventh day." So the people rested on the seventh day.

a. **Some of the people went out on the seventh day to gather**: Despite what God said, some went looking for bread from heaven when He said there would be none. Some will only learn by personal experience.

b. **But they found none**: God's word was true and they found none. This was a powerful lesson, teaching Israel to trust what God said before they had proven it true in experience.

i. People today still look for life and fulfillment in places God has said there would be none.

8. (31-36) God commands some bread from heaven be set aside as a testimony to His provision.

And the house of Israel called its name Manna. And it *was* like white coriander seed, and the taste of it *was* like wafers *made* with honey. Then Moses said, "This *is* the thing which the LORD has commanded: 'Fill an omer with it, to be kept for your generations, that they may see the bread with which I fed you in the wilderness, when I brought you out of the land of Egypt.'" And Moses said to Aaron, "Take a pot and put an omer of manna in it, and lay it up before the LORD, to be kept for your generations." As the LORD commanded Moses, so Aaron laid it up before the Testimony, to be kept. And the children of Israel ate manna forty years, until they came to an inhabited land; they ate manna until they came to the border of the land of Canaan. Now an omer *is* one-tenth of an ephah.

a. **And the house of Israel called its name Manna**: This name means, *What is that?* It is based on the question asked in Exodus 16:15.

b. **It was like white coriander seed**: This refers to the small size of the particles of the bread from heaven. It meant that it had to be humbly, carefully gathered.

c. **The taste of it was like wafers made with honey**: God gave Israel good tasting food. He didn't give them tasteless gruel or pasty porridge. Since it could be baked like bread or cake (Exodus 16:23), eating manna was like eating sweet bread every day.

d. **Fill an omer with it, to be kept for your generations**: This pot full of the bread from heaven was later put into the ark of the covenant, referred to here as **the Testimony** (Hebrews 9:4).

e. **They ate manna until they came to the border of the land of Canaan**: As important as it was for God to provide this bread from heaven, it was also important for God to *stop* providing it. It was essential that Israel be put again in the position to receive God's more normal provision, through hard work - which in itself is a blessing of God.

i. "Those who followed the cloud were always certain of their sustenance. Where the cloud brooded the manna fell." (Meyer)

ii. This **manna**, this bread from heaven, is a powerful picture of Jesus Himself. After the feeding of the 5,000, Jesus had a discussion with people who wanted Him to keep on feeding them with His miraculous power. They wanted Jesus to provide for them just as Israel was provided for with manna in the wilderness. This is what Jesus said in reply:

Most assuredly, I say to you, Moses did not give you the bread from heaven, but My Father gives you the true bread from heaven. For the bread of God is he who comes down from heaven and gives life to the world. (John 6:32-33)

iii. Jesus is the bread from heaven, and we have to receive Him like Israel received the manna.

- Aware of our need, *hungry*
- Each for himself, family by family
- Every day
- Humbly – perhaps even on our knees
- With gratitude, knowing we don't deserve it
- Eating it, taking the gift inside, to our innermost being

Exodus 17 - God's Provision and Protection of Israel

A. Water from the rock.

1. (1-4) The congregation of Israel contends with Moses.

Then all the congregation of the children of Israel set out on their journey from the Wilderness of Sin, according to the commandment of the LORD, and camped in Rephidim; but *there was* no water for the people to drink. Therefore the people contended with Moses, and said, "Give us water, that we may drink." And Moses said to them, "Why do you contend with me? Why do you tempt the LORD?" And the people thirsted there for water, and the people complained against Moses, and said, "Why *is* it you have brought us up out of Egypt, to kill us and our children and our livestock with thirst?" So Moses cried out to the LORD, saying, "What shall I do with this people? They are almost ready to stone me!"

a. **According to the commandment of the LORD…but there was no water for the people to drink**: Israel did exactly what God commanded, following the pillar of cloud and fire; yet there was no water to drink. They were in the will of God, but in a difficult time. It is possible to be completely in the will of God, yet also in a season of great problems.

i. "Thirst is the more eager appetite, so they are more eager and earnest for water than they were for bread." (Trapp)

ii. Cole on **to kill….our livestock with thirst**: "Who but a cattleman would have worried about his stock dying of thirst, if he were already dying of thirst himself? Here speaks the true Israelite farmer."

iii. **Set out on their journey**: "In Numbers 33:12-14 it is said, that when the Israelites came from *Sin* they encamped in *Dophkah*, and next in *Alush*, after which they came to *Rephidim*. Here, therefore, *two stations* are omitted, probably because nothing of moment took place at either." (Clarke)

b. **Therefore the people contended with Moses**: The people of Israel had a real problem - there was **no water for the people to drink**. This was not an imaginary problem and the people were right to be concerned. Yet when the people then **contended with Moses**, they did not respond with spiritual thinking or actions.

c. **Why do you tempt the LORD**: The people focused their complaint against Moses, but Moses understood that their problem was with the LORD.

i. When we have a problem, it is much easier to blame someone than to think through the problem carefully and spiritually. In this situation Israel could have thought, "We are in a desert; it's not surprising there isn't much water here. We need to look to God to meet this need." Instead, they blamed Moses and did nothing to *help* the problem.

d. **So Moses cried out to the LORD**: The lack of water wasn't Moses' fault. Yet as the leader of Israel, he had to lead them to the answer - and crying out to the LORD was the right way to lead them to the solution.

i. Moses knew the people were unfair to him (**What shall I do with this people? They are almost ready to stone me!**). But he still had to lead while under the pressure of unfair attack, and he did the right thing in turning to God in prayer.

ii. "One of Moses' most characteristic and praiseworthy traits was that he took his difficulties to the Lord." (Kaiser)

2. (5-6) God tells Moses how water will be provided.

And the LORD said to Moses, "Go on before the people, and take with you some of the elders of Israel. Also take in your hand your rod with which you struck the river, and go. Behold, I will stand before you there on the rock in Horeb; and you shall strike the rock, and water will come out of it, that the people may drink." And Moses did so in the sight of the elders of Israel.

a. **Take in your hand your rod with which you struck the river**: God directed Moses to get out **before the people**, to bring other leaders with him (**take with you some of the elders of Israel**), and to use what God had used before. This gave confidence to Moses, because he saw God use that same **rod** to do great miracles before.

i. Moses couldn't pick up that rod without remembering the power of God. The confidence he received by picking up the rod was confidence in God, not in himself.

b. **Behold, I will stand before you there**: One of the great themes of this journey from Egypt to Canaan was that *God was with them*. He was with them each step of the way, and here again He would show His presence to Moses and to Israel.

    i. "If God had not stood upon the rock, in vain had Moses struck it. Means must be used, but God only depended upon for success." (Trapp)

c. **You shall strike the rock, and water will come out of it**: Moses was commanded, in the presence of the LORD, to strike the rock with his rod, and water would gush forth to satisfy the thirst of God's people.

    i. *This was a remarkable miracle.* Moses (and everyone else) knew that water does not normally come from rocks in such a way.

    ii. *This was a generous miracle.* "Here again the divine patience appears, for Jehovah uttered no word of reproach, but in spite of their impatient unbelief provided water out of the rock for them." (Morgan)

    iii. *This was a meaningful miracle.* In striking the rock, Moses acted out a drama that perhaps he didn't understand. In 1 Corinthians 10:4, Paul wrote of Israel in the Exodus: *they drank of that spiritual Rock that followed them, and that Rock was Christ.* We don't know if this **rock** followed Israel just as Paul described, but we do know that when Jesus was struck, living water flowed out for all to receive. "Herein a type of Christ, 'stricken, smitten of God, and afflicted' (Isaiah 53:4; 1 Corinthians 10:4)." (Trapp)

    iv. Jesus was struck with the rod of Moses - the curse of the law - and from Him flowed water to satisfy our spiritual thirst. As the old hymn says:

> *Let the water and the blood*
> *From Thy riven side which flowed,*
> *Be of sin the double cure,*
> *Save me from its wrath and power.*

3. (7) Moses names the place as a rebuke to the children of Israel.

So he called the name of the place Massah and Meribah, because of the contention of the children of Israel, and because they tempted the LORD, saying, "Is the LORD among us or not?"

a. **So he called the name of the place**: Moses did what God told him to do and water came from the rock. This was a great miracle of God's provision and a rebuke to unbelieving and rebellious Israel.

    i. We don't know exactly how God provided water from this rock. Perhaps there was an artesian spring that God caused to burst forth when Moses struck the rock. Perhaps it was a completely unique miracle.

b. **He called the name of the place Massah and Meribah**: God remembered the way Israel tested Him at Massah and Meribah, recalling it in several passages.

- Deuteronomy 6:16: *You shall not tempt the* LORD *your God as you tempted Him in Massah*
- Deuteronomy 9:22: *at…Massah…you provoked the* LORD *to wrath*
- Deuteronomy 33:8: *Your holy one, Whom You tested at Massah, and with whom You contended at the waters of Meribah*

c. **They tempted the LORD, saying "Is the LORD among us or not"**: God dramatically said, *I will stand before you there on the rock in Horeb* (Exodus 17:6), saying that He was and would be present with Israel. Yet they still wondered, **Is the LORD among us or not?**

i. This attitude among the Israelites was their great sin. In this time of difficulty, the children of Israel - directly or indirectly - doubted the loving presence and care of God among them. "Under the stress of an immediate lack, these people doubted the one fact of which they had overwhelming evidence." (Morgan)

ii. Later, when Israel remembered God's provision in the wilderness at the Feast of Tabernacles, they had a specific ceremony where they recalled this miracle of water from a rock. In that exact context, Jesus said: *If anyone thirsts, let him come to Me and drink. He who believes in Me, as the Scripture has said, out of his heart will flow rivers of living water.* (John 7:37-38)

iii. The living water Jesus spoke of was the Holy Spirit (John 7:39); it is no less of a miracle for God to bring the love and power of the Holy Spirit out of our hearts than it is to bring water out of a rock - our hearts can be just as hard.

B. God brings victory to Israel over the Amalekites.

1. (8-9) Amalek attacks Israel.

Now Amalek came and fought with Israel in Rephidim. And Moses said to Joshua, "Choose us some men and go out, fight with Amalek. Tomorrow I will stand on the top of the hill with the rod of God in my hand."

a. **Now Amalek came and fought with Israel in Rephidim**: This was an unprovoked attack by the Amalekites against Israel. In response, Moses called **Joshua** to lead the armies of Israel into battle to defend the nation against the attack from **Amalek**.

i. "Amalek was grandson of Esau (Genesis 36:12), and although akin to Israel, proved their most inveterate foe, as subsequent history shows." (Thomas)

ii. "There is every possibility that they had known about the promise of the Land of Canaan that had been given to Esau's twin brother, Jacob; therefore, they should not have felt any threat to their interests in the Negev had this promise been remembered and taken seriously." (Kaiser)

iii. "Like many other nomads, they ranged over a wide area, roughly described as 'the Negeb' or 'south land' (Numbers 13:29)." (Cole)

b. **And fought with Israel**: The method of attack used by Amalek was despicable. Deuteronomy 25:17-18 says: *Remember what Amalek did to you on the way as you were coming out of Egypt, how he met you on the way and attacked your rear ranks, all the stragglers at your rear, when you were tired and weary; and he did not fear God.*

i. "In the most treacherous and dastardly manner; for they came at the rear of the camp...The baggage, no doubt, was the object of their avarice; but finding the women, children, aged and infirm persons, behind with the baggage, they smote them and took away their spoils." (Clarke)

c. **Go out, fight with Amalek**: This was a significant first experience of warfare for ancient Israel. They had lived for hundreds of years as slaves, and God fought the Egyptians for them. Now they had to learn to rely on God as they fought a military battle.

i. "In their first movement God led them in such a way as to avoid the possibility of war (Exodus 13:17). Now they were involved in war." (Morgan)

d. **The rod of God in my hand**: The Scriptures call this stout stick both the rod of Moses (*your rod*, Exodus 17:5) and **the rod of God**. There was the combination of the human instrument and the divine power.

i. God called it the rod of Moses, and so honored Moses. Moses called it the rod of God, and so honored God.

2. (10-11) Israel prevails in battle as Moses prays.

So Joshua did as Moses said to him, and fought with Amalek. And Moses, Aaron, and Hur went up to the top of the hill. And so it was, when Moses held up his hand, that Israel prevailed; and when he let down his hand, Amalek prevailed.

a. **So Joshua did as Moses said to him**: This is the first passage that mentions **Joshua**. We find him doing what he did until the time Moses passed from the scene - Joshua served the Lord and Moses faithfully.

i. It's always good to remember that the name *Jesus* is simply the Greek way of pronouncing the name **Joshua**. It's the same name.

ii. "Both in the Septuagint and Greek Testament he is called *Jesus*: the name signifies *Saviour*; and he is allowed to have been a very expressive type of our blessed Lord. He fought with and conquered the enemies of his people, brought them into the promised land, and divided it to them by lot. The parallel between him and the Saviour of the world is too evident to require pointing out." (Clarke)

b. **Moses, Aaron, and Hur went up to the top of the hill**: They did this so they could see, so they could be seen, and so that they could pray. **Aaron** was the brother of Moses, and some think **Hur** was his brother-in-law.

i. "Josephus (Antiquities III, 54 [ii.4]) preserves a Jewish tradition that Hur was the husband of Moses' sister, Miriam." (Kaiser)

c. **And so it was, when Moses held up his hand, that Israel prevailed**: Moses supported the battle behind the scenes, busy in prayer. The fate of Israel in battle depended on Moses' intercession because when he prayed, **Israel prevailed**, and when he stopped praying, **Amalek prevailed**.

i. **Held up his hand**: This phrase describes the Israelite posture of prayer, even as some people today might bow their head or fold their hands. Moses had to pray, and had to keep on praying. "Both the verbs 'to hold up' and 'to lower' are introduced by the perfect... Continued or frequentative action is clearly denoted." (Kaiser)

ii. This amazing passage shows us that life or death for Israel depended on the prayers of one man. Moses prayed as we should pray - with passion, believing that life and death - perhaps eternally - depended on prayer.

iii. It can be difficult to reconcile this with knowing God has a pre-ordained plan. But God didn't want Moses to concern himself with that - he was to pray as if it really mattered. Just because we can't figure out how our prayers mesh with God's pre-ordained plan, doesn't mean we should ever stop believing that prayer matters.

iv. In his early days, Moses thought the only way to win a battle was to fight (Exodus 2:11-15). Now Moses let Joshua fight while he did the more important work: pray for the victory.

3. (12-13) Moses' hands are strengthened in prayer.

But Moses' hands *became* heavy; so they took a stone and put *it* under him, and he sat on it. And Aaron and Hur supported his hands, one on one side, and the other on the other side; and his hands were steady until the going down of the sun. So Joshua defeated Amalek and his people with the edge of the sword.

a. **Moses' hands became heavy**: The job of supporting the battle in prayer was difficult and Moses could not easily continue. We might think that fighting was the hard work and praying was the easy work, but true prayer was also hard work.

i. Prayer is sometimes sweet and easy; other times it is hard work. This is why Paul described the ministry of Epaphras as *always laboring fervently for you in prayers* (Colossians 4:12), and why Paul wrote we must *continue earnestly in prayer, being vigilant in it with thanksgiving* (Colossians 4:2).

b. **Aaron and Hur supported his hands**: Aaron and Hur came alongside Moses and literally held his hands up in prayer. They helped him and partnered with him in intercession. Their help was successful: **his hands were steady until the going down of the sun.**

i. Though this was Moses' work to do, it was more than he could do by himself. Moses alone could not win the battle of prayer. He needed others to come by his side and strengthen him in prayer.

ii. "Several of the fathers consider Moses, with his stretched-out hands, as a figure of Christ on the cross, suffering for mankind, and getting a complete victory over sin and Satan." (Clarke)

c. **So Joshua defeated Amalek and his people with the edge of the sword**: Because of this work of prayer, Israel was victorious over Amalek. We are left with no other option than to say if Moses, Aaron, and Hur did not do the work in prayer, Israel would have been defeated, and history would have been changed.

i. This amazing passage shows us the great importance of prayer. Life and death - the course of history itself - depended upon prayer. We can conclude that many times the people of God are defeated today because they will not pray, or prayer does not support their work.

ii. *Nevertheless, Joshua had to fight.* Praying, Moses did not eliminate what Joshua had to do. The battle was won with prayer, but also through normal instruments – the work of the army, led by Joshua. "Prayer is a downright mockery if it does not lead us into the practical use of means likely to promote the ends for which we pray." (Spurgeon)

4. (14-16) A never-ending battle with Amalek.

Then the LORD said to Moses, "Write this *for* a memorial in the book and recount *it* in the hearing of Joshua, that I will utterly blot out the remembrance of Amalek from under heaven." And Moses built an altar and called its name, THE-LORD-IS-MY-BANNER; for he said, "Because the LORD has sworn: the LORD *will have* war with Amalek from generation to generation."

a. **Write this for a memorial in the book**: Kaiser notes that there are five places in the Pentateuch where Moses wrote something down at the command of God (Exodus 17:14, Exodus 24:4-7, Exodus 34:27, Numbers 33:1-2, and Deuteronomy 31:9, 24). Not very long ago some academics were skeptical, and said that writing was not invented in Moses' day. Further research proved that man had been writing for at least 1,500 years before the time of Moses.

b. **I will utterly blot out the remembrance of Amalek from under heaven**: Amalek had a special guilt and shame in their attack against Israel.

- Amelek had the shame of being the first nation to make war against Israel
- Amelek had the shame of going out of their way to attack Israel
- Amelek had the shame of actually fighting against God

c. **And Moses built an altar and called its name, THE-LORD-IS-MY-BANNER**: Though Moses knew his prayer was important, he wasn't foolish enough to think that *he* won the battle. As an act of worship he built an altar and praised the name of *Yahweh-Nissi* (**THE-LORD-IS-MY-BANNER**).

i. *Nissi* describes a flag or a banner. The idea is that God is victorious in battle and the flag of his victory is lifted high. The same word is used of the serpent on the pole in Numbers 21:8, and in other significant passages:

- Psalm 60:4: *You have given a banner to those who fear You, that it may be displayed because of the truth.*
- Isaiah 11:10: *And in that day there shall be a Root of Jesse, Who shall stand as a banner to the people; for the Gentiles shall seek Him, and His resting place shall be glorious.*

ii. In Exodus 17 we see examples of God's power and man's effort working together. Moses struck the rock, but only God could bring the water. Joshua fought, Moses prayed, but only God gave the victory over Amalek. In it all, *God received the glory*. It wasn't *Israel is my banner* or *Moses is my banner* or *Joshua is my banner*, rather it was *Yahweh-Nissi*: **THE-LORD-IS-MY-BANNER**.

iii. We sometimes are even *more* aware of the power and the help of God when we work together with Him than we are when God does the work all by Himself. *Jehovah-Nissi* came after the battle with Amalek, not after the dead Egyptians at the Red Sea.

d. **The LORD has sworn: the LORD will have war with Amalek from generation to generation**: This was not the last battle with or mention of the Amalekites. God continued His war against them, but gave them much time to repent of this great sin of attacking their cousin, Israel.

- Balaam prophesied of their ruin (Numbers 24:20)
- Hundreds of years later, Saul fought against them (1 Samuel 14:48)
- God then commanded Saul to continue the fight against Amalek, to bring complete judgment upon them for their ancient sin against Israel (1 Samuel 15:1-7)
- In partial obedience to God, Saul fought against the Amalekites and defeated them, but kept their king alive (and presumably others) while also enriching himself in the battle (1 Samuel 15:7-9)
- The failure to obey God in regard to Amalek was the primary act of disobedience that cost Saul the throne (1 Samuel 15:2-9 and 1 Samuel 28:18)
- The Amalekites existed after this, so we know Saul did not complete the work God gave to him (1 Samuel 27:8, 30:17; 2 Samuel 8:12)
- There are some indications that this work was completed in the late days of the divided monarchy under Hezekiah (1 Chronicles 4:41-43), but it is possible that some descendants of the Amalekites remained (such as Haman in Esther 3:1)

    i. Because of God's strong command to battle against Amalek until they were completely conquered, many see the Amalekites as a picture of our flesh, the unspiritual aspect of man that makes war against the spirit. In this sense, "Amalek" constantly battles against the spirit and must be struggled against until completely conquered (Galatians 5:17).

Exodus 18 - Jethro's Counsel to Moses

A. Jethro and Moses meet.

1. (1-6) Moses meets with Jethro, his father-in-law, in the desert of Midian.

And Jethro, the priest of Midian, Moses' father-in-law, heard of all that God had done for Moses and for Israel His people; that the LORD had brought Israel out of Egypt. Then Jethro, Moses' father-in-law, took Zipporah, Moses' wife, after he had sent her back, with her two sons, of whom the name of one *was* Gershom (for he said, "I have been a stranger in a foreign land") and the name of the other *was* Eliezer (for *he said*, "The God of my father *was* my help, and delivered me from the sword of Pharaoh"); and Jethro, Moses' father-in-law, came with his sons and his wife to Moses in the wilderness, where he was encamped at the mountain of God. Now he had said to Moses, "I, your father-in-law Jethro, am coming to you with your wife and her two sons with her."

a. **Jethro, the priest of Midian, Moses' father-in-law, heard of all that God had done for Moses and for Israel His people**: The greatness of God's work through Moses and for the people of Israel became known to surrounding peoples, especially those with an interest in Moses as Jethro.

i. Jethro was the **priest of Midian** - likely a descendant of one of Abraham's other children through Keturah named Midian (Genesis 25:1-2). Because of this connection with Abraham, we have good reason to believe he was a true priest, and worshipped the true God.

ii. "Some think that Jethro was the brother-in-law of Moses (the word is equally capable of this rendering), Reuel being his father (Exodus 3:1)." (Thomas)

b. **Jethro, Moses' father-in-law, took Zipporah, Moses' wife, after he had sent her back, with her two sons**: Moses was here reunited with his wife Zipporah and his two sons Gershon and Eliezer. Apparently Moses sent his family back to Midian at some time, perhaps during the plagues of Egypt.

i. "This is the first, and only, mention of Moses' second son, whose very name suggests a rekindling of faith in Moses' heart, compared with the despair shown in the name 'Gershom'." (Cole)

c. **I, your father-in-law Jethro, am coming to you**: Moses had a special relationship with Jethro. Even though he was raised in all the wisdom and education of Egypt, Moses perhaps learned more about real leadership from the priest and shepherd Jethro - whose flocks Moses tended until his call at Sinai.

i. "It is almost certainly quite out of its chronological place here. It most probably happened later, as the people were about to depart from Sinai. Compare Numbers 11:14-17 and Deuteronomy 1:7-14." (Morgan) Adam Clarke has a long section where he deals with the matter of this event not following chronological sequence.

2. (7-12) Jethro glorifies God when Moses reports what the LORD has done.

So Moses went out to meet his father-in-law, bowed down, and kissed him. And they asked each other about *their* well-being, and they went into the tent. And Moses told his father-in-law all that the LORD had done to Pharaoh and to the Egyptians for Israel's sake, all the hardship that had come upon them on the way, and *how* the LORD had delivered them. Then Jethro rejoiced for all the good which the LORD had done for Israel, whom He had delivered out of the hand of the Egyptians. And Jethro said, "Blessed *be* the LORD, who has delivered you out of the hand of the Egyptians and out of the hand of Pharaoh, *and* who has delivered the people from under the hand of the Egyptians. Now I know that the LORD *is* greater than all the gods; for in the very thing in which they behaved proudly, *He was* above them." Then Jethro, Moses' father-in-law, took a burnt offering and *other* sacrifices *to offer* to God. And Aaron came with all the elders of Israel to eat bread with Moses' father-in-law before God.

a. **Moses went out to meet his father-in-law, bowed down, and kissed him**: Though he was the leader of a nation, Moses honored Jethro both as his father-in-law and as a legitimate priest of God. His position of leadership did not make Moses proud.

i. "The whole scene is typical of eastern courtesy. Both men are now great chiefs in their own right and behave accordingly." (Cole)

b. **All the hardship...and how the LORD had delivered them**: Moses gave Jethro an honest report, describing both the hardships and the deliverance.

c. **Now I know that the LORD is greater than all the gods**: It is possible Jethro knew this before, because he was the *priest of Midian* (Exodus 2:16, 3:1, and 18:1). But when he heard of God's great works over the gods of Egypt, it brought this truth to Jethro more clearly than before.

> i. "This may not be true monotheism (the belief that there is only one god), but it certainly leads to monolatry (the worship of one god to the exclusion of others) as a logical sequence." (Cole)

B. Jethro's advice to Moses.

1. (13-16) Jethro observes Moses as he settles disputes.

And so it was, on the next day, that Moses sat to judge the people; and the people stood before Moses from morning until evening. So when Moses' father-in-law saw all that he did for the people, he said, "What *is* this thing that you are doing for the people? Why do you alone sit, and all the people stand before you from morning until evening?" And Moses said to his father-in-law, "Because the people come to me to inquire of God. When they have a difficulty, they come to me, and I judge between one and another; and I make known the statutes of God and His laws."

a. **Moses sat to judge the people**: Among such a large group there would naturally be many disputes and questions of interpretation to settle. Apparently Moses was virtually the only recognized judge in the nation, and the job of hearing each case occupied **Moses from morning until evening**. Jethro noted this and asked Moses about it.

> i. **Moses sat to judge...the people stood before Moses**: "*Sat... stood* are technical terms of Semitic law, denoting 'judge' and 'litigant' respectively." (Cole)

b. **And I make known the statutes of God and His laws**: Because Moses knew God and His Word, he was able to fairly settle disputes among the children of Israel. Yet taking all this responsibility by himself was a massive burden.

2. (17-18) Jethro advises Moses to change his current approach.

So Moses' father-in-law said to him, "The thing that you do *is* not good. Both you and these people who *are* with you will surely wear yourselves out. For this thing *is* too much for you; you are not able to perform it by yourself."

a. **The thing that you do is not good**: It wasn't that Moses was unfit to hear their disputes; it wasn't that he didn't care about their disputes; it wasn't that the job was beneath him, and it wasn't that the people didn't want Moses to hear their disputes. The problem was simply that the job was too big for Moses to do. His energies were spent unwisely, and justice was delayed for many in Israel.

i. Moses needed to delegate, even as in Acts 6:2-4 when the apostles insisted they needed to delegate so they would not *leave the word of God and serve tables*.

b. **This thing is too much for you; you are not able to perform it by yourself**: Much to Moses' credit, he was teachable; when Jethro said **the thing that you do is not good**, Moses listened to Jethro. Moses knew how to *not* bow to the complaints of the children of Israel (Exodus 17:3), but also knew how to hear godly counsel from a man like Jethro.

i. "Men called by God to lead are always in danger of attempting to encompass more than they are able." (Morgan)

3. (19-20) Jethro advises Moses to pray and teach.

"Listen now to my voice; I will give you counsel, and God will be with you: Stand before God for the people, so that you may bring the difficulties to God. And you shall teach them the statutes and the laws, and show them the way in which they must walk and the work they must do."

a. **Stand before God for the people**: This was the first essential step in effective delegation for Moses. He had to pray for the people; Moses had to **bring the difficulties to God**. Prayer was an essential aspect of Moses' leadership of the people.

b. **Teach them the statutes and the laws**: For Moses to effectively lead and delegate, he had to teach the Word of God not only to those who would hear the disputes, but also those who might dispute.

i. If the people knew God's Word for themselves, many disputes could be settled immediately. Also, if the people knew God's Word for themselves, they would not be discouraged if they could not bring their case to Moses himself - they could know one of Moses' delegates was able give them counsel from God's wisdom.

ii. There is a clear analogy between the leadership of Moses for Israel and the leadership of a pastor among God's people. The analogy does not fit at every point, but in many aspects.

- God was recognized as the true leader of the people
- The leader could not do the work of leadership alone
- The leader had a special responsibility for prayer and teaching
- The leader must select, train, and give authority to others to help in the work
- The people had a definite role in all this (Deuteronomy 1:13)

iii. "The Christian pastor is in some respects comparable to Moses, for he is set apart as a leader in the band of brethren; and as such his business is not only to teach the people but to plead for them with God." (Spurgeon)

4. (21-22) Jethro advises Moses to delegate the responsibility of resolving disputes.

"Moreover you shall select from all the people able men, such as fear God, men of truth, hating covetousness; and place *such* over them *to be* rulers of thousands, rulers of hundreds, rulers of fifties, and rulers of tens. And let them judge the people at all times. Then it will be *that* every great matter they shall bring to you, but every small matter they themselves shall judge. So it will be easier for you, for they will bear *the burden* with you.

a. **Select from all the people able men, such as fear God, men of truth**: This was the next step in effective delegation for Moses. Delegation fails if the job is not put into the hands of able, godly men. Only particular men were fit for this job:

- Men of ability: **able men**
- Men of godliness: **such as fear God**
- Men of God's Word: **men of truth**
- Men of honor: **hating covetousness**

i. This means that Moses had to fulfill an essential function of a leader: to develop and implement new leaders. "There is no greater art in the world than to develop the latent capacities of those around us by yoking them to useful service." (Meyer)

ii. Paul gave the same counsel to Timothy in 2 Timothy 2:2: *And the things that you have heard from me among many witnesses, commit these to faithful men who will be able to teach others also.*

b. **Every great matter they shall bring to you**: For Moses to effectively delegate, he must still have oversight and leadership over those under him. Delegation is the exercise of leadership, not the abandonment of it.

5. (23) Jethro tells Moses the good result from his advice.

"If you do this thing, and God *so* commands you, then you will be able to endure, and all this people will also go to their place in peace."

a. **If you do this thing, and God so commands you**: Jethro knew that his advice came from outside the community of Israel, and was perhaps more from a school of management than from existing holy Scripture. Therefore he was careful to tell Moses that he had to be sure that *God* commanded this approach, and not Moses.

i. "All advice which we receive from men should be tested by remitting the same to God for ratification and amendment." (Morgan)

b. **You will be able to endure**: This was the first reward for effective delegation. Moses would enjoy life more and be able to do his job better than ever, avoiding the exhaustion of having to settle every dispute.

c. **And all this people will also go to their place in peace**: The second reward was that the people would be effectively served. It is said that justice delayed is justice denied, and disputes in Israel could be both *prevented* or *settled by the parties themselves* (by the teaching of God's law), or settled *by the leaders appointed by Moses*.

i. This method also had the advantage of settling problems quickly, because people didn't need to wait in line for Moses. "The longer a controversy lasts, the worse the tangle becomes, the more hot words are spoken, the more bystanders become involved." (Meyer) Jesus said we should agree with our adversary *quickly* (Matthew 5:25).

6. (24-27) Moses follows Jethro's suggestions and Jethro departs.

So Moses heeded the voice of his father-in-law and did all that he had said. And Moses chose able men out of all Israel, and made them heads over the people: rulers of thousands, rulers of hundreds, rulers of fifties, and rulers of tens. So they judged the people at all times; the hard cases they brought to Moses, but they judged every small case themselves. Then Moses let his father-in-law depart, and he went his way to his own land.

a. **Moses heeded the voice of his father-in-law and did all that he had said**: God taught Moses by someone from the outside, and Moses listened. Moses wisely followed Jethro's counsel, and surely this extended his ministry and made him more effective.

i. "God has many ways of making known His will to His servants." (Morgan)

b. **Rulers of thousands, rulers of hundreds, rulers of fifties, and rulers of tens**: In Moses' method of administration, some had a higher position than others. Yet God honored the faithful service of the **rulers of tens** as much as the service of the **rulers of thousands**.

i. This was good for Moses. He could focus on the most important things and not be overwhelmed and overstressed by many smaller tasks.

ii. This was good for the leaders Moses chose. Capable men were given real responsibility and had the opportunity to serve God's people in meaningful ways and further God's work.

iii. This was good for the congregation. Prayed for and taught by Moses, they were able to settle more things themselves. When they did need a dispute settled, they received quicker attention and better attention from the delegated leaders than from Moses himself.

iv. "It is better to set a hundred men to work than to do the work of a hundred men." (D.L. Moody)

Exodus 19 - The Nation of Israel Comes to Mount Sinai

A. Coming to the Mountain.

1. (1-2) Israel camps at Mount Sinai.

In the third month after the children of Israel had gone out of the land of Egypt, on the same day, they came *to* the Wilderness of Sinai. For they had departed from Rephidim, had come *to* the Wilderness of Sinai, and camped in the wilderness. So Israel camped there before the mountain.

a. **They came to the Wilderness of Sinai**: It took them three months of trusting God to get to this place, but they finally arrived. They saw God's deliverance from Egypt, received His guidance on the way, saw His glorious victory at the Red Sea, received God's miraculous gifts of food and water, and they saw a prayerful victory won over the Amalekites.

i. Israel stayed in **the Wilderness of Sinai** until Numbers 10. More than 57 chapters of Scripture are devoted to what happened to Israel in the year they camped at Mount Sinai.

ii. "The word conventionally translated 'wilderness' is not a sandy desert, but grazing country, not settled by man." (Cole)

b. **So Israel camped there before the mountain**: In one sense, all that went before was meant to bring them to this place. This was the beginning of the fulfillment of what God said in Exodus 3:12: *this shall be a sign to you that I have sent you: When you have brought the people out of Egypt, you shall serve God on this mountain.*

i. Sinai was the place where Moses met God at the burning bush. The whole nation of Israel would soon experience some of what Moses experienced at the burning bush. Moses could lead them to this mountain for this experience because he had already been there. The people could not go farther than their leader.

ii. If the traditional site of Mount Sinai looks like anything, it looks like a huge pulpit - a sudden, steep outcropping of mountain out in the wilderness. Here, God preached one of the most dramatic sermons ever heard.

iii. Yet there is good reason to believe that the *traditional* site of Mount Sinai – on the Sinai Peninsula – is not the correct location of the **mountain** where all this came to pass.

- According to Exodus 2:15, 3:1, and 3:12, this mountain was in the region of *Midian*, which was on the east side of the Gulf of Aqaba, east of the Sinai Peninsula. The ancient land of Midian is in the modern nation of Saudi Arabia
- In Galatians 4:25, the Apostle Paul clearly described Mount Sinai as being *in Arabia*. Though some claim that this can also be understood as extending to the Sinai Peninsula, this isn't the normal understanding of where *Arabia* is, either in the modern or the ancient understanding
- There is significant evidence – both historic and archaeological – to associate the Arabian mountain *Jebel al-Lawz* with the site of Mount Sinai

2. (3-4) God reminds Israel of His great power and care for them.

And Moses went up to God, and the LORD called to him from the mountain, saying, "Thus you shall say to the house of Jacob, and tell the children of Israel: 'You have seen what I did to the Egyptians, and *how* I bore you on eagles' wings and brought you to Myself.'"

a. **Moses went up to God, and the LORD called to him from the mountain**: Moses, led by God, went up on the mountain to meet with God as he had before - and the LORD spoke to Moses again.

b. **Thus you shall say to the house of Jacob**: With this title, God associated the nation with the weakest and least stable of the patriarchs. At this point, they acted more like **Jacob** than like Abraham or Isaac.

c. **You have seen what I did to the Egyptians**: God gave a message to Israel through Moses, a message regarding His purpose and destiny for Israel. This destiny was based on what God already did for them in the great deliverance from Egypt.

d. **I bore you on eagles' wings**: An **eagles' wings** are strong and sure, but they also speak of careful protection. It is said that an eagle does not carry her young in her claws like other birds; the young eagles attach themselves to the back of the mother eagle and are protected as they are carried. Any arrow from a hunter must pass through the mother eagle before it could touch the young eagle on her back.

i. "This metaphor is developed most extensively in Deuteronomy 32:11, where the loving compassion, protection, strength, and watchfulness of God is compared with the majestic bird's attributes." (Kaiser)

e. **And brought you to Myself**: The *deliverance* (**I bore you on eagles' wings**) was for *fellowship* (**brought you to Myself**). God didn't deliver Israel so they could live apart from God, but so they could be God's people.

3. (5-6) God reveals His plan and destiny for Israel.

"'Now therefore, if you will indeed obey My voice and keep My covenant, then you shall be a special treasure to Me above all people; for all the earth *is* Mine. And you shall be to Me a kingdom of priests and a holy nation.' These *are* the words which you shall speak to the children of Israel."

a. **If you will indeed obey My voice and keep My covenant**: God would soon make a formal covenant with Israel at Mount Sinai. Before He did, He revealed what He wanted to do to for an obedient Israel.

i. Before God called Israel to keep His *law*, He commanded them to "**keep My covenant**." The **covenant** was greater than the law itself. The covenant God made with Israel involved law, sacrifice, and the choice to obey and be blessed or to disobey and be cursed.

b. **Then you shall be a special treasure to Me**: God intended for Israel to be **a special treasure** unto Him. He wanted them to be a people with a unique place in God's great plan, a people of great value and concern to God. It wasn't as if God ignored the rest of the world (**for all the earth is mine**), but that He was determined to use Israel to reach the earth.

i. The Apostle Paul also wanted Christians to know how great a treasure they were to God; he prayed they would know *what are the riches of the glory of His inheritance in the saints* (Ephesians 1:18).

ii. "Where his treasure is, there is a man's heart. If it is in ships on the treacherous sea, he tosses restlessly on his bed, solicitous for its safety. If it is in fabrics, he guards against moth; if in metal, against rust and thieves. And is Christ less careful for his own?" (Meyer)

c. **You shall be to Me a kingdom of priests**: God intended for Israel to be **a kingdom of priests**, where every believer could come before God himself, and as a group they represented God to the nations.

i. "The whole nation was to act as mediators of God's grace to the nations of the earth." (Kaiser) "God's 'particularist' choice of Israel has a wider 'universalist' purpose." (Cole)

ii. Peter reminds us we are a *royal priesthood* (1 Peter 2:9), those who serve God as both kings and priests (*and has made us kings and priests to His God and Father*, Revelation 1:6).

d. **And a holy nation**: God intended for Israel to be **a holy nation**, a nation and people set apart from the rest of the world, the particular possession of God, fit for His purposes.

i. Peter reminds us we are a *holy nation, His own special people, that you may proclaim the praises of Him who called you out of darkness into His marvelous light* (1 Peter 2:9). As God's people, we must be set apart, thinking and doing differently than the flow of the world in general.

4. (7-9) The people agree to obey the covenant.

So Moses came and called for the elders of the people, and laid before them all these words which the LORD commanded him. Then all the people answered together and said, "All that the LORD has spoken we will do." So Moses brought back the words of the people to the LORD. And the LORD said to Moses, "Behold, I come to you in the thick cloud, that the people may hear when I speak with you, and believe you forever." So Moses told the words of the people to the LORD.

a. **Laid before them all these words which the LORD commanded him**: The people are later challenged to receive the covenant again, after they heard its terms, and they received it again (Exodus 24:1-8).

i. Here they said, **"All that the LORD has spoken we will do."** "Their answer was sincere, but it was ignorant." (Morgan) Later they would say it again, in an even more formal arrangement (Exodus 24:1-8).

ii. "Even so with us. We say, 'All that Jehovah hath spoken we will do,' and we fail. But God never fails. He waits and pursues His own way of grace and government." (Morgan)

b. **Moses brought back the words of the people to the LORD**: Moses here acted as a true priest, as an intermediary between God and the people. Yet God spoke audibly to Moses (**that the people may hear when I speak with you**) so everyone would know that it was really God speaking to Moses.

5. (10-13) God commands that His holy presence on Sinai be respected.

Then the LORD said to Moses, "Go to the people and consecrate them today and tomorrow, and let them wash their clothes. And let them be ready for the third day. For on the third day the LORD will come down upon Mount Sinai in the sight of all the people. You shall set bounds for the people all around, saying, 'Take heed to yourselves *that* you do *not* go up to the mountain or touch its base. Whoever touches the

mountain shall surely be put to death. Not a hand shall touch him, but he shall surely be stoned or shot *with an arrow;* whether man or beast, he shall not live.' When the trumpet sounds long, they shall come near the mountain."

a. **Go to the people and consecrate them today and tomorrow**: God was going to appear to Israel in a spectacular way; and before this could happen, the people had to prepare themselves.

b. **You shall set bounds for the people all around**: As God promised to reveal Himself on Sinai He told Israel, *Stay away.* There were boundaries that could not be crossed. Israel had to keep their distance behind a barrier, and the penalty for failing to keep their distance was death (**shall surely be put to death**).

i. **Not a hand shall touch him**: Any person or animal killed for getting too close would be regarded as so unholy they could not even be touched, they had to be executed with stones or arrows.

ii. If there is anything basic to human nature, it is that we need boundaries. In setting these boundaries and providing the death penalty for breaching them, God showed Israel that obedience is more important than their feelings. We don't doubt that some bold Israelites *felt* like going beyond the boundaries, but they were to submit their feelings to obedience.

c. **When the trumpet sounds long**: The people could only come near at God's invitation, and the **trumpet** signaled that the invitation was open. At the sounding of the trumpet they could come up to the boundaries, but not beyond them.

6. (14-15) Commands for ceremonial purity and cleanliness.

So Moses went down from the mountain to the people and sanctified the people, and they washed their clothes. And he said to the people, "Be ready for the third day; do not come near *your* wives."

a. **Sanctified the people, and they washed their clothes**: The people immediately prepared for the revelation of God that was promised for **the third day**.

b. **Be ready for the third day**: The meeting with God could only come at the third day. God promised to reveal Himself on **the third day**, and they had to wait for it.

c. **Do not come near your wives**: The rest of the Scriptures do not teach that there is any inherent uncleanness in sexual relations. This command was peculiar for this event. In this situation, God wanted the people to demonstrate their desire for purity by putting on clean clothes and restraining desires, even legitimate desires.

> i. "Men must come before God with the best preparation they can get." (Trapp)

B. God's presence on the mountain.

1. (16-19) God's terrifying presence on Mount Sinai.

Then it came to pass on the third day, in the morning, that there were thunderings and lightnings, and a thick cloud on the mountain; and the sound of the trumpet was very loud, so that all the people who *were* in the camp trembled. And Moses brought the people out of the camp to meet with God, and they stood at the foot of the mountain. Now Mount Sinai *was* completely in smoke, because the Lord descended upon it in fire. Its smoke ascended like the smoke of a furnace, and the whole mountain quaked greatly. And when the blast of the trumpet sounded long and became louder and louder, Moses spoke, and God answered him by voice.

> a. **Thunderings and lightnings, and a thick cloud**: These signs of power and glory signaled the presence of God. The whole environment spoke of God's presence in a terrifying sense.

> b. **The sound of the trumpet was very loud**: What Israel saw and felt in the thunder, lightning, the cloud, the smoke, and the earthquake was terrifying; but each of these are natural (though frightening) phenomenon. Yet the **sound of the trumpet** did not come from the camp, but from heaven itself. No wonder that **all the people who were in the camp trembled**.

> c. **Moses brought the people out of the camp to meet with God**: At the sound of the trumpet, Moses led the people up to the barrier at the base of Mount Sinai where they could see, smell, hear, and virtually taste the fire which covered the mountain - as well as feel the earth shake under their feet when **the whole mountain quaked greatly**.

> d. **When the blast of the trumpet sounded long and became louder and louder**: In the midst of all this, the sound of the trumpet blast became longer and louder and longer and louder until **Moses spoke** to God, **and God answered him by voice**. Collectively, Israel heard the Lord God speak from Mount Sinai in an audible **voice**.

2. (20) Moses goes up on Mount Sinai to the immediate presence of God.

Then the Lord came down upon Mount Sinai, on the top of the mountain. And the Lord called Moses to the top of the mountain, and Moses went up.

a. **Then the LORD came down upon Mount Sinai, on the top of the mountain**: God came in a special presence to Mount Sinai, ready to meet with Moses as a representative of the whole nation of Israel.

b. **And Moses went up**: God **came down**, and **Moses went up**. As the people trembled in terror at the foot of the mountain, Moses needed courage to go to the top and meet with God. It took courage for Moses to go up in the midst of all the thunder, lightning, earthquakes, fire, and smoke.

i. Yet Moses knew God not only in terms of this awesome power, but also in terms of His gracious kindness.

3. (21-25) God tells Moses to go back down and warn the people again about respecting the holiness of His presence on Sinai.

And the LORD said to Moses, "Go down and warn the people, lest they break through to gaze at the LORD, and many of them perish. Also let the priests who come near the LORD consecrate themselves, lest the LORD break out against them." But Moses said to the LORD, "The people cannot come up to Mount Sinai; for You warned us, saying, 'Set bounds around the mountain and consecrate it.'" Then the LORD said to him, "Away! Get down and then come up, you and Aaron with you. But do not let the priests and the people break through to come up to the LORD, lest He break out against them." So Moses went down to the people and spoke to them.

a. **Go down and warn the people**: Those who through rebellion, curiosity, or simple daring presumed to go up on the mountain would **perish**. The glory and greatness of God wasn't to be a matter subjected to scientific inquiry or a way to prove one's own manhood.

b. **The people cannot come up to Mount Sinai**: Just because God called Moses and Aaron up did not mean there was an open invitation for the whole nation to meet with God on Mount Sinai.

c. **Do not let the priests and the people break through to come up to the LORD**: The whole idea at Sinai was *exclusion*. Exodus 19 describes the awe and fear each Israelite must have felt at Mount Sinai. It is easy to think that this alone inspired them to a holy lifestyle.

i. Many today feel we need to get more of the thunder and fire and trembling of Mount Sinai into people as a way of keeping them from sin. Yet, not forty days from this, the whole nation would have an orgy around a golden calf, praising *it* as the god that brought them out of Egypt.

ii. "Awe is one thing: the submission of the will is another." (Chadwick) Israel had plenty of awe, but little submission of their will.

iii. Hebrews 12:18-24 says clearly that under the New Covenant, we come to a different mountain, that our salvation and relationship with God is centered at Mount Zion, not Mount Sinai.

- Sinai speaks of fear and terror, but Zion speaks of love and forgiveness
- Sinai, with all its fear and power is earthly; but the Mount Zion we come to is heavenly and spiritual
- At Sinai, only Moses could come and meet God; at Zion, there is an innumerable company, a general assembly
- Sinai had guilty men in fear; but Zion just men made perfect
- At Sinai, Moses is the mediator; but at Zion, Jesus the mediator
- Sinai put forth an Old Covenant, ratified by the blood of animals; Zion has a New Covenant, ratified by the blood of God's precious Son
- Sinai was all about barriers and exclusion; Zion is all about invitation
- Sinai is all about Law; Zion is all about grace

iv. Therefore, we shouldn't come to Zion as if coming to Sinai. We must put away our hesitation and get bold in coming to God. Even so, there is much for us to learn at Mount Sinai. We learn of God's holy requirements and what we have to do before we can come to Him. In a similar manner to those at Mount Sinai, there are things we must to do meet with God.

- We must receive God's Word
- We must be set apart
- We must be cleansed
- We can only come after the third day
- We must respect God's boundary
- We must restrain the flesh
- We must know we come to a holy God

v. "Reader, art thou still under the influence and condemning power of that fiery law which proceeded from his right hand? Art though yet *afar off*? Remember, thou canst only *come nigh* by the blood of sprinkling; and till justified by his blood, thou are under the *curse*. Consider the terrible majesty of God. If thou have his *favour* thou hast *life;* if his *frown, death*. Be instantly reconciled to God, for though thou hast deeply *sinned,* and he is *just*, yet he is the justifier of him that believeth in Christ Jesus. Believe on him, receive his salvation; OBEY *his voice indeed*, and KEEP his *covenant*, and THEN *shalt thou be a king and a priest unto God and the Lamb,* and be finally saved with all the power of an endless life. *Amen.*" (Clarke)

Exodus 20 - The Ten Commandments

A. Four commandments regarding our conduct before God.

1. (1) Preface to the Ten Commandments.

And God spoke all these words, saying:

a. **And God spoke**: It is proper to believe that **God spoke** these words to Israel as a whole, as they assembled together at the foot of Mount Sinai. There, *God answered him* [Moses] *by voice* (Exodus 19:19), as Moses stood among the people at the foot of Mount Sinai.

i. "These commandments were after all addressed to the ordinary Israelite, not to the religious elite of the day: they are expressed in strong simple terms, understandable to all, and deal with the temptations of the common man, not of the theologian." (Cole)

ii. After this, the people asked that God not speak with them directly, and that Moses be the messenger (Exodus 20:18-19). After this, Moses went back up the mountain to receive more revelation from God for the people (Exodus 20:21).

iii. In reading and thinking through these commandments, it should be always remembered that *Israel first heard these commands spoken by God from heaven in an audible voice.* This made the strongest, most authoritative impression upon the people possible.

b. **God spoke all these words**: The following laws were not invented at Mount Sinai. A few aspects of the Mosaic Law show new revelation, but for the most part it simply, clearly and definitely lays out God's law as it was written in the heart of man since the time of Adam.

i. "It is wrong to steal, or murder, or covet, not primarily because these sins are forbidden by the Decalogue. They are forbidden by the Decalogue, because they were previously forbidden by conscience; and they are forbidden by conscience because they are forbidden by the nature of things; and the nature of things is God." (Meyer)

ii. "It has been well said that the commandments are God's nature expressed in terms of moral imperatives." (Cole)

iii. In his book *The Abolition of Man*, C.S. Lewis explained how there certainly is a universal morality among men. He gave concrete examples of how all cultures in the past were able to agree on the basics of morality because these principles are implanted in the heart and mind of mankind.

iv. All cultures have said murder is wrong, and kindness is good. All agree that we have particular obligations to our family. All say that honesty is good and that a man cannot have any woman he wants. They agree that stealing is wrong and that justice is good. There are no cultures where cowardice is good and bravery is bad.

c. **God spoke all these words**: This *God-based moral code* set the God of Israel – the God of Abraham, Isaac, and Jacob – apart from the commonly worshipped gods of the pagan world at that time. They were often just as immoral or more immoral than their human followers.

i. The *God-based moral code* also established that this people, this nation of Israel belonged to *God* and not to Moses. This wasn't Moses' law (though we often casually refer to it as such). Rather, **God spoke all these words,** and Moses nor any other man was ever to think of himself or allow others to think of him as *above* the law. God was above all, and His law was and is the expression of His will.

ii. The *Code of Hammurabi* is another well-known set of laws and principles from this same approximate period. There are some similarities between the Ten Commandments/Mosaic Law and the Code of Hammurabi, but the differences are even more profound. While Hammurabi mentions the gods of Babylon, the emphasis is clearly on *him* as the king and lawgiver (with divine authority, of course). The *Code of Hammurabi* begins with page after page of how wonderful Hammurabi is and how much he has accomplished. Hammurabi is clearly above his own law, since *he* was the embodiment of the law. Not so with Moses; the emphasis is clear: **God spoke all these words,** and *no man is above the law.*

d. **God spoke all these words**: We *need* God to morally instruct and guide us. Though these principles resonate with the human conscience (both individually and collectively), they are certainly *not* the only influence upon our thinking and behavior. We *need* to know that there is a God in heaven who expects certain moral behavior and that there are consequences for obeying or disobeying these commands.

i. The Ten Commandments (and all of the Law of Moses that follows) is a *God-based moral code*. It doesn't just say that certain behavior is unwise or unhelpful; it says that *God commands us to do or not do certain things*, and it either says or implies that:

- God sees our obedience or disobedience
- God measures our obedience or disobedience
- God, in some way, rewards our obedience and punishes our disobedience

ii. Without a *God-based moral code*, it is difficult or impossible to answer the question "*Why?*" in response to any moral demand.

iii. The idea of a *God-based moral code* seems to become less and less popular. While the idea of a moral code remains strong, the tendency grows that the moral code should be based on an individual's inner sense of right or wrong, good or bad – and not upon a standard set by God.

iv. There is a persistent impulse to make one's own moral code, apart from God or His revelation. In the late 1980s, media mogul Ted Turner suggested replacing the Ten Commandments with his own "10 Voluntary Initiatives." Mr. Turner's list is conspicuous in its failure to mention God or religion in any way. These were Mr. Turner's Voluntary Initiatives:

1. I promise to have love and respect for the planet earth and living things thereon, especially my fellow species--humankind.

2. I promise to treat all persons everywhere with dignity, respect, and friendliness.

3. I promise to have no more than two children, or no more than my nation suggests.

4. I promise to use my best efforts to save what is left of our natural world in its untouched state and to restore damaged or destroyed areas where practical.

5. I pledge to use as little nonrenewable resources as possible.

6. I pledge to use as little toxic chemicals, pesticides, and other poisons as possible and to work for their reduction by others.

7. I promise to contribute to those less fortunate than myself, to help them become self-sufficient and enjoy the benefits of a decent life, including clean air and water, adequate food and health care, housing, education, and individual rights.

8. I reject the use of force, in particular military force, and back United Nations arbitration of international disputes.

9. I support the total elimination of all nuclear, chemical, and biological weapons of mass destruction.

10. I support the United Nations and its efforts to collectively improve the conditions of the planet.

e. **God spoke all these words**: The Bible tells us that the law is holy, just, and good (Romans 7:12). It tells us that every good and perfect gift comes from God (James 1:17). These commandments are *good* gifts that came to Israel and humanity at Mount Sinai. The Ten Commandments are good because:

- They show the wise moral guidance and government of God
- They answer the need of mankind for moral guidance and government
- They give us a way to teach morality
- They would make the world so much better if obeyed
- They are good for all humanity; some of the Law of Moses is specific unto Israel, but the Ten Commandments are universal
- They are good when they are promoted and held as ideals, even when they are not perfectly obeyed

i. "The 'ten words' are at once the beginning and the heart of the Mosaic revelation." (Cole)

f. **God spoke all these words**: It is important for us to know, understand, receive, and obey all of these commandments in a fully Biblical perspective, also taking into account what the rest of the Book of Exodus and the New Testament also tells us about the law of God.

i. The Ten Commandments were never given with the thought that one might earn heaven by obeying them all perfectly or adequately. The covenant God made with Israel at Mount Sinai was much bigger than the law, though that was its first and perhaps most dramatic aspect. Another aspect of the covenant was *sacrifice*, which was given because both God and Israel knew that it was impossible for them to keep this law perfectly, and they must depend on the sacrifice of an innocent victim as a substitute for the guilty law-breaker. In this sense, the Ten Commandments were like a mirror that showed Israel their need for sacrifice.

ii. These Ten Commandments can also be summarized as Jesus did in Matthew 22:35-40: *Then one of them, a lawyer, asked Him a question, testing Him, and saying, "Teacher, which is the great commandment in the law?" Jesus said to him, "'You shall love the LORD your God with all your heart, with all your soul, and with all your mind.' This is the first and great commandment. And the second is like it: 'You shall love your neighbor as yourself.' On these two commandments hang all the Law and the Prophets."* This simplification doesn't eliminate the Ten Commandments; it fulfills them, showing us the heart and desire of God for His people. The problem is that we haven't kept the two commandments either, much less the ten.

iii. More importantly, we know that Jesus Himself was the only one to ever keep the law perfectly – either in the ten or the two. He never needed to sacrifice for His own sin, so could be the perfect sacrifice for our sin. Wonderfully, *His obedience is credited to those who put their love and trust in Him.* Romans 8:2-3 puts it this way: *For what the law could not do in that it was weak through the flesh, God did by sending His own Son in the likeness of sinful flesh, on account of sin: He condemned sin in the flesh, that the righteous requirement of the law might be fulfilled in us who do not walk according to the flesh but according to the Spirit.* This is God's amazing promise to those who repent and believe on Jesus.

iv. The law is a schoolmaster to us (Galatians 3:22-25). Before God's plan of salvation in Jesus Christ was fully evident, we were *kept under guard by the law* - both in the sense of being bound by the law, but also held in protective custody. The law, through its revelation of God's character and its exposure of our sin, prepares us to come to Jesus - but after we have come, we no longer have to live under our tutor (though we remember the behavior he has taught us).

v. From the perspective of the entire Bible, we can say that the law of God has three great purposes and uses:

- It is a guardrail, keeping humanity on a moral path
- It is a mirror, showing us our moral failure and need for a savior
- It is a guide, showing us the heart and desire of God for His people

vi. "The great message of the Christian faith is, therefore, that we are free from the Law's condemnation in order that we may be able to fulfill its obligation by the power of [Jesus] within us." (Redpath)

vii. "My obedience therefore is not legal, but inspired by love and empowered by God's Holy Spirit. Does New Testament grace allow a lower standard than Old Testament law? The standard under grace is higher." (Redpath)

viii. The Ten Commandments are often organized into two groups. The first four focus on our conduct toward God, and the next six on our conduct toward one another.

2. (2-3) The first commandment: **no other gods before Me.**

"I *am* the LORD** your God, who brought you out of the land of Egypt, out of the house of bondage. You shall have no other gods before Me."**

a. **I am the LORD your God**: In the ancient world (including Egypt), men worshipped many gods. Here Yahweh (**the LORD**), the covenant God of Israel, set Himself apart from any of the other supposed deities.

i. In these first few words, God both reminded and taught Israel essential facts or principles about who He is, about His nature.

- *God is above nature*; He is not merely the personification of fire, or the wind, or the sun, or the sky, or any other created thing
- *God is personal*; He is not a depersonalized force; He relates with and communicates to man in an understandable way. God has a mind, a will, a voice, and so forth
- *God is good*; He had done good for Israel and now does good for them in giving these commands, the keeping of which not only pleases Him, but is genuinely best for humanity
- *God is holy*; He is different from the supposed gods of the pagans, and He therefore also expects His people to be different

ii. It seems that the *structure* of these commands and covenant were familiar in the ancient world. "Most scholars point to the similarity between this historical prologue (followed by its stipulations, witnesses, and provisions for succession) and the great suzerain-vassal treaty forms of the ancient Near East." (Kaiser)

b. **Who brought you out of the land of Egypt, out of the house of bondage**: Before God commanded anything of Israel, He reminded them what He had done for them. This was a clear foundation: because of who God is, and what He has done for us, He has the right to tell us what to do - and we have the obligation to obey Him.

i. "God did not promulgate a code of laws for the children of Israel, while they were in bondage, telling them that if they would obey it, He would deliver them. He brought them out of the land of Egypt, out of the house of bondage, and then gave them His law." (Morgan)

ii. "God's blessings are binders; every deliverance is a tie to obedience." (Trapp)

c. **You shall have no other gods before Me**: The first commandment logically flowed from understanding who God was and what He had done for Israel. Because of that, nothing was to come **before** God, and He was the only God we worship and serve.

i. In the days of ancient Israel, there was great temptation to worship the gods of materialism (such as *Baal*, the god of weather and financial success) and sex (such as *Ashtoreth*, the goddess of sex, romance, and reproduction), or any number of other local deities. We are tempted to worship the same gods, but without the old-fashioned names and images.

ii. It has been said (perhaps first by John Calvin) that human nature is like an idol factory that operates constantly. We constantly deal with the temptation to set all kinds of things before God or to compete with God and His preeminent place in our life.

d. **No other gods before Me**: This does not imply that it is permissible to have other gods, as long as they line up behind the true God. Instead, the idea is that there are to be no other gods before the sight of the true God in our life. According to Cole, **before Me** is literally, *To My face.*

i. This means God demands to be more than *added* to our lives. We don't just add Jesus to the life we already have. We must give Him all our life.

ii. Failure to obey this commandment is called *idolatry*. We are to flee idolatry (1 Corinthians 10:14). Those lives marked by habitual idolatry will not inherit the kingdom of God (1 Corinthians 6:9-10, Ephesians 5:5, Revelation 21:8, 22:15). Idolatry is a work of the flesh (Galatians 5:19-20), which marks our old life instead of the new (1 Peter 4:3), and we are not to associate with those who call themselves Christians who are idolaters (1 Corinthians 5:11).

3. (4-6) The second commandment: **You shall not make for yourself any carved image...you shall not bow down to them.**

"You shall not make for yourself a carved image, or any likeness *of anything* that *is* in heaven above, or that *is* in the earth beneath, or that *is* in the water under the earth; you shall not bow down to them nor serve them. For I, the LORD your God, *am* a jealous God, visiting the iniquity of the fathers on the children to the third and fourth *generations* of those who hate Me, but showing mercy to thousands, to those who love Me and keep My commandments."

a. **You shall not make for yourself a carved image**: The second commandment prohibits not only idolatry regarding false gods (overlapping with the first commandment), it also forbids making an image of any created thing that we might worship (**you shall not bow down to them nor serve them**).

i. Some take this command to prohibit any kind of representation of God, such as with a painting of Jesus or a picture of a dove to represent the Holy Spirit, or any other representation. However, others emphasize that the prohibition is actually in the making of an image that would be or would likely be worshipped (**you shall not bow down to them nor serve them**).

ii. Speaking later of Israel's experience at Sinai, Moses wrote: *And the LORD spoke to you out of the midst of the fire. You heard the sound of the words, but saw no form; you only heard a voice* (Deuteronomy 4:12). This established the principle that the worship of God was to be *word-based* and not *image-based*.

b. **Or any likeness of anything that is in heaven above, or that is in the earth beneath**: In that day as well as in our own, worship was tied closely with images - idealized images, or even images in the mind of man. God will not allow us to depict Him with any such image, nor replace Him with another image.

i. The second commandment doesn't forbid making an image of something for artistic purposes; God Himself commanded Israel to make images of cherubim (Exodus 25:18, 26:31). It forbids the making of images as an aid or help to worship. "If the making of cherubim was permitted, then the prohibition of the 'image' will refer only to the making of direct objects of worship." (Cole)

ii. "To countenance its *image worship*, the *Roman Catholic Church* has left the whole of this second commandment out of the decalogue, and thus lost one whole commandment out of the *ten*; but to keep up the *number* they have divided the *tenth* into *two*." (Clarke)

iii. In John 4:24 Jesus explained the rationale behind the second commandment: *God is Spirit, and those who worship Him must worship in spirit and truth.* The use of images and other material things as a focus or help to worship denies who God is (*Spirit*) and how we must worship Him (*in spirit and truth*).

iv. Paul reminded us of the danger and futility of trying to make God into our own image: *Professing to be wise, they became fools, and changed the glory of the incorruptible God into an image made like corruptible man; and birds and four-footed animals and creeping things.* (Romans 1:22-23)

c. **For I, the LORD your God, am a jealous God**: God is **jealous** in the sense that He will not accept being merely added to the life; He insists on being supreme, and does this out of love.

i. "God's jealousy is love in action. He refuses to share the human heart with any rival, not because He is selfish and wants us all for Himself, but because He knows that upon that loyalty to Him depends our very moral life...God is not jealous *of* us: He is jealous *for* us." (Redpath)

ii. " 'Zealous' might be a better translation in modern English, since 'jealousy' has acquired an exclusively bad meaning." (Cole)

d. **Visiting the iniquity of the fathers on the children to the third and fourth generations of those who hate Me**: This does not mean God punishes people directly for the sins of their ancestors. The important words are **of those who hate Me**. If the descendants love God, they will not have the iniquity of the fathers visited on them.

> i. "'This necessarily implies - IF *the children walk in the steps of their fathers*; for no man can be condemned by Divine justice for a crime of which he was never guilty." (Clarke)

> ii. "Children who repeat the sins of their father evidence it in personally hating god; hence they too are punished like their fathers." (Kaiser)

> iii. Yet, the focus here is on idolatry, and this refers to judgment on a *national* scale - nations that forsake the LORD will be judged, and that judgment will have effects throughout generations.

e. **But showing mercy to thousands, to those who love Me and keep My commandments**: It's possible for everyone to receive God's **mercy**; if they will only turn to Him in **love** and obedience.

4. (7) The third commandment: **You shall not take the name of the LORD your God in vain**.

"You shall not take the name of the LORD your God in vain, for the LORD will not hold *him* guiltless who takes His name in vain."

a. **You shall not take the name of the LORD your God in vain**: There are at least three ways this command is commonly disobeyed.

- *Profanity*: Using the name of God in blasphemy and cursing
- *Frivolity*: Using the name of God in a superficial, stupid way
- *Hypocrisy*: Claiming the name of God, but acting in a way that disgraces Him

> i. Jesus communicated the idea of this command in the disciples' prayer, when He taught us to have a regard for the holiness of God's name (*Hallowed be Your name*, Matthew 6:9).

b. **For the LORD will not hold him guiltless who takes His name in vain**: The strength of this command has led to strange traditions among the Jewish people. Some go to extreme measures to avoid violating this command, refusing to even write out the word *God*, in the fear that the paper might be destroyed and the name of God be written **in vain**.

5. (8-11) The fourth commandment: **Remember the Sabbath day**.

"Remember the Sabbath day, to keep it holy. Six days you shall labor and do all your work, but the seventh day *is* the Sabbath of the LORD your God. *In it* you shall do no work: you, nor your son, nor your

daughter, nor your male servant, nor your female servant, nor your cattle, nor your stranger who *is* within your gates. For *in* six days the LORD made the heavens and the earth, the sea, and all that *is* in them, and rested the seventh day. Therefore the LORD blessed the Sabbath day and hallowed it."

a. **Remember the Sabbath day, to keep it holy**: The command is to respect the seventh day (Saturday) as a day of rest (**you shall do no work**). This rest was for all of Israel – for the **son** and the **servant** and the **stranger** – even including **cattle**.

> i. This is an important principle that might be too easily passed over. Here God declared the essential humanity and dignity of women, slaves, and strangers, and said they had the same right to a day of rest as the free Israeli man. This was certainly a radical concept in the ancient world.

> ii. "The baser sort of people in Sweden do always break the Sabbath, saying that it is for gentlemen to keep that day." (Trapp, sometime around 1660)

b. **To keep it holy**: God commanded Israel – and all humanity – to make sure that there was *sacred time* in their life, *separated* time of rest.

> i. In their traditions, the Jewish people came to carefully quantify what they thought could and could not be done on the Sabbath day, in order to **keep it holy**. For example, in Luke 6:1-2, in the mind of the Jewish leaders, the disciples were guilty of four violations of the Sabbath every time they took a bite of grain out in the field, because they reaped, threshed, winnowed, and prepared food.

> ii. Ancient Rabbis taught that on the Sabbath, a man could not carry something in his right hand or in his left hand, across his chest or on his shoulder. But he could carry something with the back of his hand, his foot, his elbow, or in his ear, his hair, or in the hem of his shirt, or in his shoe or sandal. Or on the Sabbath Israelites were forbidden to tie a knot - except a woman could tie a knot in her girdle. So, if a bucket of water had to be raised from a well, an Israelite could not tie a rope to the bucket, but a woman could tie her girdle to the bucket and pull it up from the well.

> iii. In observant Jewish homes today, one cannot turn on a light, a stove, or a switch on the Sabbath. It is forbidden to drive a certain distance or to make a telephone call - all carefully regulated by traditions seeking to spell out the law exactly.

c. **For in six days the LORD made the heavens and the earth**: God established the pattern for the Sabbath at the time of creation. When He rested from His works on the seventh day, God made the seventh day a day of rest from all our works (Genesis 2:3). It's as if God said, *Having too much to do isn't an excuse from taking the rest you need — I created the universe and found time to rest from My work.*

i. When God told them to **remember the Sabbath,** He told them to *remember the rest.* "The term 'Sabbath' is derived from the Hebrew verb 'to rest or cease from work.'" (Kaiser) The most important purpose of the Sabbath was to serve as a preview picture of the rest we have in Jesus.

ii. Like everything in the Bible, we understand this with the perspective of the whole Bible, not this single passage. With this understanding, we see that there is a real sense in which Jesus fulfilled the purpose and plan of the Sabbath *for* us and *in* us (Hebrews 4:9-11) — He is our rest. When we remember His finished work, we **remember the Sabbath,** we *remember the rest.*

iii. Therefore, the whole of Scripture makes it clear that under the New Covenant, no one is under obligation to observe a Sabbath day (Colossians 2:16-17 and Galatians 4:9-11). Galatians 4:10 tells us that Christians are not bound to observe *days and months and seasons and years.* The rest we enter into as Christians is something to experience every day, not just one day a week - the rest of knowing we don't have to work to save ourselves, but our salvation is accomplished in Jesus (Hebrews 4:9-10).

iv. The Sabbath commanded here and observed by Israel was a *shadow of things to come, but the substance is of Christ* (Colossians 2:16-17). In the New Covenant the idea isn't that there is *no* Sabbath, but that *every day* is a day of Sabbath rest in the finished work of God. Since the shadow of the Sabbath is fulfilled in Jesus, we are free to keep any particular day - or no day - as a Sabbath after the custom of ancient Israel.

v. Yet we dare not ignore the importance of a day of rest - God has built us so that we *need* one. Like a car that needs regular maintenance, we need regular rest - or we will not wear well. Some people are like high-mileage cars that haven't been maintained well, and it shows.

vi. Some Christians are also dogmatic about observing Saturday as the Sabbath as opposed to Sunday. But because we are free to regard all days as given by God, it makes no difference. But in some ways, Sunday is more appropriate; being the day Jesus rose from the dead (Mark 16:9), and first met with His disciples (John 20:19), and a day when Christians gathered for fellowship (Acts 20:7 and 1 Corinthians 16:2). Under Law, men worked towards God's rest; but after Jesus' finished work on the cross, the believer enters into rest and goes from that rest out to work.

vii. But we are also commanded to *work* six days. "He who idles his time away in the *six* days is equally culpable in the sight of God as he who works on the *seventh*." (Clarke) Many Christians should give more "leisure time" to the work of the LORD. Every Christian should have a *deliberate* way to serve God and advance the Kingdom of Jesus Christ.

B. Six commandments regarding our conduct before God and man.

1. (12) The fifth commandment: **Honor your father and your mother**.

"Honor your father and your mother, that your days may be long upon the land which the LORD your God is giving you."

a. **Honor your father and your mother**: This command is *wise* and *good*, because honor for parents is an essential building block for the stability and health of all society. If the younger generations are constantly at war with older generations, the foundations of society will be destroyed.

i. To **honor** one's parents includes to *prize* them, to *care* for them, and to *show respect* or *reverence* to them. The command is given to children, but not for only while they are children. "This is not a popular doctrine in our modern world, where youth is worshipped, and old age dreaded or despised. The result is the folly by which men or women strive to remain eternally youthful, only to find it an impossible task." (Cole)

ii. Jesus used the way the Pharisees interpreted this commandment as an example of how one might keep the law with a limited interpretation yet violate the spirit of the commandment (Matthew 15:3-6).

b. **That your days may be long**: In Ephesians 6:2 Paul repeated this command, emphasizing the *promise* stated here, **that your days may be long upon the land**. Rebellion is costly, and many have paid a high price personally for their rebellion against their parents.

i. "A good child lengtheneth his father's days; therefore God promiseth to lengthen his." (Trapp)

2. (13) The sixth commandment: **You shall not murder**.

"You shall not murder."

a. **You shall not murder**: In Hebrew as well as in English there is a distinction between *to kill* and *to* **murder**. As opposed to killing, **murder** is the taking of life without legal justification (execution after due process) or moral justification (killing in defense).

i. "Only two words are used in Hebrew, as blunt as the order 'no killing' would be in English." (Cole)

ii. Kaiser on *rasah*: "Hebrew possesses seven words for killing...If any one of the seven words could signify 'murder,' where factors of premeditation and intentionality are present, this is the verb." (Kaiser)

iii. This important distinction explains how someone can quite consistently argue for the principle of capital punishment *and* the prohibition of murder. When carried out properly, capital punishment is killing with legal justification.

b. **You shall not murder**: Jesus carefully explained the heart of this commandment. He showed that it also prohibits us from *hating* someone else (Matthew 5:21-26), because we can wish someone dead in our hearts, yet never have the nerve to commit the deed. Someone may not kill from a lack of courage or initiative, yet his or her heart is filled with hatred.

3. (14) The seventh commandment: **You shall not commit adultery**.

"You shall not commit adultery."

a. **You shall not commit adultery**: Clearly, the *act itself* is condemned. God allows no justification for the ways that many often seek to justify extra-marital sex. It is not to be done, and when it is done, it is sin and it damages.

i. "For a man to have intercourse with another man's wife was considered as heinous sin against God as well as man, long before the law, in patriarchal times (Genesis 39:9)." (Cole)

ii. Because there are different punishments for adultery (Deuteronomy 22:22) and the seduction of a virgin woman (Exodus 22:16-17, Deuteronomy 22:23-29), adultery is distinguished from pre-marital sex in the Old Testament. Each is wrong, but wrong in sometimes-different ways.

iii. Some years ago, there was a Christian music industry singer named Michael English. He lost his recording contract and marriage over adultery with another Christian singer. Afterward he said of his adultery and its aftermath: "Maybe God allowed this to happen to make me see I needed some freedom." *No!*

b. **You shall not commit adultery**: The New Testament clearly condemns adultery: *Now the works of the flesh are evident, which are: adultery, fornication uncleanness, licentiousness...*(Galatians 5:19). The act is condemned, but not *only* the act itself.

i. More than the act itself, Jesus carefully explained the *heart* of this commandment. It prohibits us from looking *at a woman to lust for her,* where we commit adultery in our heart or mind, yet may not have the courage or opportunity to do the act (Matthew 5:27-30). We aren't innocent just because we didn't have the opportunity to sin the way we really wanted to.

ii. "As to the word adultery, *adulterium*, it has probably been derived from the words *ad alterius torum, to another's bed*; for it is *going to the bed of another man* that constitutes the *act* and the *crime*." (Clarke)

4. (15) The eighth commandment: **You shall not steal**.

"You shall not steal."

a. **Not steal**: This command is another important foundation for human society, establishing the right to personal property. God has clearly entrusted certain possessions to certain individuals, and other people or states are not permitted to take that property without due process of law.

b. **Not steal**: We can also steal from God. Of course, this demands we honor God with our financial resources so we are not guilty of robbing Him (Malachi 3:8-10). But we can also rob God by refusing to give Him ourselves for obedience and His service, because He bought us and owns us: *knowing that you were not redeemed with corruptible things, like silver or gold… but with the precious blood of Christ* (1 Peter 1:18-19)

i. 1 Corinthians 6:20 gives the same idea: *For you were bought at a price; therefore glorify God in your body and in your spirit, which are God's.*

c. **Not steal**: Ephesians 4:28 gives the solution to stealing. *Let him who stole steal no longer, but rather let him labor, working with his hands what is good, that he may have something to give him who has need.*

5. (16) The ninth commandment: **You shall not bear false witness**.

"You shall not bear false witness against your neighbor."

a. **You shall not bear false witness against your neighbor**: The primary sense of this command has to do with the legal process. Yet it is common to speak in an *informal* court, where what we say is taken seriously and truth or error matters for us and for others.

i. In an extended sense, we can break the ninth commandment through slander, tale bearing, creating false impressions, by silence, by questioning the motives behind someone's actions, or even by flattery.

ii. "Slander…is a lie invented and spread with intent to do harm. That is the worst form of injury a person can do to another. Compared to one who does this, a gangster is a gentleman, and a murderer is kind, because he ends life in a moment with a stroke and with little pain.

But the man guilty of slander ruins a reputation which may never be regained, and causes lifelong suffering." (Redpath)

iii. "Talebearing…is repeating a report about a person without careful investigation. Many, many times I have known what it is to suffer with that. To repeat a story which brings discredit and dishonor to another person without making sure of the facts, is breaking this commandment…How many people, especially Christian people, revel in this, and delight in working havoc by telling tales about others. To excuse the action by saying they believed the report to be true, or that there was no intention to malign, is no justification." (Redpath)

iv. Inappropriate *silence* may also break this command. "When someone utters a falsity about another and a third person is present who knows that statement to be untrue but, for reasons of fear or being disliked, remains quiet, that third person is as guilty of breaking this law as if he had told a lie." (Redpath)

v. "Neither bear it, nor hear it; raise, nor receive wrong reports of another; [do not] make a lie, nor love it when it is made." (Trapp)

b. **You shall not bear false witness against your neighbor**: The New Testament puts it simply. *Do not lie to one another, since you have put off the old man with his deeds* (Colossians 3:9). Lying and false representations belong to the old man, not to the new life we have in Jesus.

i. "How very strange that we have ever come to think that Christian maturity is shown by the ability to speak our minds, whereas it is really expressed in controlling our tongues." (Redpath)

ii. "What a startling revelation it would be if a tape recording could be played of all that every church member has said about his fellow members in one week!" (Redpath)

iii. Satan is always there to encourage a lie (John 8:44; Acts 5:3); and Jesus Himself was the victim of *false witness* (Mark 14:57); in some ways, we might say this was the sin that sent Jesus to the cross.

6. (17) The tenth commandment: **You shall not covet.**

"You shall not covet your neighbor's house; you shall not covet your neighbor's wife, nor his male servant, nor his female servant, nor his ox, nor his donkey, nor anything that *is* your neighbor's."

a. **You shall not covet**: The first nine commands focus more on things we do; the tenth deals straight with the heart and its desires.

i. Literally, the word for **covet** here means, *to pant after.* "Hebrew *hamad*, 'desire', is in itself a neutral word. It is only when misdirected

to that which belongs to another that such 'desire' becomes wrong."
(Cole)

ii. Covetousness works like this: the eyes look upon an object, the
mind admires it, the will goes over to it, and the body moves in to
possess it. Just because you have not taken the final step does not
mean you are not in the process of coveting right now.

b. **Your neighbor's house...wife...ox...donkey**: Covetousness can be
expressed towards all sorts of things; it is the itch to have and to possess
what someone else has. It speaks of a dissatisfaction with what we have,
and a jealously towards those who have something better.

i. Hebrews 13:5 puts it well: *Let your conduct be without covetousness; be
content with such things as you have. For He Himself has said, "I will never
leave you nor forsake you."*

ii. This last commandment is closely connected with the first
commandment against idolatry: *For this you know, that no... covetous
man, who is an idolater, has any inheritance in the kingdom of Christ and God*
(Ephesians 5:5).

iii. Jesus gave a special warning about covetousness, which explained
the core philosophy of the covetous heart: *And He said to them, "Take
heed and beware of covetousness, for one's life does not consist in the abundance of
the things he possesses."* (Luke 12:15)

C. The nation's great fear of the presence of God.

1. (18) The people stand afar off.

**Now all the people witnessed the thunderings, the lightning flashes, the
sound of the trumpet, and the mountain smoking; and when the people
saw *it*, they trembled and stood afar off.**

a. **All the people witnessed the thunderings, the lightning**: Awesome
sights and sounds came from Mount Sinai together with the speaking of
the law. All of the phenomena together made for an overwhelming scene.

i. **Lightning flashes**: "The word here is unusual and might be
translated 'torches', meaning 'flashes' or 'fireballs'. This is the same
word used for the symbol of God's presence that Abraham sees at
the making of God's covenant with him (Genesis 15)." (Cole)

ii. **The mountain smoking**: Deuteronomy 5:23 explains why the
mountain smoked; it says *the mountain was burning with fire*.

b. **They trembled and stood afar off**: The awe of all the phenomena
did nothing to draw the people closer to God; it only made them stand
afar off.

2. (19) The request of the people.

Then they said to Moses, "You speak with us, and we will hear; but let not God speak with us, lest we die."

a. **Let not God speak with us**: One might think that Israel loved the dramatic experience at Mount Sinai, and especially the honor of hearing God's voice like a loudspeaker from heaven. Instead, because of the great awe and dread they felt, they *wanted God to stop* speaking to them directly.

i. Biblically speaking, an up-close encounter with God could just as often be *troubling* as it might be comforting. Israel could not see, feel, and hear this much from God, and not at the same time be acutely aware that *He* is perfect and holy and *they* were not.

ii. This was a typical reaction of those who came into the presence of God, such as Isaiah who felt *undone* before God (Isaiah 6:1-5) and John who fell as a dead man before the Lord (Revelation 1:17).

iii. "What Israel dreaded, Moses coveted (Exodus 33:18)." (Cole)

b. **You speak with us, and we will hear**: The people promised to hear and (by implication) obey the Word of God that came to them by Moses. They failed in this promise, both soon after this and in the longer term.

i. In following generations, Israel interpreted the law downward so it could be more easily obeyed, removing the *heart* and *intent* of the law. Jesus exposed this shallow understanding of the law in His Sermon on the Mount (Matthew 5:17-48). This progressed to the point where Saul of Tarsus could say and mean of himself, *concerning the righteousness which is in the law,* [I was counted] *blameless* (Philippians 3:6).

c. **Let not God speak with us, lest we die**: In drawing back from direct dealing with God, Israel wanted Moses to be their mediator, fearing death if they did not have a mediator.

i. Man's desire for a mediator - someone to act as a go-between with us and God - is only good if it is fulfilled in Jesus Christ, *for there is one God and one Mediator between God and men, the Man Christ Jesus* (1 Timothy 2:5).

3. (20) The purpose for this fear.

And Moses said to the people, "Do not fear; for God has come to test you, and that His fear may be before you, so that you may not sin."

a. **Do not fear; for God has come to test you**: The people of Israel wanted to separate themselves from the manifest presence of God, but God meant it for good to **test** them.

- The **test** revealed to them what kind of God they served: a God above nature, personal, good, and holy

- The **test** revealed to them what God's expectations were; that God is a moral God who expects moral behavior from His people
- The **test** revealed to them their own weakness and need for God's grace, help, and rescue

b. **That His fear may be before you**: This distinguishes between two kinds of fear. **Do not fear** speaks of the tormenting fear that comes from both guilt and danger. **That His fear may be before you** speaks of the attitude of honor and reverence that leads to respect and obedience.

i. *"Fear not.* And yet fear." (Trapp)

ii. Though it is better to obey God out of **fear** than to disobey Him, God's ultimate motivation for obedience is love. This is clear from 1 John 4:18-19: *There is no fear in love; but perfect love casts out fear, because fear involves torment. But he who fears has not been made perfect in love. We love Him because He first loved us.*

c. **So that you may not sin**: Israel did not learn this lesson well. In approximately 40 days, they danced around a gold calf with both idolatry and immorality (Exodus 32).

4. (21) Moses draws near.

So the people stood afar off, but Moses drew near the thick darkness where God *was.*

a. **So the people stood afar off, but Moses drew near**: Israel dreaded the powerful presence of God, but Moses longed for it. Moses would later more directly and eloquently show this desire (Exodus 33).

i. Moses had a relationship with God the common man in Israel did not have. Through the circumstances of his life and the direct revelation of God, Moses was aware of both God's holy power and also of God's glorious grace.

b. **Moses drew near the thick darkness where God was**: It wasn't that Moses was a flawless saint. *Moses was a murderer* who had been forgiven and restored by God. Moses knew what it meant to connect with God on the ground of *grace*, not what one deserved.

E. Laws concerning worship and altars.

1. (22-23) The purity of worship.

Then the LORD said to Moses, "Thus you shall say to the children of Israel: 'You have seen that I have talked with you from heaven. You shall not make *anything to be* with Me; gods of silver or gods of gold you shall not make for yourselves.'"

a. **You have seen that I have talked with you from heaven**: This makes it perfectly clear that *God spoke the Ten Commandments to Israel* **from heaven**. This happened at Mount Sinai, but God spoke from heaven.

b. **You shall not make anything to be with Me; gods of silver or gods of gold**: Because God did not reveal Himself to Israel in any *form* or *image*, they were not to make any other god of silver or gold to set beside (**be with Me**) God.

2. (24-26) Instructions for altars and sacrifice.

"'An altar of earth you shall make for Me, and you shall sacrifice on it your burnt offerings and your peace offerings, your sheep and your oxen. In every place where I record My name I will come to you, and I will bless you. And if you make Me an altar of stone, you shall not build it of hewn stone; for if you use your tool on it, you have profaned it. Nor shall you go up by steps to My altar, that your nakedness may not be exposed on it.'"

a. **An altar of earth you shall make for Me**: As God began this expanded section of His law for Israel, *the first law* mentioned had to do with sacrifice and atonement. This was in expectation that Israel would break the laws God gave them, and need to atone for their sin by sacrifice, all with a view to the ultimate sacrifice God would ultimately provide.

i. Our word **altar** comes from the Latin *altus*, meaning *high or elevated*, because altars were raised to give them prominence and dignity. Yet the Hebrew word for **altar** (*mizbach*) has the sense of a place of sacrifice or killing, coming from the Hebrew word *to kill*.

ii. **An altar of earth**: "In opposition to the costly shrines and services of those dunghill deities." (Trapp) God did not need an ornate or elaborate altar; **an altar of earth** was sufficient. With God's ultimate altar, a few wooden beams were sufficient.

b. **You shall sacrifice on it your burnt offerings and your peace offerings**: The distinction between **burnt offerings** and **peace offerings** was given later in greater detail. Yet the mere mention of them at the outset of the giving of the law indicates that man cannot keep the law, and must have sacrifice to deal with this inability.

c. **I will come to you, and I will bless you**: This wonderful promise was made in the context of *sacrifice* and *atonement*. Even in the Law of Moses, God often made the connection between trust in atoning sacrifice and the presence and blessing of God.

i. Though there was blessing in keeping the law, we ultimately are only blessed by the law if we keep the entire law - therefore we seek and find blessing from God on the basis of His atoning sacrifice.

d. **You shall not build it of hewn stone**: If an altar were made of stone, it was possible or even likely that attention would be drawn and glory would be given to the stone carver. God, at His altar, wanted to share glory with no man - the beauty and attractiveness would be found only in the provision of God, not in any fleshly display.

i. **If you use your tool on it, you have profaned it**: "Not polished it. So in preaching (1 Corinthians 2:4-5). Some mar all by over-doing." (Trapp)

e. **Nor shall you go up by steps**: God wanted *no* display of human flesh at His place of covering sacrifice. Steps might allow the leg of the priest to be seen. God doesn't want to see our flesh in worship.

i. What God *does* want from us in worship is seen by Jesus' statement in John 4:24: *God is Spirit, and those who worship Him must worship in spirit and truth*. God wants worship that is characterized by *Spirit* (as opposed to flesh) and *truth* (as opposed to deception or mere feeling).

ii. "Later on, when altars with steps were allowed to be built (Leviticus 9:22; Ezekiel 43:13-17), the priests were instructed to wear linen undershorts (Exodus 28:40-42; Ezekiel 44:18)." (Kaiser)

Exodus 21 - Laws To Direct Judges

A. Laws regarding servitude.

1. (1) **These are the judgments**.

"Now these *are* the judgments which you shall set before them:

a. **Now these are the judgments**: Exodus Chapters 21-23 contain many laws on a wide variety of subjects including:

- Employment law regarding the treatment of servants
- Murder, manslaughter, and violent assault
- Liability for one's animals and responsibility for the animals of others
- Theft, responsibility, and restitution
- Rape, dowry, and the value of a woman's virginity
- Idolatry and sorcery
- Treatment of disadvantaged people in society
- Money and property lending
- Justice and equal standing before the law

i. "THESE different regulations are as remarkable for their justice and prudence as for their humanity. Their great tendency is to show the valuableness of human life, and the necessity of having peace and good understanding in every neighbourhood; and they possess that quality which should be the object of all good and wholesome laws-the *prevention of crimes*." (Adam Clarke)

b. **Which you shall set before them**: The wide-ranging character of these laws show that God gave them both for the laws in themselves, but also for the principles and precedent they would establish for the judges appointed by Moses.

i. "These 'laws,' or, better, 'judgments' (*mispatim*), are given as precedents to guide Israel's civil magistrates in the cases of civil dispute." (Kaiser)

2. (2-4) The general law concerning Hebrew slaves (indentured servants).

"If you buy a Hebrew servant, he shall serve six years; and in the seventh he shall go out free and pay nothing. If he comes in by himself, he shall go out by himself; if he *comes in* married, then his wife shall go out with him. If his master has given him a wife, and she has borne him sons or daughters, the wife and her children shall be her master's, and he shall go out by himself."

a. **If you buy a Hebrew servant**: With ancient Israel, as in the *entire* ancient world, there were people who worked for others on the principle of servitude. They were *slaves* in some sense, though not necessarily in the brutal and degraded sense most think of slavery.

   i. Some think that the Bible is *responsible* for slavery. The opposite is true; slavery existed long before Israel or Moses. The Bible is responsible for the *elimination* of slavery, not its establishment.

   ii. "Moses did not institute slavery in any shape; the laws concerning it were made on purpose to repress it, to confine it within very narrow bounds, and ultimately to put an end to it." (Spurgeon)

   iii. "The Torah accepts slavery as an inevitable part of ancient society, much as Paul did, but the new humanitarian approach will ultimately be the death-knell of slavery...In any case, slavery in Israel was rural, domestic and small scale." (Cole)

   iv. It is significant that the *first words* of this section of law in the Book of Exodus show that God wanted Israel to respect the rights and dignity of servants. "The first words of God from Sinai had declared that He was Jehovah Who brought them out of slavery. And in this remarkable code, the first person whose rights are dealt with is the slave." (Chadwick)

b. **A Hebrew servant**: There were four basic ways a Hebrew might become a slave to another Hebrew:

- In extreme poverty, they might sell their liberty (Leviticus 25:39)
- A father might sell a daughter as a servant into a home with the intention that she would eventually marry into that family (Exodus 21:7)
- In the case of bankruptcy, a man might become servant to his creditors (2 Kings 4:1)
- If a thief had nothing with which to pay proper restitution (Exodus 22:3-4)

   i. The ideas of *man-stealing* and life-long servitude – the concepts many have of slavery – simply do not apply to the practice of slavery in the Old Testament. Normally, slavery was:

- Chosen or mutually arranged
- Of limited duration
- Highly regulated

c. **He shall serve six years; and in the seventh he shall go out free and pay nothing**: In all of the four above-mentioned cases, the servitude was never obligated to be life-long. The Hebrew servant worked for **six years** and then was set **free**.

> i. "He was, more properly an 'indentured labourer', bound for *six years*." (Cole)

> ii. "That this servitude could extend, at the utmost, only to *six* years; and that it was nearly the same as in some cases of *apprenticeship* among us." (Clarke)

> iii. G. Campbell Morgan, after looking at the laws regarding slavery, wrote: "A careful consideration of them will show that they abolished slavery, and substituted for it, covenanted labour."

> iv. "Henceforward the condition of slaves among the Hebrew people would be in marked distinction to slavery as existing among other peoples. It was the beginning of a great moral movement." (Morgan)

d. **If he comes in by himself, he shall go out by himself; if he *comes in* married, then his wife shall go out with him**: At the end of the six years, the servant went out with what he came in with. If the master provided a wife (and therefore children), the wife and children had to stay with the master until they had fulfilled their obligations or could be redeemed.

> i. **By himself**: "Literally 'with his back', *i.e.* 'bare back and nothing more'. The phrase is vivid and unique, but the meaning is clear. This provision may seem hard to us, but the wife was presumably a perpetual slave, and therefore the master's own property." (Cole)

3. (5-6) The bond-slave: a willing slave for life.

"But if the servant plainly says, 'I love my master, my wife, and my children; I will not go out free,' then his master shall bring him to the judges. He shall also bring him to the door, or to the doorpost, and his master shall pierce his ear with an awl; and he shall serve him forever."

a. **But if the servant plainly says, "I love my master"**: If after the six years of servitude, a servant wished to make a life-long commitment to his master - in light of the master's goodness and his blessings for the servant - he could, through this ceremony, make a life-long commitment to his master.

i. This commitment was not motivated by debt or obligation, only by love for the master, and the good things that the master had provided for the servant.

b. **His master shall bring him to the judges**: This describes the public and recognized ceremony for recognizing a *willing* slave, one who had fulfilled his obligation yet still wanted to serve his master out of **love**.

i. "The 'judges' changed the slave's status from temporary to permanent by a ceremony at the doorpost of the master's house." (Kaiser)

c. **His master shall pierce his ear with an awl**: In the ceremony, the servant's ear was pierced - opened - with an awl. This was done in the presence of witnesses, and then **he shall serve him forever**.

i. It's a remarkable thing to think of this ceremony being carried out. A servant said, "I know I have fulfilled my *obligations* to my master, and I have served what I have owed. Yet I love my master and am so grateful for what he has given that I will gladly obligate myself for life, not out of debt or shame or defeat, but out of love."

ii. Psalm 40:6 later spoke of this ceremony taking place between the Father and the Son, where the Psalmist spoke prophetically for the Messiah: *Sacrifice and offering You did not desire; my ears You have opened.* Jesus was a perfect bond-slave to the Father (Philippians 2:7).

iii. "That awl represents the nail that affixed Christ to the cross, and we must expect it in every true act of consecration." (Meyer)

d. **He shall serve him forever**: Jesus gave us the right to be called *friends* instead of *servants* (John 15:15). Yet the writers of the New Testament found plenty of glory in simply being considered *bondservants* of Jesus (Romans 1:1, James 1:1, 2 Peter 1:1, Jude 1:1).

i. Pagans had a custom of branding the slave with the name or the sign of the owner. Paul referred to himself as just such a slave in Galatians 6:17: *From now on, let no one trouble me, for I bear in my body the marks of the Lord Jesus.* Paul was a slave for life to Jesus.

ii. *This is a picture of the sinner's service of sin*; there comes a place where the sinner, so filled with a love of his sin, seals his heart over to sin as his master.

iii. *This is a picture of our service to Jesus.*

- We have the power to go free if we want to
- We must be willing to take the consequences of chosen service
- We must be motivated by love for our Master

4. (7-11) The rights of female servants.

"And if a man sells his daughter to be a female slave, she shall not go out as the male slaves do. If she does not please her master, who has betrothed her to himself, then he shall let her be redeemed. He shall have no right to sell her to a foreign people, since he has dealt deceitfully with her. And if he has betrothed her to his son, he shall deal with her according to the custom of daughters. If he takes another *wife,* he shall not diminish her food, her clothing, and her marriage rights. And if he does not do these three for her, then she shall go out free, without *paying* money."

a. **If a man sells his daughter to be a female slave**: The matter described here seems to describe the selling of a young female as a slave to a family with the intention of marriage. This is why the text explained, **who has betrothed her to himself.**

i. "Refers to a girl who is sold by her father, not for slavery, but for marriage." (Kaiser)

ii. "Probably the origin of the custom was the same in either case: to avoid paying a higher bride-price at a later age, and to rear the future daughter-in-law within the family, ensuring that she 'fitted in'. Such an attitude to slaves abolishes slavery, except in name." (Cole)

iii. In ancient societies (including sometimes among the Hebrews), a child might be sold as a slave in light of a debt or; especially in the case of **a female slave**, in a dowry arrangement to satisfy a debt. Such arrangements were more of what we associate with *indentured servitude* than *slavery*. Yet, these are not the circumstances regarding this particular law.

b. **He shall let her be redeemed**: If her master did not marry her or decided not to give her to his son, the master was still obligated to respect her rights under God's law. He had to treat her well and give her the opportunity to escape the obligation of servitude.

i. "Should the terms of marriage not be fulfilled, it is to be considered a breach of contract, and the purchaser must allow the girl to be redeemed." (Kaiser)

ii. **No right to sell her to a foreign people**: "Even if he has wearied of her, he cannot sell her to another master: that would be a breach of marriage obligation to her." (Cole)

c. **He shall not diminish her food, her clothing, and her marriage rights**: If the girl received into the home with the expectation of future marriage did not work out, she was not to be treated poorly. She was not to be deprived the comforts of the home; instead she must be treated

according to the custom of daughters – treated like a daughter, not a slave.

> i. "The word translated *food* should perhaps be rendered 'meat': it means, say the commentators, the wife's fair share of luxuries, not mere subsistence allowance, which any slave would get." (Cole)

d. **Then she shall go out free, without paying money**: If the household failed in their obligations toward the girl received into the home with the expectation of future marriage, she was granted freedom. These were remarkable protections of ones who might be disadvantaged.

> i. The girl in this circumstance – out of her birth home, released by her natural parents – had no natural protector in that society. God directed the judges of Israel to be her protector.

> ii. Thus, "The right of a parent to sell his daughter was carefully guarded against abuse." (Thomas)

B. Laws regarding violence and disability.

1. (12-14) Appropriate punishment for both murder and manslaughter.

"He who strikes a man so that he dies shall surely be put to death. However, if he did not lie in wait, but God delivered *him* into his hand, then I will appoint for you a place where he may flee. But if a man acts with premeditation against his neighbor, to kill him by treachery, you shall take him from My altar, that he may die."

a. **He who strikes a man so that he dies shall surely be put to death**: The principle for capital punishment goes back to Genesis 9:6: *Whoever sheds man's blood, by man his blood shall be shed; for in the image of God He made man.* The right for the state to use the sword of execution is also stated in the New Testament (Romans 13:3-4).

b. **If he did not lie in wait...if a man acts with premeditation**: God told the judges of Israel to look for evidence of **premeditation** and **treachery**. God did not place accidents or crimes of passion or neglect on the same plane as crimes of **premeditation** and **treachery**.

c. **You shall take him from My altar, that he may die**: The principle of punishing murderers is so important to God that He denied murderers refuge at His **altar**. According to almost universal custom in the ancient world, a religious altar was a place of sanctuary against justice or vengeance. An accused man might find safety if he could flee to an altar before he was apprehended.

> i. "The supplicant would catch hold of the projecting 'horns' of the altar (1 Kings 2:28). This was tantamount to dedicating himself

to YHWH, like any animal sacrifice bound with ropes to the altar horns." (Cole)

ii. Yet God told the judges of Israel there was to be no mercy in the sentencing of those guilty of the worst murders, what we might call first-degree murder. God said, "**You shall take him from My altar, that he may die.**" The murderer was to find no protection in misunderstood, misapplied faith.

iii. God said also that unpunished murderers defiled the land: *Moreover you shall take no ransom for the life of a murderer who is guilty of death, but he shall surely be put to death . . . So you shall not pollute the land where you are; for blood defiles the land, and no atonement can be made for the land, for the blood that is shed on it, except by the blood of him who shed it. Therefore do not defile the land which you inhabit, in the midst of which I dwell; for I the* LORD *dwell among the children of Israel.* (Numbers 35:31, 33-34)

iv. The principle that unpunished murderers defile a land is a sobering, humbling thought among Americans, where so many are murdered and few are brought to justice for those murders.

d. **Then I will appoint for you a place where he may flee**: Later (in Numbers 35 and Joshua 20), God commanded and Israel made cities of refuge (**a place where he may flee**). These were selected, prepared cities where one could flee in the case of manslaughter, and be protected until his case was properly heard.

i. "From the earliest times the nearest akin had a right to revenge the murder of his relation, and as this right was universally acknowledged, no law was ever made on the subject; but as this might be abused, and a person who had killed another *accidentally*, having had no previous malice against him, might be put to death by the *avenger of blood*, as the nearest kinsman was termed, therefore God provided the cities of refuge to which the accidental manslayer might flee till the affair was inquired into, and settled by the civil magistrate." (Clarke)

ii. This careful distinction between degrees of guilt and punishment in murder, and the protections for the one guilty of manslaughter as opposed to murder, show the sophistication and concern for justice in the principles given to Israelite judges.

2. (15-17) Laws concerning murder of a parent.

"And he who strikes his father or his mother shall surely be put to death. He who kidnaps a man and sells him, or if he is found in his hand, shall surely be put to death. And he who curses his father or his mother shall surely be put to death."

a. **He who strikes his father or mother: Strikes** must be taken in the context of Exodus 21:12, which says *He who strikes a man so that he dies*. A child who murdered, or attempted the murder of a parent, was to receive capital punishment.

b. **He who kidnaps a man and sells him, or if he is found in his hand, shall surely be put to death**: Kidnapping was also considered a capital offense. In the eyes of God, criminally enslaving a man was not far from murdering him.

> i. "Kidnapping for slavery was common in the ancient world" (Cole), and is here clearly prohibited.

> ii. This is a subtle yet important difference between slavery as it was (and is) commonly practiced and slavery as regulated in the Bible. Most slavery (ancient and modern) was actually a form of *kidnapping* – the taking and imprisoning of a person against their will. As regulated in the Bible (and as practiced in some other ancient cultures), slavery was received *willingly* (usually as payment for debt), or in the case of war, was an alternative to death. In ancient Israel, other cultures were not kidnapped and enslaved (as was the practice in the African slave trade).

> iii. The context and placement of this law is significant. "Kidnapping is not a property offense since no property offense draws a capital punishment, and this law is not listed under property laws. Instead, it is the theft of a human being." (Kaiser)

> iv. **Or if he is found in his hand** "should be translated 'and is caught with the money in his hand.' Unexpectedly large bank balances are still hard to explain to the Income Tax department of our own day." (Cole)

c. **He who curses his father or his mother shall surely be put to death**: The idea was of an adult child who *threatened* his parent. Though this law was severe, it preserved a critical foundation for civilized society: respect between generations.

> i. The idea of the curse here is more like what we would think of as a *death threat*. "Since to curse was to will and pray the downfall of the other with all one's heart, it represented the attitude from which sprang acts like striking or murder." (Cole)

> ii. The Law of Moses also had a built-in protection for the rights of the child, according to Deuteronomy 21:18-21. This passage states that the parent did not have the right to carry out this punishment, but they were required to bring the accused child before the elders and judges of the city. This meant that the parent - against all

contemporary custom - did *not* have the absolute power of life and death over their children. As a practical matter, the judges of Israel rarely, if ever, administered the death penalty in such cases, yet the child was held accountable.

iii. Yet the law discouraging conflict between generations is important. Each elder generation, as they grow older, is at the mercy of the younger generation. If the younger generation is allowed to carry on open warfare with the older generation, the very foundations of society are shaken – as reflected in the Fourth Commandment. Some modern laws – including developing laws regarding euthanasia – may lead to the easy murder of the older generation by the younger.

3. (18-19) Regarding compensation for personal injury.

"If men contend with each other, and one strikes the other with a stone or with *his* fist, and he does not die but is confined to *his* bed, if he rises again and walks about outside with his staff, then he who struck *him* shall be acquitted. He shall only pay *for* the loss of his time, and shall provide *for him* to be thoroughly healed."

a. **If men contend with each other, and one strikes the other**: If, because of a conflict, a man was unable to work (**is confined to his bed**) because of an injury received at the hand of another, the one who injured him must pay compensation to the man and his family.

i. These laws of compensation for personal injury have parallels in the Code of Hammurabi and in Hittite Laws.

b. **If he rises again and walks about outside with his staff**: However, if the man could recover from the injury, the guilty party was only required to pay for his medical recovery and for his lost time.

c. **And shall provide for him to be thoroughly healed**: Though these principles have been abused by the greedy in our modern day, the principles themselves still stand.

4. (20-21) Regarding the beating and death of a servant.

"And if a man beats his male or female servant with a rod, so that he dies under his hand, he shall surely be punished. Notwithstanding, if he remains alive a day or two, he shall not be punished; for he *is* his property."

a. **So that he dies under his hand, he shall surely be punished**: This shows that in ancient Israel, servants could be murdered. In many other cultures, the master was held blameless if he murdered a servant, because the servant was not considered a person.

i. "The great advance on ancient thinking is that the slave is considered here as a person." (Cole)

b. **Notwithstanding, if he remains alive a day or two, he shall not be punished**: Yet the master **not be punished** if the servant did not die immediately. Perhaps this was a way to determine intent, with the idea that if the servant lived for several days, it was an indication that the master must not have intended to murder him.

i. The idea was that if the victim did not die immediately, it was evidence that he was struck with the intention of discipline and not murder. Additionally, if the slave died through this unintentional attack, the loss of property was thought to be penalty enough to the master.

ii. Adam Clarke noted that this reflects a general principle in the Law of Moses: great consideration to the rights of the accused. "And all penal laws should be construed as favourably as possible to the accused." (Clarke)

iii. "The aim of this law was not to place the slave at the master's mercy but to restrict the master's power over him." (Kaiser)

c. **He shall surely be punished...he is his property**: These laws together paint a picture of the ideas behind slavery in ancient Israel. A servant was a *person* (who could not be murdered), yet they were also considered the **property** of the master, until their obligation was fulfilled.

i. **For he is his property:** "Is literally 'because he is his money.' The point is not that men are mere chattel...but that the owner has an investment in this slave that he stands to lose either by death...or by emancipation." (Kaiser)

ii. These principles paint a spiritual analogy. Spiritually speaking, we are the property *of whom we serve*. We are either slaves to Satan or to Jesus Christ.

5. (22-25) Laws of retribution.

"If men fight, and hurt a woman with child, so that she gives birth prematurely, yet no harm follows, he shall surely be punished accordingly as the woman's husband imposes on him; and he shall pay as the judges *determine*. But if *any* harm follows, then you shall give life for life, eye for eye, tooth for tooth, hand for hand, foot for foot, burn for burn, wound for wound, stripe for stripe."

a. **He shall surely be punished accordingly as the woman's husband imposes on him**: This is an example of a case of retribution, where a pregnant woman was injured in a conflict, and she gave birth prematurely. A penalty was only to be assessed if there was lasting damage.

i. If no lasting damage resulted, there are no damages awarded. Perhaps this was recognition that the law cannot address every loss or consequence, and that only *permanent* consequences are justly compensated.

b. **But if any harm follows**: If lasting damage resulted – short of death, which was covered by another law – there was retribution or restitution due.

i. "For the accidental assault, the offender must still pay some compensation, even though both mother and child survived….The fee would be set by the woman's husband and approved by a decision of the court." (Kaiser)

c. **But if any harm follows, then you shall give life for life, eye for eye**: If lasting damage resulted, the **eye for eye** principle always *limited* retribution. This law was meant to block man's natural desire for vengeance. It was not given as a license for revenge.

i. Our tendency is to want to do *more* against the offending party than what they did to us. This principle can apply to our modern practice of assessing huge punitive damages in lawsuits, and this law presents the principle that only the loss itself is to be compensated.

d. **You shall give life for life**: This principle leads some to wonder if, in ancient Israel, people were routinely killed for what we might consider accidental death or manslaughter. It's important to correlate this principle of **you shall give life for life** with Numbers 35:31, which allows a substitute ransom payment for loss of life that was not willful and premeditated murder.

i. Numbers 35:31: *Moreover you shall take no ransom for the life of a murderer who is guilty of death, but he shall surely be put to death.* This prohibition indicates that it *was* common practice to take ransom money for wrongful death in other circumstances.

ii. "Thus we conclude that the defendant must surrender to the deceased child's father or wife's husband the monetary value of each life if either or both were harmed." (Kaiser)

6. (26-27) The law of retribution as it regards masters and servants.

"If a man strikes the eye of his male or female servant, and destroys it, he shall let him go free for the sake of his eye. And if he knocks out the tooth of his male or female servant, he shall let him go free for the sake of his tooth."

a. **If a man strikes the eye of his male or female servant, and destroys it, he shall let him go free for the sake of his eye**: The principle of *eye for an eye* had a different application for servants. If injured by the master, the servant received something more precious than an eye - his freedom.

i. These laws don't try to make the master *feel* a certain way about his slave. Instead, the laws guide the behavior of the master, giving him incentive to protect and honor his slaves, treating them more like an employee than a work-animal.

b. **If he knocks out the tooth of his male or female servant, he shall let him go free**: "If this did not teach them *humanity*, it taught them *caution*, as one rash blow might have deprived them of all right to the future services of the slave; and this self-interest obliged them to be cautious and circumspect." (Clarke)

C. Laws regarding animal control and damage.

1. (28-32) Determining guilt when an animal kills a human.

"If an ox gores a man or a woman to death, then the ox shall surely be stoned, and its flesh shall not be eaten; but the owner of the ox *shall be* acquitted. But if the ox tended to thrust with its horn in times past, and it has been made known to his owner, and he has not kept it confined, so that it has killed a man or a woman, the ox shall be stoned and its owner also shall be put to death. If there is imposed on him a sum of money, then he shall pay to redeem his life, whatever is imposed on him. Whether it has gored a son or gored a daughter, according to this judgment it shall be done to him. If the ox gores a male or female servant, he shall give to their master thirty shekels of silver, and the ox shall be stoned."

a. **The ox shall surely be stoned...but the owner of the ox shall be acquitted**: This law illustrated the principle of *intent* and *neglect*. An owner of a man-killing ox could not be held guilty if the animal had no history of aggression towards people. Yet the animal must die, and the owner was forbidden to profit from the animal or its death (**its flesh shall not be eaten**). No one was to profit from or regard casually even accidental death.

i. "This means injury by oxen, since the Israelites kept no other animal that was capable of killing a human: horses were foreign luxuries." (Cole)

ii. "This served to keep up a due detestation of murder, whether committed by man or beast; and at the same time punished the man as far as possible, by the total loss of the beast." (Clarke)

b. **But if the ox tended to thrust with its horn in times past . . . the ox shall be stoned and its owner also shall be put to death**: Yet if an ox owner had an ox (or similar animal) whom he knew to be aggressive, and he failed to control the animal, he was guilty of murder and punished as such.

c. **If there is imposed on him a sum of money, then he shall pay to redeem his life**: It seems that if the survivors of the dead man accepted monetary restitution in lieu of the owner's death, this was an acceptable settlement.

d. **Whether it has gored a son or gored a daughter, according to this judgment it shall be done to him**: The same principles were applied in the death of a minor. They were regarded as people with rights to respect as well as adults.

e. **If the ox gores a male or female servant, he shall give to their master thirty shekels of silver**: If a servant was killed under such circumstances, the price of restitution was **thirty shekels of silver**, which was considered the price of a slave.

> i. "Even in Israel, a slave was still a man: his blood brings blood-guilt, like that of any other man." (Cole)

> ii. Significantly, this was the same price Jesus was sold for when Judas betrayed Him for thirty pieces of silver (Matthew 26:15).

2. (33-36) More laws regarding the principles of negligence and restitution.

"And if a man opens a pit, or if a man digs a pit and does not cover it, and an ox or a donkey falls in it, the owner of the pit shall make *it* good; he shall give money to their owner, but the dead *animal* shall be his. If one man's ox hurts another's, so that it dies, then they shall sell the live ox and divide the money from it; and the dead *ox* they shall also divide. Or if it was known that the ox tended to thrust in time past, and its owner has not kept it confined, he shall surely pay ox for ox, and the dead animal shall be his own."

a. **He shall give money to their owner, but the dead animal shall be his**: These laws communicate the principle of responsibility for the consequences of an individual's actions upon another. The example given had to do with necessary restitution when the digging of a pit caused the death of an animal.

> i. **If a man opens a pit**: "More likely for grain storage than water storage. Pits were also used as traps for animals (2 Samuel 23:20) or prisons for men (Genesis 37:24)." (Cole)

b. **If one man's ox hurts another's, so that it dies, then they shall sell the live ox and divide the money from it**: These laws required the investigation and analysis of judges so that the application of the law took into account findings of intent and negligence. There is a sense in which these are simply applications of the general principles of justice and fairness.

i. "To a struggling Israelite farmer, fair payment for the death of an ox might mean the difference between life and death, or at least between freedom and slavery for debt." (Cole)

Exodus 22 - More Laws to Direct Judges

A. Laws regarding personal property and restitution.

1. (1-4) Restitution required in cases of theft.

"If a man steals an ox or a sheep, and slaughters it or sells it, he shall restore five oxen for an ox and four sheep for a sheep. If the thief is found breaking in, and he is struck so that he dies, *there shall be* no guilt for his bloodshed. If the sun has risen on him, *there shall be* guilt for his bloodshed. He should make full restitution; if he has nothing, then he shall be sold for his theft. If the theft is certainly found alive in his hand, whether it is an ox or donkey or sheep, he shall restore double."

a. **If a man steals an ox or a sheep**: The command against theft was already stated in the Ten Commandments (Exodus 20:15). Here are more specific principles given to judges so they could apply that principle in the daily life and administration of justice among the people of Israel.

i. **Slaughters or sells**: "There is a heavier fine for this, since such action presumably shows deliberate intent to steal." (Cole)

b. **He shall restore**: The Mosaic Law did not send a person to jail because of theft. Instead, the thief was required to **restore** what he stole, plus an additional penalty.

i. In this passage, the penalty could be anywhere from 500% (**he shall restore five oxen for an ox**) to 200% (**he shall restore double**). "The reason for the fivefold penalty in the case of stealing an ox is probably because one man stole the means of another man's livelihood. The principle would extend to taking any of the man's plowing or cultivating implements." (Kaiser)

ii. This can be regarded as a *positive* approach to the punishment of criminals, putting them to productive restitution and compensating the victims of their theft. These principles are often ignored in the modern administration of justice.

iii. They are also, as a principle, ignored in many Christian lives. "This chapter is full of restitution, of which there is far too little in ordinary Christian life. We try to make amends for injury done to another by an extraordinary amount of civility; but we are reluctant in so many words to frankly confess that we have done wrong, and make proper reparation for the act or speech." (Meyer)

c. **He should make full restitution; if he has nothing, then he shall be sold for his theft**: If the person was unable to pay back what he stole, the thief was sold as an indentured laborer, with the money from the sale going to the victim.

d. **If the thief is found breaking in, and he is struck so that he dies, there shall be no guilt for his bloodshed. If the sun has risen on him, there shall be guilt for his bloodshed**: A property owner had the right to protect his property with force - but only with *reasonable* force. The assumption was that if it was daylight, the property owner had the ability to defend himself short of lethal force.

i. "It is typical of Israel's merciful law that even a thief has his rights." (Cole)

2. (5-8) Further application of the principle of restitution.

"If a man causes a field or vineyard to be grazed, and lets loose his animal, and it feeds in another man's field, he shall make restitution from the best of his own field and the best of his own vineyard. If fire breaks out and catches in thorns, so that stacked grain, standing grain, or the field is consumed, he who kindled the fire shall surely make restitution. If a man delivers to his neighbor money or articles to keep, and it is stolen out of the man's house, if the thief is found, he shall pay double. If the thief is not found, then the master of the house shall be brought to the judges *to see* whether he has put his hand into his neighbor's goods."

a. **If a man causes a field or vineyard to be grazed, and lets loose his animal, and it feeds in another man's field, he shall make restitution**: The owner of animals was responsible for the grazing of his animals. He was obliged to respect his neighbor's property (the grazing land).

i. "Thus men are held responsible, not only for the harm they *do*, but also for the harm they *occasion*, even though they may not have purposely designed the damage that ensued." (Kaiser)

ii. "We wrong another not only by what we do, or permit to be done, but in what we carelessly fail to do." (Meyer)

b. **He shall make restitution from the best of his own field and the best of his own vineyard**: This was a fair punishment, and significant enough to give a farmer a reason to *not* allow his animals to carelessly and destructively graze.

> i. "These laws also began by laying emphasis on the guilt of carelessness. The truth emphasized is that no man must live his life on the basis of selfishness or wholly alone and that wrong inflicted on neighbor by neighbor in the material realm becomes sin against God in the moral realm." (Morgan)

c. **He who kindled the fire shall surely make restitution**: Restitution was also required in cases of vandalism or foolish negligence, even if one kept the property of another. The Mosaic legal system had a high view of personal responsibility, even with the property of others.

> i. This translates into a proper concern for the property of others today. A Christian, if he backs into someone else's car, will certainly leave a note and make good the damage. A Christian will have proper insurance, guaranteeing he can compensate for someone else's loss.

> ii. If someone gives you something to hold for them, you are then responsible for it as a faithful steward or manager. This principle also includes what *God* gives us to manage or steward for Him.

d. **Shall surely make restitution...he shall pay double**: Restitution was paid according to a pre-determined amount or percentage; it was not left to the whim of either the victim or the judge.

3. (9-13) More application of the principle of restitution.

"For any kind of trespass, *whether it concerns* an ox, a donkey, a sheep, or clothing, *or* for any kind of lost thing which *another* claims to be his, the cause of both parties shall come before the judges; *and* whomever the judges condemn shall pay double to his neighbor. If a man delivers to his neighbor a donkey, an ox, a sheep, or any animal to keep, and it dies, is hurt, or driven away, no one seeing *it, then* an oath of the LORD shall be between them both, that he has not put his hand into his neighbor's goods; and the owner of it shall accept *that,* and he shall not make *it* good. But if, in fact, it is stolen from him, he shall make restitution to the owner of it. If it is torn to pieces *by a beast, then* he shall bring it as evidence, *and* he shall not make good what was torn."

a. **Any kind of lost thing which another claims to be his**: In the law of Israel, an owner did not lose ownership simply because the object was **lost**. If another found the object and the owner laid claim to it (with a dispute following), it was to be decided by judges.

i. "An object has been lost: the owner later sees a similar object in possession of his neighbor, and claims it as his own. The Israelites apparently did not follow the Anglo-Saxon dictum of 'finders are keepers': a lost object remains the possession of the original owner, who can claim it on sight." (Cole)

b. **The cause of both parties shall come before the judges; and whomever the judges condemn shall pay double**: If there was a dispute regarding the loss of property, the judges heard evidence, investigated, and decided who was right and who was wrong. The guilty party had to **pay double** restitution – whether they were the accused or the defendant. There was a *price* for false accusation or lawsuit.

i. **Before the judges**: "Hebrew, the gods: so judges are called, if good especially (Psalm 82:6). And the seat of judicature is called the holy place (Ecclesiastes 8:10)." (Trapp)

c. **If a man delivers to his neighbor a donkey, an ox, a sheep, or any animal to keep, and it dies, is hurt, or driven away, no one seeing it**: This law considers the situation when something suspicious happened – an animal in the care of another **dies, is hurt, or driven away**. Yet, it happened with no witnesses (**no one seeing it**). Shall the testimony of the accused be accepted in such cases?

d. **Then an oath of the LORD shall be between them both, that he has not put his hand into his neighbor's goods; and the owner of it shall accept that**: In such cases, the owner of the animal was obligated to **accept** the sworn testimony of the accused, unless there was evidence that gave reasonable doubt to the truthfulness of the accused.

i. This principle is the foundation of our idea that a *man is innocent until proven guilty*. In this case, the man's oath was taken as true unless proof to the contrary could be found.

ii. **He shall bring it as evidence**: "Production of the carcase would show that, while the shepherd could not prevent the kill, he was alert enough to stop the devouring of the prey." (Cole)

e. **The owner of it shall accept that**: Though the owner of the animal suffered loss, he was not allowed to compensate the loss by accusing and winning damages against an innocent party. He had to **accept** the outcome, even though justice left him uncompensated.

i. There is a parallel thought in the New Testament, that believers should avoid taking legal disputes among themselves to secular judges. They should allow the matter to be judged by the church (1 Corinthians 6:1-8).

4. (14-15) Restitution principles applied to borrowing and lending.

"And if a man borrows *anything* from his neighbor, and it becomes injured or dies, the owner of it not *being* with it, he shall surely make *it* good. If its owner *was* with it, he shall not make *it* good; if it *was* hired, it came for its hire."

a. **If a man borrows anything from his neighbor**: The principles of responsibility and restitution also applied to borrowing and lending.

b. **The owner of it not being with it...If its owner was with it**: The assumption was that if the owner was with the animal or tool (or whatever) as it was used by another, the owner was responsible for the care and use of the object while in his presence. If the owner was not present, the borrower was responsible.

c. **He shall surely make it good**: This was the simple principle meant to guide the judges. The guilty party had to **make it good**. Distinctions were to be made according to fairness and justice, not simply to reward whoever suffered loss. *Sometimes loss is suffered and no one is to blame.*

B. Moral and ceremonial laws.

1. (16-17) The remedy for pre-marital sex.

"If a man entices a virgin who is not betrothed, and lies with her, he shall surely pay the bride-price for her *to be* his wife. If her father utterly refuses to give her to him, he shall pay money according to the bride-price of virgins."

a. **If a man entices a virgin who is not betrothed**: Some claim this passage did not prohibit pre-marital sex; but it did prohibit (or at least strongly discourage) it in practice, because it required a man to either marry or provide for a woman he had pre-marital sex with.

i. **Virgin**: The Hebrew (*betulah*) "Was an unmarried girl who was always presumed to be a virgin." (Kaiser)

ii. **Entice a virgin**: "Hebrew, over-persuade with her by fair words, which make fools fain." (Trapp)

b. **He shall surely pay the bride-price for her to be his wife**: This law emphasized the principle that there is no such thing as *casual* sex. Both Old and New Testaments state that sexual relations carry lasting consequences (1 Corinthians 6:15-16).

i. "This was an exceedingly wise and humane law, and must have operated powerfully against seduction and fornication; because the person who might feel inclined to take the advantage of a young woman knew that he must marry her, and give her a dowry." (Clarke).

ii. This law encouraged both men and women to value the virginity of a woman. "Since a man has taken a girl without paying bride-price, bride-price he must pay, for who else will pay it now?" (Cole) It's not that the virginity of men was worthless or ignored; yet the law encouraged greater care and preservation for the virginity of women until marriage and the advantageous circumstances for child raising.

iii. It is to the great detriment of society and culture when the government works _against_ the value of virginity, and (intentionally or not) supports behavior that doesn't value it or promotes the cheapening of virginity and abstinence until marriage.

iv. A man illustrated the value of virginity with a true story about a friend who owned an antique store and had a table for sale. The table was worth $600, but was marked down to $300. A man tried to bargain her down to $200, and not only did she refuse, but she realized the true value of the table, and upped the price to its true worth - even when offered $300. The man finally bought the table for $600, and certainly treated it like a $600 table - because its worth had been recognized and fought for. Some women who know men treat them shabbily contribute to the problem by selling themselves cheaply.

c. **If her father utterly refuses to give her to him, he shall pay money according to the bride-price of virgins**: If the man who took advantage of the woman was considered a completely unacceptable husband by the **father** of the wronged woman, then that man had to **pay** the dowry _without_ receiving the bride. This was a strong incentive against taking advantage of young women.

d. **He shall pay money**: This brief presentation of the law gave no penalty to the woman involved. This was because she was thought to be disadvantaged (**if a man entices a virgin**) and needed to be recompensed. If she was not taken advantage of, then the loss of her virginity and the diminution of her marriage prospects was thought to be punishment enough.

i. "This one consideration was a powerful curb on disorderly passions, and must tend greatly to render marriages respectable, and prevent all crimes of this nature." (Cole)

2. (18-20) Three capital crimes.

"You shall not permit a sorceress to live. Whoever lies with an animal shall surely be put to death. He who sacrifices to _any_ god, except to the Lord only, he shall be utterly destroyed."

a. **A sorceress**: Among the ancients, the practice of sorcery had two associations. First, contact with dark or demonic powers or persons.

Second, altered states through drugs and potions. There was understood to be a connection between drug taking and occultist practices.

i. The law shows that such communication is *possible*, and the penalty shows that it is *dangerous*.

ii. The King James Version translates **sorceress** as *witch*. "An enchantress, sorceress, whose help was sometimes sought in enticing young maids to folly. The man-witch is also here meant, but the woman-witch mentioned; both because women are more inclinable to that sin; and also because the weaker sex is not to be spared for this fault." (Trapp)

iii. Taking this noun **sorceress**, the "verb is to use incantations, magic, sorcery, or the arts of witchcraft. Our English 'witch' is alleged to have come from 'to wit,' i.e., 'to know,' in the adjectival *wittigh* or *wittich*, contracted to witch. The Greeks rendered our word by *pharmakos* ('poisoners'), since sorcerers dealt in drugs and pharmaceutical potions." (Kaiser)

iv. "Many of the Israelites had, no doubt, learned these curious arts from their long residence with the Egyptians; and so much were the Israelites attached to them, that we find such arts in repute among them, and various practices of this kind prevailed through the whole of the Jewish history, notwithstanding the offence was capital, and in all cases punished with *death*." (Clarke)

v. "It is clearly against the will of God that in this life men should hold any communication with the spirit world, save that of direct fellowship with Himself, through His Son, by the Holy Spirit." (Morgan)

b. **You shall not permit a sorceress to live**: This was considered a severe enough threat that sorcery was considered a capital crime. This combination of occult practices and drug-induced altered states was seen as destructive to the culture and moral fabric of ancient Israel.

i. "Thus with blunt directness and complete finality, the law of God against all traffic with the world of evil spirits was promulgated." (Morgan)

ii. "Witchcraft is equally condemned in New Testament days (Acts 13:10; 19:19), but in spite of the practices of the church in the Middle Ages, there is no hint in the New Testament that mediums or witches should be put to death." (Cole)

iii. **Shall utterly be destroyed**: This uses the ancient Hebrew word *herem*. "*Herem* is something devoted to God; however, it is not a voluntary but an involuntary dedication. It is now set apart to be banned from the earth." (Kaiser)

c. **Whoever lies with an animal shall surely be put to death**: Bestiality was practiced in the ancient world, and here God commanded specifically against it.

i. "This offensive sex act apparently was prevalent among the Canaanites." (Kaiser) "Bestiality was not only an obvious perversion: it figured so often in the Canaanite cycle 'Tales of Baal' that it probably had a religious significance for the Canaanites." (Cole)

ii. It is surprising to some that bestiality is legal in some European nations, and a subculture practices and promotes it. Yet there should be no surprise; if God's standard is rejected in one area of sexual morality, then the standards are often left up to the individual to decide. It is Christian civilization and morality that has discouraged and condemned fornication, adultery, pedophilia, polygamy, prostitution, homosexuality, gender confusion and the like. As Christian civilization and morality are increasingly mocked and rejected, it is no surprise that *all* of these sexual practices are increasingly practiced, supported, and encouraged.

iii. Some years ago, a student group at a university responded to the school's sponsorship of GLAD (Gay/Lesbian Awareness Days), with a mocking parody they called BAD (Bestiality Awareness Days). University administration did not allow them to promote or carry out their parody celebration; but there was no *rational* reason to prohibit this apart from a Biblical foundation for morality.

iv. If the moral measure for a sexual act is, *If it feels good, do it* – then there is no moral measure, and the culture will become increasingly depraved until this changes.

d. **He who sacrifices to any god, except to the LORD only, he shall be utterly destroyed**: In ancient Israel, it was strictly prohibited to sacrifice to the pagan gods. This law was often broken, and this penalty was rarely applied. One rare example of its application was when Elijah executed the prophets of Baal in 1 Kings 18:40.

3. (21) Compassion for the stranger.

"You shall neither mistreat a stranger nor oppress him, for you were strangers in the land of Egypt."

a. **You shall neither mistreat a stranger nor oppress him**: A good measure of our moral character is found in how we treat **a stranger**. People often find it easy to treat their own flesh and blood well, but God commands us to have a concern for others - including the **stranger**.

i. The enduring hatred and strife between ethnic and national groups shows just how little humanity has progressed.

ii. It is fair to examine how accommodating are we to the strangers among us. If we stay with our own safe group and enjoy all the blessings, and fail to be outreaching and out-looking as a blessing to others, we **mistreat a stranger**.

b. **For you were strangers in the land of Egypt**: Israel's own experience of being **strangers** should have given them appropriate sympathy for strangers in their midst.

i. God's command that there be kindness and good treatment towards the **stranger** does not mean that it is not good or fitting that strangers receive *permission* to live among a new community. The people of Israel **were strangers in the land of Egypt**, but at the express invitation of Pharaoh (Genesis 47:5-6). Israel *was not* welcomed into Canaan, and their coming was rightly regarded as a war of conquest. Governments have the right and responsibility to control borders and immigration; yet there is no doubt of the individual's responsibility to **neither mistreat a stranger nor oppress him**.

4. (22-24) Compassion for the weak and vulnerable.

"You shall not afflict any widow or fatherless child. If you afflict them in any way, *and* they cry at all to Me, I will surely hear their cry; and My wrath will become hot, and I will kill you with the sword; your wives shall be widows, and your children fatherless."

a. **You shall not afflict any widow or fatherless child**: The **widow** and **fatherless child** were the weakest and most vulnerable members of society. In an unrestrained, survival-of-the-fittest society, they would be the first to suffer abuse and destruction. God here commanded that at the very least, they *not* be afflicted.

i. "It was the prophets who chided Israel for their neglect in this area of oppressing the poor and the weak." (Kaiser)

b. **I will kill you with the sword**: Because of their special vulnerability, God commanded a special care and concern for them, promising to protect them.

i. "The society that lacks social justice will itself come under God's judgment." (Cole)

5. (25-27) Compassion for the poor.

"If you lend money to *any of* My people *who are* poor among you, you shall not be like a moneylender to him; you shall not charge him interest. If you ever take your neighbor's garment as a pledge, you

shall return it to him before the sun goes down. For that *is* his only covering, it *is* his garment for his skin. What will he sleep in? And it will be that when he cries to Me, I will hear, for I *am* gracious."

a. **If you lend money to any of My people who are poor among you, you shall not be like a moneylender to him**: Interest was prohibited on loans made to the poor and the taking of collateral had to be reasonable.

i. "The reason for the prohibition is presumably that the poor man borrows in his need. The loan is seen as assistance to a neighbor, and to make money from his need would be immoral." (Cole)

ii. This only prohibited the taking of interest on loans for relief of the poor. Adam Clarke said of the word translated **interest**: "*Neshech*, from *nashach*, to *bite, cut,* or *pierce* with the *teeth; biting usury.* So the Latins call it *usura vorax, devouring usury*… Perhaps *usury* may be more properly defined *unlawful interest*, receiving more for the loan of money than it is really worth, and more than the law allows." Trapp commented on the word **interest**: "Hebrew, Biting usury."

iii. "The prohibition against interest was written with the poor in mind. Commercial loans were not explicitly banned because they were not considered. Out of sixteen biblical passages dealing with loans (but not with interest), not one deals with a commercial loan. Commercial loans simply did not come under the biblical purview." (Gamoran, cited in Kaiser)

b. **If you ever take your neighbor's garment as a pledge**: The fact that one's garment could be used as collateral (under regulated circumstances) shows that these were *loans*, with repayment expected and secured with collateral. They were not gifts, but loans.

i. "Retaining one's outer garment (used as temporary collateral) overnight was strictly forbidden, for even an interest-free loan apparently required some type of pledge or security." (Kaiser)

c. **And it will be that when he cries to Me, I will hear**: God promised to hear the prayer of the poor man when he cried out to the Lord. God's general sympathy for the poor is reflected in the fact that Jesus came from a poor family. When He was dedicated in the temple, shortly after His birth, the sacrifice was that of a poor family: two birds (Luke 2:24).

6. (28-31) Laws regarding holiness and separation unto God.

"You shall not revile God, nor curse a ruler of your people. You shall not delay *to offer* the first of your ripe produce and your juices. The firstborn of your sons you shall give to Me. Likewise you shall do with your oxen *and* your sheep. It shall be with its mother seven days; on the eighth day you shall give it to Me. And you shall be holy men to Me:

you shall not eat meat torn *by beasts* in the field; you shall throw it to the dogs."

a. **You shall not revile God, nor curse a ruler of your people**: The most basic measure of holiness is what we *say*. God cares how we talk about Him and those in rightful authority over us.

> i. According to Clarke and others, the context shows that **God** (*elohim*) here is a reference to *judges*. There were laws against blaspheming God, but here – combined with **nor curse a ruler of your people** – suggests that *elohim* here refers to Israel's legal judges, as it sometimes does (Exodus 22:9, Psalm 82:6).

> ii. "This is the famous verse quoted by Paul at his trial before the high priest (Acts 23:5)." (Cole)

b. **You shall not delay to offer the first of your ripe produce and your juices**: Another way to honor God is by giving Him his due. When we are commanded to give something to God, it is a sin to not give it – or to **delay** in giving it.

> i. "True obedience is prompt and present, ready and speedy, without demurs and consults." (Trapp)

c. **The firstborn of your sons you shall give to Me**: According to Exodus 13:11-12, this command was to be obeyed *when they came into the land of Canaan*. Much of the Mosaic Law didn't make sense for Israel in the wilderness, and was given to prepare them for life in Canaan.

> i. Had they obeyed and trusted God the way they should have, they were at this point only a little more than a year away from Canaan. Because of unbelief and disobedience, they were some 40 years from Canaan, but they didn't know that at this giving of the law.

d. **The firstborn of your sons you shall give to Me**: This was done through *redemption*, the giving of money to substitute for the son (Exodus 34:19-20). Money was also substituted for the firstborn among unclean animals, but the firstborn among clean animals was sacrificed to the LORD.

> i. This law regarding the given of the firstborn to God was important because:

> - Since the firstborn was always regarded as best, it was a demonstrated way to give the best to God
> - It reminded Israel that God regarded them as His firstborn, His favored people
> - It reminded Israel that God spared their firstborn when He judged the firstborn of Egypt

e. **And you shall be holy men to Me: you shall not eat meat torn by beasts in the field**: This was a command to act differently than the animals, who freely scavenge dead carcasses. God called Israel to be **holy men**, not to act like scavengers who tear at carcasses as animals. This reinforces the basic idea of holiness: that we are set apart, different.

i. Kaiser adds two more thoughts: "Animals killed by another were unclean for two reasons: (1) the carnivorous beasts that tore it were unclean, and (2) the blood of such a slain animal would remain in its tissues, leaving it unclean. Instead, the people were to toss that meat to the dogs."

ii. "In the conclusion of this chapter we see the grand reason of all the ordinances and laws which it contains. No command was issued merely from the *sovereignty* of God. He gave them to the people as restraints on disorderly passions, and incentives to holiness; and hence he says, *Ye shall be holy men unto me.*" (Clarke)

Exodus 23 - More Laws Directed to Judges

A. Laws promoting justice.

1. (1-3) Commands to respect the law, not convenience or the crowd.

"You shall not circulate a false report. Do not put your hand with the wicked to be an unrighteous witness. You shall not follow a crowd to do evil; nor shall you testify in a dispute so as to turn aside after many to pervert *justice*. You shall not show partiality to a poor man in his dispute."

a. **You shall not circulate a false report**: This command is connected with the next, because the circulation of **a false report** was and is a fundamental way to **put your hand with the wicked** and **follow a crowd to do evil**.

i. The only way to obey this command is to put a *stop* to a false report. Doing nothing or remaining neutral is to allow the **false report** to **circulate**. "The *inventor* and *receiver* of false and slanderous reports, are almost equally criminal. The word seems to refer to *either*, and our translators have very properly retained both senses." (Clarke)

ii. Since the issue was *a **false** report*, it was proper to ask and require *proof* from the person bringing the report, and proof as required in the Bible - from two or three witnesses (Deuteronomy 19:15).

iii. **An unrighteous witness**: "Better translated 'witness in a charge of violence', for the thought is that a verdict will be fatal to the defendant." (Cole)

b. **You shall not follow a crowd to do evil**: It has always been in the nature of man to **follow a crowd to do evil**, since the time Adam followed Eve into sin.

i. It is easy and dangerous **to turn aside after many to pervert justice**, to follow with our peers and popular opinion. When doing so promotes **a false report** or perverts **justice**, then it is sin.

ii. This is why it is so important for us to choose our **crowd** carefully: *Do not be deceived: "Evil company corrupts good habits."* (1 Corinthians 15:33).

iii. "The history of all right movements has been in the first place the history of lonely souls, who, having heard the authentic voice of God, have stood alone or in small minorities." (Morgan)

c. **You shall not show partiality to a poor man in his dispute**: No partiality was to be shown **to a poor man**; the poor were not to be favored just because they were poor, any more than the rich should be favored because they were rich. The facts of a case and the principles of justice should decide a dispute, not the high or low standing or perceived victim status of those involved.

2. (4-9) Laws promoting kindness and righteous civil conduct.

"If you meet your enemy's ox or his donkey going astray, you shall surely bring it back to him again. If you see the donkey of one who hates you lying under its burden, and you would refrain from helping it, you shall surely help him with it. You shall not pervert the judgment of your poor in his dispute. Keep yourself far from a false matter; do not kill the innocent and righteous. For I will not justify the wicked. And you shall take no bribe, for a bribe blinds the discerning and perverts the words of the righteous. Also you shall not oppress a stranger, for you know the heart of a stranger, because you were strangers in the land of Egypt."

a. **If you meet your enemy's ox or his donkey going astray, you shall surely bring it back to him again**: This command to do good for **your enemy** was important. It showed that goodness and kindness in Israel was not only required for those ones liked and loved, but to all. One might not need a command to do this for a friend, but it was necessary for the **enemy** and **one who hates you**.

i. The principle was clear: *How you feel about someone does not determine right and wrong behavior towards them.* There are principles of justice that must be observed above our feelings.

ii. "*Enemy* in this context probably means 'legal adversary'. Justice demands that we treat him like any other neighbor." (Cole)

b. **You shall not pervert the judgment of your poor in his dispute**: God knew that it was always easy for the **poor** to be neglected in the administration of justice. Being poor did not make one right in a legal dispute, but it should never keep them from getting a fair hearing and justice.

c. **Keep yourself far from a false matter; do not kill the innocent and righteous**: The promotion of *truth* was essential under God's law. God knew how much evil and injustice is justified among men by lies, so He emphasized truth telling in Israel's daily life and legal practices.

i. The command **do not kill the innocent and righteous** not only spoke to the need to protect life in the womb, but also that there are instances where justice requires the death of the guilty and wicked.

d. **You shall take no bribe, for a bribe blinds the discerning and perverts the words of the righteous**: In the promotion of justice, God also commanded against bribery. Specifically, He commanded against the *taking* of a bribe; bribe makers can't exist without bribe takers.

e. **Your enemy's ox...one who hates you...you shall not oppress a stranger**: God commanded Israel to show kindness and fairness towards those who they might not be kind towards by nature. In later times, some rabbis taught there was an obligation - or at least a permission - to hate one's enemy. Here, fairness and kindness were commanded even to **one who hates you** - even as Jesus made clear in the parable of the Good Samaritan (Luke 10:30-37).

i. **You know the heart of a stranger**: "The Hebrew is not the usual word for 'heart' but *nepes*, which can be translated 'life' or 'self'. Here it seems to have more the meaning of 'desires and longings'." (Cole)

ii. Jesus simply summarized these laws promoting kindness and fair conduct in the community of Israel: *You shall love...your neighbor as yourself* (Luke 10:27).

B. Laws of ceremonial devotion.

1. (10-13) The Sabbath principle.

"Six years you shall sow your land and gather in its produce, but the seventh *year* you shall let it rest and lie fallow, that the poor of your people may eat; and what they leave, the beasts of the field may eat. In like manner you shall do with your vineyard *and* your olive grove. Six days you shall do your work, and on the seventh day you shall rest, that your ox and your donkey may rest, and the son of your female servant and the stranger may be refreshed. And in all that I have said to you, be circumspect and make no mention of the name of other gods, nor let it be heard from your mouth."

a. **Six years you shall sow your land**: The principle of the Sabbath applied to more than the workweek. There were also Sabbath **years**, where the land was to **rest and lie fallow** one year out of seven.

i. "The law of the Sabbatical Year. This was unique in the world, and associated only with Israel." (Thomas)

b. **The seventh year you shall let it rest and lie fallow**: By tradition, some in Israel accomplished this by only cultivating six-sevenths of their land at any one time, and practicing a method of crop rotation.

i. **That the poor of your people may eat**: One reason God commanded the Sabbath year was to give the poor something to eat, in that they were allowed to harvest and process that which grew unplanted from the **fallow** ground. This was a way to help the poor which demanded both that the landowners hold themselves back from maximum profit, and that the poor work to help themselves.

ii. Failure of Israel to give the land its Sabbath-years determined the *certainty* and the *duration* of the Babylonian exile (Leviticus 26:32-35, 2 Chronicles 36:21).

c. **On the seventh day you shall rest, that your ox and your donkey may rest**: The principle of Sabbath rest was intended for all people, and even for animals. In the same pattern, the Sabbath rest fulfilled in Jesus is intended for all people (2 Peter 3:9), and even for all creation (Romans 8:21).

d. **Make no mention of the name of other gods**: The Sabbath was to be dedicated to the LORD God, and not to any foreign or false god.

2. (14-17) Three national feasts.

"Three times you shall keep a feast to Me in the year: You shall keep the Feast of Unleavened Bread (you shall eat unleavened bread seven days, as I commanded you, at the time appointed in the month of Abib, for in it you came out of Egypt; none shall appear before Me empty); and the Feast of Harvest, the firstfruits of your labors which you have sown in the field; and the Feast of Ingathering at the end of the year, when you have gathered in *the fruit of* your labors from the field. Three times in the year all your males shall appear before the Lord GOD."

a. **Three times you shall keep a feast to Me in the year**: God commanded that three times a year, all men in Israel had to come together to keep the most important feasts. These included Unleavened Bread (connected to Passover), Firstfruits, and Ingathering (Pentecost).

i. "*Old* men, *sick* men, *male idiots*, and *male children* under *thirteen* years of age, excepted; for so the Jewish doctors understand this command." (Clarke)

b. **Feast of Unleavened Bread...Feast of Harvest...Feast of Ingathering**: Details regarding the observance of these feasts will be given later in the Book of Leviticus.

3. (18-19) Laws regarding sacrifice and firstfruits offering.

"You shall not offer the blood of My sacrifice with leavened bread; nor shall the fat of My sacrifice remain until morning. The first of the firstfruits of your land you shall bring into the house of the LORD your God. You shall not boil a young goat in its mother's milk."

a. **You shall not offer the blood of My sacrifice with leavened bread**: Since leaven was a symbol of sin and corruption, atoning blood could never be offered with leavened bread.

> i. "It means that individual Israelites were not to kill the Passover lamb while leaven was still in their houses." (Kaiser)

b. **Nor shall the fat of My sacrifice remain until morning**: If atonement was to be regarded as a complete work, it must be wholly offered unto the LORD - *everything* must be given to God, not a portion reserved for later. This especially included **the fat of My sacrifice**, the best portion of the sacrificed animal.

c. **The first of the firstfruits of your land you shall bring into the house of the LORD**: When Israel came into Canaan, they had a special responsibility to make a firstfruit offering to God, in addition to their regular firstfruit offering (Exodus 23:16). Giving God the first and the best honored Him as the Good Provider of all things.

d. **You shall not boil a young kid in its mother's milk**: This strange-sounding command was actually a command to not imitate a common pagan fertility ritual.

> i. "The Canaanite texts show this to be a magic spell, so the prescription is more ritual than humane." (Cole)

> ii. "It was a custom of the ancient heathens, when they had gathered in all their fruits, to take a kid and boil it in the milk of its dam; and then, in a magical way, to go about and besprinkle with it all their trees and fields, gardens and orchards; thinking by these means to make them fruitful, that they might bring forth more abundantly in the following year." (Cudworth cited in Clarke)

> iii. But because of strange rabbinical interpretations, today this command is the reason why an observant Jew cannot eat a kosher cheeseburger. Observant Jews today will not eat milk and meat at the same meal (or even on the same plates with the same utensils cooked in the same pots), because the rabbis insisted that the meat

in the hamburger may have come from the calf of the cow that gave the milk for the cheese, and the cheese and the meat would "boil" together in one's stomach, and be a violation of this command.

iv. This law also speaks of keeping distance between a mother and the death of her offspring. Meyer says this law was meant "to inculcate a tender appreciation of the natural order, and of the relation subsisting between the mother and her offspring. It was against nature to make the mother an accomplice in the death of her child."

C. The promise of God's presence and blessing.

1. (20-21) The Angel who has the name of God **in Him**.

"Behold, I send an Angel before you to keep you in the way and to bring you into the place which I have prepared. Beware of Him and obey His voice; do not provoke Him, for He will not pardon your transgressions; for My name *is* in Him."

a. **I send an Angel before you**: This unique angel commanded obedience from Israel and had the right of judgment over the nation. Most of all, the name of God was in this angel (**for My name is in Him**).

i. We only know a few angels by name, and in a sense, *Micha-el* and *Gabri-el* each have the name of God in their name. But neither Michael nor Gabriel commanded this kind of obedience from Israel or presumed to sit in judgment over them. This is the specific **Angel** *of the* LORD, Jesus appearing in the Old Testament, before His incarnation in Bethlehem, who often speaks directly as the LORD.

ii. "The Angel (v. 20) was not a created angel but a divine manifestation, the Second Person of the Trinity in angelic form." (Thomas) *"My name is in him* seems to translate the 'messenger' into the supernatural realm, for God's 'name' is the equivalent of His revealed nature." (Cole)

iii. **My name is in Him**: Of course, the name Yahweh is **in** Jesus. His name is literally *Yah-shua*. Jesus was with Israel in all their wilderness experience. "This Angel with the authority and prestige of the name of God was evidence enough that God himself was present in his Son." (Kaiser)

b. **And to bring you into the place which I have prepared**: The **Angel** would go before them **into the place which I have prepared**. The same principle is true of our life with Jesus today. Not only is it true that Jesus goes before us to prepare a place for us in heaven (John 14:2-3), but the place we walk today was prepared by God, and where we will walk tomorrow is prepared by Him also.

2. (22-26) Blessing promised to an obedient Israel.

"But if you indeed obey His voice and do all that I speak, then I will be an enemy to your enemies and an adversary to your adversaries. For My Angel will go before you and bring you in to the Amorites and the Hittites and the Perizzites and the Canaanites and the Hivites and the Jebusites; and I will cut them off. You shall not bow down to their gods, nor serve them, nor do according to their works; but you shall utterly overthrow them and completely break down their *sacred* pillars. So you shall serve the LORD your God, and He will bless your bread and your water. And I will take sickness away from the midst of you. No one shall suffer miscarriage or be barren in your land; I will fulfill the number of your days."

a. **But if you indeed obey His voice and do all that I speak**: It was characteristic of the Mosaic covenant that blessing was based *almost* purely on Israel's performance. If they obeyed, they would be blessed. If they disobeyed, they would be cursed.

i. Under the New Covenant, we operate on a different principle. Though there are inevitable consequences of sin and God's loving correction for disobedience, we are blessed in Jesus, and not because we have been obedient (Ephesians 1:3).

b. **My Angel will go before you**: God did not bring Israel out of Egypt to leave them in the wilderness. His plan was to bring them into His land of promise and abundance. Though there were mighty nations in Canaan, His **Angel** would bring an obedient Israel into the Promised Land.

c. **You shall not bow down to their gods**: The Canaanite people were deeply depraved and morally degraded, and this was a natural result of the depraved and degraded idol gods they served. Therefore it was essential that Israel did not imitate their idol worship or allow it to continue.

i. "Concerning the people to be driven out, it is worthy of note that this paragraph shows that 'their gods' were their undoing. Everything in the life of a man or a nation depends on the character of its worship." (Morgan)

d. **So you shall serve the LORD your God, and He will bless your bread and your water**: If they did reject the gods of the Canaanites and continue in faithfulness to God, He promised to bring blessing through their whole life.

3. (27-30) How God will help Israel take possession of the land.

"I will send My fear before you, I will cause confusion among all the people to whom you come, and will make all your enemies turn *their* backs to you. And I will send hornets before you, which shall drive

out the Hivite, the Canaanite, and the Hittite from before you. I will not drive them out from before you in one year, lest the land become desolate and the beast of the field become too numerous for you. Little by little I will drive them out from before you, until you have increased, and you inherit the land."

a. **I will send My fear before you...and will make all your enemies turn their backs to you**: God promised that He would go before Israel and with the land for them, using both obviously supernatural methods (**send My fear**) and seemingly natural phenomenon (**send hornets before you**).

i. "*My terror* explains the method that God will use to subdue the Canaanites before Israel: a divine panic will grip them." This was fulfilled in passages such as Joshua 2:11. (Cole)

ii. "From Joshua 24:12, we find that two kings of the Amorites were actually driven out of the land by these hornets, so that the Israelites were not obliged to use either sword or bow in the conquest." (Clarke)

iii. "He who is an angel to the saint is a hornet to His foes." (Meyer)

b. **Little by little**: God promised to drive out the enemies of Israel from Canaan, but He would not drive them out all at once. Israel may have wanted to have the land all cleared out before them, but God knew it was not best for the *land* or for *them*.

i. Though it sometimes frustrates us, this is often the way God works in our lives. He clears things out little by little, though we might prefer it all at once. But God wanted Israel to **have increased** in the process of taking the Promised Land. He wanted them to grow. God cares that we grow, and so He often grows us **little by little**.

ii. "God crumbles his mercies to us; we have his blessings by retail. So the cloud empties not itself at a sudden burst, but dissolves upon the earth drop by drop." (Trapp)

c. **Lest the land become desolate and the beast of the field become too numerous**: This was just one reason why it was better for God to defeat their enemies **little by little**. Doing it by what seemed to be the easy way - clearing out all of Israel's enemies out at once - had consequences Israel could not see or appreciate.

4. (31-33) Boundaries of Israel's inheritance.

"And I will set your bounds from the Red Sea to the sea, Philistia, and from the desert to the River. For I will deliver the inhabitants of the land into your hand, and you shall drive them out before you. You shall make no covenant with them, nor with their gods. They shall not dwell

in your land, lest they make you sin against Me. For *if* you serve their gods, it will surely be a snare to you."

a. **From the Red Sea to the Sea of the Philistines, and from the desert to the River**: This encompassed a huge portion of land, one that Israel has never fully possessed. Many suppose that the closest they came was in the days of King David and Solomon.

> i. Yet this was a territory that at some points stretched all the way to the Euphrates River. " 'The river' in the Bible is always 'the great river', *i.e.* the Euphrates, just as 'the sea' is normally the Mediterranean." (Cole)

> i. There is a spiritual principle here. God may grant, but we must possess. He withholds our possession of many blessings until we will partner with Him in bold faith and obedience. We have been granted *every spiritual blessing in the heavenly places in Christ* (Ephesians 1:3); but will only possess what we will partner with Him in faith and obedience to receive.

> iii. God is not an indulgent, spoiling father, pouring out on His children resources, blessings, and gifts they are not ready to receive or be responsible with. When His people are ready to possess in faith, what was promised becomes realized.

b. **You shall make no covenant with them**: Through lack of discernment, Israel did end up making a covenant with some of the people of the land (Joshua 9). There is no area of the law that Israel - or anyone - has ever kept perfectly.

Exodus 24 - The Covenant Is Made

A. The signing of the Mosaic covenant.

1. (1-3) Moses relates **all the words of the LORD and all the judgments** to Israel.

Now He said to Moses, "Come up to the LORD, you and Aaron, Nadab and Abihu, and seventy of the elders of Israel, and worship from afar. And Moses alone shall come near the LORD, but they shall not come near; nor shall the people go up with him." So Moses came and told the people all the words of the LORD and all the judgments. And all the people answered with one voice and said, "All the words which the LORD has said we will do."

a. **Come up to the LORD, you and Aaron, Nadab and Abihu, and seventy of the elders of Israel**: We are reminded that God spoke Exodus Chapters 20:22 through 23:33 to Moses alone. Now others were to come up on the mountain and keep their distance (**worship from afar**), yet **Moses alone shall come near**. Moses was allowed special access to God, so God spoke to Moses and Moses spoke to the nation.

b. **So Moses came and told the people all the words of the LORD and all the judgments**: When the people heard the law of God, they responded with complete agreement (**all the people answered with one voice**). Then they verbally agreed to obey the LORD (**All the words which the LORD has said we will do**).

i. Israel here was perhaps guilty of tremendous over-confidence. The way they seemed to easily say to God, "We will keep Your law" seemed to lack appreciation for how complete and deeply comprehensive God's law is.

ii. However, a nation that had been terrified by God's awesome presence at Sinai was in no state of mind to do anything *but* agree with God.

2. (4-8) The nation confirms their solemn covenant with God.

And Moses wrote all the words of the LORD. And he rose early in the morning, and built an altar at the foot of the mountain, and twelve pillars according to the twelve tribes of Israel. Then he sent young men of the children of Israel, who offered burnt offerings and sacrificed peace offerings of oxen to the LORD. And Moses took half the blood and put *it* in basins, and half the blood he sprinkled on the altar. Then he took the Book of the Covenant and read in the hearing of the people. And they said, "All that the LORD has said we will do, and be obedient." And Moses took the blood, sprinkled *it* on the people, and said, "This is the blood of the covenant which the LORD has made with you according to all these words."

a. **And Moses wrote all the words of the LORD**: In the previous verse (Exodus 24:3), Israel verbally agreed to a covenant-relationship with God; but there is a sense in which this is simply not good enough. They must do specific things to confirm their covenant with God. First, the Word of God must be written: **Moses wrote all the words of the LORD**. God's Word was important enough that it was not to be left up to human recollection and the creative nature of memory. It had to be written down.

i. God did not make an individual covenant with its own arrangement for each Israelite. There was one covenant. The same is true today under the New Covenant. You do have a personal relationship with God; you don't have your own private agreement with Him that contradicts the revealed **words of the LORD**.

ii. With the same idea, God spoke through Habakkuk: *Write the vision and make it plain on tablets, that he may run who reads it.* (Habakkuk 2:2)

b. **Who offered burnt offerings and sacrificed peace offerings of oxen to the LORD**: Second, covenant was only made in the context of sacrifice. Sacrifice admits our own sin and failing before God, and it addresses that need through the death of a substitute.

i. **He sent the young men**: "This is a primitive touch, coming from before the time of a specialized priesthood...There is nothing magical in the choice of young men for the task: it is purely a practical consideration. To bind cattle to a stone altar required strength and agility. A young man was a natural warrior, so he was a natural 'priest'." (Cole)

c. **He took the Book of the Covenant and read in the hearing of the people**: Third, covenant was made when God's Word is heard and responded to. Our covenant with God is based on His words and His terms, not our own words and terms.

i. Additionally, there must be a response to God's word: **All that the Lord has said we will do, and be obedient**. Just as much as God would not negotiate His covenant with Israel, neither would He force it upon them. They must freely respond.

ii. **Book of the Covenant**: "The book (Exodus 24:7) is doubtless the germ of the Old Testament." (Thomas)

d. **Moses took the blood, sprinkled it on the people**: Fourth, covenant was made with the application of blood. As the nation received the blood of the covenant, the covenant was sealed.

i. There was nothing magical about blood, but because it represents the *life* of a being (*For the life of the flesh is in the blood*, Leviticus 17:11), blood represents the outpouring of life, of one life being given for another.

ii. "Blood-ritual of some kind is common to most forms of covenant: witness the custom in many lands of making 'blood-brothers' by allowing the blood from two persons to mingle and flow together in one." (Cole)

iii. "*Half of the blood being sprinkled on the* ALTAR, and *half of it sprinkled on the* PEOPLE, showed that both GOD and THEY were mutually bound by this covenant." (Clarke)

iv. Almost a thousand years later, God did not forget the blood of this covenant: *Because of the blood of your covenant, I will set your prisoners free from the waterless pit.* (Zechariah 9:11)

v. The blood of Jesus' covenant saves us: *this is My blood of the new covenant, which is shed for many for the remission of sins.* (Matthew 26:28)

vi. The blood of Jesus' covenant is also the foundation for all our growth and maturity in Christ: *Now may the God of peace who brought up our Lord Jesus from the dead, that great Shepherd of the sheep, through the blood of the everlasting covenant, make you complete in every good work to do His will, working in you what is well pleasing in His sight, through Jesus Christ, to whom be glory forever and ever. Amen.* (Hebrews 13:20-21)

iv. Our dealing with God through the New Covenant follows the same covenant pattern:

- Words of God read
- Sacrifice must be made
- Receiving God's words
- Receiving the Blood of Sacrifice

B. The elders and priests of Israel with God on Sinai.

1. (9-11) The elders of Israel meet with God.

Then Moses went up, also Aaron, Nadab, and Abihu, and seventy of the elders of Israel, and they saw the God of Israel. And *there was* under His feet as it were a paved work of sapphire stone, and it was like the very heavens in *its* clarity. But on the nobles of the children of Israel He did not lay His hand. So they saw God, and they ate and drank.

a. **And they saw the God of Israel**: It is difficult to say exactly what they saw. What they saw **under His feet** suggests that at the most, they saw the *footstool* of God. Most likely they saw some aspect of a heavenly vision of God, after the pattern of Isaiah (Isaiah 6) or Ezekiel (Ezekiel 1).

i. "In this verse it is equally stressed that the elders did not dare to raise their eyes above His footstool." (Cole)

ii. The blue of the **sapphire** may suggest that the elders saw the sea of glass before the throne of God (Revelation 4:6). "Ezekiel 1:26 sees God as seated on a sapphire throne, over a crystal 'firmament' (verse 22), and the thought is taken up again in the book of Revelation." (Cole)

iii. **A paved work of sapphire stone**: "To show that God had now changed their condition, their *bricks*, made in their bondage, to *sapphire*."

b. **But on the nobles of the children of Israel He did not lay His hand**: This indicates that as glorious as this experience was, there was something missing or incomplete in the encounter. This was not a "face-to-face" encounter with God. These elders of Israel could see God, but there was no fellowship or communication between them and God.

i. **Nobles**: "Literally 'corner pegs', an unusual and archaic word, whose meaning is clear from the context. Similar metaphors will be used elsewhere in the Old Testament (Isaiah 22:23; Zechariah 10:4)."

c. **So they saw God**: God allowed the elders of Israel to see such a spectacular vision to impress on them the reality of His presence. After this experience, they would be more likely to trust God when He spoke through Moses.

i. "The account of this experience is reverently reticent. No description is given of the form which the manifestation took. All the description attempted is that of the footstool of Deity." (Morgan)

ii. "It is impossible to say what is meant by 'they saw God.' It was some appearance of the divine presence (Numbers 12:8; Isaiah 6:1; Ezekiel 1:26)." (Thomas)

iii. "That Moses and his company 'saw the God of Israel' at first appears to contradict Exodus 33:20; John 1:18; and 1 Timothy 6:16;

but what they saw was a 'form [similitude] of the LORD' (Numbers 12:8, just as Ezekiel (Ezekiel 1:26) and Isaiah (Isaiah 6:1) saw an approximation, a faint resemblance and a sensible adumbration of the incarnate Christ who was to come." (Kaiser)

d. **And they ate and drank**: God wanted them to eat and drink in His presence because He wanted to communicate a sense of fellowship with these leaders of Israel.

i. "Seventy-four men were gathered together around the manifested presence of God, and in that Presence they did eat and drink." (Morgan)

ii. "It is true that a shared meal (especially involving salt) was a common way of sealing a covenant, from biblical times to modern days. However, it is also true that any form of worship which involved the sacrifice of 'peace offerings' (Exodus 24:5) would be naturally followed by a sacrificial feast." (Cole)

iii. F.B. Meyer noted that eating and drinking are entirely normal, daily activities, and that these men experienced God profoundly in something so normal. He then observed:

- Some eat and drink, and do not behold God
- Some behold God, and do not eat and drink
- Some behold God, and eat and drink

2. (12-18) Moses goes up on the mountain to meet with God and to receive the tablets of the Ten Commandments.

Then the LORD said to Moses, "Come up to Me on the mountain and be there; and I will give you tablets of stone, and the law and commandments which I have written, that you may teach them." So Moses arose with his assistant Joshua, and Moses went up to the mountain of God. And he said to the elders, "Wait here for us until we come back to you. Indeed Aaron and Hur *are* with you. If any man has a difficulty, let him go to them." Then Moses went up into the mountain, and a cloud covered the mountain. Now the glory of the LORD rested on Mount Sinai, and the cloud covered it six days. And on the seventh day He called to Moses out of the midst of the cloud. The sight of the glory of the LORD *was* like a consuming fire on the top of the mountain in the eyes of the children of Israel. So Moses went into the midst of the cloud and went up into the mountain. And Moses was on the mountain forty days and forty nights.

a. **Come up to Me on the mountain and be there**: Moses went up at God's invitation and he also brought with him **his assistant Joshua**. This same Joshua became the great leader God used to bring Israel into the

Promised Land, but he began as Moses' **assistant** - first, helping Moses in battle (Exodus 17:8-16); then by assisting him here in spiritual things.

i. "Joshua accompanied Moses for a distance and there waited six days (a solemn reminder of God's unapproachableness), when Moses was called higher to a personal and private interview with God, which lasted nearly six weeks (Deuteronomy 9:9)." (Thomas)

ii. The nation of Israel assembled at the foot of the mountain. Aaron, his sons, and the 70 elders of Israel were halfway up the mountain. Joshua and Moses went up further, and Moses alone met with God.

b. **Indeed Aaron and Hur are with you**: Moses had good reason to believe that these two men could supervise the camp of Israel. They already proved themselves as men capable of assisting Moses in prayer (Exodus 17:10-13). Yet **Aaron and Hur** didn't do a good job guarding the camp – as will be demonstrated in the following chapters.

c. **The sight of the glory of the LORD was like a consuming fire on the top of the mountain in the eyes of the children of Israel**: Perhaps this looked like glowing, radiant embers of a hot fire (**a consuming fire**). The glorious presence of God on Sinai lingered the forty days Moses was on the mount. Though the people could not see God, and could not see Moses, God left them reminders of His glory and presence to help them trust what they could not see.

i. **Rested on Mount Sinai**: "The Hebrew verb is 'dwelt'. It is used in a technical sense later of God's 'shekinah', the outward manifestation of His presence to men." (Cole)

ii. "When the glory of God 'settled' on the mountain, the same word (*sakan*) is used as the 'shekinah' glory (cf. John 1:14, the Word 'tabernacling' among us)." The ancient Greek word for *dwelt* in John 1:14 sounds very much like the Hebrew *sakan*. (Kaiser)

d. **He called to Moses out of the midst of the cloud**: This was not a welcoming place; the harsh and dangerous environment said, "Stay away." But God **called to Moses** and told him, "Come close to me."

i. As harsh and as dangerous as the environment was, there was something of the glory of God in it. These images of the cloud, the smoke, the fire are all Biblical images of God's revealed glory. They are connected to His cloud of shekinah glory, and also with Jesus' presence among men.

ii. In all of this God said to Moses, "*You can draw near. I will keep you safe and reveal Myself to you.*" Under the New Covenant, in light of the Word of God, and under the sacrifice of Jesus, God dares us to draw near to Him.

Exodus 25 - Supplies and Directions for the Tabernacle

A. The supplies for this building project.

1. (1-2) God tells Moses to ask for an offering.

Then the LORD spoke to Moses, saying: "Speak to the children of Israel, that they bring Me an offering. From everyone who gives it willingly with his heart you shall take My offering."

a. **Speak to the children of Israel, that they bring Me an offering**: Before God told Moses what the offering was for, He told Moses to take an offering. God wanted Israel to be motivated by a willing heart more than by a specific need.

i. Our giving should not be *primarily* because of need. We should primarily give because our willing heart compels us.

b. **Bring Me an offering**: God is a rich God and can use any method of providing He wants. Yet He usually uses the willing hearts of His people as the way to support His work.

i. "All the materials for the building of the Tabernacle were to be supplied by the people themselves. This was not because God could not have provided everything in some other way." (Morgan)

ii. This is because God wants to develop giving hearts within us. When we become givers, we become more like God, who is the greatest giver: *For God so loved the world, He gave His only begotten Son* (John 3:16).

iii. Therefore we must be givers, not so much because God or the church needs our money, but because we must be conformed into the image of God's Son (Romans 8:29).

c. **From everyone who gives it willingly with his heart**: God only wanted contributions from those who gave **willingly**. God is not interested in coerced or manipulated giving. In the New Testament, this idea is echoed in 2 Corinthians 9:7: *So let each one give as he purposes in his heart, not grudgingly or of necessity; for God loves a cheerful giver.*

d. **You shall take My offering**: The offering didn't belong to Moses, it didn't belong to the elders, and it didn't belong to Israel itself. God said **you shall take *My* offering**. The offering belonged to God, and was held by Moses and the nation on God's behalf.

2. (3-7) The specific materials to be gathered.

"And this *is* the offering which you shall take from them: gold, silver, and bronze; blue, purple, and scarlet *thread,* fine linen, and goats' *hair;* ram skins dyed red, badger skins, and acacia wood; oil for the light, and spices for the anointing oil and for the sweet incense; onyx stones, and stones to be set in the ephod and in the breastplate."

a. **This is the offering which you shall take from them**: Each of these materials were used in building a structure God commanded Moses to build. Each of these materials has a symbolic or a spiritual representation relevant to the building.

　　i. In the proportion of the finished tabernacle, the present day value of these materials total more than $13 million (DeWitt). Their combined weight would be almost 19,000 pounds (8,600 kilos).

b. **Blue**: The dye for this color was extracted from a shellfish, seemingly in several different hues.

c. **Purple**: The dye for this color came from the murex snail. It was a purple-red color.

d. **Scarlet**: The dye for this color came from the dried and powdered eggs and bodies of a particular worm (*coccus ilicis*) which attaches itself to the holly plant.

e. **Fine linen**: This term translates an Egyptian word. The Egyptians knew (and undoubtedly taught the Jews) how to make fine linen.

　　i. "Egypt excelled in the production of linen, especially *twined linen,* where every thread was twisted from many strands." (Cole)

f. **Goat hair**: Coverings made from this material were typically black and coarse, similar to our modern felt.

g. **Rams' skins**: This customarily had the wool removed and was like fine leather.

h. **Badger skins**: This difficult to translate phrase may also refer to the skins of porpoises or manatees (the sea cow).

i. **Acacia wood**: This wood is harder and darker than oak. It is also very durable because wood-eating insects avoid it.

i. "This acacia is known to have been plentiful in Egypt, and it abounds in Arabia Desert, the very place in which Moses was when he built the tabernacle; and hence it is reasonable to suppose that he built it of that wood, which was every way proper for his purpose." (Clarke)

3. (8-9) The purpose and pattern of the tabernacle.

"And let them make Me a sanctuary, that I may dwell among them. According to all that I show you, *that is,* the pattern of the tabernacle and the pattern of all its furnishings, just so you shall make *it.*"

a. **Let them make Me a sanctuary, that I may dwell among them**: The purpose of the tabernacle was to be the dwelling place of God. The idea was not that God exclusively lived in that place, but that it was the specific place where men could come and meet God.

i. **Sanctuary**: "Means 'holy' place or 'the place set apart.' Everything about the tabernacle was holy. The same word in 1 and 2 Chronicles refers to the temple." (Kaiser)

b. **The pattern of the tabernacle**: This first representation of God's dwelling place would be a **tabernacle** – a *tent* – and not a permanent structure.

i. "The word 'tabernacle' (*miskan*) appears for the first time here of its 139 OT occurrences. It is from the word 'to dwell' (*sakan*) and is the place where God dwells among his people." (Kaiser)

ii. "The Hebrews were meant to feel that the God of their fathers was a fellow-pilgrim, that where they pitched He pitched, that their enemies, difficulties, and long toilsome marches were His." (Meyer)

c. **According to all that I show you, that is, the pattern of the tabernacle and the pattern of all its furnishings**: It is evident that God not only *described* the tabernacle and its furnishings to Moses, but also did **show** him something of its structure and arrangement. There was a vision that accompanied the giving of these words.

i. The pattern of the tabernacle was according to a heavenly reality. It was a *copy and shadow of the heavenly things* (Hebrews 8:5). Therefore, it had to be made according to exact dimensions, being somewhat of a "scale model" of the area around God's throne in heaven.

ii. "*The pattern* means almost 'architect's model.'" (Cole)

B. Instructions for building the Ark of the Covenant.

1. (10-11) The basic structure of the Ark of the Covenant.

"And they shall make an ark of acacia wood; two and a half cubits *shall be* its length, a cubit and a half its width, and a cubit and a half its

height. And you shall overlay it with pure gold, inside and out you shall overlay it, and shall make on it a molding of gold all around."

a. **They shall make an ark**: The first item God told Moses to build was the **ark**, later called the *Ark of the Covenant*. This was the most important single item associated with the tabernacle, modeled after the throne of God in heaven.

i. "The most important feature is described first of all, because it was the symbol of the approach to God." (Thomas)

b. **They shall make an ark of acacia wood**: The Ark of the Covenant was essentially a box (an **ark** is a box, not a boat). It was made of acacia wood, overlaid with gold, 3 foot 9 inches long; 2 foot 3 inches wide; and 2 foot 3 inches high.

2. (12-15) The rings and the poles for the Ark of the Covenant.

"You shall cast four rings of gold for it, and put *them* in its four corners; two rings *shall be* on one side, and two rings on the other side. And you shall make poles *of* acacia wood, and overlay them with gold. You shall put the poles into the rings on the sides of the ark, that the ark may be carried by them. The poles shall be in the rings of the ark; they shall not be taken from it."

a. **You shall cast four rings of gold for it**: The Ark didn't have handles and was not to be carried by lifting it directly in one's hands. Instead, it was to be carried by inserting gold-overlaid wood poles into gold rings at each corner of the Ark.

b. **The poles shall be in the rings of the ark; they shall not be taken from it**: The poles were to remain inserted in the rings, and to be the only proper source of contact with the Ark. Apart from touching the poles, it was forbidden to touch the Ark of the Covenant.

i. In 2 Samuel 6:6-7, Uzzah touched the Ark to keep it from falling off a cart, but he did not touch it at the poles, and God struck him dead. Uzzah was wrong in his thinking that God would let the Ark be damaged; in fact, it *did not* fall off the cart, and no thanks to Uzzah. Uzzah was also wrong in his thinking that there was something less pure about the ground than his act of pure disobedience.

3. (16) The contents of the Ark.

"And you shall put into the ark the Testimony which I will give you."

a. **You shall put into the ark the Testimony**: God instructed Moses to put **the Testimony** - that is, a copy of the law - into the Ark of the Covenant.

b. **Which I will give you**: God told Moses to build the Ark of the Covenant to hold the law even before the law was given. Later, God would instruct Israel to put other things in the Ark as well - *the golden pot that had the manna, Aaron's rod that budded, and the tablets of the covenant* (Hebrews 9:4).

3. (17-22) The mercy seat.

"You shall make a mercy seat of pure gold; two and a half cubits *shall be* its length and a cubit and a half its width. And you shall make two cherubim of gold; of hammered work you shall make them at the two ends of the mercy seat. Make one cherub at one end, and the other cherub at the other end; you shall make the cherubim at the two ends of it *of one piece* with the mercy seat. And the cherubim shall stretch out *their* wings above, covering the mercy seat with their wings, and they shall face one another; the faces of the cherubim *shall be* toward the mercy seat. You shall put the mercy seat on top of the ark, and in the ark you shall put the Testimony that I will give you. And there I will meet with you, and I will speak with you from above the mercy seat, from between the two cherubim which *are* on the ark of the Testimony, about everything which I will give you in commandment to the children of Israel."

a. **You shall make a mercy seat of pure gold**: The **mercy seat** - actually, the lid to the Ark - was to be made of pure gold, and made with the sculpted figures of cherubim. In the picture provided by the Ark of the Covenant, it was as if God dwelt **between the two cherubim**, and met Israel there.

i. "In Israel, *cherubim* symbolized God's attendant and messenger spirits (Psalm 104:3,4) and so were not considered a breach of Exodus 20:4, since no man worshipped them." (Cole)

ii. Kaiser translates the ancient Hebrew word *kapporet* with the phrase "atonement cover." "The ark was the place of atonement or propitiation, hence the place where God was rendered favorable to his people." (Kaiser)

b. **And there I will meet with you**: God met with Israel in the sense that He met with the representative of Israel (the high priest) in peace because of the atoning blood on the Day of Atonement (Leviticus 16:14-15).

c. **I will speak with you from above the mercy seat, from between the two cherubim**: It was as if God, looking down from His dwelling place between the cherubim, saw the law in the Ark - and knew we were guilty of breaking His law. But atoning blood of sacrifice was sprinkled on the mercy seat so that God saw the blood covering the breaking of His law, and forgiveness could be offered.

i. It is remarkable that *even before God gave Moses the tablets of the Ten Commandments*, God made provision for Israel's failure under the law.

ii. In Romans 3:25, the Greek word for *propitiation* (*hilasterion*) is also used in the Septuagint (an early translation of the Old Testament from Hebrew into Greek, read in the days of the New Testament) for the "mercy seat." Therefore it can be rightly said that "Jesus is our mercy seat." He is the *place* and the *means* of our redemption.

C. Instructions for building the table of showbread.

1. (23-29) Dimensions and materials for the table of showbread.

"You shall also make a table of acacia wood; two cubits *shall be* its length, a cubit its width, and a cubit and a half its height. And you shall overlay it with pure gold, and make a molding of gold all around. You shall make for it a frame of a handbreadth all around, and you shall make a gold molding for the frame all around. And you shall make for it four rings of gold, and put the rings on the four corners that *are* at its four legs. The rings shall be close to the frame, as holders for the poles to bear the table. And you shall make the poles of acacia wood, and overlay them with gold, that the table may be carried with them. You shall make its dishes, its pans, its pitchers, and its bowls for pouring. You shall make them of pure gold."

a. **You shall also make a table of acacia wood**: This table was to be made of acacia wood, overlaid with gold; 3 feet (1 meter) long; 1 foot, 6 inches (one half meter) wide; and 2 feet, 3 inches (.75 meter) high.

b. **The rings shall be close to the frame, as holders for the poles to bear the table**: This table was also to have rings and poles necessary to carry it as well as accompanying dishes, pans, and so forth, all made out of pure gold.

i. "We are fortunate in having, on the Arch of Titus, a carved representation of this table (as well as of the golden lampstand). The model pictured is that from Herod's Temple but, to judge from the description in Exodus, it followed closely the Exodus pattern." (Cole)

2. (30) The purpose for the table of showbread.

"And you shall set the showbread on the table before Me always."

a. **And you shall set the showbread on the table before Me always**: On the table of showbread were set twelve loaves of **showbread** - literally "bread of faces." This was bread associated with, and to be eaten before, the face of God.

i. "In the East a table was always the symbol of fellowship. Thus the people were reminded of the possibility created of constant communion with God." (Morgan)

ii. Meyer calls the **showbread** "presence-bread." Bread is necessary for survival, and the link was a reminder that fellowship with God was just as necessary for man.

iii. "*Lechem panim* literally, *bread of faces*; so called, either because they were placed *before the presence* or *face of God* in the sanctuary, or because they were made *square*, as the Jews will have it." (Clarke)

b. **Showbread**: According to Leviticus 24:5-9, **showbread** was made of fine flour, and twelve cakes of showbread - one for each tribe of Israel - set on the table, sprinkled lightly with frankincense. Once a week, the bread was replaced, and normally only priests could eat the old bread.

D. Instructions for building the lampstand.

1. (31-36) The lampstand itself.

"You shall also make a lampstand of pure gold; the lampstand shall be of hammered work. Its shaft, its branches, its bowls, its *ornamental* knobs, and flowers shall be *of one piece*. And six branches shall come out of its sides: three branches of the lampstand out of one side, and three branches of the lampstand out of the other side. Three bowls *shall be* made like almond *blossoms* on one branch, *with* an *ornamental* knob and a flower, and three bowls made like almond *blossoms* on the other branch, *with* an *ornamental* knob and a flower; and so for the six branches that come out of the lampstand. On the lampstand itself four bowls *shall be* made like almond *blossoms, each with* its *ornamental* knob and flower. And *there shall be* a knob under the *first* two branches of the same, a knob under the *second* two branches of the same, and a knob under the *third* two branches of the same, according to the six branches that extend from the lampstand. Their knobs and their branches *shall be of one piece;* all of it *shall be* one hammered piece of pure gold."

a. **You shall also make a lampstand of pure gold**: The lampstand was hammered out of pure gold, with no specific dimensions given, but after the pattern of a modern-day menorah. It had one middle shaft with three branches coming out of each side, for a total of seven places for lamps.

b. **Three bowls shall be made like almond blossoms on one branch**: The repetition of the **almond blossom** motif was important, because it was the first tree to blossom in the springtime. It reminded everyone of new life and the fresh nature of God's ongoing work.

i. "A glance at any reproduction of the Arch of Titus will make the main outline plain, although the exact metaphorical sense of some of the technical terms used is not quite clear." (Cole)

2. (37-40) The lamps for the lampstand.

"You shall make seven lamps for it, and they shall arrange its lamps so that they give light in front of it. And its wick-trimmers and their trays *shall be* of pure gold. It shall be made of a talent of pure gold, with all these utensils. And see to it that you make *them* according to the pattern which was shown you on the mountain."

a. **You shall make seven lamps for it**: The tabernacle represented the court of God's throne, and Revelation 4:5 describes *Seven lamps of fire were burning before the throne, which are the seven Spirits of God.* The **seven lamps** represent the presence of the Holy Spirit in heaven.

b. **So that they give light in front of it**: Since the tabernacle itself was a completely covered tent, the only source of light was the lamps of the lampstand.

i. "The symbolism might be that of the light which God's presence brings to His people (Numbers 6:25), remembering that light, in the Old Testament, is also a symbol of life and victory (Psalm 27:1)." (Cole)

ii. " 'A talent of pure gold' was about seventy-five pounds." (Kaiser)

c. **According to the pattern which was shown you on the mountain**: The principle first mentioned in Exodus 25:9 - that the tabernacle and its furnishings were to be built according to the specific, revealed pattern - is here again emphasized. It had to be a proper representation of the heavenly reality.

Exodus 26 - Coverings and Curtains for the Tabernacle

A. Four sets of curtains for the tent itself.

1. (1-6) The fine linen curtain.

"Moreover you shall make the tabernacle *with* ten curtains *of* fine woven linen and blue, purple, and scarlet *thread;* with artistic designs of cherubim you shall weave them. The length of each curtain *shall be* twenty-eight cubits, and the width of each curtain four cubits. And every one of the curtains shall have the same measurements. Five curtains shall be coupled to one another, and *the other* five curtains *shall be* coupled to one another. And you shall make loops of blue *yarn* on the edge of the curtain on the selvedge of *one* set, and likewise you shall do on the outer edge of *the other* curtain of the second set. Fifty loops you shall make in the one curtain, and fifty loops you shall make on the edge of the curtain that *is* on the end of the second set, that the loops may be clasped to one another. And you shall make fifty clasps of gold, and couple the curtains together with the clasps, so that it may be one tabernacle."

a. **Make the tabernacle with ten curtains of fine woven linen**: The tabernacle was a tent with a frame and a series of elaborate coverings. This section describes the first covering, the one seen from the interior of the tabernacle.

i. The plans for the tabernacle were revealed to Moses from the inside out, starting with the interior furniture and then working out. We approach the sanctuary from the outside in, but God builds the sanctuary from the inside out. He works in His people according to the same pattern.

b. **Fine woven linen...with artistic designs of cherubim**: The designs on this covering were visible only from the inside of the tabernacle.

Therefore, on the inside of the tabernacle, one saw cherubim all around - as one would see in heaven (Psalm 80:1, Isaiah 37:16, and Ezekiel 10:3).

> i. In association with the **cherubim** on the ark of the covenant, Trapp noted: "Golden-winged images, made by God's special appointment, and set out of sight. Hence then is no warrant for the use of images in churches."

c. **Five curtains shall be coupled**: The fine linen curtain was made by sewing together **five curtains**, each one 42 feet (14 meters) long and 6 feet (2 meters) wide. They were first joined in sets of five, and then joined together for a covering 42 feet (14 meters) by 60 feet (20 meters).

d. **Make fifty clasps of gold, and couple the curtains together with the clasps**: The sets of five curtains were not to be sewn to each other, but joined by a system of loops on the fabric and gold clasps to link the loops from one set of five curtains to the other set of five curtains.

e. **So that it may be one tabernacle**: The spiritual principle illustrated with this method of joining the curtains is unity in diversity. It is the same idea of Romans 12:5: *we, being many, are one body in Christ, and individually members of one another.*

> i. Trapp suggested a slightly different application of this idea: "The coupling of these two great curtains together, to make one tabernacle, might signify that the saints both in heaven and earth to make but one Church." (Trapp)

2. (7-13) The curtain made of goats' hair.

"You shall also make curtains of goats' *hair,* to be a tent over the tabernacle. You shall make eleven curtains. The length of each curtain *shall be* thirty cubits, and the width of each curtain four cubits; and the eleven curtains shall all have the same measurements. And you shall couple five curtains by themselves and six curtains by themselves, and you shall double over the sixth curtain at the forefront of the tent. You shall make fifty loops on the edge of the curtain that is outermost in *one* set, and fifty loops on the edge of the curtain of the second set. And you shall make fifty bronze clasps, put the clasps into the loops, and couple the tent together, that it may be one. The remnant that remains of the curtains of the tent, the half curtain that remains, shall hang over the back of the tabernacle. And a cubit on one side and a cubit on the other side, of what remains of the length of the curtains of the tent, shall hang over the sides of the tabernacle, on this side and on that side, to cover it."

a. **Make curtains of goats' hair**: The second covering was made of goats' hair producing a fabric dark, thick, and coarse - somewhat like felt.

This covering was made by joining together five and six strips of fabric with each strip being 45 feet (15 meters) long and 6 feet (2 meters) wide.

> i. According to Kaiser, this **goat hair** "Came from long-haired goats and most likely was black in color. It was a coarse material that often was used to weave tents. Felt would be a modern equivalent."

b. **Couple the tent together, that it may be one**: The set of five strips and the set of six strips were joined together with a series of loops and bronze clasps. The inner covering or curtain used gold clasps, but this second covering used bronze.

c. **The remnant that remains...shall hang over the back of the tabernacle**: Since the goats' hair layer was 6 feet (2 meters) longer than the fine linen layer, the extra length covered over the back portion of the tent.

d. **A cubit on one side, and a cubit on the other side**: Since the goats' hair covering was wider by 3 feet (2 meters), this layer completely covered over the fine linen layer.

> i. Therefore, the fine linen layer - the "heavenly" set of coverings - was completely obscured and overlapped by the dark covering of goats' hair. It was not open to observation, even in part. Heaven remained hidden to all except those who entered in through the door of the tabernacle.

3. (14) Two sets of coverings: ram skin dyed red, and badger skin.

"You shall also make a covering of ram skins dyed red for the tent, and a covering of badger skins above that."

a. **You shall also make a covering of ram skins**: The covering of **ram skins** was like fine leather dyed red. No specific size or arrangement is mentioned for the assembling of this covering.

> i. Kaiser described the **ram skins** as, "Skins that had all the wool removed and then were dyed red; it was like our morocco leather."

b. **A covering of badger skins above that**: The outer covering of **badger skins** (or perhaps porpoise or sea-cow skins) was a durable and water resistant outer covering. It wasn't particularly beautiful to look at, but it was extremely comfortable.

> i. When these four layers of curtains were laid on one another, the result was a very dry and very dark tent. The only light came from the lampstand described in the previous chapter.

B. The framing system for the tabernacle.

1. (15-25) Boards for the sides of the tent.

"And for the tabernacle you shall make the boards of acacia wood, standing upright. Ten cubits *shall be* the length of a board, and a cubit and a half *shall be* the width of each board. Two tenons *shall be* in each board for binding one to another. Thus you shall make for all the boards of the tabernacle. And you shall make the boards for the tabernacle, twenty boards for the south side. You shall make forty sockets of silver under the twenty boards: two sockets under each of the boards for its two tenons. And for the second side of the tabernacle, the north side, *there shall be* twenty boards and their forty sockets of silver: two sockets under each of the boards. For the far side of the tabernacle, westward, you shall make six boards. And you shall also make two boards for the two back corners of the tabernacle. They shall be coupled together at the bottom and they shall be coupled together at the top by one ring. Thus it shall be for both of them. They shall be for the two corners. So there shall be eight boards with their sockets of silver; sixteen sockets; two sockets under each board."

a. **For the tabernacle you shall make the boards of acacia wood**: Each board was made of acacia wood and overlaid with gold. Each board was 15 feet (5 meters) high and 2 feet, 3 inches (about .75 meter) wide.

b. **Twenty boards for the south side**: The north and south sides of the tabernacle had 20 boards each. The back (**westward**) side was six boards wide with two corner boards, for a total of eight boards across the back.

i. Scholars debate if the surrounding boards made a solid wall around the tabernacle or were more of a frame with the fabric coverings providing the wall. The idea of a solid wall seems more likely.

c. **Coupled together at the top by one ring**: Each board was joined together by a system of **tenons** (tabs) with **rings**, through which ran bars. Each board had four rings through which the bars ran, and the corner boards had eight rings, four on two sides to accommodate the corners.

d. **So there shall be eight boards with their sockets of silver; sixteen sockets**: Each board rested on two sockets of silver, each socket made with one talent of silver. Therefore each board rested on a base of 264 pounds (120 kilos) of silver.

i. Silver is the metal associated with redemption and payment for sin (Exodus 21:32, Leviticus 5:15, 27:3, 27:6, Numbers 18:16, and Deuteronomy 22:19). Jesus was betrayed for silver (Matthew 26:15). The tabernacle's foundation was silver - pointing to the redeeming work of Jesus Christ.

ii. Perhaps the dual nature of the foundation had to do with the two sources of revelation - the Old and New Testaments.

iii. The silver of redemption also separated the tabernacle from the dirt of the desert floor. This is an illustration of the truth that Jesus' redeeming work separates us from the world.

2. (26-30) Bars to join together the boards.

"And you shall make bars of acacia wood: five for the boards on one side of the tabernacle, five bars for the boards on the other side of the tabernacle, and five bars for the boards of the side of the tabernacle, for the far side westward. The middle bar shall pass through the midst of the boards from end to end. You shall overlay the boards with gold, make their rings of gold *as* holders for the bars, and overlay the bars with gold. And you shall raise up the tabernacle according to its pattern which you were shown on the mountain."

a. **And you shall make bars of acacia wood**: Each bar was made of acacia wood and overlaid in gold. Seemingly, the bars ran the entire length of each side, linking together each board into one system.

b. **The middle bar shall pass through the midst of the boards from end to end**: Four bars ran horizontally on each side, linking each board. One bar - **the middle bar** - was invisible, running in the middle of each board.

i. This speaks to both the visible and the invisible unity among God's people. The system of linking bars was both visible and invisible.

c. **According to its pattern which you were shown on the mountain**: The repetition of this phrase (Exodus 25:9, 25:40 and here in 26:30) suggests that Moses received a vision of exactly how the tabernacle should look. He had to communicate this vision to the craftsmen who did the actual building.

i. God works the same way in leaders today. He gives them a vision of what His work should be, and the leader passes it on to others who will do much of the actual work. Moses could not have remained silent about what God had shown him, or the work would never have gotten done.

C. Two barriers: the veil and the screen.

1. (31-33) The veil.

"You shall make a veil woven of blue, purple, and scarlet *thread,* and fine woven linen. It shall be woven with an artistic design of cherubim. You shall hang it upon the four pillars of acacia *wood* overlaid with gold. Their hooks *shall be* gold, upon four sockets of silver. And you shall hang the veil from the clasps. Then you shall bring the ark of the

Testimony in there, behind the veil. The veil shall be a divider for you between the holy *place* and the Most Holy."

a. **You shall make a veil**: The veil, made of **fine linen and blue and purple and scarlet yarn, with artistic design of cherubim**, hung on four pillars made of acacia wood overlaid with gold, set on silver sockets.

i. The ancient Jews said the later veil of the temple was as wide as four fingers, so that no one could possibly see into the Most Holy place.

b. **With an artistic design of cherubim**: From this, we know that the interior of the tabernacle was filled with gold and the pattern of cherubim.

c. **The veil shall be a divider for you between the holy place and the Most Holy**: The veil separated the tent into two compartments. The first compartment was **the holy place**, which was the larger room, first entered, with the table of showbread, the lampstand, and the altar of incense. The second compartment was **the Most Holy** place, a smaller room with the Ark of the Covenant.

i. This veil was a barrier, and no priest could go beyond the veil into the Most Holy place except the high priest. He could only enter once a year, and that on the Day of Atonement.

ii. Spiritually speaking, in dying for our sins, Jesus *with His own blood He entered the Most Holy Place once for all, having obtained eternal redemption* (Hebrews 9:12).

iii. In the temple, this veil was torn from top to bottom at the death of Jesus (Matthew 27:51), showing that through His death, there is no longer a barrier to the Most Holy place.

iv. Now the Most Holy Place is open to us: *brethren, having boldness to enter the Holiest by the blood of Jesus, by a new and living way which He consecrated for us, through the veil, that is His flesh* (Hebrews 10:19-20). The torn veil of Matthew 27:51 also symbolizes the broken body of Jesus, through which we have access to the Most Holy Place.

v. "When at last the Man in whom all perfections were realized, had made full atonement for sins, the symbol of separation was destroyed." (Morgan)

vi. "How many there are who never get beyond the dividing vail! They know the brazen altar of Atonement, the laver of daily washing, the golden altar of intercession; but they are never admitted to that blessed intimacy of communion which sees the Shechinah glory between the cherubim and blood-sprinkled mercy-seat." (Meyer)

vii. Centuries later (in 63 B.C.), the ancient Roman general Pompey pushed aside the priests and walked right into the Most Holy place of the temple - and was astonished to see there was no idol or statue (Josephus, *Antiquities of the Jews*, book 14 chapter 4).

2. (34-35) The arrangement of furniture in the two rooms of the tabernacle.

"You shall put the mercy seat upon the ark of the Testimony in the Most Holy. You shall set the table outside the veil, and the lampstand across from the table on the side of the tabernacle toward the south; and you shall put the table on the north side."

a. **Put the mercy seat upon the ark of the Testimony in the Most Holy**: The Ark of the Covenant (here called **the ark of the Testimony**) was behind the veil in the **Most Holy** place.

b. **Set the table outside the veil**: The **table** of showbread was on the **north side** of the tabernacle (on the right as one entered the tabernacle), and the **lampstand** was **toward the south** (on the left as one entered the tabernacle).

i. The furniture in the holy place spoke of three great obligations of walking with God: prayer (the altar of incense), fellowship (the table of showbread), and to receive illumination (the lampstand).

3. (36-37) The screen for a door.

"You shall make a screen for the door of the tabernacle, *woven of* blue, purple, and scarlet *thread,* and fine woven linen, made by a weaver. And you shall make for the screen five pillars of acacia *wood,* and overlay them with gold; their hooks *shall be of* gold, and you shall cast five sockets of bronze for them."

a. **Make a screen for the door of the tabernacle**: The same color scheme - **blue and purple and scarlet yarn, and fine linen thread** was used to make a covering for the east entrance of the tabernacle. This was the only way to enter the structure.

b. **Five pillars of acacia wood**: The screen hung from hooks on five pillars. Each pillar was made of acacia wood overlaid with gold and set on a foundation of bronze.

i. Since bronze (or brass) must be made with a refining fire, it pictures purity and endurance through trial. The entrance to the tabernacle hung on a symbolic foundation of what Jesus did for us.

Exodus 27 - The Court of the Tabernacle

A. The altar of burnt offering.

1. (1-2) The basic structure of the bronze altar.

"You shall make an altar of acacia wood, five cubits long and five cubits wide; the altar shall be square; and its height *shall be* three cubits. You shall make its horns on its four corners; its horns shall be of one piece with it. And you shall overlay it with bronze."

a. **You shall make an altar**: The idea behind the Hebrew word for **altar** is essentially "killing-place." It was a place of death and sacrifice, where atonement for sin was made and consecration unto God was marked.

i. "This was the only altar of sacrifice in Israel's sanctuary in early days: blood would be smeared on its 'horns' in ceremonial atonement, and on it 'holocausts' or 'whole burnt offerings' would be laid. Libations were poured at its side, and blood dashed over it." (Cole)

ii. Under the new covenant, we also have an altar: *We have an altar from which those who serve the tabernacle have no right to eat* (Hebrews 13:10). Our altar - our "killing-place" - is the cross where Jesus died for our sins, and we follow by dying unto self and living for Jesus.

iii. We lay down our lives on that same altar: *I have been crucified with Christ; it is no longer I who live, but Christ lives in me; and the life which I now live in the flesh I live by faith in the Son of God, who loved me and gave Himself for me....But God forbid that I should boast except in the cross of our Lord Jesus Christ, by whom the world has been crucified to me, and I to the world.* (Galatians 2:20 and 6:14)

b. **Make an altar of acacia wood...overlay it with bronze**: The altar was a box-like structure, and because of its overlay of bronze it could survive high temperatures. The altar was 7 feet, 6 inches (2.5 meters) square; and 4 feet, 6 inches (1.5 meters) high.

i. For years, the sides of this altar were smooth and shiny bronze. But Numbers 16 describes the rebellion of Korah, who challenged the leadership of Moses: *You take too much upon yourselves, for all the congregation is holy . . . Why then do you exalt yourselves above the congregation of the* LORD*?* (Numbers 16:3). In confirming the leadership of Moses, God judged Korah and his followers, and caused the ground to split and swallow up all the rebels of Korah. The LORD then commanded the priests to take the bronze incense-censers held by Korah and his followers, to hammer them flat, and to cover the altar of burnt offering with them, *to be a memorial to the children of Israel* (Numbers 16:40).

ii. From then on, every time someone came to the altar of burnt offering, they noticed the rough, hammered finish of the bronze - and were reminded of Korah's rebellion and God's judgment against him and those who followed him.

c. **Make its horns on its four corners**: There were to be **horns** on the altar, so the altar would "reach out" to all directions. **Horns** were also thought of as a display of strength and power. In sacrifice, atoning blood was applied to each horn.

i. The horns were "To bind the beasts unto, that were to be slain in sacrifice (Psalm 118:27). And to signify the power of Christ's priesthood (Habakkuk 3:4)." (Trapp)

2. (3-8) Accessories for the altar.

"Also you shall make its pans to receive its ashes, and its shovels and its basins and its forks and its firepans; you shall make all its utensils of bronze. You shall make a grate for it, a network of bronze; and on the network you shall make four bronze rings at its four corners. You shall put it under the rim of the altar beneath, that the network may be midway up the altar. And you shall make poles for the altar, poles of acacia wood, and overlay them with bronze. The poles shall be put in the rings, and the poles shall be on the two sides of the altar to bear it. You shall make it hollow with boards; as it was shown you on the mountain, so shall they make *it*."

a. **Make its pans to receive its ashes, and its shovels and its basins and its forks and its firepans**: These utensils were used in the preparation of the offerings and the maintenance of the altar. Each was specially made for the tabernacle out of bronze and each was set-aside for the work of the tabernacle.

i. **Pans**: "To hold the fat-soaked ashes when they were removed from the hearth by the **shovels**." (Kaiser)

ii. **Basins**: "To catch the blood of the animals slain beside the altar to be sprinkled on the altar's base." (Kaiser)

iii. **Forks**: "Three-pronged forks for arranging the sacrifice or retracting the priest's portion (1 Samuel 2:13)." (Kaiser)

iv. **Firepans**: "For carrying fire from the altar of incense inside the Holy Place (Leviticus 10:1; 16:12; 1 Kings 7:50)." (Kaiser)

b. **Make a grate for it, a network of bronze**: The **grate** provided a floor for the altar so the ashes and burnt remains fell down through the **network of bronze**. The grate also had the **rings** and the **poles** with which the altar was carried.

B. The courtyard and the gate.

1. (9-15) The hangings for the perimeter of the courtyard.

"You shall also make the court of the tabernacle. For the south side *there shall be* hangings for the court *made of* fine woven linen, one hundred cubits long for one side. And its twenty pillars and their twenty sockets *shall be* bronze. The hooks of the pillars and their bands *shall be* silver. Likewise along the length of the north side *there shall be* hangings one hundred *cubits* long, with its twenty pillars and their twenty sockets of bronze, and the hooks of the pillars and their bands of silver. And along the width of the court on the west side *shall be* hangings of fifty cubits, with their ten pillars and their ten sockets. The width of the court on the east side *shall be* fifty cubits. The hangings on *one* side *of the gate shall be* fifteen cubits, *with* their three pillars and their three sockets. And on the other side *shall be* hangings of fifteen *cubits*, *with* their three pillars and their three sockets."

a. **Also make the court of the tabernacle**: A fine linen fence marked off the courtyard, white in color. It provided an area of 150 feet (50 meters) by 75 feet (25 meters).

i. "As the Tent itself took up only about one-fifteenth [about 7%] of the area of the courtyard, there was plenty of room." (Cole)

ii. "Its purposes were fourfold: (1) it was a barrier in that it prevented unlawful approach; (2) it was a protection, keeping out all wild animals; (3) it was a positive line of demarcation between the world and the holy presence of God; and (4) with its single gate, it was a way of approach to God." (Kaiser)

b. **Its twenty pillars and their twenty sockets shall be bronze**: The short linen fence surrounding the courtyard was held up by a system of bronze **pillars**, twenty on the long sides and ten pillars on the short side of the rectangular-shaped court, with three pillars on the side with the entrance to the tabernacle.

> i. Exodus 27:18 tells us that the pillars were 7.5 feet (2.5 meters) high. Each had a bronze base and silver top piece, and a silver hook for hanging the linen upon.

2. (16) The gate to the courtyard.

"For the gate of the court *there shall be* a screen twenty cubits long, *woven of* blue, purple, and scarlet *thread,* and fine woven linen, made by a weaver. It *shall have* four pillars and four sockets."

> a. **For the gate of the court**: The gate was on the east side, the same side as the gate to the tent of the tabernacle. It was woven from the four colors used for the weavings of the tabernacle: **blue and purple and scarlet yarn, and fine linen thread**.

> b. **A screen twenty cubits long**: Though there was only one gate to the courtyard, it was large - 30 feet (10 meters) wide. This was the only entrance to the court of the tent of meeting.

3. (17-19) Other details regarding the courtyard.

"All the pillars around the court shall have bands of silver; their hooks *shall be* of silver and their sockets of bronze. The length of the court *shall be* one hundred cubits, the width fifty throughout, and the height five cubits, *made of* fine woven linen, and its sockets of bronze. All the utensils of the tabernacle for all its service, all its pegs, and all the pegs of the court, *shall be* of bronze."

> a. **All the pillars around the court shall have bands of silver**: Each pillar had a top of silver, making it shiny and visible from afar in the bright desert. Each pillar also had a **socket of bronze**, or a base of bronze. Refining through the fire makes bronze.

>> i. Silver (a metal illustrating redemption) was the foundation for the tent of meeting. It was also the top - the most visible part - of the pillars surrounding the courtyard. But the courtyard fence hung on a foundation of refined bronze, a metal associated with judgment because it is forged in the fire. One could say that the tabernacle court was based on, founded upon the judgment Jesus took in our place.

> b. **The pegs of the court**: These helped anchor down the flaps of the tabernacle and the gates, and were made of bronze.

> c. **All the pillars around the court**: The *court* of the tabernacle or the temple is an important theme throughout the rest of the Old Testament. This is mainly because the temple itself was inaccessible except to a few

priests. All others in Israel met God in the court. We can say by application that God also invites us to come into His courts to praise Him.

- *Blessed is the man You choose, and cause to approach You, that he may dwell in Your courts. We shall be satisfied with the goodness of Your house, of Your holy temple.* (Psalm 65:4)
- *My soul longs, yes, even faints for the courts of the* LORD*; my heart and my flesh cry out for the living God.* (Psalm 84:2)
- *For a day in Your courts is better than a thousand. I would rather be a doorkeeper in the house of my God than dwell in the tents of wickedness.* (Psalm 84:10)
- *Those who are planted in the house of the* LORD *shall flourish in the courts of our God.* (Psalm 92:13)
- *Give to the* LORD *the glory due His name; bring an offering, and come into His courts.* (Psalm 96:8)
- *Enter into His gates with thanksgiving, and into His courts with praise. Be thankful to Him, and bless His name.* (Psalm 100:4)
- *I will offer to You the sacrifice of thanksgiving, and will call upon the name of the* LORD*. I will pay my vows to the* LORD *now in the presence of all His people, in the courts of the Lord's house, in the midst of you, O Jerusalem. Praise the* LORD*!* (Psalm 116:17-19)
- *Praise the* LORD*! Praise the name of the* LORD*; praise Him, O you servants of the* LORD*! You who stand in the house of the* LORD*, in the courts of the house of our God.* (Psalm 135:1-2)

i. Under the New Covenant we appreciate this longing for the court of God's house, but we don't need to stop there. Because of the perfect sacrifice of Jesus and His finished work on our behalf, we can come - not only to the courts, but also right on into the holy presence of God. We thank God for the right to come into His courts, but we don't have to stop there.

d. **All the pillars around the court**: In overview, in coming to the tabernacle, one saw a white linen fence with shiny spots of silver on the posts holding up the fence, surrounded by thousands of black tents with the pillar of cloud over an unassuming tent in the midst of the courtyard covered with badger's skin.

i. The entire tabernacle was a *tent* - a moveable structure. God wanted Israel to know He was with them wherever they went. It wasn't a case of "You come to Me," but the idea was "I have come to You."

ii. "The Hebrews were meant to feel that the God of their fathers was a fellow-pilgrim, that where they pitched He pitched, that their enemies, difficulties, and long toilsome marches were His." (Meyer)

4. (20-21) The oil for the lamps on the lampstand.

"And you shall command the children of Israel that they bring you pure oil of pressed olives for the light, to cause the lamp to burn continually. In the tabernacle of meeting, outside the veil which *is* before the Testimony, Aaron and his sons shall tend it from evening until morning before the LORD. *It shall be* a statute forever to their generations on behalf of the children of Israel."

a. **That they bring you pure oil of pressed olives for the light**: The oil for the lamps on the lampstand - the only light in the tabernacle - came from **pressed olives**, not beaten olives.

i. "*Beaten* olive oil, so the Mishnah tells us, refers to the method of production of the very best oil." (Cole)

ii. God uses a *pressing* work in the life of His people. We, like Paul, may be *hard pressed on every side, yet not crushed* (2 Corinthians 4:8) - and God uses our times of pressing for His glory.

iii. "The saintly McCheyne used to say, when urging his brother ministers to diligent preparation for the pulpit: 'Beaten oil for the sanctuary.' And he strove to never present to his people truth which had not been beaten out by careful devout meditation." (Meyer)

iv. "Oil is uniformly the symbol of the Holy Spirit of God. Here, then, is the true value and meaning of this sacred oil. The elect light-bearers of the world are only able to fulfill their function by the Holy Spirit." (Morgan)

b. **Aaron and his sons shall tend it from evening until morning**: The priests were to **tend** the lamps, making sure that the lamps had oil to burn and that their wicks were trimmed, so that the lamps would never go out - especially during the night.

i. God never wanted the lamps to lose their fire. Only a continual supply of oil and trimming of the wicks could keep them burning. We can only continue to be on fire for God if we are continually supplied with the oil of the Holy Spirit, and are "trimmed" by God to bear more light.

ii. In dark days, there is all the more reason to be filled with the Holy Spirit and to be "trimmed wicks" for the LORD. *For it is the God who commanded light to shine out of darkness, who has shone in our hearts to give the light of the knowledge of the glory of God in the face of Jesus Christ.* (2 Corinthians 4:6) *For once you were darkness, but now you are light in the Lord. Walk as children of light* (Ephesians 5:8).

Exodus 28 - Garments for Priests

A. The command to make garments for the priests.

1. (1-2) The purpose of the garments.

"Now take Aaron your brother, and his sons with him, from among the children of Israel, that he may minister to Me as priest, Aaron *and* Aaron's sons: Nadab, Abihu, Eleazar, and Ithamar. And you shall make holy garments for Aaron your brother, for glory and for beauty."

a. **Take Aaron your brother, and his sons with him**: The priesthood of Israel was not earned by effort nor aspired to by ambition; it could only be inherited by birthright. One must be born into a priestly family.

i. The priesthood was no place for ambition or self-glory. It was only entered into by God's call and invitation. In the New Covenant, our priesthood is also not earned nor aspired to. We are priests because of our new birth into Jesus' priestly family (1 Peter 2:5).

b. **Make holy garments for Aaron your brother, for glory and for beauty**: The priestly garments were made **for glory and for beauty**. Since there was something glorious and beautiful - indeed, *heavenly* about the priestly service, it was appropriate to make the garments glorious and beautiful.

i. "Is then the dismal *black*, now worn by almost all kinds of priests and ministers, *for glory and for beauty?* Is it emblematic of any thing that is good, glorious, or excellent? How unbecoming the *glad tidings* announced by Christian ministers is a colour emblematical of nothing but *mourning* and *woe, sin, desolation*, and *death!*" (Clarke)

2. (3-4) What to make and who must make it.

"So you shall speak to all *who are* gifted artisans, whom I have filled with the spirit of wisdom, that they may make Aaron's garments, to consecrate him, that he may minister to Me as priest. And these *are* the garments which they shall make: a breastplate, an ephod, a robe,

a skillfully woven tunic, a turban, and a sash. So they shall make holy garments for Aaron your brother and his sons, that he may minister to Me as priest."

a. **Speak to all who are gifted artisans, whom I have filled with the spirit of wisdom, that they may make Aaron's garments**: God promised a special gifting from the Holy Spirit given to the craftsmen of these garments.

i. If it is really done to the glory of God, practical, manual service requires the leading of the Holy Spirit just as much as what we normally consider to be *spiritual* service.

ii. "The Hebrew slaves must have learned many Egyptian arts and crafts, such as metalwork, spinning, weaving and embroidery during their stay in Egypt." (Cole)

b. **That he may minister to Me**: Three times in these first four verses this command is repeated. Priests - under the old or new covenants - have their first ministry to God Himself.

c. **And these are the garments which they shall make**: Here are listed the various garments for the clothing of the priests and the High Priest. Each item on this list will be described in the section following.

B. Garments for the High Priest.

1. (5-14) The ephod.

"They shall take the gold, blue, purple, and scarlet *thread,* and fine linen, and they shall make the ephod of gold, blue, purple, *and* scarlet *thread,* and fine woven linen, artistically worked. It shall have two shoulder straps joined at its two edges, and *so* it shall be joined together. And the intricately woven band of the ephod, which *is* on it, shall be of the same workmanship, *made of* gold, blue, purple, and scarlet *thread,* and fine woven linen. Then you shall take two onyx stones and engrave on them the names of the sons of Israel: six of their names on one stone, and six names on the other stone, in order of their birth. With the work of an engraver in stone, *like* the engravings of a signet, you shall engrave the two stones with the names of the sons of Israel. You shall set them in settings of gold. And you shall put the two stones on the shoulders of the ephod *as* memorial stones for the sons of Israel. So Aaron shall bear their names before the LORD on his two shoulders as a memorial. You shall also make settings of gold, and you shall make two chains of pure gold like braided cords, and fasten the braided chains to the settings."

a. **Make the ephod of gold, blue, purple, and scarlet thread, and fine woven linen, artistically worked**: The **ephod** was essentially an ornate apron-like garment, made of gold, blue, purple and scarlet thread.

i. "Linen was the dress of the noble and the priest in Egypt, chosen both for coolness and cleanliness." (Cole)

b. **Take two onyx stones and engrave on them the names of the sons of Israel**: On the shoulder straps were polished gemstones on each strap, with the inscription of six of the tribes on each stone. Therefore, the High Priest would **bear their names before the LORD on his two shoulders as a memorial**.

i. "Aaron bears Israel's names before God whenever he enters the Tent, identifying himself with them." (Cole)

ii. While the first ministry of a priest is always unto God Himself, a priest also is constantly connected to the people, bearing them on his shoulders. The shoulders are a place of *work*; therefore, in the priest's ministry unto the LORD, he also worked for and with the people.

2. (15-30) The breastplate.

"You shall make the breastplate of judgment. Artistically woven according to the workmanship of the ephod you shall make it: of gold, blue, purple, and scarlet *thread,* and fine woven linen, you shall make it. It shall be doubled into a square: a span *shall be* its length, and a span *shall be* its width. And you shall put settings of stones in it, four rows of stones: *The first* row *shall be* a sardius, a topaz, and an emerald; *this shall be* the first row; the second row *shall be* a turquoise, a sapphire, and a diamond; the third row, a jacinth, an agate, and an amethyst; and the fourth row, a beryl, an onyx, and a jasper. They shall be set in gold settings. And the stones shall have the names of the sons of Israel, twelve according to their names, *like* the engravings of a signet, each one with its own name; they shall be according to the twelve tribes. You shall make chains for the breastplate at the end, like braided cords of pure gold. And you shall make two rings of gold for the breastplate, and put the two rings on the two ends of the breastplate. Then you shall put the two braided *chains* of gold in the two rings which are on the ends of the breastplate; and the *other* two ends of the two braided *chains* you shall fasten to the two settings, and put them on the shoulder straps of the ephod in the front. You shall make two rings of gold, and put them on the two ends of the breastplate, on the edge of it, which is on the inner side of the ephod. And two *other* rings of gold you shall make, and put them on the two shoulder straps, underneath the ephod toward its front, right at the seam above the intricately woven band of the ephod. They shall bind the breastplate by means of its rings to the rings of the ephod, using a blue cord, so that it is above the intricately woven band of the ephod, and so that the breastplate does not come loose from the ephod. So Aaron shall bear the names of the sons of

Israel on the breastplate of judgment over his heart, when he goes into the holy *place*, as a memorial before the LORD** continually. And you shall put in the breastplate of judgment the Urim and the Thummim, and they shall be over Aaron's heart when he goes in before the L**ORD**. So Aaron shall bear the judgment of the children of Israel over his heart before the L**ORD** continually."**

a. **Make the breastplate of judgment**: The breastplate was also made with gold, blue, purple, and scarlet thread. It was attached to the ephod with gold chains.

i. "This explains why the garment may be called the 'breastplate of judgment', since it contains the two oracular stones, by means of which God's 'judgment' might be made known." (Cole)

b. **Put settings of stones in it, four rows of stones**: On the breastplate were four rows of three gemstones, each stone having one of the names of the twelve tribes inscribed on it. In wearing the breastplate, the High Priest would **bear the names of the sons of Israel...over his heart**.

i. It was not enough that the High Priest worked for the people (having them on his shoulders). He must also *love* the people - that is, bear them on his heart.

ii. It isn't enough for a priest to have a heart for God. He must also have a heart for the people, and bear them on his heart in his entire ministry unto the L**ORD**.

c. **A sardius, a topaz, and an emerald**: This begins a list of twelve gemstones set in the breastplate of the high priest. It is impossible to know exactly what all of these gemstones were, but we can come to some likely conclusions. Revelation 21:19-20 describes the foundations of the walls of the New Jerusalem with a series of twelve gemstones, which may answer to these stones in the breastplate.

i. We cannot neglect the fact God commanded the tribes to have their names inscribed on *gemstones* - truly precious things. God's people are indeed precious to Him.

d. **Put in the breastplate of judgment the Urim and the Thummim**: Three times in this passage the breastplate is called **the breastplate of judgment** because it held the **Urim and Thummim** which were tools for discerning God's will.

i. The use of the discerning tools of **Urim and Thummim** is described on a few occasions (Numbers 27:21, 1 Samuel 28:6, Ezra 2:63, and Nehemiah 7:65), and their use may be implied in other passages (Judges 1:1; 20:18, 23).

ii. The names **Urim and Thummim** mean "Lights and Perfections." We aren't sure what they were or how they were used. The best guess is that they were a pair of stones, one light and another dark, and each stone indicated a "yes" or "no" from God. The High Priest would ask God a question, reach into the breastplate, and pull out either a "yes" or a "no."

iii. Meyer suggests the **Urim and Thummim** were brilliant diamonds, which flashed brightly with a "yes" or dimly with a "no" answer from God.

iv. Many consider the **Urim and Thummim** as crude tools of discernment. In fact, they are better than the tools many Christians use today. It would be better to use the **Urim and Thummim** than rely on feelings, or outward appearances, or to simply use no discernment at all.

v. The key to the effectiveness of the **Urim and Thummim** was that *God's Word* gave them. In seeking God through the **Urim and Thummim**, one was really going back to God's Word for guidance, because it was the Word of God that commanded their place and allowed their use. Today, if we have the same focus on God's Word, He will guide us also. One old preacher was asked to explain the **Urim and Thummim**. He said, "Well, this is how I understand it. When I need to know God's will, I get out my Bible and I do a lot of *usin' and thummin'* through my Bible, and God always speaks to me." More Christians would know God's will if they did more *usin' and thummin'*.

3. (31-35) The robe.

"You shall make the robe of the ephod all of blue. There shall be an opening for his head in the middle of it; it shall have a woven binding all around its opening, like the opening in a coat of mail, so that it does not tear. And upon its hem you shall make pomegranates of blue, purple, and scarlet, all around its hem, and bells of gold between them all around: a golden bell and a pomegranate, a golden bell and a pomegranate, upon the hem of the robe all around. And it shall be upon Aaron when he ministers, and its sound will be heard when he goes into the holy *place* before the LORD and when he comes out, that he may not die."

a. **Make the robe of the ephod all of blue**: This was the basic covering of the priest, made of all blue, seamless, and with no tear for the head opening.

b. **Bells of gold between them all around**: On its hem, between the ornate **pomegranates of blue and purple**, were bells so the priest could be heard while ministering before God - if he were to die, the bells would stop ringing and he could be pulled out of the Most Holy Place. The sound of the bells would remind the priest of the solemn nature of his work, and remind him so **that he may not die**.

i. "The tinkling bells were presumably so that the people outside could trace the movements of the priest within, who was of course invisible to them. By this they would know that his offering had been accepted, and that he had not been struck dead." (Cole)

ii. "The *pomegranates* (symbols of fruitfulness) were either hanging as 'bobbles' between the bells, or else embroidered on the fabric." (Cole)

iii. "The alternating bell and pomegranate on the skirts of the priest's robe were typical of his obligation to testimony and fruit bearing." (Morgan)

4. (36-38) The turban and its engraving.

"You shall also make a plate of pure gold and engrave on it, *like* the engraving of a signet: HOLINESS TO THE LORD. And you shall put it on a blue cord, that it may be on the turban; it shall be on the front of the turban. So it shall be on Aaron's forehead, that Aaron may bear the iniquity of the holy things which the children of Israel hallow in all their holy gifts; and it shall always be on his forehead, that they may be accepted before the LORD."

a. **It shall be on the front of the turban**: The turban was a simple wound linen headpiece. More important than the turban itself was the gold plate with the inscription HOLINESS TO THE LORD.

i. "The *turban* (literally something wound around: the Talmud tells us that eight yards of material were used)." (Cole)

ii. The inscription HOLINESS TO THE LORD indicated that first and foremost the high priest was the servant of God, not man. "Hence it was not lawful for the high priest, say the Jews, to put off his bonnet to whomsoever he met, were he never so great a man; lest the same name and glory of God, whose person he sustained, should seem to submit to any man." (Trapp)

b. **That Aaron may bear the iniquity of the holy things which the children of Israel hallow in all their holy gifts**: Even the gifts and sacrifices Aaron and the other priests brought before the Lord were touched with **iniquity**. Yet when God's appointed priest in God brought them in God's appointed way, God **accepted** them.

c. **That they might be accepted before the LORD**: Holiness - not as a legalistic list of rules, but in the power of a life separated to God - is essential for anyone who will appear before God. Hebrews 12:14 reinforced this principle: *Pursue peace with all people, and holiness, without which no one will see the Lord.*

5. (39) The tunic, the turban, and the sash.

"You shall skillfully weave the tunic of fine linen *thread,* you shall make the turban of fine linen, and you shall make the sash of woven work."

a. **Skillfully weave the tunic of fine linen**: These basic garments are simply described as being woven of fine linen.

6. (40-43) Garments for the sons of Aaron.

"For Aaron's sons you shall make tunics, and you shall make sashes for them. And you shall make hats for them, for glory and beauty. So you shall put them on Aaron your brother and on his sons with him. You shall anoint them, consecrate them, and sanctify them, that they may minister to Me as priests. And you shall make for them linen trousers to cover their nakedness; they shall reach from the waist to the thighs. They shall be on Aaron and on his sons when they come into the tabernacle of meeting, or when they come near the altar to minister in the holy *place,* that they do not incur iniquity and die. *It shall be* a statute forever to him and his descendants after him."

a. **For Aaron's sons you shall make tunics**: Though the regular priests had special garments, they were simple clothes of fine linen. They were special, but not much compared to the glory and beauty of the High Priest's garments.

i. This is because the regular priests, though important, had a far lesser office than the High Priest - and were appropriately clothed for this lower position.

ii. Even so, the High Priest's clothing, in total, speaks more of Jesus' glory and beauty than of ours. We are (or should be) content with simple linen robes.

b. **You shall anoint them, consecrate them, and sanctify them, that they may minister to Me as priests**: Here God explained three important and essential aspects to the preparation of His servants: *anointing, consecration,* and *sanctification.* They are separated because here they indicated three different ideas.

i. **Anoint** describes the application of the sacred oil upon the head. In the consistent idiom of the Bible, it represents the filling and continual reliance upon the power and work of the Holy Spirit.

ii. **Consecrate** "Is the translation of two Hebrew words, meaning the filling of the open hand, and signifies the perfect equipment of the anointed one for the discharge of that ministry." (Morgan)

iii. **Sanctify** "Means literally, to make clean, and refers to the spiritual and moral separation of the priest from all defilement." (Morgan)

c. **Linen trousers to cover their nakedness**: The priests - all of the priests - were to wear undergarments so it would be impossible for their nakedness to be exposed while ministering.

i. This was probably a reaction to the nakedness of many pagan priests while performing their rituals. "This command had in view the necessity of *purity* and *decency* in every part of the Divine worship, in opposition to the shocking indecency of the pagan worship in general, in which the priests often ministered *naked*, as in the sacrifices to Bacchus." (Clarke)

ii. Also, the trousers were to be made of cool **linen** instead of warm wool. God doesn't want His servants to sweat.

C. A Contrast between Jesus' clothing when He accomplished His great priestly work and the garments of the High Priest.

1. Jesus wore no beautiful ephod - only a purple robe for mocking.

2. Jesus had no precious gems on His shoulders, only a cross that we deserved.

3. Jesus had no breastplate with "Israel on His heart," yet He died of a broken heart for Israel - and all of mankind.

4. As the High Priest, Jesus had a seamless robe that was not torn, but it was stripped away at the cross.

5. Jesus heard no delicate sound of bells proving that the High Priest was alive, only the sound of pounding nails ensuring our High Priest's death.

6. Jesus wore no fine linen turban, rather a painful crown of thorns.

7. Jesus had no headplate reading HOLINESS TO THE LORD, but a life and death showing nothing but holiness to the LORD!

8. Jesus had no linen trousers to hide His nakedness, rather He bore our sins on the cross in a naked shame.

Exodus 29 - The Consecration of the Priests

A. Preparation for consecration.

1. (1a) The purpose of the ceremony.

And this is what you shall do to them to hallow them for ministering to Me as priests:

a. **This is what you shall do**: These are only the instructions for the ceremony, which was actually carried out in Leviticus 8.

b. **To hallow them for ministering to Me as priests**: The purpose of the ceremony was to **hallow them**; that is, to set the priests aside for God's purpose.

2. (1b-3) Ingredients needed for consecration.

Take one young bull and two rams without blemish, and unleavened bread, unleavened cakes mixed with oil, and unleavened wafers anointed with oil (you shall make them of wheat flour). You shall put them in one basket and bring them in the basket, with the bull and the two rams.

a. **One young bull and two rams without blemish**: The ceremony for consecration required animals intended for sacrifice. Consecration couldn't happen without shedding sacrificial blood.

b. **Unleavened bread, unleavened cakes**: The ceremony for consecration required bread for fellowship with God. Consecration couldn't happen without true fellowship with God.

3. (4) The washing.

And Aaron and his sons you shall bring to the door of the tabernacle of meeting, and you shall wash them with water.

a. **Aaron and his sons**: This was not a ceremony for just anyone in Israel. There were special consecration ceremonies available to anyone, such as the Nazirite vow in Numbers 6. But the ceremony described here and carried out in Leviticus 8 was for *priests*, for **Aaron and his sons**.

b. **You shall bring to the door of the tabernacle of meeting**: This process of consecration didn't take place *inside* the tabernacle. It happened outside, at **the door of the tabernacle of meeting**. It was something others could see.

c. **And you shall wash them with water**: The process of consecration began with cleansing. All priestly ministries began with cleansing, and a cleansing that was *received*: **you shall wash them**. Aaron and his sons did not wash themselves; they *received* a washing.

> i. This was humbling, because it took place publicly at **the door of the tabernacle of meeting**. We cannot be cleansed from our sin without being humbled first.

> ii. This great cleansing was a one-time thing. From then on, they just needed to cleanse their hands and their feet.

> iii. Like these ancient priests, every Christian is washed by the work of God's Word (Ephesians 5:26), by the regenerating work of the Holy Spirit (Titus 3:5). This cleansing work was accomplished by the death of Jesus for us (Revelation 1:5) and appropriated by faith.

4. (5-9) The clothing and the anointing.

Then you shall take the garments, put the tunic on Aaron, and the robe of the ephod, the ephod, and the breastplate, and gird him with the intricately woven band of the ephod. You shall put the turban on his head, and put the holy crown on the turban. And you shall take the anointing oil, pour *it* on his head, and anoint him. Then you shall bring his sons and put tunics on them. And you shall gird them with sashes, Aaron and his sons, and put the hats on them. The priesthood shall be theirs for a perpetual statute. So you shall consecrate Aaron and his sons.

a. **Take the garments, put the tunic on Aaron**: After being cleansed, the priest had to be clothed, but not in his own clothes. He had to put on garments given by God.

> i. Like these ancient priests, every believer is clothed in Jesus Christ and in his righteousness (Revelation 3:5). These are clothes that are given freely by Jesus, but received and "worn" by faith.

> ii. "Note, that *these garments were provided for the*m. They were at no expense in buying them, nor labor in weaving them, nor skill in making them; they had simply to put them on. And you, dear child of God, are to put on the garments which Jesus Christ has provided for

you, at his own cost, and freely bestows upon you out of boundless love." (Spurgeon)

b. **And you shall take the anointing oil, pour it on his head, and anoint him**: Priests must be anointed. The oil (a picture of the Holy Spirit) was *poured* over their heads, indicating that it was given in great measure, not in small measure (Psalm 133:2).

> i. Like these ancient priests, every believer has an anointing (1 John 2:20) that they may receive and walk in by faith.

5. (10-14) The sin offering.

You shall also have the bull brought before the tabernacle of meeting, and Aaron and his sons shall put their hands on the head of the bull. Then you shall kill the bull before the LORD, *by* the door of the tabernacle of meeting. You shall take *some* of the blood of the bull and put *it* on the horns of the altar with your finger, and pour all the blood beside the base of the altar. And you shall take all the fat that covers the entrails, the fatty lobe *attached* to the liver, and the two kidneys and the fat that *is* on them, and burn *them* on the altar. But the flesh of the bull, with its skin and its offal, you shall burn with fire outside the camp. It *is* a sin offering.

a. **Aaron and his sons shall put their hands on the head of the bull**: The washing at the door of the tabernacle was only one aspect of the symbolic cleansing from sin. There had to be the punishment of the guilty, and this happened. As Aaron and his sons **put their hands on the head of the bull**, they symbolically transferred their sin to the bull.

> i. "The Hebrew word means more than lightly placing the hand, it gives the idea of pressing hard upon the bullock's head. They came each one and leaned upon the victim, loading him with their burden, signifying their acceptance of its substitution, their joy that the Lord would accept that victim in their stead. When they put their hands on the bullock, they made a confession of sin." (Spurgeon)

> ii. Like these ancient priests, every believer can only be consecrated to God through sacrifice. Our consecration should be greater, because it was made through a far greater sacrifice - the sacrifice of God's own Son.

b. **You shall take some of the blood of the bull and put it on the horns of the altar with your finger**: The altar was sanctified with the blood of the **sin offering**, and the best of the animal was burnt before the LORD; the rest was destroyed outside the camp. The sin offering said, "We have failed to give our best to God. This animal now gives its best to atone for our failure, and we decide to live now giving our best, even as this animal who dies in our place."

> i. The idea behind the ancient Hebrew word for **altar** is essentially, "killing-place." The ancient altar, a place of death, was made holy and was consecrated to God. Like that ancient altar, the altar of the New Covenant, the cross, is transformed from a place of death to a place set apart to bring life.

6. (15-18) The burnt offering.

You shall also take one ram, and Aaron and his sons shall put their hands on the head of the ram; and you shall kill the ram, and you shall take its blood and sprinkle *it* all around on the altar. Then you shall cut the ram in pieces, wash its entrails and its legs, and put *them* with its pieces and with its head. And you shall burn the whole ram on the altar. It *is* a burnt offering to the LORD; it *is* a sweet aroma, an offering made by fire to the LORD.

> a. **Aaron and his sons shall put their hands on the head of the ram; and you shall kill the ram**: As the sin offering before it, the **burnt offering** also symbolically received the sins of the priests, and they laid their hands on the head of the animal and confessed their sin.

> b. **And you shall burn the whole ram on the altar**: The ram was completely burnt before the LORD, with its blood sprinkled on the altar. The burnt offering said, "We have failed to give our all to God. This animal now gives its all to atone for our failure, and we decide to live now giving our all, even as this animal who dies in our place."

B. The consecration offering.

1. (19-21) The application of blood.

You shall also take the other ram, and Aaron and his sons shall put their hands on the head of the ram. Then you shall kill the ram, and take some of its blood and put *it* on the tip of the right ear of Aaron and on the tip of the right ear of his sons, on the thumb of their right hand and on the big toe of their right foot, and sprinkle the blood all around on the altar. And you shall take some of the blood that is on the altar, and some of the anointing oil, and sprinkle *it* on Aaron and on his garments, on his sons and on the garments of his sons with him; and he and his garments shall be hallowed, and his sons and his sons' garments with him.

> a. **Also take the other ram, and Aaron and his sons shall put their hands on the head of the ram**: Atonement for sin was performed with the sin offering and the burnt offering. Yet in their consecration, the

priests still had to identify with the sacrificial victim. Their identification with the sacrifice went beyond atonement.

b. **Kill the ram, and take some of its blood and put it on the tip of the right ear of Aaron**: To express the idea of consecration, blood from the ram was placed on the ear, thumb, and toe of the priest. It was blood from the ram, not the wool, not the fat. God wanted the "life" of the sacrificial victim to mark His consecrated priests.

i. Leviticus 17:11 is one of many passages that expresses this principle: *For the life of the flesh is in the blood.* God wanted the *life* of the sacrificial victim to be evident in the *body* of the priest.

c. **Tip of the right ear...thumb of their right hand...big toe of their right foot**: These consecrated priests were stained with the blood of sacrifice. They should *hear* differently because the blood was on their **ear**. They should *work* differently because the blood was on their **thumb**. They should *walk* differently because the blood was on their **toe**.

i. Specifically, it was applied to the **right** ear, hand, and foot. This isn't because God felt they could do whatever they wanted to with their left ear, hand, and foot. It is because the **right** side was considered superior, with more strength and skill (because most people are right-handed). God wanted their *best* to be dedicated to Him.

d. **You shall take some of the blood that is on the altar, and some of the anointing oil, and sprinkle it on Aaron and on his garments**: The blood alone wasn't enough. God wanted **blood** mixed with **oil**, and to have the *mixture* sprinkled on the priests. There was to be a combination of both the sacrifice and the spirit (represented by the **anointing oil**).

i. "Yes, brethren, we need to know that double anointing, the blood of Jesus which cleanses, and the oil of the Holy Spirit which perfumes us. It is well to see how these two blend in one...It is a terrible blunder to set the blood and the oil in opposition, they must always go together." (Spurgeon)

2. (22-28) The wave offering.

Also you shall take the fat of the ram, the fat tail, the fat that covers the entrails, the fatty lobe *attached* to the liver, the two kidneys and the fat on them, the right thigh (for it *is* a ram of consecration), one loaf of bread, one cake *made with* oil, and one wafer from the basket of the unleavened bread that *is* before the LORD; and you shall put all these in the hands of Aaron and in the hands of his sons, and you shall wave them *as* a wave offering before the LORD. You shall receive them back from their hands and burn *them* on the altar as a burnt offering, as a sweet aroma before the LORD. It *is* an offering made by fire to the LORD.

Then you shall take the breast of the ram of Aaron's consecration and wave it *as* **a wave offering before the** Lord**; and it shall be your portion. And from the ram of the consecration you shall consecrate the breast of the wave offering which is waved, and the thigh of the heave offering which is raised, of** *that* **which** *is* **for Aaron and of** *that* **which is for his sons. It shall be from the children of Israel** *for* **Aaron and his sons by a statute forever. For it is a heave offering; it shall be a heave offering from the children of Israel from the sacrifices of their peace offerings,** *that is,* **their heave offering to the** Lord**.**

a. **Also you shall take the fat of the ram**: The second ram used in the consecration ceremony - the ram whose blood was applied to the ear, hand, and foot of the priest - was used as a **heave offering** and **peace offerings**.

b. **You shall wave them before the** Lord**...burn them on the altar as a burnt offering**: Part of this second ram - the best parts - was put together with the **bread**, **cake**, and the **wafer** and was first *waved* before God in an act of presentation. Then these portions were burnt on the altar as an act of complete devotion.

c. **It shall be your portion**: The remaining meat portions of this ram were given to Aaron and the other priests, after those portions were presented to God as a **wave offering**. It was then cooked and eaten by the priests during the days of their consecration ceremony.

i. The second ram - after the ram presented as a burnt offering - had its *life* applied to the consecrated priests. First, its life was applied with the application of blood to the ear, hand, and foot of the priest. Then through a ritual meal, its life was applied to the priest taking the ram in to himself.

ii. The eating did not *begin* the process of consecration. It came *after* the washing, the clothing, and the blood-atonement of the priests. The eating speaks of the *continuing relationship* of the priest with God. "Let not this distinction be forgotten; the eating of the sacrifice is not intended to give life, for no dead man can eat, but to sustain the life which is there already. A believing look at Christ makes you live, but spiritual life must be fed and sustained." (Spurgeon)

iii. In this way, eating is a good picture of a healthy, continuing relationship with Jesus.

- Eating is *personal*. No one can eat for you, and no one can have a relationship with Jesus on your behalf

- Eating is *inward*. It does no good to be around food or to rub food on the outside of your body; you must *take it in*. We must take Jesus unto ourselves *inwardly*, not merely in an external way
- Eating is *active*. Some medicines are received passively. They are injected under the skin and go to work. Such medicines could even be received while one sleeps, but no one can eat while asleep. We must *actively* take Jesus unto ourselves
- Eating arises *out of a sense of need* and produces *a sense of satisfaction*. We will have a healthy relationship with Jesus when we *sense our need* for Him and *receive the satisfaction* the relationship brings

3. (29-37) The week of consecration.

And the holy garments of Aaron shall be his sons' after him, to be anointed in them and to be consecrated in them. That son who becomes priest in his place shall put them on for seven days, when he enters the tabernacle of meeting to minister in the holy *place*. And you shall take the ram of the consecration and boil its flesh in the holy place. Then Aaron and his sons shall eat the flesh of the ram, and the bread that *is* in the basket, *by* the door of the tabernacle of meeting. They shall eat those things with which the atonement was made, to consecrate *and* to sanctify them; but an outsider shall not eat *them,* because they *are* holy. And if any of the flesh of the consecration offerings, or of the bread, remains until the morning, then you shall burn the remainder with fire. It shall not be eaten, because it *is* holy. Thus you shall do to Aaron and his sons, according to all that I have commanded you. Seven days you shall consecrate them. And you shall offer a bull every day *as* a sin offering for atonement. You shall cleanse the altar when you make atonement for it, and you shall anoint it to sanctify it. Seven days you shall make atonement for the altar and sanctify it. And the altar shall be most holy. Whatever touches the altar must be holy.

a. **That son who becomes priest in his place shall put them on for seven days**: With the coming generations, new descendants of Aaron would qualify for the priesthood and would be consecrated the same way. For Aaron and his descendants, the consecration process took **seven days**.

b. **They shall eat those things with which the atonement was made, to consecrate and to sanctify them**: For **seven days**, they lived at the tabernacle and ate the **ram of the consecration** and the bread of consecration. The consecration ceremony wasn't quick and easy. It took time, reflection, and a constant awareness of sacrifice and atonement.

i. "The Lord's part was consumed with fire upon the altar, and another portion was eaten by man in the holy place. The peace offering was thus an open declaration of the communion which had been established between God and man, so that they ate together, rejoicing in the same offering." (Spurgeon)

ii. "I know some good people who are very busy indeed in the services of God, and I am very delighted that they should be, but I would caution them against working and never eating. They give up attending the means of grace as hearers, because they have so much to do as workers." (Spurgeon)

c. **But an outsider shall not eat them, because they are holy**: Few among us today are of the lineage of Aaron, but we have the right to receive and enjoy this priestly consecration and relationship based not only on the clear declaration of the New Testament (1 Peter 2:5 and 2:9), but also upon principles of the *Old Covenant*.

i. Leviticus 22:11 says, *But if the priest buys a person with his money, he may eat it; and one who is born in his house may eat his food.* Since Jesus, our High Priest, has purchased us with His own life, we may eat of the priestly portion. And since we are born again as children of God - *born in his house*, the family of our High Priest - we also *may eat his food* and enjoy the priestly privileges of our High Priest.

d. **And you shall offer a bull every day as a sin offering for atonement**: Every day there was another large animal to sacrifice and use its blood for atonement. This daily ritual, for **seven days** in a row, reminded Aaron and the priests that any animal sacrifice could not take away sin, but only provided a temporary covering.

4. (38-41) The continual consecration.

Now this *is* what you shall offer on the altar: two lambs of the first year, day by day continually. One lamb you shall offer in the morning, and the other lamb you shall offer at twilight. With the one lamb shall be one-tenth *of an ephah* of flour mixed with one-fourth of a hin of pressed oil, and one-fourth of a hin of wine *as* a drink offering. And the other lamb you shall offer at twilight; and you shall offer with it the grain offering and the drink offering, as in the morning, for a sweet aroma, an offering made by fire to the LORD.

a. **Two lambs...day by day continually**: After the ceremony of consecration, the priests continued with daily sacrifices, one **in the morning** and the other **at twilight**. Every day was given to God, beginning and ending by sacrifices of atonement and consecration.

b. **A drink offering**: This was wine given to God as a sacrifice, poured out before Him as a demonstration of completely emptying one's self to God.

> i. The Apostle Paul used the terminology of the **drink offering** to express his complete devotion to God, and his possibly soon martyrdom (Philippians 2:17).

c. **For a sweet aroma, an offering made by fire to the LORD**: These burnt offerings - completely consumed by fire - pleased God and "smelled good" to Him. God is honored and glorified by our complete surrender to Him.

5. (42-43) Why God wanted the daily sacrifices and continual consecration.

This shall be **a continual burnt offering throughout your generations** *at* **the door of the tabernacle of meeting before the LORD, where I will meet you to speak with you. And there I will meet with the children of Israel, and** *the tabernacle* **shall be sanctified by My glory.**

a. **This shall be a continual burnt offering throughout your generations**: Except for times of captivity and national apostasy, these daily sacrifices continued in Israel up through the time of the New Testament. Luke 1 describes Zacharias (the father of John the Baptist) ministering at a morning sacrifice, which developed into what we might call "morning devotions" for ancient Israel.

b. **I will meet you**: God wanted consecrated priests and a worshipping nation, and not because He simply wanted a "well-trained work-force." God wanted consecrated priests and daily sacrifice so He could **meet** with and **speak** to His people.

> i. This is the great reason for consecration, for a sense of full surrender to God. It isn't primarily so we can be better *workers* for God, but so that we can enjoy deeper and more meaningful relationship with Him. If this is of little interest to us, we will never be properly motivated to true consecration.

c. **And the tabernacle shall be sanctified by My glory**: It was the *presence of God* that truly sanctified and consecrated the **tabernacle** and the priests. It wasn't primarily because of what the priests did. What the priests did in consecration was to *remove the barriers* to the radiant glory of God.

6. (44-46) **So I will sanctify**.

So I will consecrate the tabernacle of meeting and the altar. I will also consecrate both Aaron and his sons to minister to Me as priests. I will dwell among the children of Israel and will be their God. And they

shall know that I *am* the LORD their God, who brought them up out of the land of Egypt, that I may dwell among them. I *am* the LORD their God.

a. **So I will consecrate**: God made it clear *who* performs the work of consecration. We are tempted to think that *we sanctify our self* because we are so immersed in the sanctifying process and because it draws so much out of us. Yet God does the work - what we do is remove barriers and spend time with the focus on Him.

b. **To minister to Me as priests**: Aaron and his sons had a ministry to the people of Israel, but their first ministry was to the LORD. They might be successful in ministry to the people, but if they failed in their ministry to the LORD, their ministry failed.

i. "The best part of all Christian work is that part which only God sees." (Andrew Bonar)

c. **And they shall know that I am the LORD their God**: God promised to show His glory through consecrated priests. When Moses and Aaron performed this ceremony of consecration, Leviticus 9:23-24 tells us the result: *Then the glory of the LORD appeared to all the people, and fire came out from before the LORD and consumed the burnt offering and the fat on the altar. When all the people saw it, they shouted and fell on their faces.*

i. There is a price to pay for being fully surrendered to God. The ceremony of consecration was long, bloody, and it took persistence to complete. Yet the reward was far greater than the cost - the glory of the LORD was revealed not only to the consecrated priests, but to the people in general.

d. **I will dwell among the children of Israel and will be their God**: God again stressed the idea of *relationship* in the process of consecration. This worship-filled relationship with God is both the *instrument* and the *fruit* of consecration.

Exodus 30 - More Tabernacle Related Subjects

A. The altar of incense.

1. (1-5) How to make the altar of incense.

"You shall make an altar to burn incense on; you shall make it of acacia wood. A cubit *shall be* its length and a cubit its width; it shall be square; and two cubits *shall be* its height. Its horns *shall be* of one piece with it. And you shall overlay its top, its sides all around, and its horns with pure gold; and you shall make for it a molding of gold all around. Two gold rings you shall make for it, under the molding on both its sides. You shall place *them* on its two sides, and they will be holders for the poles with which to bear it. You shall make the poles of acacia wood, and overlay them with gold."

a. **Make an altar to burn incense on**: The altar of incense was made of acacia wood overlaid with gold. It was 18 inches (0.5 meter) square and 3 feet (1 meter) high.

b. **Two gold rings you shall make for it...they will be holders for the poles with which to bear it**: The altar of incense was also carried by the system of rings and poles, just like the Ark of the Covenant, the table of showbread, and the brazen altar with its grate.

2. (6-10) The use of the altar of incense.

"And you shall put it before the veil that *is* before the ark of the Testimony, before the mercy seat that *is* over the Testimony, where I will meet with you. Aaron shall burn on it sweet incense every morning; when he tends the lamps, he shall burn incense on it. And when Aaron lights the lamps at twilight, he shall burn incense on it, a perpetual incense before the LORD throughout your generations. You shall not offer strange incense on it, or a burnt offering, or a grain offering; nor shall you pour a drink offering on it. And Aaron shall make atonement upon its horns once a year with the blood of the sin

offering of atonement; once a year he shall make atonement upon it throughout your generations. It *is* most holy to the LORD."

a. **You shall put it before the veil that is before the ark of the Testimony**: The altar of incense stood outside the veil, in the holy place (not in the most holy place). Therefore it was fairly close to the Ark of the Covenant, yet separated by the veil.

i. It was in the holy place of the tabernacle, together with the golden lampstand and the table of showbread. "The table of showbread represented communion with God, the lampstand spoke of testimony to the world, and now the golden altar speaks of the offering of adoration." (Morgan)

b. **Where I will meet with you**: Sprinkled throughout this description of the tabernacle and the furnishings were reminders of the purpose of the tabernacle. It was a place for man to meet with God.

c. **Aaron shall burn on it sweet incense every morning**: Aaron (and other priests after him) were instructed to burn incense on this altar every day as part of their normal priestly duties, both in the morning and in the evening (**when Aaron lights the lamps at twilight, he shall burn incense on it**).

i. Incense is a picture of prayer, in the sweetness of its smell and the way it ascends to heaven (*golden bowls of incense, which are the prayers of the saints*, according to Revelation 5:8). The ministry at the altar of incense speaks of how God's people should continually come to Him in prayer.

ii. Revelation 8:3-4 describes the golden altar of incense standing before Gods' throne: *Then another angel, having a golden censer, came and stood at the altar. He was given much incense, that he should offer it with the prayers of all the saints upon the golden altar which was before the throne. And the smoke of the incense, with the prayers of the saints, ascended before God from the angel's hand.*

d. **You shall not offer strange incense on it**: Priests were not permitted to offer God whatever they wanted on the altar of incense. **Strange incense** was prohibited.

e. **You shall not offer strange incense on it, or a burnt offering, or a grain offering; nor shall you pour a drink offering on it**: It was called *the altar* of incense, but an animal sacrifice or drink offering was never placed upon it.

i. Prayer is not the place sacrificial atonement is made; it is the place sacrificial atonement is enjoyed. We don't *save* ourselves through prayer; we pray because of Jesus' saving work on the cross.

f. **Aaron shall make atonement upon its horns once a year with the blood of the sin offering of atonement**: The altar of incense was not a place of sacrifice, but it was a place for atoning blood. On the Day of Atonement, Aaron had to anoint the horns of the altar of incense with blood from the atoning sacrifice.

i. Once a year the altar of incense received the blood of atonement, but it was a place where atonement was remembered and enjoyed, not made.

ii. This illustrates the principle that prayer does not atone for our sins, but must always be made in reference to Jesus' atoning blood. The Day of Atonement was only once a year, but every day when the priests brought a morning and evening offering of incense, they saw the blood-stained horns of the altar. This was a constant reminder of the work of atoning blood.

B. The ransom money for a census.

1. (11-12) The reason for the ransom money.

Then the LORD spoke to Moses, saying: "When you take the census of the children of Israel for their number, then every man shall give a ransom for himself to the LORD, when you number them, that there may be no plague among them when *you* number them."

a. **When you take the census of the children of Israel for their number**: Later in the Book of Numbers, two significant censuses were recorded of the nation of Israel. Here, God made provision to make a census without being plagued.

b. **That there may be no plague among them when you number them**: A census put Israel at risk of **plague** because a census (a numbering) signified ownership. This spoke against God's ownership of Israel, because in their thinking, a man only had the right to count or number what belonged to him. Israel didn't belong to Israel; Israel belonged to God. It was up to Him to command a counting.

i. If a count was made without receiving the ransom money, a census communicated the idea that a king or a human leader owned Israel, when God alone did. This was David's problem in 2 Samuel 24:1-25, when David took a census without the ransom money and God plagued Israel.

2. (13-16) How to take a census with ransom money.

"This is what everyone among those who are numbered shall give: half a shekel according to the shekel of the sanctuary (a shekel *is* twenty gerahs). The half-shekel *shall be* an offering to the LORD. Everyone

included among those who are numbered, from twenty years old and above, shall give an offering to the LORD. The rich shall not give more and the poor shall not give less than half a shekel, when *you* give an offering to the LORD, to make atonement for yourselves. And you shall take the atonement money of the children of Israel, and shall appoint it for the service of the tabernacle of meeting, that it may be a memorial for the children of Israel before the LORD, to make atonement for yourselves."

a. **Everyone included among those who are numbered, from twenty years old and above, shall give an offering to the LORD**: The census was to include everyone aged twenty and over. This seems to be the Israelite age of full adulthood in this sense. Everyone also had to give an equal amount, one-half shekel.

i. This ransom money spoke clearly: *everyone owes God; everyone is obligated to Him.* "The Lord commanded that every male over twenty years of age should pay half a shekel as redemption money, confessing that he deserved to die, owning that he was in debt to God, and bringing the sum demanded as a type of a great redemption which would by-and-by be paid for the souls of the sons of men." (Spurgeon)

ii. "Later, the 'half-shekel' became an annual temple tax (Matthew 17:24)." (Cole)

b. **The rich shall not give more and the poor shall not give less... to make atonement for yourselves**: This was not a request for a free-will offering, nor was it a proportional tithe. This was more like a flat tax where everyone paid the same amount, rich or poor, because this was **to make atonement**. It wasn't that the money was the atonement, but it marked the ones who were atoned.

i. In this sense, it is not a pattern for our giving under the New Covenant. New Covenant giving should be proportional, under the principle that we should give in proportion to our blessing (1 Corinthians 16:2).

ii. Instead of a pattern of our own giving, this money was a picture of the cost of our own redemption. "The *rich* were not to give *more*, the *poor* not to give less; to signify that all souls were equally precious in the sight of God, and that no difference of *outward* circumstances could affect the state of the soul; all had sinned, and all must be redeemed by the same price." (Clarke)

iii. "The half-shekel was not a gift in the sense of a free-will offering. It was a recognition of redemption, a sign of atonement, made and received. Here the rich and the poor stood upon a perfect equality." (Morgan)

iv. As well, *everyone* had to pay their own redemption money. No lump sum for every member of the tribe or family could satisfy this obligation.

c. **Appoint it for the service of the tabernacle of meeting**: This money was given to the service of the tabernacle. There was a large amount of silver needed in the building of the tabernacle, and this is how it was obtained.

i. "It must have weighed something over four tons, and this was dedicated to the use of the tabernacle: the special application of the precious metal was to make sockets into which the boards which made the walls of the tabernacle should be placed." (Spurgeon)

C. Other needs for the tabernacle.

1. (17-21) The bronze laver.

Then the LORD spoke to Moses, saying: "You shall also make a laver of bronze, with its base also of bronze, for washing. You shall put it between the tabernacle of meeting and the altar. And you shall put water in it, for Aaron and his sons shall wash their hands and their feet in water from it. When they go into the tabernacle of meeting, or when they come near the altar to minister, to burn an offering made by fire to the LORD, they shall wash with water, lest they die. So they shall wash their hands and their feet, lest they die. And it shall be a statute forever to them; to him and his descendants throughout their generations."

a. **Make a laver of bronze**: The bronze laver had no specific dimensions. It was essentially a pool for ceremonial washings, set between the brazen altar and the tent of meeting.

b. **Of bronze, with its base also of bronze**: When it was made, the metal for the bronze laver came from the mirrors of the women of Israel (Exodus 38:8). It was a wonderful thing for people to give up the measure of their own appearance for God's cleansing.

c. **You shall put it between the tabernacle of meeting and the altar**: "The laver then was to stand in the great courtyard, before men entered the Tent itself…Priests must certainly have needed to wash after sacrifice and blood ritual, so it had practical value as well." (Cole)

d. **So they shall wash their hands and their feet, lest they die**: The bronze laver speaks of the washing that is necessary for anyone who would come into the presence God.

i. The idea was later expressed in a Psalm: *Who may ascend into the hill of the LORD? Or who may stand in His holy place? He who has clean hands and pure heart.* (Psalm 24:3-4)

ii. When Jesus washed the disciples' feet, He told them: *He who is bathed needs only to wash his feet, but is completely clean* (John 13:10). When we come to Jesus, we are initially cleansed (1 Corinthians 6:11), but must also be continually washed from the dust and dirt of the world by having our feet washed by Jesus.

iii. An important way this washing takes place is through God's Word: *the washing of water by the word.* (Ephesians 5:26)

2. (22-33) The holy anointing oil.

Moreover the LORD spoke to Moses, saying: "Also take for yourself quality spices; five hundred *shekels* of liquid myrrh, half as much sweet-smelling cinnamon (two hundred and fifty *shekels),* two hundred and fifty *shekels* of sweet-smelling cane, five hundred *shekels* of cassia, according to the shekel of the sanctuary, and a hin of olive oil. And you shall make from these a holy anointing oil, an ointment compounded according to the art of the perfumer. It shall be a holy anointing oil. With it you shall anoint the tabernacle of meeting and the ark of the Testimony; the table and all its utensils, the lampstand and its utensils, and the altar of incense; the altar of burnt offering with all its utensils, and the laver and its base. You shall consecrate them, that they may be most holy; whatever touches them must be holy. And you shall anoint Aaron and his sons, and consecrate them, that *they* may minister to Me as priests. And you shall speak to the children of Israel, saying: 'This shall be a holy anointing oil to Me throughout your generations. It shall not be poured on man's flesh; nor shall you make *any other* like it, according to its composition. It *is* holy, *and* it shall be holy to you. Whoever compounds *any* like it, or whoever puts *any* of it on an outsider, shall be cut off from his people.' "

a. **Make from these a holy anointing oil, an ointment compounded according to the art of the perfumer:** This oil was used for anointing the priests and the articles pertaining to service. It was regarded as a sacred compound that could not be imitated nor used as normal perfuming oil.

b. **It shall not be poured on man's flesh:** Since oil is emblematic of the Holy Spirit, we see that the Holy Spirit is not poured out to enhance our flesh, but to glorify Himself.

c. **Nor shall you make any other like it...it is holy, and it shall be holy to you:** This shows that the work of the Holy Spirit is never to be imitated. There is to be no place for encouraging a man-made imitation of the gifts or operations of the Holy Spirit. To do this denies the holiness of the Holy Spirit, regarding His work as something we can do just as well on our own.

> i. "Very solemn are the injunctions that neither the sacred oil nor the holy incense was to be used in any way for personal gratification." (Morgan)

3. (34-38) The holy incense.

And the LORD said to Moses: "Take sweet spices, stacte and onycha and galbanum, and pure frankincense with *these* sweet spices; there shall be equal amounts of each. You shall make of these an incense, a compound according to the art of the perfumer, salted, pure, *and* holy. And you shall beat *some* of it very fine, and put some of it before the Testimony in the tabernacle of meeting where I will meet with you. It shall be most holy to you. But *as for* the incense which you shall make, you shall not make any for yourselves, according to its composition. It shall be to you holy for the LORD. Whoever makes *any* like it, to smell it, he shall be cut off from his people."

a. **Make of these an incense, a compound according to the art of the perfumer, salted, pure, and holy**: The special incense for the tabernacle was made according to the same principles as the anointing oil. God didn't want this sacred smell, symbolizing the sweetness of prayer, to be used for human attraction or adornment.

> i. "Where so many sacrifices were offered it was essentially necessary to have some pleasing perfume to counteract the disagreeable smells that must have arisen from the slaughter of so many animals, the sprinkling of so much blood, and the burning of so much flesh." (Clarke)

> ii. **Salted**: "This 'salting' of the mixture was probably designed to secure rapid burning, through the addition of sodium chloride. Perhaps it was also done for the preservative value of the salt." (Cole)

b. **Whoever makes any like it, to smell it, he shall be cut off from his people**: God was so concerned to protect the unique character of the tabernacle incense that He commanded excommunication for anyone who would make these holy things common.

Exodus 31 - The Call of Bezalel and Aholiab

A. The unique gifts of Bezalel and Aholiab.

1. (1-6) The call of Bezalel and Aholiab.

Then the LORD spoke to Moses, saying: "See, I have called by name Bezalel the son of Uri, the son of Hur, of the tribe of Judah. And I have filled him with the Spirit of God, in wisdom, in understanding, in knowledge, and in all *manner of* workmanship, to design artistic works, to work in gold, in silver, in bronze, in cutting jewels for setting, in carving wood, and to work in all *manner of* workmanship. And I, indeed I, have appointed with him Aholiab the son of Ahisamach, of the tribe of Dan; and I have put wisdom in the hearts of all who are gifted artisans, that they may make all that I have commanded you:"

a. **See, I have called by name Bezalel the son of Uri, the son of Hur**: Even as God specifically chose Moses and Aaron, He also specifically chose these craftsmen for His service.

b. **I have filled him with the Spirit of God, in wisdom, in understanding, in knowledge, and in all manner of workmanship**: God supernaturally enabled Bezalel to do the work of building the Tabernacle. God saw this work as just as spiritual, and just as dependent on the Holy Spirit's power, as the work Moses and Aaron did.

i. This divine empowering wasn't restricted only to Bezalel: **I have put wisdom in the hearts of all who are gifted artisans**. God wanted every worker's labor to be blessed and prompted by the Holy Spirit.

ii. Yet they were filled with the Holy Spirit not to work unto themselves, but unto the LORD: **that they may make all that I have commanded you**. God's empowering isn't to be used for our own selfish ends. *Whatever you do, do it heartily, as to the Lord and not to men* (Colossians 3:23).

2. (7-11) The list of items to be built in the construction of the tabernacle and its furnishings.

"The tabernacle of meeting, the ark of the Testimony and the mercy seat that *is* on it, and all the furniture of the tabernacle; the table and its utensils, the pure *gold* lampstand with all its utensils, the altar of incense, the altar of burnt offering with all its utensils, and the laver and its base; the garments of ministry, the holy garments for Aaron the priest and the garments of his sons, to minister as priests, and the anointing oil and sweet incense for the holy *place.* According to all that I have commanded you they shall do."

a. **The tabernacle of meeting, the ark of the Testimony and the mercy seat that is on it...**: The list seems to be given because God wanted the work organized and attentive to each detail. Nothing should be forgotten or neglected.

b. **According to all that I have commanded you they shall do**: This reminds us that God wanted the tabernacle and its furnishings built according to a specific pattern. It was a deliberate model of a heavenly reality.

B. The Sabbath.

1. (12-17) The command to respect the Sabbath.

And the LORD spoke to Moses, saying, "Speak also to the children of Israel, saying: 'Surely My Sabbaths you shall keep, for it *is* a sign between Me and you throughout your generations, that *you* may know that I *am* the LORD who sanctifies you. You shall keep the Sabbath, therefore, for *it is* holy to you. Everyone who profanes it shall surely be put to death; for whoever does *any* work on it, that person shall be cut off from among his people. Work shall be done for six days, but the seventh *is* the Sabbath of rest, holy to the LORD. Whoever does *any* work on the Sabbath day, he shall surely be put to death. Therefore the children of Israel shall keep the Sabbath, to observe the Sabbath throughout their generations *as* a perpetual covenant. It *is* a sign between Me and the children of Israel forever; for *in* six days the LORD made the heavens and the earth, and on the seventh day He rested and was refreshed.' "

a. **Surely My Sabbaths you shall keep**: This command was strategically placed, at the very end of all the commands to build the tabernacle. Though God gave Israel a work to do in building the tabernacle, He did not want them to do that work on the Sabbath. The rest of God still had to be respected.

b. **It is a sign between Me and the children of Israel forever**: Though in the New Covenant we are not bound by the Sabbath (Romans 14:5; Colossians 2:16-17), the principle is still important. Our rest in the finished work of Jesus is never to be eclipsed by our work for God. When workers for God are burnt-out, they have almost always allowed their work for God to be bigger in their minds than His work for them.

i. The difference between what Jesus has done for us and what we do for Him is like the difference between the sun and the moon, and the sun is almost unbelievably larger than the moon. Yet if the moon is in exactly the right (or wrong) place, it is possible for the moon to eclipse the sun. Some Christians live in a constant state of total eclipse, allowing what they do for Jesus to seem more important than what Jesus did for them.

2. (18) God gives Moses the tablets of stone, written with His finger.

And when He had made an end of speaking with him on Mount Sinai, He gave Moses two tablets of the Testimony, tablets of stone, written with the finger of God.

a. **Tablets of stone, written with the finger of God**: We often say that something can be changed because "It is not written in stone." These commandments *were* written in **stone**.

b. **Two tablets of the Testimony**: These tablets of stone were placed in the Ark of the Testimony, also known as the Ark of the Covenant. They were kept in the ark, later joined by Aaron's rod that budded and a jar of manna.

Exodus 32 - The Golden Calf

A. Israel steps into idolatry.

1. (1) The people make a request.

Now when the people saw that Moses delayed coming down from the mountain, the people gathered together to Aaron, and said to him, "Come, make us gods that shall go before us; for *as for* this Moses, the man who brought us up out of the land of Egypt, we do not know what has become of him."

a. **Moses delayed coming down from the mountain**: This troubled the people of Israel. It is true that **Moses delayed**, but God had a wonderful purpose for Moses' delay, and it would soon be over. Yet because the people couldn't see the reason for the delay, they allowed it to stumble them.

i. Moses was gone for forty days (Exodus 24:18). This probably seemed like a long time to the people, but a short time to Moses. Certainly it was a short time related to the outworking of God's plan for Israel.

ii. How we handle God's ordained delays is a good measure of our spiritual maturity. If we allow such delays to make us drift off into sin or lapse into resignation to fate, then we react poorly to His ordained delays. If we allow such times to deepen our perseverance in following God, then they are of good use.

b. **The people gathered together to Aaron, and said to him**: This sinful impulse came first from the people, not Aaron. The episode of sin described in this chapter started at the impulse of popular opinion. This is an example of where the will of the people is not always the will of God.

i. This is true in society in general, but it is also true among God's people. When it comes to representing God in the world and in serving mankind, there is danger in starting in what people want or what they feel that they need.

c. **Come, make us gods that shall go before us**: The people wanted gods to go **before** them, leading them to the Promised Land. They knew the LORD led them out of Egypt and they knew the LORD God had revealed Himself at Mount Sinai. Yet, they were willing to trust a god they could *make* to finish what the LORD began.

i. "As later Israel wanted a human king, not the invisible divine king (1 Samuel 8:4-8), so now they want a god 'with a face', like everybody else." (Cole)

ii. Centuries later, the Apostle Paul dealt with the same error with the Galatians: *Are you so foolish? Having begun in the Spirit, are you now being made perfect by the flesh?* (Galatians 3:3) It is possible to begin the Christian life trusting Jesus, and then at a later time to trust self or one's own spirituality. Following our own gods is no better for us than it was for ancient Israel.

d. **We do not know what has become of him**: *Not knowing* led Israel into sin. Frustrated because of this uncertainty, Israel turned to idolatry and sin.

i. "It is likely they might have supposed that Moses had perished in the fire, which they saw had invested the top of the mountain into which he went." (Clarke)

ii. "The clause, 'as for this fellow Moses who brought us up out of Egypt' is deliberately cast in coarse language, thus revealing the attitude of the people who had relegated God's works to a mere mortal." (Kaiser)

2. (2-4) Aaron responds to the peoples' request.

And Aaron said to them, "Break off the golden earrings which *are* in the ears of your wives, your sons, and your daughters, and bring *them* to me." So all the people broke off the golden earrings which *were* in their ears, and brought *them* to Aaron. And he received *the gold* from their hand, and he fashioned it with an engraving tool, and made a molded calf. Then they said, "This *is* your god, O Israel, that brought you out of the land of Egypt!"

a. **Break off the golden earrings...and bring them to me**: God told Moses to receive a free-will offering to gather materials for the tabernacle (Exodus 25:1-7). Before Moses came down from Mount Sinai and received this God-commanded offering, Aaron received this offering of gold to make an idol.

i. The people were generous in response - **all the people broke off the golden earrings...and brought them to Aaron**. By nature, people are generous in what they give to their idols. We should be even *more* generous with what we give to the Living God.

ii. "Aaron instructed the people to 'take off' (*paraq*, lit. 'tear off'; contrast *laqah* ['take'] in 35:5) their 'gold earrings.'" (Kaiser)

b. **He fashioned it with an engraving tool**: This wasn't the Spirit-inspired craftsmanship of Bezalel and Aholiab mentioned in Exodus 31:1-6. This was the sin-inspired work of Aaron. He thought it out, melted the gold, molded it, and **fashioned it** carefully with an **engraving tool**.

i. **A molded calf**: "*Calf* is not a good translation of the Hebrew *egel*. A young bull in his first strength is meant: for instance, the word can describe a three-year-old animal (Genesis 15:9)."

c. **Then they said, "This is your god"**: Aaron did not anoint this thing as their god; he simply went along with the people as **they** proclaimed it as their god. He was probably flattered at their admiration of his creation.

i. True leadership would have cried out, "This is idolatry! We must destroy this golden calf. You people are wrong in calling this creation of man your god." But Aaron wasn't a true leader. He was an example of the one who leads by following popular opinion.

ii. "Jeroboam borrowed this statement when he installed the two golden calves at the division of the kingdom in 931 B.C. (1 Kings 12:28)." (Kaiser)

d. **That brought you out of the land of Egypt**: This shows the foolishness of idolatry. This statue of a calf did not exist the day before, yet they worshipped it as the god that brought them out of Egypt.

3. (5-6) Ungodly and immoral worship at the golden calf.

So when Aaron saw *it*, he built an altar before it. And Aaron made a proclamation and said, "Tomorrow *is* a feast to the LORD." Then they rose early on the next day, offered burnt offerings, and brought peace offerings; and the people sat down to eat and drink, and rose up to play.

a. **When Aaron saw it**: Aaron was flattered by the enthusiastic response of the people. When he saw their devotion to this idol, **he built an altar before it**. He began to organize the worship of the idol he just made.

i. It was bad enough to have a golden calf the people praised for their escape from Egypt. This second step of Aaron's was worse. He *honored* and *sanctified* the idol with animal sacrifice. He made the calf, and then he made the altar to worship it.

b. **Tomorrow is a feast to the LORD**: This shows that the creation and the worship of the golden calf was not a *conscious* rejection of the LORD. Aaron and the rest of Israel probably thought that they could give honor to the LORD *through* the golden calf.

i. Aaron was not crass enough to say, "Let's do away with the LORD God." As Israel saw it, Aaron didn't take away the LORD God; he simply added the golden calf.

c. **They rose early on the next day**: They served their idol with eagerness, energy, and personal sacrifice. People usually find a way to rise early for the things that are really important to them. This shows that Israel was willing to give their time, their sleep, and their money in the service of this idol.

i. **Offered burnt offerings, and brought peace offerings**: "Aaron might make a calf, but the people made it a god, by adoring it." (Trapp)

d. **And rose up to play**: This is a tasteful way to speak of gross immorality among the people of Israel. Their worship included eating, drinking (in the sense of drunkenness) and sexual immorality.

i. "The verb translated *play* suggests sex-play in Hebrew...and therefore we are probably to understand drunken orgies." (Cole)

ii. "The verb *sahaq* signifies drunken, immoral orgies and sexual play." (Kaiser) One Hebrew dictionary uses the phrase "conjugal caresses," as found in Genesis 26:8, 39:14 and 39:17.

iii. Less than two months before this, Israel heard the voice of God Himself thunder from heaven, audibly speaking the Ten Commandments to the nation. That dramatic experience, in and of itself, did not change their hearts. It made many of them desire a *less demanding* god.

iv. "It seems impossible that, so soon after receiving such a lofty revelation, Israel could fall so low: but Christian experience today is often the same." (Cole)

B. The nature and result of Moses' intercession.

1. (7-8) God tells Moses what is happening at the camp of Israel.

And the LORD said to Moses, "Go, get down! For your people whom you brought out of the land of Egypt have corrupted *themselves*. They have turned aside quickly out of the way which I commanded them. They have made themselves a molded calf, and worshiped it and sacrificed to it, and said, 'This *is* your god, O Israel, that brought you out of the land of Egypt!'"

a. **For your people whom you brought out of the land of Egypt**: God called Israel **your people**, in the sense that they belonged to Moses, not to God. In this God suggested to Moses that He had already or was about to *disown* Israel.

b. **They have turned aside quickly**: This is almost an understatement. They didn't wait long to go their own sinful way.

c. **They have made themselves a molded calf, and worshiped it and sacrificed to it**: God described to Moses everything that happened, and even quoted the words of the people in their idolatry. God knew *exactly* what happened. The people ignored God, but He did not ignore them.

2. (9-10) God's amazing offer to Moses.

And the LORD said to Moses, "I have seen this people, and indeed it *is* a stiff-necked people! Now therefore, let Me alone, that My wrath may burn hot against them and I may consume them. And I will make of you a great nation."

a. **I have seen this people, and indeed it is a stiff-necked people**: God spoke as if He had seen enough, and He made a remarkable offer to Moses. If Moses would only agree, God would **consume** Israel and start over again with Moses (**I will make of you a great nation**).

i. Hypothetically, God could have done this and still fulfilled every promise made to Abraham, Isaac, and Jacob. It would completely change the place of Moses, making him the new "Abraham" of God's plan for Israel. Moses had the opportunity to be as revered as Abraham was, and to be honored by every following generation.

ii. **Stiff-necked**: "This phrase, common in the Bible, is a farmer's metaphor of an ox or a horse that will not respond to the rope when tugged." (Cole)

b. **Let Me alone, that My wrath may burn hot against them**: God did not ask for the opinion or participation of Moses in this matter. He simply told Moses, "**Let Me alone** so I can do this." The clear impression was that if Moses did *nothing*, the plan would go ahead.

3. (11-13) Moses intercedes for Israel.

Then Moses pleaded with the LORD his God, and said: "LORD, why does Your wrath burn hot against Your people whom You have brought out of the land of Egypt with great power and with a mighty hand? Why should the Egyptians speak, and say, 'He brought them out to harm them, to kill them in the mountains, and to consume them from the face of the earth'? Turn from Your fierce wrath, and relent from this harm to Your people. Remember Abraham, Isaac, and Israel, Your servants,

to whom You swore by Your own self, and said to them, 'I will multiply your descendants as the stars of heaven; and all this land that I have spoken of I give to your descendants, and they shall inherit *it* forever.'"

a. **Then Moses pleaded with the LORD his God**: Moses refused to do *nothing*. He did not fatalistically say, "Well, whatever God will do, God will do." He **pleaded with the LORD**, according to what he believed to be God's heart.

> i. "Moses' prayer was not long, but it was strong. "It is not the *length*, but the *strength* of prayer that appeals to heaven." (Meyer)

> ii. "Thus did Jehovah lead His servant into fellowship with the deepest things of His own heart. Therefore his intercession prevailed." (Morgan)

b. **Your people whom You brought out of the land of Egypt**: In his prayer, Moses first gave the people back to God. "LORD, they belong to You and not to me. I don't want to be god over these people; only You can do that."

c. **Your people whom You brought out of the land of Egypt**: Moses then appealed to God on the basis of grace. "LORD, we didn't deserve to be brought out of Egypt to begin with. You did it by Your grace, not because we deserved it. Please don't stop dealing with us by grace."

d. **Why should the Egyptians speak**: Moses next appealed to God on the basis of glory. "LORD, this will bring discredit to You in the eyes of the nations. The Egyptians will think of You as a cruel God who led your people out to the desert to kill them. Don't let anyone think that of You, God."

> i. "Undoubtedly Moses was filled with compassion for the people, but his chief concern was for the honor of the name of God." (Morgan)

e. **Remember Abraham, Isaac, and Israel, Your servants, to whom You swore by Your own self**: Finally, Moses appealed to God on the basis of His goodness. "LORD, keep Your promises. You are a good God who is always faithful. Don't break Your promises to Abraham, Isaac, and Israel."

> i. "In the want of other rhetoric, let Christians in their prayers urge with repetition. Lord, thou hast promised, thou hast promised. Put the promises into suit, and you have anything. God cannot deny himself." (Trapp)

4. (14) God relents from His anger.

So the LORD relented from the harm which He said He would do to His people.

a. **So the LORD relented**: God answered Moses' prayer. God was going to destroy the nation - all Moses had to do was leave God alone and let Him do it. But Moses did not leave God alone; he labored in intercession according to what He knew of the heart of God.

b. **So the LORD relented**: In the King James Version, this phrase is translated *the LORD repented of the evil which he thought to do unto his people*. Based on this, some believe God sometimes needs to repent of evil or that God changes His mind.

    i. It is helpful to read other translations of this passage.

- *Then the Lord relented* (NIV)
- *So the Lord changed His mind about the harm which He said He would do to His people* (NASB)
- *The Lord turned from the evil which He had thought to do* (Amplified)
- *The Lord was moved with compassion to save His people* (Septuagint Bible)

    ii. Numbers 23:19 says, *God is not a man, that He should lie, nor a son of man, that He should repent. Has He said, and will He not do?* Some say that these two passages contradict each other, and that Exodus 32 shows God repenting and changing, while Numbers 23 says God never changes or repents. We can understand these passages by understanding that Moses wrote with what we call *anthropomorphic* or "man-centered" language. He described the actions of God as they appeared to him. Moses' prayer did not change God, but it did change the standing of the people in God's sight; the people were now in a place of mercy, when before they were in a place of judgment.

    iii. Also, we can say that God *did not* go back on His word to either Moses or Israel. We understand the principle that God's promises of judgment are inherently meant to call men to repentance and prayer and therefore avert the judgment (Ezekiel 33:13-16).

    iv. Some are frustrated because the Bible describes God's actions in human terms, but they really cannot be described in any other way. "I suppose that I need not say that this verse speaks after the manner of men. I do not know after what other manner we can speak. To speak of God after the manner of God, is reserved for God himself; and mortal men could not comprehend such speech. In this sense, the LORD often speaks, not according to the literal fact, but according to the appearance of things to us, in order that we may understand so far as the human can comprehend the divine." (Spurgeon)

c. **The LORD relented from the harm which He said He would do**: God did not destroy Israel, and He *knew* that He would not destroy Israel.

Yet He deliberately put Moses into this crucial place of intercession so that Moses would display and develop God's heart for the people, a heart of love and compassion. Moses prayed just as God wanted him to - as if heaven and earth, salvation or destruction, depended on his prayer. This is how God waits for us to pray.

i. "We are not to think of Moses as altering God's purpose towards Israel by this prayer, but as carrying it out: Moses was never more like God than in such moments, for he shared God's mind and loving purpose." (Cole)

ii. Living under the New Covenant, we do not have *less* privilege in prayer than Moses had. We do not have *less* access to God than Moses had. The only thing we may have *less* of is Moses' heart for the people.

C. Moses confronts Aaron.

1. (15-18) Moses and Joshua hear the people in the camp.

And Moses turned and went down from the mountain, and the two tablets of the Testimony *were* in his hand. The tablets *were* written on both sides; on the one *side* and on the other they were written. Now the tablets *were* the work of God, and the writing *was* the writing of God engraved on the tablets. And when Joshua heard the noise of the people as they shouted, he said to Moses, *"There is* a noise of war in the camp."* But he said: *"It is* not the noise of the shout of victory, nor the noise of the cry of defeat, *but* the sound of singing I hear."

a. **Moses turned and went down from the mountain**: In the midst of this great idolatry, Moses and Joshua came down from their extended time up on Mount Sinai. He carried **the two tablets of the Testimony**, written direction by the hand of God.

b. **The tablets were the work of God, and the writing was the writing of God**: It is significant that the tablets were written by God's direct hand. All law and morality must come from God's standard and character or be up to the opinion or changing values of men.

i. "For as he is the sole author of *law* and *justice*, so he alone can write them on the heart of man." (Clarke)

ii. Under the New Covenant, God also promised to write His law: *I will put My law in their minds, and write it on their hearts; and I will be their God, and they shall be My people.* (Jeremiah 31:33)

c. **There is a noise of war in the camp**: We might say that Joshua was correct when he said this; however, the noise reflected a spiritual war instead of a material war.

2. (19-21) Moses puts an end to the disgrace and confronts Aaron.

So it was, as soon as he came near the camp, that he saw the calf *and the dancing*. So Moses' anger became hot, and he cast the tablets out of his hands and broke them at the foot of the mountain. Then he took the calf which they had made, burned *it* in the fire, and ground *it* to powder; and he scattered *it* on the water and made the children of Israel drink *it*. And Moses said to Aaron, "What did this people do to you that you have brought *so* great a sin upon them?"

a. **Moses' anger became hot, and he cast the tablets out of his hands and broke them**: Israel broke the covenant by their idolatry and immorality with the golden calf. There was something appropriate about Moses breaking the stone tablets of the covenant at Israel's breaking of the covenant.

> i. Cole called the breaking of the tablets "a significant ceremonial act, not a mere exhibition of anger." Moses acted out the broken law and covenant.

> ii. Nevertheless, Moses had to deal with **anger** through much of his life. In anger, he killed an Egyptian (Exodus 2:11-12). In anger, he broke the tablets written by the finger of God. In anger, he beat the rock God commanded him to speak to (Numbers 20:10-11). This last display of anger kept Moses out of the Promised Land.

b. **He took the calf which they had made, burned it in the fire, and ground it to powder**: This idol had been the object of adoration and immoral rites; yet it seems that no one challenged Moses when he did this. Moses came down from Mount Sinai with the authority and strength of a man who had been with God – and all Israel knew it.

c. **Made the children of Israel drink it**: Moses ground up the calf and made the people drink it for several reasons.

- To show that the so-called god was nothing and could be destroyed easily
- To completely obliterate this idol
- To make the people pay an immediate consequence of their sin
- To make the gold of the idol absolutely unusable, being corrupted with bodily waste

> i. "The gold dust sprinkled on the water of the wady, flowing down from the mountain, the water that Israel must drink, reminds us of the 'water of bitterness' to be drunk by the wife suspected of unfaithfulness (Numbers 5:18-22)." (Cole)

d. **What did this people do to you that you have brought so great a sin upon them**: This was a perceptive question. Moses understood that this plan didn't originate with Aaron, but that he allowed it and implemented it.

3. (22-24) Aaron's excuse.

So Aaron said, "Do not let the anger of my lord become hot. You know the people, that they *are set* on evil. For they said to me, 'Make us gods that shall go before us; *as for* this Moses, the man who brought us out of the land of Egypt, we do not know what has become of him.' And I said to them, 'Whoever has any gold, let them break *it* off.' So they gave *it* to me, and I cast it into the fire, and this calf came out."

a. **Do not let the anger of my lord become hot**: Aaron essentially asked Moses to calm down, and to not be so angry. Aaron had no sense of the greatness of his sin. He had no significant sense of the fear of the LORD.

b. **You know the people, that they are set on evil**: Moses knew this as well as Aaron did. Yet Moses had a sense of his need to *restrain* the evil of the people, while in this case Aaron actually encouraged and supported the sin of the people.

c. **Make us gods that shall go before us**: Aaron quoted the people exactly, but he lied when he described his own actions (**I cast it into the fire, and this calf came out**).

i. Aaron no doubt meant that this calf was produced by a miracle, it just happened. But Moses, and everyone else, could see the human engraving marks on it (Exodus 32:4). Aaron claimed this was a miraculous work, but the evidence of his workmanship were all over it.

ii. Aaron gave the classic "it just happened" excuse, but it *didn't* just happen. Aaron thought it out, melted the gold, molded it, and fashioned it carefully with an engraving tool (Exodus 32:4).

iii. Aaron did this evil thing and made his excuse, because at that moment it seemed harder to stand for the LORD than to go along with the people, and Aaron took the path of least resistance. He was lazy. "Lazy people always find fault with their tools, and those who do not intend to work always find some excuse or other; and then they make up for their laziness by having a delicious spiritual dream. Half the nominally Christian people about us are dreaming; and they consider that thus they are doing the work of the LORD. They are only doing it deceitfully by putting dreaming into the place of real service." (Spurgeon)

iv. "What a silly and ridiculous subterfuge!...Just like the popish legend of the *falling* of the *shrine of our Lady of Loretta out of heaven*! These legends come from the same quarter. Satan can provide more when necessary for his purpose." (Clarke)

v. Aaron's sin was so great that only the intercession of Moses saved his life. *And the LORD was very angry with Aaron and would have destroyed him; so I prayed for Aaron also at the same time.* (Deuteronomy 9:20)

D. The call to side with either God or idolatry.

1. (25-26) Moses issues a challenge.

Now when Moses saw that the people *were* unrestrained (for Aaron had not restrained them, to *their* shame among their enemies), then Moses stood in the entrance of the camp, and said, "Whoever *is* on the LORD's side; *come* to me." And all the sons of Levi gathered themselves together to him.

a. **The people were unrestrained**: This shows how great the problem was. There is no greater danger than for people to cast off all restraint and do whatever seems right in their own eyes. The darkest days of Israel's national history were characterized by the phrase, *everyone did what was right in his own eyes.* (Judges 17:6)

i. "The idea of the verb 'to cast off all restraints' is that of loosening or uncovering. It would appear that there was a type of religious prostitution connected with the people's worship of the golden calf." (Kaiser)

ii. In our modern culture, we regard the absence of restraint as heaven on earth. But the Bible and common sense tell us that this kind of moral, spiritual, and social anarchy brings nothing but destruction.

iii. *There is a way that seems right to a man, but its end is the way of death.* (Proverbs 14:12) When man follows his own instincts, his own inclinations, it leads to ruin. We need to follow God's way, not our own.

iv. **Unrestrained...no restrained**: "The exact word used twice in this verse is found in the warning of Proverbs 29:18: 'Where there is no revelation [i.e., the message from or attention to the Word of God], the people cast off all moral restraints [i.e., they become ungovernable]'." (Kaiser)

v. God has given many restraints to us: the curbs of the fear of God, of family, of culture, of conscience, of law, even of necessity. But these restraints can be - and are being - broken down.

b. **Whoever is on the LORD's side; come to me**: Moses gave the people of Israel the opportunity to make a stand for the LORD. The Levites, to their honor, sided with the LORD and with Moses. Sadly, they were the only significant group to come out clearly for God's cause at the golden calf incident.

> i. It only makes sense for us to be on our LORD's side. He is our Creator, our Redeemer, our Preserver, and our Best Friend. Yet being on the LORD's side requires something.
>
> - Being on the LORD's side requires *decision*
> - Being on the LORD's side requires *action*
> - Being on the LORD's side requires *separation*

2. (27-29) The execution of 3,000.

And he said to them, "Thus says the LORD God of Israel: 'Let every man put his sword on his side, and go in and out from entrance to entrance throughout the camp, and let every man kill his brother, every man his companion, and every man his neighbor.'" So the sons of Levi did according to the word of Moses. And about three thousand men of the people fell that day. Then Moses said, "Consecrate yourselves today to the LORD, that He may bestow on you a blessing this day, for every man has opposed his son and his brother."

> a. **Let every man kill his brother, every man his companion, and every man his neighbor**: In this case, siding with the LORD meant siding against some people. Those who were more interested in siding with *all* the people could never do what these Levites did.
>
> > i. "My one interest is into this separation between those who are 'on the Lord's side' and those who worship their own god, and their own ideas, and their own thoughts." (Lloyd-Jones)
>
> b. **About three thousand men of the people fell that day**: It seems that the sin of Israel at the golden calf involved more than these 3,000 people. Yet these were undoubtedly those most flagrant in their idolatry and immorality, or these were the leaders of the sinful conduct.

E. Moses' second intercession.

1. (30) Moses returns to intercede for the people.

Now it came to pass on the next day that Moses said to the people, "You have committed a great sin. So now I will go up to the LORD; perhaps I can make atonement for your sin."

> a. **Now I will go up to the LORD; perhaps I can make atonement for your sin**: Moses already interceded for the people in Exodus 32:11-14. But he prayed again for them, because now he saw the sin with his own eyes, and was struck with the depth of the people's sin.
>
> b. **Perhaps I can make atonement for your sin**: Moses also learned on Mount Sinai that God's penalty for idolatry was death. *He who sacrifices to*

any god, except to the L*ORD* *only, he shall be utterly destroyed* (Exodus 22:20). He was more aware than ever of the distance between the people and God, and sensed the urgency to intercede.

2. (31-32) Moses' bold request on behalf of the people.

Then Moses returned to the LO**RD and said, "Oh, these people have committed a great sin, and have made for themselves a god of gold! Yet now, if You will forgive their sin; but if not, I pray, blot me out of Your book which You have written."**

a. **Oh, these people have committed a great sin**: Moses did not minimize the sin of the people or put it in soft terms. They were guilty of worshipping a **god of gold**.

i. People still worship gods of gold. In August of 1990, a man staggered to the steps of his Los Angeles office. Before he died of the gunshot wound to his chest, he called out the names of his three children. But he still had his $10,000 Rolex watch clutched in his hand. He gave his life for a god of gold.

b. **Yet now, if You will forgive their sin**: Moses knew the enormity of the people's sin, yet he still asked for forgiveness. This was an appeal to the mercy and grace of God.

c. **If not, I pray, blot me out of Your book which You have written**: Moses asked God to forgive Israel on the basis of his own sacrificial identification with the sinful people. If God would not forgive, Moses asked to be *damned* in sacrificial identification with his sinful people.

i. Moses felt that Israel had sinned so terribly that the blood of a goat or an ox couldn't cover it; it had to be a man who suffered in their place. Therefore he offered to be blotted out of God's Book if it could somehow rescue the people. God said "no" to the request of Moses; yet we can say that God looked ahead to the sacrifice of One greater than Moses, who would give Himself for the people, bringing full and complete atonement.

ii. "He stands between the people and the wrath of God and says, 'Punish me.' He could not have borne it, of course, it was too much. And yet the noble spirit of Moses shines out so clearly in this great incident." (Lloyd-Jones)

iii. Of course, this sacrificial heart was the same heart Jesus had in dying for our sins (1 Peter 3:18 and 2 Corinthians 5:21). The Apostle Paul also had some of this same heart of Jesus (Romans 9:3).

3. (33-35) The L*ORD*'s response to the plea of Moses.

And the L<small>ORD</small> said to Moses, "Whoever has sinned against Me, I will blot him out of My book. Now therefore, go, lead the people to *the place* of which I have spoken to you. Behold, My Angel shall go before you. Nevertheless, in the day when I visit for punishment, I will visit punishment upon them for their sin." So the L<small>ORD</small> plagued the people because of what they did with the calf which Aaron made.

a. **Whoever has sinned against Me, I will blot him out of My book:** God agreed to spare the nation as a whole, but He definitely reserved the right to judge individual sinners.

b. **Now therefore, go, lead the people to the place of which I have spoken to you:** This was God's promise to stay faithful to Israel and to keep His presence with them (**My Angel shall go before you**).

c. **I will visit punishment upon them for their sin:** That entire generation of adult Israelites would never enter the Promised Land. That specific judgment had yet to be pronounced, but God knew it would happen.

d. **So the L<small>ORD</small> plagued the people:** This probably describes the death of the 3,000 already mentioned in Exodus 32:28.

Exodus 33 - Israel's Path of Restored Fellowship

A. Israel's repentance and restoration.

1. (1-3) The people learn of God's heart towards their sin.

Then the Lord said to Moses, "Depart *and* go up from here, you and the people whom you have brought out of the land of Egypt, to the land of which I swore to Abraham, Isaac, and Jacob, saying, 'To your descendants I will give it.' And I will send *My* Angel before you, and I will drive out the Canaanite and the Amorite and the Hittite and the Perizzite and the Hivite and the Jebusite. *Go up* to a land flowing with milk and honey; for I will not go up in your midst, lest I consume you on the way, for you *are* a stiff-necked people."

a. **Depart and go up from here....to the land...to your descendants I will give it**: After the sin of the golden calf, God did not deny the children of Israel the Promised Land. He said they could continue on to possess what He had promised to them and to Abraham, Isaac, and Jacob.

b. **And I will send My Angel before you, and I will drive out the Canaanite**: After the sin of the golden calf, God did not deny Israel His protection. He promised to be with them in some way (**I will send My Angel**), and to fight for them in the Promised Land.

i. Isaiah 63:9 looks back at the Exodus, and says: *In all their affliction He was afflicted, and the Angel of His Presence saved them.* The *Angel of His Presence* describes the presence of God with His Israel in Exodus 23:20-23, the angel that had the name of God in Him. The angel described here in Exodus 33:2 was simply an angelic being, not the Lord Himself.

c. **I will not go up in your midst**: God did say He would deny Israel His *presence*, or at least the near sense of His presence. We might say that God said, "I won't stay so close to you, because I might judge you along the way - but go on and take the Promised Land."

i. This was a challenge to Moses and the nation as a whole. God told them they could have the Promised Land, but He would not remain with them in a close, personal way. If they were satisfied with that arrangement, it would prove they only loved God's blessings and not God Himself. If they challenged God - pleading with Him for His presence, not only His blessings - it would show a genuine heart for God Himself. This was the first step towards spiritual restoration and revival in Israel.

ii. "To be given every other blessing is of no value if God is not with you. What is the value of Canaan? What is the value of milk and honey? What is the value of having possessions, if God was not with them? They saw that the realization of the presence of God, having this fellowship and company, was infinitely more important than everything else." (Lloyd-Jones)

2. (4-6) The people repent and mourn.

And when the people heard this bad news, they mourned, and no one put on his ornaments. For the LORD had said to Moses, "Say to the children of Israel, 'You *are* a stiff-necked people. I could come up into your midst in one moment and consume you. Now therefore, take off your ornaments, that I may know what to do to you.'" So the children of Israel stripped themselves of their ornaments by Mount Horeb.

a. **They mourned, and no one put on his ornaments**: This was a good response on behalf of Israel. To them, it was **bad news**. They mourned the potential loss of God's close presence. They cared about their relationship with the LORD, not only what He could give them.

i. "It is clear that the people felt that the promise of an angel to be sent before them was the lowering of a privilege." (Morgan)

ii. This was a significant issue for Israel, because they could *see* the presence of the LORD in the pillar of cloud by day and fire by night. If God withdrew His presence, it could be clearly seen.

iii. **They mourned** here, because with the golden idol they couldn't have their fun obediently and responsibly. It was good for them to be sad for a while.

b. **You are a stiff-necked people**: This phrase is repeated again. The idea isn't only that they were stubborn, but that they stubbornly resisted God. The picture is of an ox or donkey resisting the farmer and making its neck stiff.

c. **So the children of Israel stripped themselves of their ornaments by Mount Horeb**: The people displayed their repentance and mourning by not wearing their **ornaments**. They knew this was not the time for decorating the external, but it was time to bring the heart right with God. This was the second step towards spiritual restoration and revival in Israel.

i. "The people who are concerned about revival, in a true sense, are not just out for a little bit of excitement, or interest, or some happiness, or phenomena, or coming with an attitude of 'something marvelous is going to happen and we are going to have a great good time.' That is not how they think about it at all. And if you, my dear friends, are simply thinking about meetings, and excitement, and something wonderful, you have not begun to understand this matter." (Lloyd-Jones)

ii. Exodus 35:22 describes how these ornaments went to the building of the tabernacle. "The very ornaments that could make a golden idol in the past could now be dedicated to God for the use of His sanctuary." (Cole)

3. (7) Moses makes his tent the tabernacle of meeting.

Moses took his tent and pitched it outside the camp, far from the camp, and called it the tabernacle of meeting. And it came to pass *that* everyone who sought the LORD went out to the tabernacle of meeting which *was* outside the camp.

a. **Moses took his tent and pitched it outside the camp, far from the camp, and called it the tabernacle of meeting**: After Israel's heart was turned towards God, and after they humbled themselves by removing their ornaments, Moses took the next step towards revival and restored relationship. *He* initiated a determined effort to seek God, making his own tent a **tabernacle of meeting**.

i. God told Moses to make a tabernacle of meeting when Moses was on Mount Sinai (Exodus 25-28), but the tabernacle wasn't built yet. This wouldn't stop Moses from taking extraordinary measures to seek God. He determined to make his own tent a **tabernacle of meeting**.

ii. This was not something that Moses organized or planned or strategized. He sought God, radically and spontaneously. When Moses did that, God touched the hearts of the people.

iii. **Far from the camp**: "Sanctuaries were usually built a little distance from towns in the ancient world: Israel had therefore lost their uniqueness, as the nation among whom God dwells in the very midst." (Cole)

b. **Everyone who sought the LORD went out to the tabernacle of meeting which was outside the camp**: By making the place of worship outside the camp, Moses clearly drew a line to see who really wanted to draw close to the LORD.

i. When Moses put the temporary **tabernacle of meeting… outside the camp**, it meant that everyone who wanted to seek the Lord had to separate in some sense. We can assume that not everyone wanted to do this.

ii. "When the Holy Spirit of God begins to deal with any one of us, there will be this separation. It will not be paraded, it will not be the Pharisees' 'I am holier than thou' attitude. No, once a man begins to be burdened for the glory of God and the state of the Church, he immediately feels the call to consecration, he 'goes out' as it were." (Lloyd-Jones)

4. (8-10) The presence of God shows itself at the tent of Moses.

So it was, whenever Moses went out to the tabernacle, *that* **all the people rose, and each man stood** *at* **his tent door and watched Moses until he had gone into the tabernacle. And it came to pass, when Moses entered the tabernacle, that the pillar of cloud descended and stood** *at* **the door of the tabernacle, and** *the LORD* **talked with Moses. All the people saw the pillar of cloud standing** *at* **the tabernacle door, and all the people rose and worshiped, each man** *in* **his tent door.**

a. **Whenever Moses went out to the tabernacle, that all the people rose**: The people watched and noticed when Moses worshipped. When Moses worshipped, they also worshipped. Moses prompted the people to draw close to God by his own example.

b. **The pillar of cloud descended and stood at the door of the tabernacle**: Moses' tent did not become the tabernacle of meeting simply because he named it so. It became that because *God actually came there to meet Moses*, displayed by the pillar of cloud.

i. The **pillar of cloud** became like the flag of royalty or of an admiral indicates that they are present, so the pillar of cloud (which Cole describes as literally, a "standing thing") indicated the presence of God.

ii. Everyone saw this **pillar of cloud** come to the tent of Moses, and they knew Moses worshipped and met with God there. This was a great comfort to the people to know that their leader really did meet with God and hear from Him.

c. **And the LORD talked with Moses**: We read a lot about God talking with Moses, but we don't know all that much about what God said. There was probably much more said than what is recorded in Exodus 33, and probably much of it was of a personal, strengthening nature to Moses.

d. **And all the people rose and worshipped**: This was their natural response. Something about Moses and his relationship with God made others want to also worship God.

5. (11) God speaks to Moses at his tent, the tabernacle.

So the LORD spoke to Moses face to face, as a man speaks to his friend. And he would return to the camp, but his servant Joshua the son of Nun, a young man, did not depart from the tabernacle.

a. **The LORD spoke to Moses face to face, as a man speaks to his friend**: Numbers 12:8 clarifies what this meant. There God contrasted how He spoke to Moses with how He spoke to other prophets; Moses heard clearly and plainly, and other prophets heard in dreams and visions.

i. It is also *possible* this meant that God appeared to Moses in human form, as He did to Abraham in Genesis 18. More likely, the phrase **face to face** is simply a figurative expression, meaning free and open fellowship.

ii. Moses had not - and could not - see the actual face of God the Father in His glory. No one has seen the face of God the Father in glory, and this is why John wrote, *No one has seen God at any time* (1 John 4:12).

b. **Joshua the son of Nun, a young man, did not depart from the tabernacle**: The personal revival in the life of Moses was an example to the entire nation, but it was a special example to his servant Joshua. When Moses drew close to God, it also drew Joshua close to God so much so that Joshua **did not depart from the tabernacle**.

B. Moses prays and draws near to God.

1. (12-13) Moses prays for the people.

Then Moses said to the LORD, "See, You say to me, 'Bring up this people.' But You have not let me know whom You will send with me. Yet You have said, 'I know you by name, and you have also found grace in My sight.' Now therefore, I pray, if I have found grace in Your sight, show me now Your way, that I may know You and that I may find grace in Your sight. And consider that this nation *is* Your people."

a. **But You have not let me know whom You will send with me**: For Moses, it wasn't enough to know that he and Israel would make it to the Promised Land. In his estimation, the Promised Land was nothing special without the special presence of the LORD. God previously promised to send an angel with Israel (Exodus 33:2). Moses pressed God on this point, wanting to know *exactly* whom God would send.

i. "Moses is now concerned to obtain both a guarantee of that presence for his people, and also the enjoyment of a closer experience of it for himself." (Cole)

ii. This was bold - almost rude - drawing near to God. Moses was determined to have God's presence with Israel as close as possible. This was the next step towards revival and restoration of Israel's relationship with God.

b. **If I have found grace in Your sight**: Moses was bold in drawing near to God, but he based the boldness on the **grace** God had already shown to him. This was a good ground for drawing near.

c. **Your sight…Your way, that I may know You…grace in Your sight…Your people**: Moses was almost obsessed with God. He was still on earth, but he connected everything to God in heaven.

i. Another strong theme in this section is *to know*. In some form, the word is used repeatedly in these verses. In the sense of relationship, God knew Israel and Moses, and Moses wanted to know God.

2. (14-17) God answers Moses' prayer, giving the promise of His Presence.

And He said, "My Presence will go *with you,* and I will give you rest." Then he said to Him, "If Your Presence does not go *with us,* do not bring us up from here. For how then will it be known that Your people and I have found grace in Your sight, except You go with us? So we shall be separate, Your people and I, from all the people who *are* upon the face of the earth." So the LORD said to Moses, "I will also do this thing that you have spoken; for you have found grace in My sight, and I know you by name."

a. **My Presence will go with you**: God seemed to answer Moses' prayer, but Moses did not rest. He continued to press God for affirmation of the promise. This shows how boldly Moses sought after God for the sake of his own relationship with God *and* for the benefit of the nation.

i. **My Presence will go with you** is literally "My Face will go with you." This helps us to understand what it means when it says Moses met with God *face to face* (Exodus 32:11). It has the sense of "in the immediate presence of God."

ii. "This means that the heavenly 'messenger' sent with them will now be 'the angel of his presence' (Isaiah 63:9), *i.e.* a full manifestation of God as in Exodus 23:20." (Cole)

iii. **And I will give you rest**: The Presence of God means **rest** and peace in life. This was an important and necessary gift from God to Moses and Israel.

b. **If Your Presence does not go with us, do not bring us**: Moses continued his bold way of speaking with God. God had just promised His presence; Moses responded by warning or cautioning God of the consequences of *not* keeping His promise.

c. **For how then will it be known that Your people and I have found grace in Your sight, except You go with us**: Moses knew that nothing the LORD could *give* them would make them truly different from the nations. Only the strong presence of the LORD Himself could do that.

> i. Moses wanted something for Israel that would show that they were not just like all the other nations, and that could only be the unique, powerful presence of their God. Israel's relationship with Yahweh – a unique example of ethical monotheism in the ancient world – did make them different from all other ancient peoples. *God among them made them different*. It was important for *Israel* to know this for themselves; it was also important for the *other nations* to know this.

> ii. " 'Now,' said Moses to God, 'I am asking for this something extra, because I am concerned. Here we are thy people. How are all the other nations to know that we really are your people? They are looking on at us, they are laughing at us, mocking us and jeering at us, they are ready to overwhelm us. Now, I am asking for something,' said Moses, 'that will make it absolutely clear that we are not just one of the nations of the world, but that we are thy people, that we are separate, unique, altogether apart.' " (Lloyd-Jones)

d. **I will also do this thing that you have spoken; for you have found grace in My sight, and I know you by name**: God honored the bold intercession of Moses, and He promised to restore His relationship with Israel.

3. (18) Moses' desire to draw closer.

And he said, "Please, show me Your glory."

a. **Please, show me Your glory**: Moses won a "yes" answer from God when he asked for the special presence of God to remain with Israel on the way to the Promised Land (Exodus 33:12-17). He also won a confirmation of the promise from God and an affirmation of close relationship. Yet he was still not satisfied. He wanted *more* in his personal relationship with God.

> i. Spurgeon thought that perhaps Moses, when he asked for this, was somewhat like Peter on the Mount of Transfiguration when he asked for something, not really understanding what he said. This was such a bold and brave request that it might have been beyond Moses to really

experience; yet God was still pleased with Moses and his longing to know the LORD in greater and deeper ways.

ii. This hunger for more of God, for more of an *experience* with God, is a mark of true revival and restoration of relationship. Whatever Moses had experienced with God, he now wanted more. "The more a man knows of God, the more desirous he is to know him." (Trapp)

iii. "We may have been Christians for many years, but have we ever really longed for some personal, direct knowledge and experience of God? Oh, I know, we pray for causes, we pray for the Church, we pray for missionaries, we pray for our own efforts that we organize, yes, but that is not what I am concerned about. We all ask for personal blessings, but how much do we know of this desire for God himself? That is what Moses asked for: 'Show me thy glory. Take me yet a step nearer.' " (Lloyd-Jones)

b. **Show me Your glory**: This was an interesting request. Moses already saw something of the glory of God (Exodus 16:10 and 24:16-17), yet he wanted more. He sensed that he had not seen anything yet.

i. "Now Moses' prayer is to see the *kabod*, the manifested glory (literally 'weight') of YHWH." (Cole)

ii. "In other words, by revival we do not mean the Church being blessed by God, and conscious of his presence, and enabled to do his work. Moses, in a sense, was already conscious of all that . . . But Moses was not satisfied. And revival, I repeat, is not the Church being blessed and being conscious of God's presence, and being enabled to do her work. Revival goes beyond all that." (Lloyd-Jones)

4. (19-20) God tells Moses what He will show him.

Then He said, "I will make all My goodness pass before you, and I will proclaim the name of the LORD before you. I will be gracious to whom I will be gracious, and I will have compassion on whom I will have compassion." But He said, "You cannot see My face; for no man shall see Me, and live."

a. **I will make all My goodness pass before you**: Moses asked to see the glory of God (Exodus 33:18), and God promised to show Moses His **goodness**. God's glory lies in His **goodness**. When Moses saw the glory of God, His first understanding was that God was good. If we don't know that God is good, we don't know much about Him at all.

i. God didn't reveal His *justice* to Moses, not His *power*, and not His *wrath against sin*. All those are truly aspects of God's nature, but when He showed Himself to Moses, He displayed His **goodness**.

ii. Sometimes people think they must "balance" God, supposing there is something like a Yin and Yang to the universe in the sense of light and dark, good and evil, law and grace. But God Himself is "unbalanced" in this sense. He is entirely good. Even His justice and power and wrath must be understood as aspects of His **goodness**.

b. **I will proclaim the name of the LORD before you**: In the thinking of the ancient Hebrews (and also in other ancient cultures), the **name** represented a person's character and nature. God promised to reveal His character to Moses, not merely a title.

i. Lloyd-Jones gives the idea of what God said to Moses: "I will stoop to your weakness. I will let you see something. But, much more important than that, I will cause all my goodness to pass before you. I will give you a deeper insight and understanding into myself, into my character, into what I am. That is what you really need to know."

c. **You cannot see My face; for no man shall see Me, and live**: God would not, and could not, literally show Moses His face. This helps us to understand what was meant in Exodus 33:11 when it said, *the LORD spoke to Moses face to face, as a man speaks to his friend.*

i. "But at the same time he assures him that he *could not see his face*-the fulness of his perfections and the grandeur of his designs, *and live*, as no human being could bear, in the present state, this full discovery. But he adds, *Thou shalt see my back parts.*" (Clarke)

5. (21-23) How God will protect Moses when God passes before Moses.

And the LORD said, "Here is a place by Me, and you shall stand on the rock. So it shall be, while My glory passes by, that I will put you in the cleft of the rock, and will cover you with My hand while I pass by. Then I will take away My hand, and you shall see My back; but My face shall not be seen."

a. **Here is a place by Me, and you shall stand on the rock**: God was about to reveal Himself to Moses in a unique way. God prepared the event carefully, giving Moses a specific place to stand.

i. Later, Elijah met God in what may have been the same place (1 Kings 19:8-18).

b. **While My glory passes by, that I will put you in the cleft of the rock**: God's glory could not *remain* in front of Moses; it had to pass by him. Even with that, Moses had to be protected by the **hand** of God and **the cleft of the rock** when the glory of God passed before him.

i. This is a vivid and endearing image: protected both by the **hand** of God and hidden away in the **rock** of refuge He provides. The shelter in the **cleft of the rock** gave the image for Augustus Toplady in his famous hymn *Rock of Ages*:

Rock of Ages, cleft for me;
Let me hide myself in Thee.

ii. Protected by God, Moses could endure the glory of God passing before him. Isaiah had a glimpse of the glory of God, and it moved him to mourn his own sin and unworthiness (Isaiah 6). John experienced some of the glory of God and fell at the feet of Jesus like a dead man (Revelation 1:17). Paul experienced the glory of God on the Damascus Road, but also in the experience described in 2 Corinthians 12. It was such an amazing experience that he could only barely describe it.

iii. Others, beyond the times of the Bible, have also experienced glimpses of this glory. Lloyd-Jones mentioned a few:

- Jonathan Edwards described a time of praying in the forest, kneeling for an hour that seemed to pass in just a few moments because of the powerful sense of God's glory and presence
- David Brainerd, a great colonial-era missionary to the Native Americans, knelt in the snow and prayed for hours – literally sweating in his body though it was freezing cold in the air. The sweat was a physical reaction to the intensity of the spiritual experience
- D.L. Moody asked God for such an experience, and when God gave it to him he had to ask God to pull back His hand, because he felt like it was killing him

iv. *What many people speak of today as the presence and the glory of God seems very trivial compared to what Moses and these others experienced.* There is no *kabod* – no *weight* to their experience of glory.

v. We also should have an earnest desire to experience God deeply. Paul made it clear that we cannot fully see the glory of God - we see it as in a piece of polished metal, dimly (1 Corinthians 13:12) - *but we can see something of it.* Paul didn't say we see *nothing* of the glory of God, only that we can't fully see it or comprehend it.

c. **I will take away My hand, and you shall see My back; but My face shall not be seen**: Moses could only see God's **back** (a unique term often not used for anatomy). The idea is that Moses could only see behind God, not God Himself.

i. "The word…could just as well and more accurately be rendered 'the after-effects' of his radiant glory, which had just passed by." (Kaiser)

ii. Poole puts it like this: "Thou shalt see a shadow or obscure delineation of my glory, as much as thou canst bear, though not as much as thou dost desire."

iii. "These four things are happening at the same time, whenever God draws near to his people - revealing and concealing, blessing and protecting, all happening together at one and the same time. You cannot separate these things." (Lloyd-Jones)

iv. With these special protections, God rewarded the desire of Moses to see His glory as much as humanly possible. This demonstrates that God rewards the seeking heart. And as marvelous as this experience was for Moses, it still cannot compare to the revelation of God given to us in Jesus Christ.

- *And the Word became flesh and dwelt among us, and we beheld His glory, the glory as of the only begotten of the Father, full of grace and truth* (John 1:14)
- *But we all, with unveiled face, beholding as in a mirror the glory of the Lord, are being transformed into the same image from glory to glory, just as by the Spirit of the Lord* (2 Corinthians 3:18)

Exodus 34 - The Covenant Renewed

A. Moses meets with God again on the mountain.

1. (1-4) God calls Moses up Mount Sinai again.

And the LORD said to Moses, "Cut two tablets of stone like the first ones, and I will write on *these* tablets the words that were on the first tablets which you broke. So be ready in the morning, and come up in the morning to Mount Sinai, and present yourself to Me there on the top of the mountain. And no man shall come up with you, and let no man be seen throughout all the mountain; let neither flocks nor herds feed before that mountain." So he cut two tablets of stone like the first *ones*. Then Moses rose early in the morning and went up Mount Sinai, as the LORD had commanded him; and he took in his hand the two tablets of stone.

a. **Cut two tablets of stone like the first ones**: Moses broke the first set of stone tablets, the ones written with the finger of God (Exodus 32:19). He broke the tablets because Israel broke the covenant.

b. **I will write on these tablets the words that were on the first tablets which you broke**: After their great sin with the golden idol (Exodus 32), Moses interceded for Israel, Israel repented, and God restored. It was appropriate to give then new stone tablets.

c. **No man shall come up with you...let neither flocks nor herds feed before the mountain**: When God first spoke the Ten Commandments to Israel at Mount Sinai, He commanded that they not come near the mountain (Exodus 19:12-13). At this second giving of the commandments, they were also to stay away, all except Moses.

i. Moses again acted as a mediator between God and the people. The people couldn't deal with God directly because of their own sin and rebellion, so Moses bridged the gap between the people and God.

2. (5-6a) The revelation of God's presence to Moses.

Now the Lord descended in the cloud and stood with him there, and proclaimed the name of the Lord. And the Lord passed before him

a. **Now the Lord descended in the cloud and stood with him there**: The **cloud** mentioned was no doubt the cloud of glory known as the *Shekinah*. This cloud is mentioned many times in the Bible.

- It covered Mount Sinai (Exodus 19:16)
- It went with Israel by day (Exodus 13:21-22)
- It stood at the tent of Moses (Exodus 33:9-10)
- It filled Solomon's temple with glory (2 Chronicles 7:2)
- It overshadowed Mary at the conception of Jesus (Luke 1:35)
- It was present at the transfiguration of Jesus (Luke 9:34-35)
- It will be present at the return of Jesus (Revelation 1:7)

i. **And stood with him there**: In some way, God appeared to Moses **in the cloud** at Sinai. This was what Moses asked for when he said, *Please, show me Your glory* (Exodus 33:18).

b. **Proclaimed the name of the Lord**: This means that God revealed His *character* to Moses. The specific aspects of His character are mentioned in this passage, yet this was far more than a lecture on the nature of God. Moses *experienced* the character of God in a dramatic way.

c. **And the Lord passed before him**: As Moses did what God told him to do in Exodus 33:21-23, he experienced what God said he would. Hidden in the cleft of the rock, Moses saw "behind" the Lord - as much of God's glory as he could possibly take in.

i. In Exodus 33:18 Moses boldly asked, *Please, show me Your glory*. After that, God *promised* to reveal His presence to Moses (Exodus 33:19-23), or as much as His presence as Moses could bear to experience.

3. (6b-7) The revelation of God's character to Moses.

And proclaimed, "The Lord, the Lord God, merciful and gracious, longsuffering, and abounding in goodness and truth, keeping mercy for thousands, forgiving iniquity and transgression and sin, by no means clearing *the guilty,* visiting the iniquity of the fathers upon the children and the children's children to the third and the fourth generation."

a. **And proclaimed**: God *said* this to Moses, revealing His character to Moses by *words*; He **proclaimed** it to Moses. As this happened, Moses had a power spiritual experience, rich with feeling and emotion. Yet God didn't want His revelation to only be in feeling and emotion, but connecting to the whole person through His Word.

b. **The LORD, the LORD God**: This *name* Yahweh was the same name for God that Abraham, Isaac, and Jacob knew; this was no new revelation of God. God presented Himself as the eternal, immutable God.

i. "The *name* of YHWH expresses all that He is and does, so this means proclamation of the saving acts of God . . . Here is God's Self-revelation, proclaiming His very self to Moses." (Cole)

ii. Knowing God should be the active interest of every human being, and especially of every Christian. "It has been said by someone that 'the proper study of mankind is man.' I will not oppose the idea, but I believe it is equally true that the proper study of God's elect is God; the proper study of a Christian is the Godhead. The highest science, the loftiest speculation, the mightiest philosophy which can ever engage the attention of a child of God, is the name, the nature, the person, the work, the doings, and the existence of the great God whom he calls his Father." (Spurgeon)

iii. "The Lord's self-disclosure is prefaced by the repetition of his name: 'The LORD, the LORD,' repeated perhaps to emphasize his unchangeableness." (Kaiser)

b. **Merciful and gracious**: **Merciful** is better translated, *full of compassion*. In five of the 13 times it is used, this word is translated *full of compassion* in the NKJV. F.B. Meyer wrote, "the word means 'tenderly pitiful.'"

i. The same word was also used regarding Israel and the Exodus in Psalm 78:38: *But He, being full of compassion, forgave their iniquity, and did not destroy them. Yes, many a time He turned His anger away, and did not stir up all His wrath.* This is compassion in *action*.

ii. The word translated **gracious** comes from the idea "to bend or stoop in kindness to an inferior; to favor, or to bestow" (Erwin). It is grace, giving to the undeserving.

iii. F.B. Meyer on this word **gracious**: "That word has gone out of fashion. Our fathers petrified it; they made it the foundation-stone of a structure of granite, in which the souls of men could find no rest, and therefore we rather dread that word - Grace. And yet there is no greater word in the language than the word that stands for the undeserved, free gift of the Love of God."

c. **Longsuffering, and abounding in goodness and truth**: The idea behind the word **longsuffering** means that God is *slow to anger*. He doesn't have a short fuse and is patient with us.

i. We all know what it is like to deal with people who have a short fuse, offended or even outraged at the slightest offense or the slightest perceived wrong. God isn't like that. He is **longsuffering**.

ii. "Not merely adequate, but abounding is this great God of glory. He has barns and silos full of love and faithfulness; he is stacking it in the streets looking for a distribution system." (Erwin)

d. **Keeping mercy for thousands, forgiving iniquity and transgression and sin**: God shows His goodness towards us in His forgiving character.

i. **Iniquity and transgression and sin** are all mentioned so that no one would think there were some types of sin God is unable to forgive.

ii. This revelation of the character of God to Moses forever puts away the idea there is a bad God of the Old Testament. This is in contrast to the good God of the New Testament. God's character of love and mercy and grace is present in the Old Testament as well as in the New Testament.

iii. Psalm 86:15 repeats this exact same revelation of God: *But You, O LORD, are a God full of compassion, and gracious, longsuffering and abundant in mercy and truth.*

e. **By no means clearing the guilty**: If His love and forgiveness are rejected, God will punish, and that punishment will have repercussions through the generations that hate Him (Exodus 20:5).

i. His loving, gracious, and giving character do not cancel out His righteousness. Because of the work of Jesus, the righteousness of God is satisfied and the grace and mercy of God are righteously given.

ii. "*To the third and fourth generation*: a common Semitic idiom to express continuance." (Cole)

3. (8-9) Moses reacts to the revelation of God.

So Moses made haste and bowed his head toward the earth, and worshiped. Then he said, "If now I have found grace in Your sight, O Lord, let my Lord, I pray, go among us, even though we *are* a stiff-necked people; and pardon our iniquity and our sin, and take us as Your inheritance."

a. **So Moses made haste and bowed his head toward the earth, and worshiped**: The first and primary reaction of Moses was to simply worship. When we come to know who God is and all His great love for us, the most practical thing it causes us to do is to worship Him more than ever.

i. "The elements of God's character are striking, suggesting both grace and truth. The effect on Moses was adoration and prayer." (Thomas)

ii. Indeed, Moses **made haste** to worship. He was compelled to worship God when he saw so clearly whom God was. When we don't have a compelling drive to worship God, it's clear evidence we don't really appreciate who He is.

b. **If now I have found grace in Your sight, O Lord, let my Lord, I pray, go among us**: Moses asked for the goodness, grace, and mercy of God be extended to himself and the nation. Moses knew they did not deserve it (**we are a stiff-necked people; and pardon our iniquity and our sin**), but he asked for God's **grace** and not His justice.

i. When we see the goodness of God for what it is, we should not hesitate to ask that it be extended to us. If we know God is good, we should ask Him to be good to us. If we know He is forgiving, we should ask Him to forgive us. The knowledge of God is therefore not a passive exercise. When we know Him, it leads us to receive from Him.

ii. Moses went even a step further than this, going beyond only asking these things for himself. He also asked for them on behalf of Israel.

B. Renewal of the covenant.

1. (10-11) What God will do for Israel.

And He said: "Behold, I make a covenant. Before all your people I will do marvels such as have not been done in all the earth, nor in any nation; and all the people among whom you *are* shall see the work of the LORD. For it *is* an awesome thing that I will do with you. Observe what I command you this day. Behold, I am driving out from before you the Amorite and the Canaanite and the Hittite and the Perizzite and the Hivite and the Jebusite."

a. **I will make a covenant**: This was *God's* covenant that Israel was invited to join. He did not negotiate the terms with Israel. Instead He dictated the terms to the people of Israel through Moses.

b. **I will do marvels…all the people among whom you are shall see the work of the LORD**: God's plan was to glorify Himself to all the nations (**all the people**) through Israel, and to show His glory through the great things He did among them.

i. Israel had a choice regarding those great things. Either the great things would be blessings so impressive that every nation would know that God alone had blessed Israel (as was the case with Solomon), or the great things would be curses so horrible that every nation would know God had chastised Israel and yet kept them a nation (as was the case with the exile). Either way, God would glorify Himself through Israel among the nations.

ii. Surely, that was **an awesome thing** that God promised to do with Israel. For their own good, it was essential that they obey God (**Observe what I command you this day**) and enjoy the blessings of covenant obedience.

iii. **I will do marvels**: "This seems to refer to what God did in putting them in possession of the land of Canaan, causing the walls of Jericho to fall down; making the sun and moon to stand still, [and so forth]." (Clarke)

c. **I am driving out**: God promised to do what Israel could not do by itself, drive out the nations of Canaan, allowing Israel to take possession of what God promised to give them.

2. (12-16) Israel must be separate from the Canaanites in worship, politics, fellowship and marriage.

"Take heed to yourself, lest you make a covenant with the inhabitants of the land where you are going, lest it be a snare in your midst. But you shall destroy their altars, break their *sacred* pillars, and cut down their *wooden* images (for you shall worship no other god, for the LORD, whose name *is* Jealous, *is* a jealous God), lest you make a covenant with the inhabitants of the land, and they play the harlot with their gods and make sacrifice to their gods, and *one of them* invites you and you eat of his sacrifice, and you take of his daughters for your sons, and his daughters play the harlot with their gods and make your sons play the harlot with their gods."

a. **You shall destroy their altars, break their sacred pillars, and cut down their wooden images**: As previously stated in Exodus 23:24, showing that the culture of the Canaanites was so corrupt that it was beyond redemption. God did not want Israel to assume any of the sinful practices found in the culture of the Canaanites.

i. "To worship a statue while calling it YHWH is not to worship YHWH." (Cole)

b. **And they play the harlot with their gods and make sacrifice to their gods**: There was a definite connection between the worship of the Canaanite gods and sexual immorality. Many of the Canaanite gods were fertility gods and were worshipped with ritual prostitutes and sex.

3. (17) Israel must renounce idolatry.

"You shall make no molded gods for yourselves."

a. **No molded gods**: The repetition of this command (the idea is in Exodus 20:4, the second commandment) was especially meaningful in light of the golden calf debacle. No molded image could come close to displaying the glory of God, even in the partial sense of what Moses saw on Mount Sinai.

4. (18) Israel must keep the feast of Unleavened Bread.

"The Feast of Unleavened Bread you shall keep. Seven days you shall eat unleavened bread, as I commanded you, in the appointed time of the month of Abib; for in the month of Abib you came out from Egypt."

a. **The Feast of Unleavened Bread**: First mentioned in Exodus 12:14-20, this feast spoke of the purity God desired among Israel before Him, when all leaven, a symbol of sin, was put away and Israel walked in a symbolic purity.

5. (19-26) Various laws, mostly regarding Israel's separation from other nations and separating unto the LORD.

"All that open the womb *are* Mine, and every male firstborn among your livestock, *whether* ox or sheep. But the firstborn of a donkey you shall redeem with a lamb. And if you will not redeem *him,* then you shall break his neck. All the firstborn of your sons you shall redeem. And none shall appear before Me empty-handed. Six days you shall work, but on the seventh day you shall rest; in plowing time and in harvest you shall rest. And you shall observe the Feast of Weeks, of the firstfruits of wheat harvest, and the Feast of Ingathering at the year's end. Three times in the year all your men shall appear before the Lord, the LORD God of Israel. For I will cast out the nations before you and enlarge your borders; neither will any man covet your land when you go up to appear before the LORD your God three times in the year. You shall not offer the blood of My sacrifice with leaven, nor shall the sacrifice of the Feast of the Passover be left until morning. The first of the firstfruits of your land you shall bring to the house of the LORD your God. You shall not boil a young goat in its mother's milk."

a. **All that open the womb are Mine**: Here God repeated the laws regarding the firstborn and their dedication to Him, first stated in Exodus 13:11-13 and 22:29-30.

b. **None shall appear before Me empty-handed**: God gave this command in the context of daily work (**Six days you shall work**) and festival observance (**you shall observe the feast....**). The idea is that everyone should have some work and something to give unto the Lord.

i. It is simply appropriate for the creature to honor the Creator by giving unto Him. It is even more appropriate for the redeemed to honor their Redeemer this way.

c. **Three times in the year all your men shall appear before the Lord**: God commanded that at three feasts each year (Passover, Pentecost, and the Feast of Tabernacles), each Israelite man should gather before the LORD (Exodus 23:14-17). Here, God even promised a supernatural protection for an obedient Israel when they went to the feasts (**neither will any man covet your land when you go up to appear before the LORD your God three times in the year**).

> i. **Neither will any man covet your land when you go up**: "What a manifest proof was this of the power and particular providence of God! How easy would it have been for the surrounding nations to have taken possession of the whole Israelitish land, with all their fenced cities, when there were none left to protect them but women and children! Was not this a standing proof of the Divine origin of their religion?" (Clarke)

d. **You shall not offer the blood of My sacrifice with leaven**: Leaven (yeast) is often a picture of sin in the Bible. Therefore, it was forbidden to include any kind of leaven in a blood sacrifice (as previous stated in Exodus 23:18).

e. **The first of the firstfruits of your land you shall bring into the house of the LORD**: When Israel came into Canaan, they had a special responsibility to make a firstfruit offering to God, in addition to their regular firstfruit offering (Exodus 23:16). Giving God the first and the best honored Him as the Good Provider of all things.

f. **You shall not boil a young goat in its mother's milk**: This command is repeated from Exodus 23:19. It was a command not to imitate the cruel pagan fertility rituals practiced among the Canaanites.

6. (27-28) Moses is commanded to write and is miraculously sustained.

Then the LORD said to Moses, "Write these words, for according to the tenor of these words I have made a covenant with you and with Israel." So he was there with the LORD forty days and forty nights; he neither ate bread nor drank water. And He wrote on the tablets the words of the covenant, the Ten Commandments.

a. **Write these words**: Since God's covenant with Israel was based on these and other words, it was important for Moses to **write** them. They should not only be left to memory.

b. **So he was there with the LORD forty days and forty nights; he neither ate bread nor drank water**: This was a completely unique and supernatural fast. It is definitely possible (yet remarkable) for someone to live without food for 40 days, but by any account it is a miracle to go without **water** for this long. This kind of fasting is never repeated or recommended in the Scriptures.

i. "It is impossible to exaggerate the stupendous things suggested in this simple statement." (Morgan) It was a powerful evidence of the truth that *man shall not live by bread alone, but by every word that comes from the mouth of God.*

c. **He wrote on the tablets the words of the covenant, the Ten Commandments**: These tablets were eventually placed into the ark of the covenant (Deuteronomy 10:5).

C. The shining face of Moses.

1. (29-30) Moses' face shines when he comes down from Mount Sinai.

Now it was so, when Moses came down from Mount Sinai (and the two tablets of the Testimony *were* in Moses' hand when he came down from the mountain), that Moses did not know that the skin of his face shone while he talked with Him. So when Aaron and all the children of Israel saw Moses, behold, the skin of his face shone, and they were afraid to come near him.

a. **Moses did not know that the skin of his face shone while he talked with Him**: Close communion with God physically affected Moses. His face had a shining appearance that was so noticeable that both the leaders and the people of Israel were **afraid to come near him.**

i. After such a remarkable fast, we would expect that Moses looked pale and sickly. Apparently not; instead **his face shone** with a radiance and glory so great that it made others hesitant to come near him.

ii. It is true that a life lived with God affects physical appearance, especially the face. The peace, joy, love, and goodness of God should be evident on the face of the one who follows Jesus. Yet what Moses experienced seems beyond that general principle, and a direct result from his remarkable communication with God (**his face shone while he talked with Him**).

iii. The radiance of Moses' shining face was a *reflected* radiance, a *received* glory. The source was the face of God, and as Moses communicated so directly with God his face received some of this shining glory. "The face of Moses shone because he had long looked upon the face of God." (Spurgeon)

b. **Moses did not know that the skin of his face shone**: Wonderfully, Moses **did not know** this. He was unaware of the greatness of his own spiritual radiance. This was because Moses was a genuinely and deeply humble man (Numbers 12:3).

i. "Directly people become conscious of their superiority to others, and boast of it, it is certain that they have never really seen the beauty of God's holiness, and have no clear knowledge of the condition of their own hearts." (Meyer)

ii. We read of only two men in the Bible whose faces shone like this: Moses and Stephen (Acts 6:15). Both were humble men. "I am afraid, brethren, that God could not afford to make our faces shine: we should grow too proud. It needs a very meek and lowly spirit to bear the shinings of God." (Spurgeon)

iii. "We are always praying, 'Lord, make my face to shine'; but Moses never had such a wish; and, therefore, when it did shine, he did not know it. He had not laid his plans for such an honor. Let us not set traps for personal reputation, or even glance a thought that way." (Spurgeon)

2. (31-32) Moses relates the covenant of God to the leaders of Israel.

Then Moses called to them, and Aaron and all the rulers of the congregation returned to him; and Moses talked with them. Afterward all the children of Israel came near, and he gave them as commandments all that the LORD had spoken with him on Mount Sinai.

a. **Moses called to them, and Aaron and all the rulers of the congregation returned to him**: They had all gone away from Moses because the radiance of his face so greatly intimidated them. He had to persuade them to come back. First the leaders, then **all the children of Israel came near.**

b. **And he gave them as commandments all that the Lord had spoken with him on Mount Sinai**: Moses experienced glorious, transforming communion with God on Sinai. Yet as he came down to the people, he once again involved himself directly in the work of governing and leading.

i. "From that experience he returned, not to be a dreamer, for ever thinking and talking of a past rapture; but to be, as never before, a man of affairs, directing, controlling all the earthly life according to the standards received in the mount." (Morgan)

3. (33-35) The veil on Moses' face.

And when Moses had finished speaking with them, he put a veil on his face. But whenever Moses went in before the LORD to speak with Him, he would take the veil off until he came out; and he would come out and speak to the children of Israel whatever he had been commanded. And whenever the children of Israel saw the face of Moses, that the skin of Moses' face shone, then Moses would put the veil on his face again, until he went in to speak with Him.

a. **He put a veil on his face…whenever Moses went in before the Lord to speak with Him, he would take the veil off**: In the presence of God (presumably at his own tent, which had become the tabernacle of meeting according to Exodus 33:7), Moses took the veil off. Yet among the people, **he put a veil on his face**.

b. **He put a veil on his face**: It is easy to think that Moses wore the veil so the people would not be *afraid to come near him* (Exodus 34:30), or that the purpose of the veil was to protect others from the glorious radiance of Moses' face. Yet the Apostle Paul explained the real purpose of the veil: not to hide the shining face of Moses, but so that the diminishing glory of his face would not be observed because the glory was fading.

  i. *Moses, who put a veil over his face, so that the children of Israel could not look steadily at the end of what was passing away* (2 Corinthians 3:13). The Old Covenant had a glory, but it was a fading glory. God didn't want people to see the fading glory of the Old Covenant, and lose confidence in Moses.

  ii. The Old Covenant was great and glorious, but it looks pretty pale in comparison to the New Covenant. A bright autumn moon may look beautiful and give great light, but it is nothing compared to the noonday sun.

c. **The skin of Moses' face shone**: The Hebrew verb for **shone** literally means, "shot forth beams" (Cole). It is also related to a Hebrew noun for "horn." This is why the Latin Vulgate mistranslated this verb as "having horns," and so in most medieval works of art Moses wears a pair of horns on his head.

Exodus 35 - Offerings For the Tabernacle

A. The call to receive the offering.

1. (1-3) The command to keep the Sabbath.

Then Moses gathered all the congregation of the children of Israel together, and said to them, "These *are* the words which the LORD has commanded *you* to do: Work shall be done for six days, but the seventh day shall be a holy day for you, a Sabbath of rest to the LORD. Whoever does any work on it shall be put to death. You shall kindle no fire throughout your dwellings on the Sabbath day."

a. **Work shall be done for six days, but the seventh day shall be a holy day for you, a Sabbath of rest to the LORD**: In the coming chapters, there was a lot of work for Israel to do. They had to build a complex and exact tabernacle of meeting. Yet before they did anything, they should be reminded to enter into God's rest and to respect the Sabbath.

i. The same principle holds true for our walk with God. Anything we do for the LORD must grow out of our rest in Him, and rest in His finished work on our behalf.

b. **Whoever does any work on it shall be put to death**: This was a strict call to obedience. Before they did the work of building the tabernacle, God first called Israel to the work of simple obedience. Basic obedience is a pre-requisite for doing work for the LORD.

i. "Why was it necessary to refer so often to the Sabbath? (16:23-30; 20:8-11; 23:12; 31:13-17). The observance was the best guarantee of continued loyalty to God." (Thomas)

ii. The Hebrew language has two words for **work**: *avodah* and *melachah*. *Avodah* is a general term meaning work, while *melachah* is a word more related to *business* and things specifically forbidden on the Sabbath. One might say that here, God allowed some work (*avodah*) to be done on the Sabbath, but did not allow certain things on the Sabbath, especially business-related things (*melachah*).

iii. **Kindle no fire**: "The Jews understand this precept as forbidding the kindling of fire *only* for the purpose of *doing work* or *dressing victuals*; but to give them *light* and *heat*, they judge it lawful to light a fire on the Sabbath day." (Clarke)

2. (4-9) Receiving what is needed to build the tabernacle.

And Moses spoke to all the congregation of the children of Israel, saying, "This *is* the thing which the LORD commanded, saying: 'Take from among you an offering to the LORD. Whoever *is* of a willing heart, let him bring it as an offering to the LORD: gold, silver, and bronze; blue, purple, and scarlet *thread,* fine linen, and goats' *hair*; ram skins dyed red, badger skins, and acacia wood; oil for the light, and spices for the anointing oil and for the sweet incense; onyx stones, and stones to be set in the ephod and in the breastplate.'"

a. **This is the thing which the LORD commanded**: Now it was time to do what God originally commanded Moses in Exodus 25-31 regarding the building of the tabernacle and its associated items.

i. "If it is a reduplication, it is a deliberate one, to point out the lesson of the faithfulness of Moses in carrying out God's instruction (Exodus 25:9)." (Cole)

b. **Take from among you an offering to the LORD. Whoever is of a willing heart, let him bring it as an offering to the LORD**: This offering came from God's command, not from Moses' clever fund-raising techniques. This shows God's normal way of channeling resources to His work – by the gifts given from His people with a **willing heart**.

i. God could cause the money and materials to appear by a miracle. Yet He chose to fund His work through the willing gifts of His people. He works this way because we need to be a giving people.

ii. This idea is echoed in 2 Corinthians 9:7: *So let each one give as he purposes in his heart, not grudgingly or of necessity; for God loves a cheerful giver.*

c. **Gold, silver, and bronze; blue, purple, and scarlet *thread,* fine linen, and goats' *hair*; ram skins dyed red**: These were the materials necessary to build the tabernacle as commanded in Exodus 25-31.

3. (10-19) Coordinating the labor and planning the work for the tabernacle.

"'All *who are* gifted artisans among you shall come and make all that the LORD has commanded: the tabernacle, its tent, its covering, its clasps, its boards, its bars, its pillars, and its sockets; the ark and its poles, *with* the mercy seat, and the veil of the covering; the table and

its poles, all its utensils, and the showbread; also the lampstand for the light, its utensils, its lamps, and the oil for the light; the incense altar, its poles, the anointing oil, the sweet incense, and the screen for the door at the entrance of the tabernacle; the altar of burnt offering with its bronze grating, its poles, all its utensils, *and* the laver and its base; the hangings of the court, its pillars, their sockets, and the screen for the gate of the court; the pegs of the tabernacle, the pegs of the court, and their cords; the garments of ministry, for ministering in the holy *place;* the holy garments for Aaron the priest and the garments of his sons, to minister as priests.'"

a. **All who are gifted artisans among you shall come and make all that the** LORD **has commanded**: God commanded that the labor to make the tabernacle and its furnishings come from the **gifted artisans** among the Israelites.

b. **The tabernacle, its tent, its covering…**: This lists the items of the tabernacle that must be made, repeating from Exodus 25-31.

4. (20-29) Receiving the offering for building the tabernacle.

And all the congregation of the children of Israel departed from the presence of Moses. Then everyone came whose heart was stirred, and everyone whose spirit was willing, *and* they brought the LORD**'s offering for the work of the tabernacle of meeting, for all its service, and for the holy garments. They came, both men and women, as many as had a willing heart, *and* brought earrings and nose rings, rings and necklaces, all jewelry of gold, that is, every man who *made* an offering of gold to the** LORD**. And every man, with whom was found blue, purple, and scarlet *thread,* fine linen, and goats' *hair,* red skins of rams, and badger skins, brought *them.* Everyone who offered an offering of silver or bronze brought the** LORD**'s offering. And everyone with whom was found acacia wood for any work of the service, brought *it.* All the women *who were* gifted artisans spun yarn with their hands, and brought what they had spun, of blue, purple, *and* scarlet, and fine linen. And all the women whose heart stirred with wisdom spun yarn of goats' *hair.* The rulers brought onyx stones, and the stones to be set in the ephod and in the breastplate, and spices and oil for the light, for the anointing oil, and for the sweet incense. The children of Israel brought a freewill offering to the** LORD**, all the men and women whose hearts were willing to bring *material* for all kinds of work which the** LORD**, by the hand of Moses, had commanded to be done.**

a. **All the congregation of the children of Israel departed from the presence of Moses**: After Moses asked them to give, he sent them home to decide what they would give. This shows that Moses did not use manipulative techniques, such as asking people to make quick, public decisions about their giving. There was no manipulation at all in Moses' request.

> i. Moses didn't have a contest setting one tribe against another to see which tribe could raise the most money or any other such nonsense. God did the work in the hearts of the people.

b. **Everyone came whose heart was stirred...everyone whose spirit was willing...as many as had a willing heart...all the women whose hearts were stirred...a freewill offering to the LORD...whose hearts were willing**: The idea of the freedom and lack of coercion in the offering is repeated and emphasized.

> i. "The willingness of the people is mentioned repeatedly (vv. 21, 22, 26, 29; 36:2)." (Kaiser)

> ii. Though their hearts were willing, they didn't know what to give, when to give, or how to give until Moses led them. Willing hearts still need to be told when there is a need and how they can meet that need.

c. **The LORD's offering...an offering of gold to the LORD...the LORD's offering...a freewill offering to the LORD**: It was also clear exactly to Whom they gave - the LORD, not to Moses or even to the nation.

d. **Both men and women...every man...every man with whom was found blue and purple and scarlet...everyone with whom was found acacia wood...all the women who were gifted artisans...all the women whose hearts stirred with wisdom...the rulers brought onyx stones**: In this, we see just *how many* among Israel gave to the work. It wasn't only the wealthy, but **everyone** who could and who had a willing heart gave. There were many willing hearts.

> i. "All have a part in building the sanctuary for YHWH, and, without each playing his peculiar part, it cannot be completed (*cf.* Ephesians 4:16)." (Cole)

> ii. The people gave what they could. Not all could give gold or precious gems, but they could give some goat's hair. Certainly, a gift of goat's hair could be just as welcome in God's sight as a gift of gold, if it was given with the right heart.

B. Coordinating the construction of the tabernacle.

1. (30-35) The call of Bezalel and Aholiab.

And Moses said to the children of Israel, "See, the LORD has called by name Bezalel the son of Uri, the son of Hur, of the tribe of Judah; and He has filled him with the Spirit of God, in wisdom and understanding,

in knowledge and all manner of workmanship, to design artistic works, to work in gold and silver and bronze, in cutting jewels for setting, in carving wood, and to work in all manner of artistic workmanship. And He has put in his heart the ability to teach, *in* him and Aholiab the son of Ahisamach, of the tribe of Dan. He has filled them with skill to do all manner of work of the engraver and the designer and the tapestry maker, in blue, purple, and scarlet *thread,* and fine linen, and of the weaver; those who do every work and those who design artistic works."

a. **He has filled him with the Spirit of God, in wisdom and understanding, in knowledge and all manner of workmanship**: God chose Bezalel and Aholiab to be the general contractors for this building project. He equipped them with a special outpouring of the Holy Spirit to do the work.

b. **Those who do every work and those who design artistic works**: The leaders of the work of building the tabernacle had a unique inspiration of the Holy Spirit to do this important and practical work. Since God wanted the work done according to a certain *pattern* (Exodus 25:9), it made sense that He specially inspired some to do the work.

2. (36:1) The coordination of the work.

"And Bezalel and Aholiab, and every gifted artisan in whom the LORD has put wisdom and understanding, to know how to do all manner of work for the service of the sanctuary, shall do according to all that the LORD has commanded."

a. **Every gifted artisan…shall do according to all the LORD has commanded**: It was up to the workers under Bezalel and Aholiab to follow what the LORD instructed them to do.

Exodus 36 - Building the Tent of Meeting

A. The people bring an offering.

1. (2-3) The offering is asked for.

Then Moses called Bezalel and Aholiab, and every gifted artisan in whose heart the LORD had put wisdom, everyone whose heart was stirred, to come and do the work. And they received from Moses all the offering which the children of Israel had brought for the work of the service of making the sanctuary. So they continued bringing to him freewill offerings every morning.

a. **To come and do the work**: The planning and preparation were over. It was time to actually **do the work** of building the tabernacle and its furnishings.

i. **Then everyone came whose heart was stirred**: "Literally, *whose heart was lifted up*-whose affections were set on the work, being cordially engaged in the service of God." (Clarke)

b. **They continued bringing to him freewill offerings every morning**: Again, even willing hearts need to be told, *now is the time to give*. Moses let them know, and the people started bringing their offering to the LORD.

2. (4-7) The people bring more than enough.

Then all the craftsmen who were doing all the work of the sanctuary came, each from the work he was doing, and they spoke to Moses, saying, "The people bring much more than enough for the service of the work which the LORD commanded *us* to do." So Moses gave a commandment, and they caused it to be proclaimed throughout the camp, saying, "Let neither man nor woman do any more work for the offering of the sanctuary." And the people were restrained from bringing, for the material they had was sufficient for all the work to be done; indeed too much.

a. **The people bring much more than enough**: This shows how blessed giving can be when free from human manipulation and tricks. Willing hearts will always give enough as God blesses the work - indeed, **the people were restrained from bringing**.

 i. "When the heart is truly stirred, and the spirit makes willing, giving is robbed of all meanness; indeed, it ceases to be calculating. Nothing is too precious to be given, no amount is too great." (Morgan)

 ii. "Compare the story of the anointing at Bethany (Matthew 26:7), and the generosity of the Philippian church (Philippians 4:14-19)." (Cole)

 iii. This also shows that Moses and the planners of the work *knew how much was* **enough**. The job was organized and planned to the extent that they understood what they needed, and when they had more than enough. When God's people are asked to give to something, they should expect that it be well organized, planned, and managed.

b. **And the people were restrained from bringing, for the material they had was sufficient**: Moses showed great integrity by not gathering more than the project needed. God told him to take an offering for the building of a tabernacle, and when the tabernacle was provided for, the offering was over. The purpose wasn't to amass endless resources, but to properly put those resources into action.

 i. **Indeed too much**: This follows the pattern of God's giving to us. God gives us *much more* than we ever need, and our giving is simply a response to His.

 ii. "It must have been both a disappointment and a frustration to those who had delayed their gifts because they could not bear to part with their treasures, and who now found that God had no further need of them. His work was finished, but they had excluded themselves from any share in it: God deliver us from such a frustration." (Cole)

B. The building and assembling of the curtains, boards, pillars, and veils of the tabernacle.

This begins a long section, almost to the end of the Book of Exodus, where the Tabernacle described in Exodus 26-31 is actually built. Cole rightly noted, "As an architect delights to pore over plans or blueprints, so the pious priest would have rejoiced in this meticulous re-listing of specifications already given."

1. (8-13) The curtains of an artistic design of cherubim (according to the command and description in Exodus 26:1-6).

Then all the gifted artisans among them who worked on the tabernacle made ten curtains woven of fine linen, and of blue, purple, and scarlet

thread; with artistic designs of cherubim they made them. The length of each curtain *was* twenty-eight cubits, and the width of each curtain four cubits; the curtains *were* all the same size. And he coupled five curtains to one another, and *the other* five curtains he coupled to one another. He made loops of blue *yarn* on the edge of the curtain on the selvedge of one set; likewise he did on the outer edge of *the other* curtain of the second set. Fifty loops he made on one curtain, and fifty loops he made on the edge of the curtain on the end of the second set; the loops held one *curtain* to another. And he made fifty clasps of gold, and coupled the curtains to one another with the clasps, that it might be one tabernacle.

2. (14-18) The curtains of goat's hair (according to the command and description in Exodus 26:7-13).

He made curtains of goats' *hair* for the tent over the tabernacle; he made eleven curtains. The length of each curtain *was* thirty cubits, and the width of each curtain four cubits; the eleven curtains *were* the same size. He coupled five curtains by themselves and six curtains by themselves. And he made fifty loops on the edge of the curtain that is outermost in one set, and fifty loops he made on the edge of the curtain of the second set. He also made fifty bronze clasps to couple the tent together, that it might be one.

3. (19) The curtains of ram's skin dyed red and badger skins (according to the command and description in Exodus 26:14).

Then he made a covering for the tent of ram skins dyed red, and a covering of badger skins above *that.*

4. (20-34) The boards and connecting bars for the frame and walls of the tabernacle (according to the command and description in Exodus 26:15-30).

For the tabernacle he made boards of acacia wood, standing upright. The length of each board *was* ten cubits, and the width of each board a cubit and a half. Each board had two tenons for binding one to another. Thus he made for all the boards of the tabernacle. And he made boards for the tabernacle, twenty boards for the south side. Forty sockets of silver he made to go under the twenty boards: two sockets under each of the boards for its two tenons. And for the other side of the tabernacle, the north side, he made twenty boards and their forty sockets of silver: two sockets under each of the boards. For the west side of the tabernacle he made six boards. He also made two boards for the two back corners of the tabernacle. And they were coupled at the bottom and coupled together at the top by one ring. Thus he made both of them for the two corners. So there were eight boards and their sockets; sixteen sockets of silver; two sockets under each of the boards.

And he made bars of acacia wood: five for the boards on one side of the tabernacle, five bars for the boards on the other side of the tabernacle, and five bars for the boards of the tabernacle on the far side westward. And he made the middle bar to pass through the boards from one end to the other. He overlaid the boards with gold, made their rings of gold *to be* holders for the bars, and overlaid the bars with gold.

5. (35-38) The veil with its four pillars, and the screen with its five pillars (according to the command and description in Exodus 26:31-33, 36-37).

And he made a veil of blue, purple, and scarlet *thread,* and fine woven linen; it was worked *with* an artistic design of cherubim. He made for it four pillars of acacia *wood,* and overlaid them with gold, with their hooks of gold; and he cast four sockets of silver for them. He also made a screen for the tabernacle door, of blue, purple, and scarlet *thread,* and fine woven linen, made by a weaver, and its five pillars with their hooks. And he overlaid their capitals and their rings with gold, but their five sockets *were* bronze.

Exodus 37 - Building the Tabernacle Furniture

A. The furniture of the Most Holy Place.

1. (1-5) The Ark of the Covenant (according the command and description in Exodus 25:10-16).

Then Bezalel made the ark of acacia wood; two and a half cubits *was* its length, a cubit and a half its width, and a cubit and a half its height. He overlaid it with pure gold inside and outside, and made a molding of gold all around it. And he cast for it four rings of gold *to be set* in its four corners: two rings on one side, and two rings on the other side of it. He made poles of acacia wood, and overlaid them with gold. And he put the poles into the rings at the sides of the ark, to bear the ark.

2. (6-9) The mercy seat (the gold lid to the Ark of the Covenant, according to the command and description in Exodus 25:17-22).

He also made the mercy seat of pure gold; two and a half cubits *was* its length and a cubit and a half its width. He made two cherubim of beaten gold; he made them of one piece at the two ends of the mercy seat: one cherub at one end on this side, and the other cherub at the *other* end on that side. He made the cherubim at the two ends *of one piece* with the mercy seat. The cherubim spread out *their* wings above, *and* covered the mercy seat with their wings. They faced one another; the faces of the cherubim were toward the mercy seat.

B. The furniture of the holy place.

1. (10-16) The Table of Showbread with its utensils (according to the command and description in Exodus 25:23-30).

He made the table of acacia wood; two cubits *was* its length, a cubit its width, and a cubit and a half its height. And he overlaid it with pure gold, and made a molding of gold all around it. Also he made a frame of a handbreadth all around it, and made a molding of gold for the frame all around it. And he cast for it four rings of gold, and put the rings on

the four corners that *were* at its four legs. The rings were close to the frame, as holders for the poles to bear the table. And he made the poles of acacia wood to bear the table, and overlaid them with gold. He made of pure gold the utensils which were on the table: its dishes, its cups, its bowls, and its pitchers for pouring.

2. (17-24) The gold lampstand (according to the command and description in Exodus 25:31-40).

He also made the lampstand of pure gold; of hammered work he made the lampstand. Its shaft, its branches, its bowls, its *ornamental* knobs, and its flowers were of the same piece. And six branches came out of its sides: three branches of the lampstand out of one side, and three branches of the lampstand out of the other side. There were three bowls made like almond *blossoms* on one branch, with an *ornamental* knob and a flower, and three bowls made like almond *blossoms* on the other branch, with an *ornamental* knob and a flower; and so for the six branches coming out of the lampstand. And on the lampstand itself *were* four bowls made like almond *blossoms, each with* its *ornamental* knob and flower. *There was* a knob under the *first* two branches of the same, a knob under the *second* two branches of the same, and a knob under the *third* two branches of the same, according to the six branches extending from it. Their knobs and their branches were of one piece; all of it *was* one hammered piece of pure gold. And he made its seven lamps, its wick-trimmers, and its trays of pure gold. Of a talent of pure gold he made it, with all its utensils.

3. (25-28) The Altar of Incense (according to the command and description in Exodus 30:1-10).

He made the incense altar of acacia wood. Its length *was* a cubit and its width a cubit; *it was* square; and two cubits *was* its height. Its horns were *of one piece* with it. And he overlaid it with pure gold: its top, its sides all around, and its horns. He also made for it a molding of gold all around it. He made two rings of gold for it under its molding, by its two corners on both sides, as holders for the poles with which to bear it. And he made the poles of acacia wood, and overlaid them with gold.

4. (29) The anointing oil and incense (according to the command and description in Exodus 30:22-38).

He also made the holy anointing oil and the pure incense of sweet spices, according to the work of the perfumer.

Exodus 38 - More on Building the Tabernacle

A. Items associated with the outer court.

1. (1-7) The altar (according to the command and description in Exodus 27:1-8).

He made the altar of burnt offering of acacia wood; five cubits *was* its length and five cubits its width; *it was* square; and its height *was* three cubits. He made its horns on its four corners; the horns were *of one piece* with it. And he overlaid it with bronze. He made all the utensils for the altar: the pans, the shovels, the basins, the forks, and the firepans; all its utensils he made of bronze. And he made a grate of bronze network for the altar, under its rim, midway from the bottom. He cast four rings for the four corners of the bronze grating, *as* holders for the poles. And he made the poles of acacia wood, and overlaid them with bronze. Then he put the poles into the rings on the sides of the altar, with which to bear it. He made the altar hollow with boards.

2. (8) The bronze laver (according to the command and description in Exodus 30:17-21).

He made the laver of bronze and its base of bronze, from the bronze mirrors of the serving women who assembled at the door of the tabernacle of meeting.

a. **From the bronze mirrors of the serving women**: Exodus 30:17-21 gave the original command to build this container for the water of ceremonial washing. Here only are we told that the bronze used to make the **laver** came, at least in part, from the polished metal **mirrors** of some of the women of Israel.

i. It is wonderful to think that these women gave up their ability to measure their own physical beauty to make this reservoir for the water of ceremonial washing. By analogy, it may be said that some are so focused on looking at themselves that they fail to look to Jesus. It is always time to surrender such a mirror to Jesus.

ii. From a New Testament perspective, one may say that believers experience *the washing of water by the word* (Ephesians 5:26), and that the Word of God is like a mirror (James 1:22-25).

iii. "It was highly significant that the brass of these mirrors was employed to construct that laver in which the priests must wash on approaching the altar or entering the Tabernacle. It is in the beauty of holiness men must worship, and by the surrender of everything of the flesh." (Morgan)

iv. "Let those who view themselves oft in their looking-glasses take his counsel who said, 'Art thou fair? Be not like an Egyptian temple, varnish without and vermin within. Art thou foul? Let thy soul be like a rich pearl in a rude shell.'" (Trapp)

b. **The serving women who assembled at the door of the tabernacle of meeting**: Apparently, there were a group of women in Israel who served God by regularly meeting to help the priests and the work of the **tabernacle**.

i. "The verb translated *minister* is rare and interesting, and is used in only one other place of women in the service of the sanctuary (1 Samuel 2:22). It really means 'organized in bands for war', but it is used of ordinary Levitical service (Numbers 4:23, *etc.*)." (Cole)

3. (9-20) The court with its pillars and linen fence (according to the command and description in Exodus 27:9-19).

Then he made the court on the south side; the hangings of the court *were of* **fine woven linen, one hundred cubits long. There** *were* **twenty pillars for them, with twenty bronze sockets. The hooks of the pillars and their bands** *were* **silver. On the north side** *the hangings were* **one hundred cubits** *long,* **with twenty pillars and their twenty bronze sockets. The hooks of the pillars and their bands** *were* **silver. And on the west side** *there were* **hangings of fifty cubits, with ten pillars and their ten sockets. The hooks of the pillars and their bands** *were* **silver. For the east side** *the hangings were* **fifty cubits. The hangings of one side** *of the gate were* **fifteen cubits** *long,* **with their three pillars and their three sockets, and the same for the other side of the court gate; on this side and that** *were* **hangings of fifteen cubits,** *with* **their three pillars and their three sockets. All the hangings of the court all around** *were of* **fine woven linen. The sockets for the pillars** *were* **bronze, the hooks of the pillars and their bands** *were* **silver, and the overlay of their capitals** *was* **silver; and all the pillars of the court had bands of silver. The screen for the gate of the court** *was* **woven of blue, purple, and scarlet** *thread,* **and of fine woven linen. The length** *was* **twenty cubits, and the height along its width** *was* **five cubits, corresponding to the hangings of the court.**

And *there were* four pillars *with* their four sockets of bronze; their hooks *were* silver, and the overlay of their capitals and their bands *was* silver. All the pegs of the tabernacle, and of the court all around, *were* bronze.

B. An inventory of the materials for the building of the tabernacle.

1. (21-23) The leaders of the work.

This is the inventory of the tabernacle, the tabernacle of the Testimony, which was counted according to the commandment of Moses, for the service of the Levites, by the hand of Ithamar, son of Aaron the priest. Bezalel the son of Uri, the son of Hur, of the tribe of Judah, made all that the LORD had commanded Moses. And with him *was* Aholiab the son of Ahisamach, of the tribe of Dan, an engraver and designer, a weaver of blue, purple, and scarlet *thread,* and of fine linen.

a. **By the hand of Ithamar, son of Aaron the priest**: This priest named **Ithamar** oversaw the Levites who had the responsibility of managing all these resources. They had a big job to do and seemed to do it well.

b. **Which was counted according to the commandment of Moses**: By some estimations, the present day value of the materials used in the tabernacle would total more than $13 million (DeWitt). Their combined weight would be almost 19,000 pounds (more than 9 tons or 8,500 kilograms). This was a significant project to manage.

i. "The exact calculation teaches the necessity of thoroughness and accuracy in all things connected with money for religious work." (Thomas)

ii. Some wonder where Israel got all these resources out in the middle of the desert. But Exodus 12:36 reminds us that the children of Israel left Egypt with great resources because they had plundered the Egyptians, who willingly gave Israel what amounted to back wages for their years of slavery.

2. (24) The inventory of gold.

All the gold that was used in all the work of the holy *place,* that is, the gold of the offering, was twenty-nine talents and seven hundred and thirty shekels, according to the shekel of the sanctuary.

a. **Twenty-nine talents**: Some estimate a talent to equal about 70 pounds (32 kilograms). This means there was something like 2,030 pounds (920 kilograms) of gold used in the tabernacle.

3. (25-28) The inventory of silver.

And the silver from those who were numbered of the congregation *was* one hundred talents and one thousand seven hundred and seventy-five shekels, according to the shekel of the sanctuary: a bekah for each man *(that is,* half a shekel, according to the shekel of the sanctuary), for everyone included in the numbering from twenty years old and above, for six hundred and three thousand, five hundred and fifty *men*. And from the hundred talents of silver were cast the sockets of the sanctuary and the bases of the veil: one hundred sockets from the hundred talents, one talent for each socket. Then from the one thousand seven hundred and seventy-five *shekels* he made hooks for the pillars, overlaid their capitals, and made bands for them.

a. **The silver from those who were numbered**: Exodus 30:13-16 described how the Israelites were to give silver as part of a census, a counting of the nation. This accounts for the high amount of silver given.

4. (29-31) The inventory of bronze.

The offering of bronze *was* seventy talents and two thousand four hundred shekels. And with it he made the sockets for the door of the tabernacle of meeting, the bronze altar, the bronze grating for it, and all the utensils for the altar, the sockets for the court all around, the bases for the court gate, all the pegs for the tabernacle, and all the pegs for the court all around.

Exodus 39 - The Priestly Garments

A. Making of the Priestly garments.

1. (1-7) The ephod for the high priest (according to the command and description in Exodus 28:5-14).

Of the blue, purple, and scarlet *thread* **they made garments of ministry, for ministering in the holy** *place,* **and made the holy garments for Aaron, as the LORD had commanded Moses. He made the ephod of gold, blue, purple, and scarlet** *thread,* **and of fine woven linen. And they beat the gold into thin sheets and cut** *it into* **threads, to work** *it* **in** *with* **the blue, purple, and scarlet** *thread* **and the fine linen,** *into* **artistic designs. They made shoulder straps for it to couple** *it* **together; it was coupled together at its two edges. And the intricately woven band of his ephod that** *was* **on it** *was* **of the same workmanship,** *woven of* **gold, blue, purple, and scarlet** *thread,* **and of fine woven linen, as the LORD had commanded Moses. And they set onyx stones, enclosed in settings of gold; they were engraved, as signets are engraved, with the names of the sons of Israel. He put them on the shoulders of the ephod** *as* **memorial stones for the sons of Israel, as the LORD had commanded Moses.**

2. (8-21) The breastplate for the high priest (according to the command and description in Exodus 28:15-29).

And he made the breastplate, artistically woven like the workmanship of the ephod, of gold, blue, purple, and scarlet *thread,* **and of fine woven linen. They made the breastplate square by doubling it; a span** *was* **its length and a span its width when doubled. And they set in it four rows of stones: a row with a sardius, a topaz, and an emerald was the first row; the second row, a turquoise, a sapphire, and a diamond; the third row, a jacinth, an agate, and an amethyst; the fourth row, a beryl, an onyx, and a jasper.** *They were* **enclosed in settings of gold in their mountings.** *There were* **twelve stones according to the names of**

the sons of Israel: according to their names, *engraved like* a signet, each one with its own name according to the twelve tribes. And they made chains for the breastplate at the ends, like braided cords of pure gold. They also made two settings of gold and two gold rings, and put the two rings on the two ends of the breastplate. And they put the two braided chains of gold in the two rings on the ends of the breastplate. The two ends of the two braided chains they fastened in the two settings, and put them on the shoulder straps of the ephod in the front. And they made two rings of gold and put *them* on the two ends of the breastplate, on the edge of it, which *was* on the inward side of the ephod. They made two *other* gold rings and put them on the two shoulder straps, underneath the ephod toward its front, right at the seam above the intricately woven band of the ephod. And they bound the breastplate by means of its rings to the rings of the ephod with a blue cord, so that it would be above the intricately woven band of the ephod, and that the breastplate would not come loose from the ephod, as the Lord had commanded Moses.

3. (22-26) The robe for the high priest (according to the command and description in Exodus 28:31-35).

He made the robe of the ephod of woven work, all of blue. And *there was* an opening in the middle of the robe, like the opening in a coat of mail, *with* a woven binding all around the opening, so that it would not tear. They made on the hem of the robe pomegranates of blue, purple, and scarlet, and of fine woven *linen*. And they made bells of pure gold, and put the bells between the pomegranates on the hem of the robe all around between the pomegranates: a bell and a pomegranate, a bell and a pomegranate, all around the hem of the robe to minister in, as the Lord had commanded Moses.

4. (27-29) Tunics, turbans, sashes, trousers, for all the priests (according to the command and description in Exodus 28:39-43).

They made tunics, artistically woven of fine linen, for Aaron and his sons, a turban of fine linen, exquisite hats of fine linen, short trousers of fine woven linen, and a sash of fine woven linen with blue, purple, and scarlet *thread*, made by a weaver, as the Lord had commanded Moses.

5. (30-31) The turban for the high priest (according to the command and description in Exodus 28:36-38).

Then they made the plate of the holy crown of pure gold, and wrote on it an inscription *like* the engraving of a signet: Holiness to the Lord. And they tied to it a blue cord, to fasten *it* above on the turban, as the Lord had commanded Moses.

B. Moses looks over the work.

1. (32-41) An overview of the whole construction project.

Thus all the work of the tabernacle of the tent of meeting was finished. And the children of Israel did according to all that the LORD had commanded Moses; so they did. And they brought the tabernacle to Moses, the tent and all its furnishings: its clasps, its boards, its bars, its pillars, and its sockets; the covering of ram skins dyed red, the covering of badger skins, and the veil of the covering; the ark of the Testimony with its poles, and the mercy seat; the table, all its utensils, and the showbread; the pure *gold* lampstand with its lamps (the lamps set in order), all its utensils, and the oil for light; the gold altar, the anointing oil, and the sweet incense; the screen for the tabernacle door; the bronze altar, its grate of bronze, its poles, and all its utensils; the laver with its base; the hangings of the court, its pillars and its sockets, the screen for the court gate, its cords, and its pegs; all the utensils for the service of the tabernacle, for the tent of meeting; and the garments of ministry, to minister in the holy *place:* the holy garments for Aaron the priest, and his sons' garments, to minister as priests.

2. (42-43) Moses inspects the work.

According to all that the LORD had commanded Moses, so the children of Israel did all the work. Then Moses looked over all the work, and indeed they had done it; as the LORD had commanded, just so they had done it. And Moses blessed them.

a. **Then Moses looked over all the work**: Moses was the leader with the command from God and with the best knowledge of the pattern God wanted the tabernacle built according to (Exodus 25:9). Therefore it was right and proper for him to supervise every detail of the construction.

b. **As the LORD had commanded, just so they had done it**: This was wonderful obedience. No wonder **Moses blessed them**.

Exodus 40 - The Completion of the Tabernacle

A. God tells Moses how to assemble everything.

1. (1-5) How to arrange the furniture within the tabernacle.

Then the LORD spoke to Moses, saying: "On the first day of the first month you shall set up the tabernacle of the tent of meeting. You shall put in it the ark of the Testimony, and partition off the ark with the veil. You shall bring in the table and arrange the things that are to be set in order on it; and you shall bring in the lampstand and light its lamps. You shall also set the altar of gold for the incense before the ark of the Testimony, and put up the screen for the door of the tabernacle."

a. **On the first day of the first month**: This indicates that it was a year since Israel came out of Egypt. This was an amazing year in the history of Israel. They could count the great works of God and measure their own spiritual growth.

i. It is fair to use the passing of time to see how far we have come with God. Some Christians never grow much beyond their initial experience with God. Some who have been Christians for 10 years have only the maturity of a one-year-old Christian - they simply repeat their first year over and over again.

b. **You shall put in it the ark of the Testimony**: The tabernacle had to be *built* according to pattern and *assembled* according to pattern.

2. (6-11) How to arrange the items in the courtyard.

"Then you shall set the altar of the burnt offering before the door of the tabernacle of the tent of meeting. And you shall set the laver between the tabernacle of meeting and the altar, and put water in it. You shall set up the court all around, and hang up the screen at the court gate. And you shall take the anointing oil, and anoint the tabernacle and all that *is* in it; and you shall hallow it and all its utensils, and it shall be holy. You shall anoint the altar of the burnt offering and all its utensils,

and consecrate the altar. The altar shall be most holy. And you shall anoint the laver and its base, and consecrate it.

3. (12-16) Anointing Aaron and his sons to minister as priests.

"Then you shall bring Aaron and his sons to the door of the tabernacle of meeting and wash them with water. You shall put the holy garments on Aaron, and anoint him and consecrate him, that he may minister to Me as priest. And you shall bring his sons and clothe them with tunics. You shall anoint them, as you anointed their father, that they may minister to Me as priests; for their anointing shall surely be an everlasting priesthood throughout their generations." Thus Moses did; according to all that the Lord had commanded him, so he did.

a. **Thus Moses did; according to all that the Lord had commanded him, so he did**: The full description of this dedication ceremony for the priests is found in Leviticus 8 and 9.

B. Moses oversees the assembly of the tabernacle.

1. (17-19) The tent of meeting goes up by setting up the boards, covering with the curtains.

And it came to pass in the first month of the second year, on the first *day* of the month, *that* the tabernacle was raised up. So Moses raised up the tabernacle, fastened its sockets, set up its boards, put in its bars, and raised up its pillars. And he spread out the tent over the tabernacle and put the covering of the tent on top of it, as the Lord had commanded Moses.

2. (20-21) The Ark of the Covenant is set in the Most Holy Place, and the veil is set in place.

He took the Testimony and put *it* into the ark, inserted the poles through the rings of the ark, and put the mercy seat on top of the ark. And he brought the ark into the tabernacle, hung up the veil of the covering, and partitioned off the ark of the Testimony, as the Lord had commanded Moses.

3. (22-23) The table of showbread is put in the Holy Place.

He put the table in the tabernacle of meeting, on the north side of the tabernacle, outside the veil; and he set the bread in order upon it before the Lord, as the Lord had commanded Moses.

4. (24-25) The lampstand is put in the Holy Place.

He put the lampstand in the tabernacle of meeting, across from the table, on the south side of the tabernacle; and he lit the lamps before the Lord, as the Lord had commanded Moses.

5. (26-27) The golden altar of incense is put in the Holy Place.

He put the gold altar in the tabernacle of meeting in front of the veil; and he burned sweet incense on it, as the LORD had commanded Moses.

6. (28) The screen is hung at the entrance of the tabernacle.

He hung up the screen *at* the door of the tabernacle.

7. (29) The brazen altar is put in its place.

And he put the altar of burnt offering *before* the door of the tabernacle of the tent of meeting, and offered upon it the burnt offering and the grain offering, as the LORD had commanded Moses.

8. (30-32) The laver for washing is put in between the altar and the tent.

He set the laver between the tabernacle of meeting and the altar, and put water there for washing; and Moses, Aaron, and his sons would wash their hands and their feet *with water* from it. Whenever they went into the tabernacle of meeting, and when they came near the altar, they washed, as the LORD had commanded Moses.

a. **Whenever they went into the tabernacle of meeting, and when they came near the altar, they washed**: This describes the priestly use of the laver. They could not properly perform their duties without a ritual cleansing, indicating that God wanted service from pure hands and feet.

b. **As the LORD had commanded Moses**: In this section (Exodus 36-40), these words (or something similar) are repeated at least 19 times. The obedience had to be complete and exact – and it was.

i. "All things (not some only) are to be made according to the Divine pattern (Hebrews 8:5)." (Thomas)

ii. "It reminds us that Divine work must always be done according to the Divine pattern, and most strictly in the Divine way. The truth is so self evident, that it would seem needless to stress it. Yet a perpetual temptation to the mind of man is to endeavour to improve upon a Divine plan." (Morgan)

9. (33) The outer court is set up.

And he raised up the court all around the tabernacle and the altar, and hung up the screen of the court gate. So Moses finished the work.

a. **So Moses finished the work**: When the tabernacle was finally assembled, it was an earthly model of a heavenly reality. Since Moses was instructed to build and arrange everything according to pattern, it isn't surprising that we see elements of this tabernacle arrangement in the Bible's descriptions of heaven.

- In Revelation 4:1-6, the ark of the covenant (representing the throne of God), the lampstand, and the laver all correspond to a heavenly reality
- In Revelation 8:2-4, the altar of incense in heaven is mentioned
- In Isaiah 6:1-7, the tabernacle structure is implied by the mention of the temple, and the brazen altar is described
- In Hebrews 9:23-24, it tells us that at some point in time (after the cross), Jesus entered the heavenly reality represented on earth by the tabernacle, and appeared in the presence of God to offer a perfect atonement for our sins. Therefore, every time before this event, when the High Priest made atonement in the earthly tabernacle, it was "play acting" - and looking forward to - the perfect atonement the Son of God would offer

C. The glory of God and the tabernacle.

1. (34-35) God's glory fills the tabernacle.

Then the cloud covered the tabernacle of meeting, and the glory of the LORD filled the tabernacle. And Moses was not able to enter the tabernacle of meeting, because the cloud rested above it, and the glory of the LORD filled the tabernacle.

a. **The cloud covered the tabernacle of meeting, and the glory of the LORD filled the tabernacle**: Obviously, God was pleased with the obedience of Israel. This was not so much because it showed His superiority over them, but it was more so because it proved they really did believe Him and love Him.

i. There is a real and significant connection between the continually mentioned obedience of Moses and Israel (*as the LORD had commanded Moses*) and this remarkable display of glory. We shouldn't think that Moses or Israel *earned* this display of glory because of their obedience; yet their obedience *welcomed* it.

ii. This is an enduring principle. We don't earn our rescue, and God doesn't love us more when we obey. Yet, undeniably, when we walk in God's light and truth, there is blessing. Proverbs 3:5-6 speaks beautifully to this: *Trust in the LORD with all your heart, and lean not on your own understanding; in all your ways acknowledge Him, and He shall direct your paths.*

b. **Moses was not able to enter the tabernacle of meeting, because the cloud rested above it**: The same thing happened when Solomon completed and dedicated the temple - the glory of God so filled the temple, they couldn't stay in it (1 Kings 8:10-11).

i. *Without* the glory, it was just a fancy tent. The same could be said of a church, of a home, or of the human tent.

2. (36-38) God's glory abides with Israel in the pillar of cloud by day and the pillar of fire by night.

Whenever the cloud was taken up from above the tabernacle, the children of Israel would go onward in all their journeys. But if the cloud was not taken up, then they did not journey till the day that it was taken up. For the cloud of the LORD *was* above the tabernacle by day, and fire was over it by night, in the sight of all the house of Israel, throughout all their journeys.

a. **Whenever the cloud was taken up from above the tabernacle, the children of Israel would go onward**: This is beautiful evidence that God did answer Moses' prayer in Exodus 33:14. God's presence was with Israel, despite the golden calf debacle.

i. "The book ends with the fulfillment of the promise of Exodus 29:45. YHWH is living among His people: the theology of the presence of God has become the fact of His presence." (Cole)

b. **Throughout all their journeys**: The Book of Exodus ends with great hope and trust in God. Though Israel was in the middle of a desolate desert, had fierce enemies in the Promised Land, and was weak and liable to sin and rebellion, God was with them. This gave them great cause for faith and confidence.

i. "To speak of a journey is to look for an arrival: He who has begun a work of salvation for Israel will complete it (Philippians 1:6)." (Cole)

Exodus Bibliography

Buckingham, Jamie *A Way Through the Wilderness* (Grand Rapids, Michigan: Revell 1986)

Chadwick, G.A. *The Book of Exodus* (New York: Hodder and Stoughton, ?)

Clarke, Adam *The Old Testament with A Commentary and Critical Notes, Volume I* (New York: Eaton & Mains, 1831)

Cole, R. Alan *Exodus, An Introduction and Commentary* (London: Inter-Varsity Press, 1973)

DeWitt, Roy Lee *Teaching from The Tabernacle* (Grand Rapids, Michigan: Baker Book House, 1986)

Erwin, Gayle D. *The Father Style* (Cathedral City, California: Yahshua Publishing, 1994)

Ginzberg, Louis *The Legends of the Jews, Volumes 1-7* (Philadelphia: The Jewish Publication Society of America, 1968)

Kaiser, Walter C. Jr. "Exodus" *The Expositor's Bible Commentary Volume 2* (Grand Rapids, Michigan: Zondervan, 1990)

Lloyd-Jones, *Revival* (Wheaton, Illinois: Crossway Books, 1987)

Maclaren, Alexander *Expostions of Holy Scripture, Volume 1* (Grand Rapids, Michigan: Baker Book House, 1984)

McMillen, S.I. *None of These Diseases* (Old Tappan, New Jersey: Fleming H. Revell Company, 1968)

Meyer, F.B. *Our Daily Homily* (Westwood, New Jersey: Revell, 1966)

Meyer, F.B. *Devotional Commentary on Exodus* (Grand Rapids, Michigan: Kregel, 1978)

Morgan, G. Campbell *An Exposition of the Whole Bible* (Old Tappan, New Jersey: Revell, 1959)

Morgan, G. Campbell *Searchlights from the Word* (New York, Revell: 1936)

Pfeiffer, Charles F. *Egypt and the Exodus* (Grand Rapids, Michigan: Baker Book House, 1964)

Poole, Matthew *A Commentary on the Holy Bible, Volume 1 (London, Banner of Truth Trust, 1968)*

Redpath, Alan *Law and Liberty: The Ten Commandments for Today* (Grand Rapids, Michigan: Revell 1993)

Spurgeon, Charles Haddon *The New Park Street Pulpit, Volumes 1-6 and The Metropolitan Tabernacle Pulpit, Volumes 7-63* (Pasadena, Texas: Pilgrim Publications, 1990)

Thomas, W.H. Griffith *The Pentateuch, A Chapter-by-Chapter Study* (Grand Rapids, Michigan: Kregel, 1985)

Trapp, John *A Commentary on the Old and New Testaments, Volume One* (Eureka, California: Tanski Publications, 1997)

As the years pass I love the work of studying, learning, and teaching the Bible more than ever. I'm so grateful that God is faithful to meet me in His Word.

Thanks once again to Debbie Pollacia for her proofreading help. She's remarkably patient with my work, even when I make the same mistakes through a manuscript. All these years and I still haven't figured out commas. I especially thank Debbie for her prayer support through the years.

We use the same cover format and artwork for this commentary series, so continued thanks to Craig Brewer who created the cover and helped with the layout. Kara Valeri helped with graphic design. Gayle Erwin provided both inspiration and practical guidance. I am often amazed at the remarkable kindness of others, and thanks to all who give the gift of encouragement. With each year that passes, faithful friends and supporters become all the more precious. Through you all, God has been better to me than I have ever deserved.

After more than 20 years of pastoral ministry in California and 7 years of work with Calvary Chapel Bible College Germany, David Guzik accepted the call to serve the congregation of Calvary Chapel Santa Barbara in July 2010. David and Inga-Lill live in Santa Barbara.

You can e-mail David at
enduringwordbooks@gmail.com

For more resources by David Guzik, go to
www.enduringword.com

For more Bible resources by
David Guzik, go to:

www.enduringword.com

CPSIA information can be obtained
at www.ICGtesting.com
Printed in the USA
BVHW03s1209250618
519964BV00002B/90/P